This book is due for return on or before the

1 6 MAY 2001
- 7 OCT 2001
2 9 JAN 2008

Don Gresswell Ltd., London, N21   Cat. No. 1207   DG 02242/71

ROME

Its People Life and Customs

UGO ENRICO PAOLI

University of Florence

Translated from the Italian by R.D. Macnaghten

Assistant Master, Sherbourne School, Dorset

Bristol Classical Press

937

PAO

9 475 7

© Casa Editrice Felice le Monnier Firenze 1958
First Published as VITA ROMANA 1940
Eighth impression 1958

© English Language Edition
Longmans Green & Co. Ltd. 1963

This edition of *Rome: Its People, Life and Customs*:
First edition is published in 1990 by arrangement with
Longman Group UK Limited, London, by:

Bristol Classical Press
226 North Street
Bedminster
Bristol BS3 1JD.

ISBN 1-85399-121-X

A CIP catalogue record for this book is available from
the British Library.

Printed and bound in Great Britain by Short Run Press Ltd., Exeter.

TRANSLATOR'S NOTE

The short bibliographies at the end of most chapters are intended only as signposts for the non-specialist reader who may wish to investigate a subject in greater detail. With a few exceptions, all books are in English and contain detailed bibliographies themselves.

My thanks are due to Messrs Wm Heinemann Ltd for permission to use translations from the Loeb Classics. In some instances I have adapted them or produced my own translation.

Thanks are also due to my wife, who has criticised my English, and to Messrs John Roberts and Mark Morford, whose patient and detailed scrutiny of the typescript has saved me from a multitude of errors.

R. D. M.

Contents

CONTENTS

ix

CONTENTS

Plates

xi

ABBREVIATIONS

References to classical authors are to the Oxford Classical Texts
or to the Teubner edition.
The following abbreviations may be unfamiliar:

CIL   *Corpus Inscriptionum Latinarum.*
Mon. Ancyr. The *Monumentum Ancyranum* (see note, page 41).
Bruns   *Fontes iuris Romani* edited by Bruns-Mommsen-
            Gradenwitz.
References to Festus are to the page and line of Lindsay's Teubner
edition.

ACKNOWLEDGMENTS

For permission to reproduce photographs we are indebted to the
following :
Alinari: Plates 1, 2, 5-13, 15, 17, 18, 20-43, 45-51, 54-56, 60, 61,
66-68 ; Anderson : Plates 14, 16, 53, 65 ; Brogi : Plates 19, 52 ;
British Museum: Plates 4, 57, 64 ; F. Frith & Co., Ltd., Reigate, and
David Baker : Plate 58 ; London Museum : Plate 44 ; R.I.B.A. (Sir
Banister Fletcher Library) : Plates 62, 63 ; State Museum, Munich :
Plate 59 ; Herr Leonard Von Matt : Plate 3.

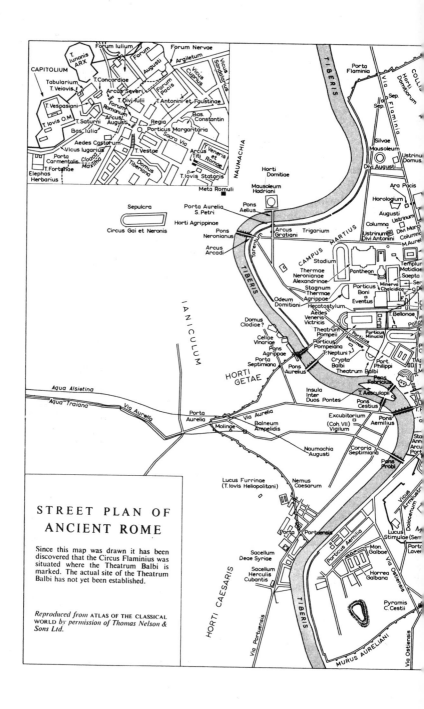

STREET PLAN OF ANCIENT ROME

Since this map was drawn it has been discovered that the Circus Flaminius was situated where the Theatrum Balbi is marked. The actual site of the Theatrum Balbi has not yet been established.

Reproduced from ATLAS OF THE CLASSICAL WORLD *by permission of Thomas Nelson & Sons Ltd.*

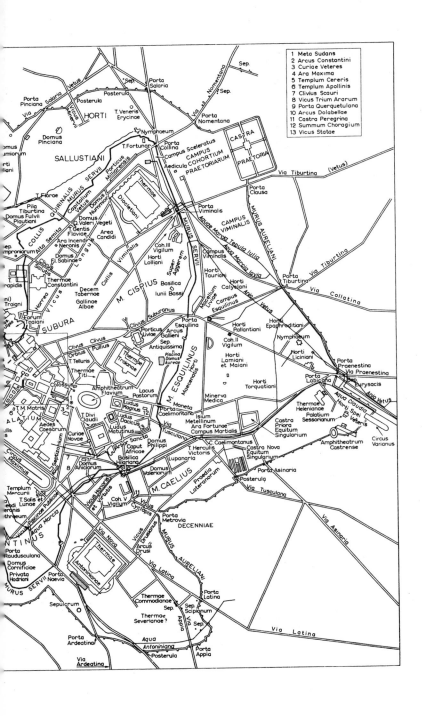

1	Meta Sudans
2	Arcus Constantini
3	Curiae Veteres
4	Ara Maxima
5	Templum Cereris
6	Templum Apollinis
7	Clivius Scauri
8	Vicus Trium Ararum
9	Porta Querquetulana
10	Arcus Dolabellae
11	Castra Peregrina
12	Summum Choragium
13	Vicus Statae

Urbs

From Romulus to Constantine. From Roma Quadrata *to the fourteen regions of Augustus and the Rome of Marcus Aurelius. The heart of Rome. The Forum. The Imperial Forums. Life in the Forums. The popular quarters; shops; the* Subura. *The monumental area of Rome. The Circus Maximus; the Aventine. The great markets on the Tiber. The district of the great warehouses and of foreign trade. The Palatine from the origins of Rome to Nero. The* Domus Aurea *of Nero. The Palatine from the age of the Flavians to the late Empire. The Capitol. The enlarged centre of Rome. The Caelian, the Quirinal and the Viminal. The Pincian,* collis hortorum. *The* Campus Martius. *The Esquiline. Walls and gates.* Trans Tiberim. *Street life. Rome at night.*

ROME grew from a small hamlet on the Palatine into the greatest city of the ancient world. Her earliest inhabitants descended to feed their sheep and bury their dead in the damp and narrow valley where later the Forum was to stand. After ten centuries, when Constantine transferred the capital of the Empire to Byzantium, Rome covered an area almost twelve miles in circumference and had a large and closely packed population. The banks of the Tiber from the *Porta Trigemina* to the southern slopes of the Aventine had been covered with docks and quays to ensure an abundant and regular supply of provisions. Eleven aqueducts furnished a daily water supply calculated at 350 million gallons.

In the fourth century A.D.[1] the city had 11 public and 856 private baths, 37 gates, 423 parishes (*vici*), 29 main roads from the centre to the outskirts, to which must be added an enormous number of minor streets, alleys and *areae*, small squares scattered among the network of streets; 25 suburban roads; 8 bridges, 2 Capitols,[2] 190 granaries, 2 large markets (*macella*), 254 mills, 8 large parks (all the open land that was left), 11 forums, 10 basilicas, 37 marble arches, 1,352 fountains, 28 libraries, 2 circuses, 2 amphitheatres, 2 *naumachiae* for naval shows and 4 gladiatorial barracks (*ludi*).

From the earliest times the population of Rome increased steadily, first through the assimilation of the neighbouring peoples, who came to live in the city, and secondly through the growth of Rome's power. The city grew gradually, and at various stages new systems of dividing it were devised, better suited to meet the changing administrative needs of a growing population.

The various stages of growth which reflect the history of the city are marked by the successive enlargements by which *Roma Quadrata* on the Palatine grew into the *Septimontium* (fig. 1),[3]

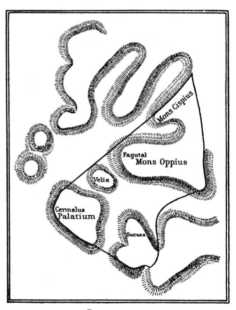

1. SEPTIMONTIUM

the city *quattuor regionum* (fig. 2),[4] the Servian city, the Rome of Augustus, and finally of Marcus Aurelius. The density of the population varied with the times, reaching its peak in the second century A.D. But even at that time a large part of the city area remained open land (fig. 3).

Augustus gave the city, which had already grown extensively since the last days of the Republic, an administrative system which remained effective throughout the Empire. He defined the city limits with a boundary line,[5] and divided it into fourteen regions[6] (thirteen on the left bank of the river, one, *Trans Tiberim*, on the right). These regions were administrative divisions, which (with the exception of the Capitol and the Palatine) disregarded the geographical, architectural and historical unity of the city.[7] An annually appointed magistrate was in charge of each region; each had a barracks (*excubitorium*), the headquarters of the *Vigiles*,[8]

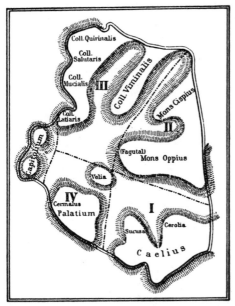

2. URBS QUATTUOR REGIONUM

a body of policemen created for fighting fires.[9] When a public health service was introduced in the fourth century A.D.,[10] each region had its own doctors. The region of Augustus was made up of a number of smaller districts (*vici*[11]), under the control of *magistri* or *vicomagistri* (forty-eight for each region) elected by the inhabitants. In the third century A.D. the perimeter of the city was fortified by the Aurelian wall, which followed roughly the boundary line of Vespasian and Titus.

Under Augustus and the Empire, Rome reached its greatest extent, and most of the surviving monuments date from that age.

Even when Rome had grown so much that the outskirts of the city were a very considerable distance from the ancient 'furrow of Romulus', the centre of Roman life did not move. The heart of

3

Rome remained where it had always been. Life was at its busiest in the valley at the foot of the Capitol and the Palatine; politics, business, the administration of justice, official meetings, as well

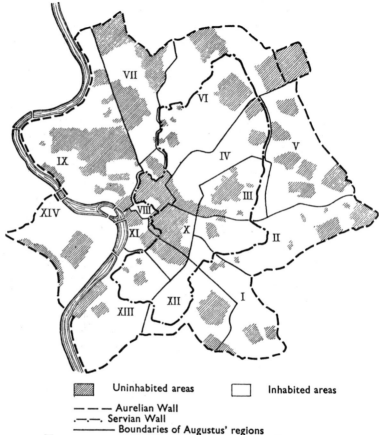

| ▨ | Uninhabited areas | □ | Inhabited areas |

— — — Aurelian Wall
.—.—. Servian Wall
————— Boundaries of Augustus' regions

3. The inhabited and uninhabited areas of Imperial Rome
(according to the calculations of A. von Gerkan)

as the city's daily market, had their main centre in the Forum and its immediate neighbourhood. Besides the Forum itself, the centre of Rome consisted of the district round the Circus Maximus, between the Palatine and the Aventine, the stretch along the Tiber opposite the Capitol and the Palatine, the district of the *Velabrum* and the *Forum Boarium* between the Capitol, the Palatine, the Aventine and the river, and on the opposite side, the

4

quarter of the *Argiletum* and the *Subura*, which stretched along the lower slopes of the Esquiline.

In the earliest days of Rome, the Forum[12] was an uninhabited swamp. But very soon the Palatine, the cradle of Rome, was not large enough to contain the rapidly growing population. The marshy valley at the foot of the hill was drained, and the first buildings and paved streets, such as the *Via Sacra*, were built. The most famous of the early temples was the temple of Janus, whose gates were closed only in time of peace ; they remained open for centuries until the time of Augustus. No trace of it remains today, but its appearance has been preserved on coins (Plate 64). The temple of Vesta (Plate 64) also dated from the earliest times; in spite of being frequently destroyed by fire, it was always rebuilt.

The *Cloaca Maxima*[13] ran the whole length of the Forum and discharged into the Tiber after crossing the *Velabrum*. The face of the Forum changed frequently, but it always remained the pulsating centre of the life of the city. In the early centuries political activity was restricted to the *Comitium* in the northern corner of the Forum; businessmen met in the *Basilica Porcia*;[14] the rest of the square was occupied by the market. Some lines of Plautus[15] show that in the second century B.C. the Forum, besides being the centre of public life, was the main market as well:

> In case you wish to meet a perjurer, go to the Comitium; for a liar and braggart, try the temple of Venus Cloacina; for wealthy married wasters, the Basilica. There too will be harlots, well-ripened ones, and men ready for a bargain, while at the Fish-market are the members of eating clubs.

In 179 B.C.[16] all the largest shops of the Forum were combined into one large *Macellum*, or general provision market.[17]

In the last century of the Republic and the early days of the Empire, the growing demands of political life overwhelmed those of trade and marketing. The ancient shops disappeared, the *Tabernae Novae* (so called when rebuilt in 210 B.C.[18] after their destruction by fire) to the north of the Forum, and the *Tabernae Veteres* to the south; the *Macellum* disappeared to make room for the Forums of Caesar and Augustus, and was replaced by the *Macellum Liviae* on the Esquiline.[19] The whole of the Forum was occupied by temples and public buildings; innumerable shops crowded together in the neighbouring districts.

The Forum changed steadily, gradually acquiring greater architectural splendour, to which its imposing ruins still bear witness. The era of the Forum's greatest splendour began when Caesar built the *Basilica Iulia* and the *Rostra*.[20] In 42 B.C. Munatius Plancus, a loyal friend of the dead dictator, rebuilt the *Templum Saturni*. Thereafter every emperor helped to increase the Forum's splendour. Augustus built the *Templum Divi Iulii*, Tiberius rebuilt the *Templum Concordiae* on the eastern slopes of the Capitol and the temple of Castor and Pollux at the foot of the Palatine. Under Titus the *Templum Divi Vespasiani* was built. Domitian placed a large equestrian statue of himself in the Forum, celebrated by Statius[21] in the first of his *Silvae*; today this somewhat tedious poem[22] is its only memorial. The two large wells near the *Rostra* (*anaglyphi Traiani*), still in a good state of preservation, are attributed to Trajan. Antoninus built a temple in honour of his wife Faustina, which the Senate dedicated after his death under the name of *Templum Antonini et Faustinae*. At the opposite end to the Arch of Titus, Septimius Severus built another large arch near the foot of the Capitol. Constantine finished the building of a new basilica, begun by Maxentius, and had an equestrian statue (*equus Constantinus*) erected, of which only the base has survived.[23] In the Byzantine age (A.D. 602) Phocas raised a column with his statue on top in the middle of the Forum.[24]

Even when the Forum was at its largest and most splendid, the new did not completely destroy the old and some of the monuments and buildings of an earlier age survived. The most important of these were the *Basilica Aemilia*, and, on the slope of the Capitol, the *Tabularium* and the *Curia*, where the Senate normally met.

All roads radiated from the centre of the city near the *Rostra*. Leaving the confines of the Forum, they became broader and straighter in the outskirts, and, once through the gates, they ran straight and well surfaced, joining others as they drew farther away from Rome, until they reached the boundaries of the Empire. Augustus marked this central point with the *miliarium aureum*, a stone covered with gilded bronze, and Constantine with the *umbilicus Romae*.

The oldest and most important road in the Forum was the *Via Sacra*, off which ran two main roads, the *Vicus Iugarius*[25] and the *Vicus Tuscus*.[26] The *Via Sacra*[27] started at the *Sacellum*

Streniae, which stood on the present site of the Colosseum, and reached the Forum after crossing the Velia.[28]

Caesar built the *Basilica Iulia* (fig. 4) on one side of the *Via Sacra* in the Forum. Along the stretch of the *Via Sacra* beyond the Forum clustered private houses, many of them belonging to the noblest families in Rome, and a considerable number of shops.

With the growth of the Roman Empire and the corresponding increase in the population, the Forum began to seem cramped, and spread beyond its original limits with the addition of the Imperial Forums (fig. 5). The *Forum Iulium* (left unfinished by Caesar and completed by Augustus) with its temple of *Venus Genetrix,* and the *Forum Augusti,* with the temple of *Mars Ultor,* extended towards the open ground between the Capitol and the Quirinal.

To the east of the *Forum Augusti* Vespasian built the *Templum Pacis,* whose precincts later took the name of *Forum Vespasiani.* In the gap between the Forums of Caesar and Augustus, Domitian began and Nerva completed the building of the *Forum Nervae,* called the *Forum Transitorium* since it was used as a passageway. When the congestion between the Capitol and the Quirinal increased,[29] Trajan extended the *Forum Augusti* with the *Forum Traiani* and the *Basilica Ulpia,* where he erected his high sculptured column.

The centre of Rome was not confined to the Forum; but that was the heart of the centre, the rendezvous of the majority of the population until noon. The Forum had a very different appearance in the morning and the afternoon. The life of the Forum reached its height at the fifth hour[30] (about eleven o'clock), but went on with decreasing vigour until the sixth and seventh hour. The passage of wheeled vehicles was forbidden from sunrise until the tenth hour; pedestrians and litter-bearers alone made up the huge crowd.

During these hours a great number of Romans thronged the Forum. Affairs of state were discussed in the offices, while in the *Basilica* near the statue of Marsyas[31] the leading financiers met to hatch their crooked and involved schemes. The money-changers were in the same quarter; as they waited for clients (Plate 45), they made their piles of coins dance and tinkle to advertise

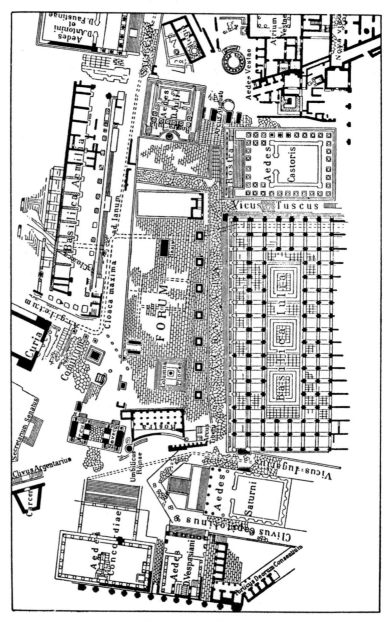

4. THE FORUM ROMANUM

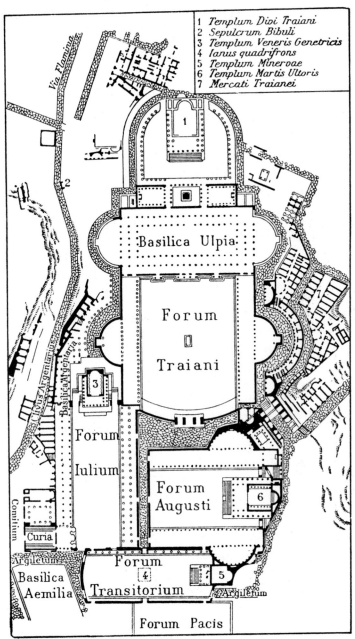

1 Templum Divi Traiani
2 Sepulcrum Bibuli
3 Templum Veneris Genetricis
4 Ianus quadrifrons
5 Templum Minervae
6 Templum Martis Ultoris
7 Mercati Traianei

Basilica Ulpia

Forum

Traiani

Basilica Argentaria

Clivus Argentarius

Via Flaminia

Forum
Iulium

Comitium

Curia

Forum
Augusti

Argiletum

Basilica
Aemilia

Forum
Transitorium

Argiletum

Forum Pacis

5. The Imperial Forums

9

their presence and their willingness to carry out any sort of transaction.[32] From the area between the temple of Castor and the temple of Vesta near the *puteal Libonis*[33] (where the Praetor's *Tribunal* stood) the shouts of the crowd and the voices of barristers raised in defence of their clients could be heard to a considerable distance. From time to time came the howls and curses of the participants in a brawl, the prelude to a lawsuit (see p. 195). If a distinguished Roman had died, his splendid funeral procession (see p. 130) filed slowly across the Forum (Plate 40). The orders of those in charge of the rites, the muted conversation of the dense crowd, the lamentations of the relatives, the cries of the *praeficae* and the blasts of the trumpets[34] made such an uproar, that, as Seneca[35] says, 'even the dead man could have heard it'. Horace describes funerals as the noisiest occasions in Rome,[36] and from the earliest days of the Republic the law tried to restrain female lamentations. The Twelve Tables laid down: *mulieres genas ne radunto, neve lessum funeris ergo habento.*[37] ('At funerals women are not to tear their cheeks, nor cry.') But such edicts were disregarded.[38]

With the growth of the Empire, the crowd in the Forum grew at certain times still thicker and more varied. All the activity of city life was concentrated on the morning bustle of the Forum, which reflected all its most ill-assorted aspects. This was not true of other districts, each of which had its individual character and appearance according to the type of people who lived and went there; there were the streets of the rich, and the streets of the poor, magnificent squares and squalid corners. The wealthy could be found near the temple of Diana[39] on the Aventine, the goal of the Romans' favourite stroll, or near the *Saepta* (see p. 14) in the Campus Martius, among the luxury shops; not for them the *Velabrum* (see p. 17) or the *Subura* (see p. 13). Arches, crossroads, alleys[40] and the paths below the walls (see p. 29) were notoriously dangerous. The smart *demi-monde* gathered near the temple of Isis and Serapis;[41] from the banks of the Tiber came the hubbub of carters, porters and bargemen;[42] there were greedy folk anxious to make full use of their money; near the gates coachmen waited for passengers; on bridges[43] and street-corners[44] beggars lay in wait for the kind-hearted. As today in all large cities, the people and the scene changed completely from one district to another often at a very short distance. But everybody poured into the

Forum during the morning, and the great throng showed the countless faces of Rome.

Every sect, nationality, interest and ambition had its representatives there. A glance at the Forum made one realise the size and variety of the population of Rome. Among the toga-clad magistrates, leading citizens and their clients, among the crowd milling round the praetor's *Tribunal*, could be seen working men in their tunics, [45] slaves with shaved heads, and Greek-speaking Orientals, with a finger in every pie.

These Orientals disgusted everybody; they were shrewd, gossiping, thrusting people, who succeeded in making themselves indispensable; nobody liked them, but nobody could do without them.

I cannot abide [says Juvenal[46]] a Rome of Greeks. The Syrian Orontes has long since poured into the Tiber, bringing with it its lingo and its manners, its flutes and its slanting harp-strings; bringing too the timbrels of the breed, and prostitutes who are bidden to ply their trade at the Circus. They come from all over the world, Sicyon, Amydon, Andros, Samos, Tralles and Alabanda; all making for the Esquiline or the Viminal; all ready to worm their way into the houses of the great and become their masters. Quick of wit and of unbounded impudence, they are as ready of speech as Isaeus, and more torrential. Say, what do you think that fellow there is? He has brought with him any character you please; grammarian, orator, geometer; painter, trainer, or rope-dancer; augur, doctor or astrologer:

> All sciences a fasting monsieur knows,
> And bid him go to Hell, to Hell he goes.

In the hours when the crowd in the Forum was at its thickest, these Orientals were always at your elbow, ready to do your bidding.

Every so often a small, haughty procession passed through the crowd; a great noble stretched on his litter carried by strongly built[47] oriental, [48] German [49] or Dalmatian[50] slaves in ostentatious liveries, was crossing the Forum followed by a train of toga clad clients.[51] The arrogance of riches was flaunted in various unpleasant ways: they struck negligent poses,[52] moved their arms in a way calculated to display rings,[53] played with rare and expensive animals, such as a baboon,[54] read, wrote or dozed.[55] The crowd opened for the procession to pass through. Or there was a solemn father ceremonially taking his son, wearing his toga that day for the first time, to the Forum as custom demanded.[56]

At these hours there were people busily concerned with the important things they had to do,[57] idlers with their heads in the clouds, serious men and scandalmongers. Also ('Who could believe it?', asks Ovid,[58] but it does not seem hard to do so) there were young engaged couples and love affairs that began amidst the hubbub of the Forum.

Et fora conveniunt (quis credere possit?) amori,
Flammaque in arguto saepe reperta foro.

The curtains of the litters carrying married women were not always as tightly drawn as their position and the severity of custom demanded.[59]

Everywhere in the Forum many doubtful characters were at large; many of that parasitic riff-raff which lives at the expense of the wealthy in every large city, and which Horace[60] so admirably described in two well-known lines:

Ambubaiarum collegia, pharmacopolae,
Mendici, mimae, balatrones. . . .

('Flute-girls, drug-quacks, beggars, actresses, buffoons.')

Towards two o'clock (the eighth hour) business stopped,[61] and then from all sides poured into the Forum a crowd of idlers, who stayed there for hours, whiling away the time pleasantly as they strolled among the handsome buildings. The Forum changed completely and took on an almost provincial air. To some this atmosphere was particularly congenial; Horace, who found all the bustle of the morning a great nervous strain, deliberately went there for his evening stroll, pausing now and again to listen with amusement to a witch foretelling the future to some simple countrymen.[62] Nothing gave him a better appetite for his dinner.

With the growth of the Forum, the market had been forced to move elsewhere (see p. 5). Driven from the Forum, shop-keepers looked for other centres, but shops were thickest in the immediate neighbourhood, stretching in two opposite directions, on one side towards the Tiber, on the other to the slopes of the

Esquiline. Near the Tiber trade assumed gigantic proportions; the *Vicus Tuscus*, where Horace tells us that scents and spices were sold,[63] and the *Vicus Iugarius* (see p. 6) led into the district of the *Velabrum*, which continued to spread southwards into the plain beyond the Aventine, where the largest commercial district of Rome grew up (see p. 17). In the opposite direction, the *Argiletum*, a street of bookshops and shoeshops (see p. 34), ran into the thickly inhabited *Subura*, a stinking and noisy district,[64] always teeming with activity,[65] where the lower classes and the slaves in charge of the household stores did their shopping.[66] On to the streets swarming with people opened the shops of barbers, shoemakers, wool merchants, linen weavers, blacksmiths[67] and hairdressers, who found other ways of earning their living besides cutting hair.[68] In this hubbub everybody could find everything. It was a district of workshops and stores with an industrious, basically plebeian, atmosphere. The centre (*media Subura*), was the Soho of Rome, where the poor could buy their eggs, chickens, cabbages and turnips cheaply, and could have themselves shaved, or their shoes mended, for a few coppers; but brawls between gangs were frequent,[69] and so coarse was the language of the inhabitants and so unpleasant the sights to be seen, that it was a place to be avoided if possible. It was thought wise not to send a boy there until he had put on his toga.[70] It was not, however, a district of complete squalor and brutality, for, just as today we find mansions and churches in the poorest quarters of our cities, so there were temples and aristocratic houses in the *Subura*; complete uniformity can be imposed artificially on a large area, as we can see, unfortunately, in many modern cities, but it will never be the result of the spontaneous development of a city's architecture over the years.

Caesar, until he became *Pontifex Maximus*,[71] lived in a humble lodging-house in the *Subura*, and the hospitable mansion of L. Arruntius Stella,[72] a distinguished figure of the Flavian age, a poet and man of letters, consul in A.D. 101, stood on the edge of the *Subura*. Yet it was as well not to venture into certain dark and dirty quarters, where shady characters were to be met with at every step and loose women beckoned passers-by from ground floor windows.[73]

Famae non nimium bonae puellam,
Quales in media sedent Subura,[74]

says Martial. Certainly, the ladies of these quarters were models neither of virtue nor of good breeding.

Luxury shops stood in another district altogether, a slightly outlying, airy part of Rome, not far from the Forum, near the *Saepta*[75] on the nearest part of the *Campus Martius*. Under the Empire they became the rendezvous of the rich, to whom money was no object, as well as the smart, who went there simply to be seen.[76] This was the obvious hunting ground for those in search of expensive trifles, costly materials or high quality slaves.[77]

The architectural genius of Rome reached its fullest expression in two areas in the valley which continued the open ground of the Forum to the foot of the Palatine, broken only by the gentle slope of the Velia between the Esquiline and the Caelian, and, further south, between the Caelian and the Palatine. Here stood the *Domus Aurea* (see p. 21) and the *Colossus* (see p. 147) and later the Flavian amphitheatre, the Arch of Titus, the Baths of Trajan,[78] the *Templum Urbis* and the Arch of Constantine.

The *Templum Urbis et Veneris* was the largest and most magnificent of the temples of Rome. Built on a vast level space (540 ft. × 340 ft.), previously the site of the *atrium* of the *Domus Aurea*, it was designed, according to Dio Cassius,[79] by Hadrian himself. He spared no expense in his determination to produce a novel and striking building. The floor shone with rare and expensive marbles; one hundred and fifty granite columns supported the arcade surrounding the temple; other huge columns decorated the two *atria* leading into the two parts of the double temple facing east and west; the roof was covered with plates of gilded bronze. This was the temple of Rome and of the goddess who in her love had guided Rome along the path to Empire; all must be as bright as a flame, as impressive as the unquenchable glory of Rome. The preparations for clearing the area were on a grand scale. The architect Decrianus[80] succeeded in removing the *Colossus* (see p. 147) and replacing it elsewhere; by a miracle of engineering twenty-four elephants transported the vast bulk upright without its touching the ground. Hadrian, who had conceived and designed this temple, regarded it as his own. From a technical point of view it provided experts with grounds for criticism. The colossal dimensions of the statues of Venus and Rome were out of proportion to the rest of the building. Apollodorus, the greatest architect of the time, who had the frankness to point out the shortcomings of this amateur effort, observed that if the two seated deities stood up, they would bang their heads on the roof and be unable to go through the door. His criticism was justified, but his frankness cost him his life. When a powerful man prides himself on his artistic skill, criticism is liable to be dangerous.

The *Templum Urbis* was built in spite of all its architectural shortcomings, but it fought a losing battle with the centuries. It was restored by Maxentius after its destruction by fire in A.D. 307, but later it fell into ruins. Its very splendour was an invitation to plunderers. The precious marbles of the floor were removed, and very few remain; the gilded tiles were carried off to roof St Peter's; the bases of the columns, only recently raised from the ground where they had lain for centuries, are the sole surviving evidence of the great arcade. Of the two apses, one has largely fallen, the other has been embodied in the church of Santa Francesca Romana. We can, however, obtain a vague idea of the whole building from various reliefs and from the view of the temple shown on some of the coins of Hadrian and Antoninus Pius (see Plate 4).

In wealth of buildings the *Campus Martius* (see p. 25) came next and with the Forums, the Palatine and the Capitol made up the most magnificent district of Rome under the Empire. In the last centuries of the Empire important buildings rose also in the outlying regions, the Baths of Caracalla (fig. 6) in Region I, the Baths of Diocletian in Region VI.

The district of the Circus Maximus in the *Vallis Murcia* between the Palatine and the Aventine, also formed part of the centre of Rome; the gathering place of the people during their struggles with the patricians, it was at all periods a populous and animated district. The long narrow Circus followed the contours of the Palatine, and public buildings and temples stood not far away, among them the offices of the Plebeian Aediles. It was a central quarter, but not so crowded as the Forum; the amenities of city life could be enjoyed there unimpeded by the continual presence of the crowd.

The district of the Circus Maximus was bounded on the south by the Aventine, which was for a long time a wooded and sparsely inhabited hill,[81] separated from the rest of Rome by a strip of marshland.[82] It was an important strongpoint in the Servian wall, but remained outside the *pomerium* until the reign of Claudius.[83] During the secessions of the people and the Gracchan riots, it became the temporary refuge of the rebels. The city life of the

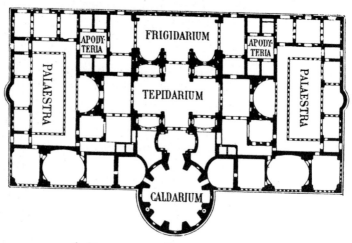

6. PLAN OF THE BATHS OF CARACALLA

Forum, which spread quickly to the neighbouring district of the Circus Maximus, made no further advance for a long time, and even when it did begin to spread towards the Aventine, it confined itself chiefly to its northern slope facing the Circus Maximus, where during the last decades of the third century B.C.[84] the *Clivus Publicius* was paved.[85] Later on, it became more thickly inhabited, and under the Empire it was one of the most densely populated of the hills of Rome. There seems every reason to suppose that the northern slope looked very different from the centre and the southern slope. It faced towards the centre of Rome, and the *Clivus Publicius*, leading to the temple of Diana, one of the favourite walks in Rome (see p. 10) was flanked by aristocratic houses,[86] while the southern slope, entirely enclosed by the Servian wall and closely connected with the business district of Rome by three gates leading from the Aventine, must have been little more than a popular trading district (see p. 30).

The level ground between the Forum and the Tiber had its own characteristic buildings and life. While the smaller shops

1. The Roman Forum. General view from the Capitol. (*p. 292 et seq.*)

2. From an Ostian tomb painting. The Isis Giminiana being loaded with grain for Rome. In the stern the master (*magister*), Farnaces, watches the corn measurers checking the cargo. (*p. 17*)

3. A detail from Trajan's Column, showing soldiers building fortifications.

(see p. 7) were centred on the roads leading out of the Forum (*Via Sacra, Vicus Tuscus, Vicus Iugarius*), and on the other side on the *Argiletum* and the *Subura*, wholesale trade was concentrated on the river banks. Here the first wharves in Rome were built, and goods from all over the world were brought, after being transhipped at Ostia, the port of Rome, and brought up the Tiber by barge (see plate 2). Here were the great salt works

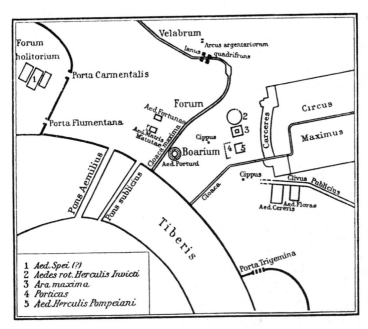

7. THE MARKET DISTRICT

(*salinae*), the huge markets of the *Velabrum* (the general market), the *Forum Boarium* (the meat market), and the *Forum Cuppedinis* for luxury goods, often referred to as the source of delicacies for the gourmet's table. Huge quantities of oil,[87] wheat, wine[88] and cheese[89] were stored in the *Velabrum*.

The *Velabrum* was for Horace[90] 'the stomach of Rome', as *les Halles* are the stomach of Paris. The steady flow of goods to satisfy the hunger of a large population and the sophisticated tastes of the wealthy involved such large sums of money that big companies were formed to deal with it. In the time of Constantine the arch of Janus, or Quadrifrons (the symbol and seat of all financial speculation), was built as a meeting place for merchants and bankers, the ancient equivalent of the Stock Exchange.

Under the Empire, the district grew steadily, until, besides the narrow space between the western slopes of the Aventine and the river, it occupied the large plain south of the Aventine. Here the largest docks on the Tiber were built, and there were enormous granaries (*horrea*), and warehouses for oil, wine, *garum*,[91] etc. Here, in the *Emporium*, imported goods of every sort were stored. A small hill, the *Mons Testaceus*, arose from discarded broken amphoras, as slag heaps in the north of England are made out of coal waste.

From above, the Palatine and the Capitol dominated the centre of Rome, just as they still dominate the Forum with their impressive ruins. The visitor who turns his eyes from the Forum and the Circus Maximus to the Palatine sees closely-packed lines of superimposed vaults, the remains of enormous buildings, and serried rows of arches with dark empty holes beneath them like the gaping eye-sockets of a skull. Time has stripped these buildings of their marble, and, after destroying the superstructure, has laid their foundations bare. The remains belong to the imperial palace of the last centuries of the Empire. More than any other of the hills of Rome, the Palatine has traced the history of Rome in its successive stages. It grew as the Empire grew, and its appearance often changed. What we see today are the mighty ruins of its last stage. Its importance changed with its outward aspect. From being the original centre of Rome, the *Roma Quadrata* of Romulus, it became the seat of the Emperors; the name adapted itself to the times, and the *Palatinus* became the *Palatium* of the Emperors. During the centuries, the walls of that formidable palace saw the formation and elaboration of a rigid court etiquette; they were the dumb witnesses of all the court intrigues, the plots, hatred, meanness and murky family and political dramas, through which Rome made her history in alternating periods of glory and of bloodshed.

Architecturally, the history of Rome begins with the Palatine and is summed up by it. In the *Aeneid*[92] Virgil describes the Palatine in the days before Romulus with its *rara domorum tecta*, the home of Evander, the poor and simple shepherd king. On this hill the shepherd village became a city within the walls marked out by

Romulus. At the corners of the original city, within the limits of the ancient *pomerium*,[93] stood its first shrines, among them the *Ara Maxima* of Hercules; the first gates were made in its walls, and on the country roads leading down from the *pomerium* to the plain, the early Romans revered the *Lupercal*, where the wolf had reared the twins, the *Casa Romuli* on the *Cermalus*, a ridge of the Palatine, and the *Tugurium Faustuli*, the hovel where Romulus and Remus had been brought up. The shrines and temples of a strange variety of deities stood on the Palatine. The *Curia* of the Salii, the temple of Victory (traditionally ascribed to the time of Evander) and the temple of the *Magna Mater* went back to the earliest days. The presence of an old temple of the Moon (*Luna Noctiluca*) may explain Elagabalus' choice of this spot for his temple of the Sun. Other deities whose shrines appeared later were: *Iuppiter Propugnator, Iuno Sospita*, Bacchus, Cybele, Venus Loyalty (*Fides*), Fortune (*Fortuna Respiciens*) and Fever (*Febris*). One of the most bizarre, Viriplaca[94], played a vital part in conjugal disputes. Before matrimonial quarrels could develop into bitterness a couple went to this shrine and were compelled to explain their case calmly one at a time. After one side had convinced the other, they returned peacefully home.

Amongst this assembly of gods many of the leading men in Rome had their homes. Under the Republic the Palatine was the home of politicians, and when political feelings had been roused, popular fury would hurl itself on one of these houses and destroy it. In this way the house of an early traitor, M. Vitruvius Vaccus,[95] was destroyed in 331 B.C., the house of Fulvius Flaccus[96] in the times of the Gracchi, and the house of Cicero during the riots stirred up by Clodius. Cicero succeeded with much difficulty in rebuilding his house; even after he had received permission to do so[97], he had to deal with an infuriated mob, determined to delay the work by threatening the workmen and hurling stones and lighted torches.[98] Grass grew for centuries, however, on the site of Vaccus' house (*Vacci prata*), while on the site of Fulvius Flaccus' house, after it had remained empty for some decades, a portico was built by Q. Lutatius Catulus, conqueror of the Cimbri, enemy, and finally victim, of the popular party. This too was destroyed by the people, who built a temple of Liberty on the site. This was destroyed in its turn by a *senatus consultum*, which decreed the rebuilding of the portico of Catulus.[99]

The orator Crassus, whose house is described as the most magnificent in Rome, lived on the Palatine, as did Licinius Calvus, the well known poet and advocate and friend of Catullus, the

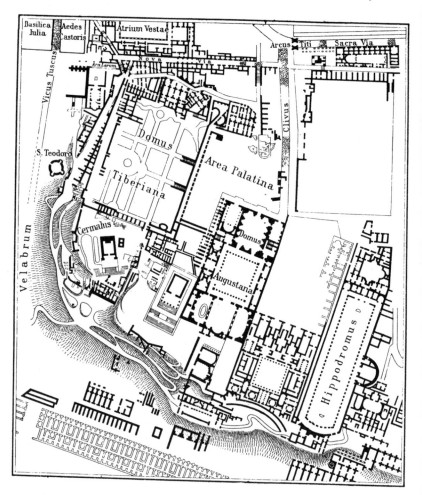

8. THE PALATINE

orator Hortensius, Milo, the assassin of Clodius, Cicero in the previously mentioned house of Crassus, with his brother Quintus nearby, M. Antonius the triumvir, and in the time of Augustus, Agrippa and Messalla; remains of the house of Tiberius Nero, the husband of Livia and father of the Emperor Tiberius (*Domus Liviae*) still exist.

Augustus was born on the Palatine, and returned to live there after Actium (*Domus Augustana*); after his death a temple was built there in his honour by Caligula (Plate 4). The hill where the leading Romans of the Republic had lived became the home of the Emperors; this home grew from the simple private house of Augustus—who, although he had gathered into his hands the reins of power, continued to live *ut unus e populo*[100] —into the palace, as the principate gradually developed into an absolute monarchy. Tiberius built a large new residence near the house of Augustus (*Domus Tiberiana*); Caligula enlarged it (*Domus Gaiana*), extending it along the slope until its hall reached the temple of Castor and Pollux in the Forum. Here it was sometimes one of his whims to stand between the two gods and receive the adoration of visitors.[101]

To the reckless madness of Nero, the Palatine seemed cramped; in his megalomania he built his house on the level ground between the Palatine, the Caelian and the Esquiline (*Domus Transitoria*). When the fire of A.D. 64 had destroyed part of Rome and the calamity was used as an opportunity for rebuilding a more beautiful city, Nero built the *Domus Aurea* on the ruins of his gutted house. This was no simple building, but a harmonious combination of buildings of every type with long colonnades, a huge lake surrounded by houses *ad urbium speciem*, meadows, vineyards, woods, and cultivated fields.[102] 'Here, at last,' he said, ' is a house for a man',[103] but the Romans grumbled that there was no longer room for anybody else, and pasquinades of the ancient type began to appear on the walls, among them, 'All Rome will become a house; citizens, make off for Veii, unless this house is to occupy Veii as well'.[104] Nero paid no attention; for all his faults he was not vindictive.[105]

The Flavians brought the imperial residence back to the Palatine; on the site of the *Domus* of Nero they erected buildings for the use and enjoyment of the people, including the *Amphitheatrum Flavium* (the *Colosseum*)[106] on the site of the lake of the *Domus Aurea*, which was drained. It was not entirely flattery for Martial to say[107] that Titus had restored Rome to itself:

Reddita Roma sibi est et sunt, te praeside, Caesar,
Deliciae populi, quae fuerant domini.

Domitian rebuilt the *Domus Augustana* with great magnificence; the still larger *Domus Flaviana* was built later with an extensive garden along one side, called the *Hippodromus*[108] from its long elliptical shape.

About a century later, Septimius Severus completed the work by surrounding the *Hippodromus* with colonnades, and raising a mighty building (*Septizonium*) on the south side of the hill (*Domus Severiana*). Under Septimius Severus the principate finally became an absolute monarchy, and the private *domus* of Augustus had become the most magnificent palace in the world. As everyday experience shows, the history of buildings follows the history of men, and stones make institutions holy.

The Capitol with its two peaks, the *Capitolium* and the *Arx*, was the smallest but holiest of the hills of Rome. Although private houses stood on its slopes, its character was essentially sacred. Here, more than anywhere else, the deities of Rome were felt to be present.[109]

The temple of *Iuppiter Capitolinus*, the chief temple of Rome because of the importance of the cult, stood on the peak of the *Capitolium*; on the *Arx* stood the temple of *Iuno Moneta* with its adjoining mint. Lower down, in the hollow between the two peaks, was the Record Office (*Tabularium*); at the foot of the hill, on the edge of the Forum, the temple of Saturn with the state Treasury (*Aerarium*), and the *Porticus Deorum Consentium*. To the south was the sheer drop of the Tarpeian rock from which traitors were hurled. At the foot of the rock opened a grim prison, the *Tullianum*, an ancient Etruscan cistern, dark and damp, where state prisoners were executed by starvation or strangulation. Their bodies were dragged down the nearby *Scalae Gemoniae*.

The Capitol, the bulwark of Rome, her last defence in the critical moments of her history, later the concrete symbol of her power and the final point in Triumphs, was a hallowed place, where the greatest of Roman deities, *Iuppiter Optimus Maximus*, had his cult. In his rites a Vestal, accompanied by the Pontifex, climbed the Capitol to offer prayers for the eternal greatness of Rome.[110] 'And if the gods did not hear these prayers,' says Cicero,[111] 'the state could not survive.' Here the statues of the great were erected, the highest of all honours. Here treaties with foreign nations were displayed inscribed on marble or bronze. The Capitol was the symbol of Rome's loyalty to her pledged word, of her austere religion, her recognition of her most distinguished sons, her relentless severity to those who had been unworthy of her.

There was no more sacred spot in Rome.

The Roman Forum, with its surrounding hills and the neighbouring open spaces in the Circus Maximus and at the foot of the Esquiline, was the centre of Rome. But Rome was always spreading steadily beyond the boundaries of this turbulent centre. On the hills, previously uninhabited, or only sparsely inhabited, new groups of houses, palaces, public buildings, gardens and fountains were constantly springing up. In the thick network of streets, as in the heart of the city, squares (*areae*) and crossroads (*trivia*) developed. By day they were meeting-places[112] and rendezvous;[113] dandies lounged there to quiz the passing beauties at leisure; their affectations[114] and their gallantry showed their character. By night refuse was heaped there[115] and all sorts of tricks were played.[116]

As Rome spread eastwards, the Caelian sacrificed its fair covering of oak woods[117] to the needs of the growing city. In early days this had given it the name of *Mons Querquetulanus*, still preserved in the name of one of the gates (*Porta Querquetulana*); its pleasant position, situated as it was between the Palatine to the west and the extensive high airy ground to the east, was favourable to this development. There were few public buildings, but a great many aristocratic houses and groups of buildings. On the Caelian lived the Mamurrae, no less famous in the days of Caesar for their loyal devotion to the dictator than for the novel refinements in the decoration of their splendid home.[118] Under the Empire, the Caelian largely replaced the Palatine (see p. 19) as the favourite district of the leading men of the day. The *limina potentiorum*[119] stood on this hill, and here more than anywhere else were to be seen toga-clad clients running to the *salutatio matutina*.

Domitian, the first to convert Augustus' house on the Palatine into a palace, also built on the Caelian his own Petit Trianon, his 'golden crumb' (*mica aurea*),[120] as he called it, for intimate dinners with his friends. Constantine moved to the Caelian, to the *egregiae*

Lateranorum aedes,[121] which had belonged to the Emperors since the reign of Nero.[122] Marcus Aurelius was born and brought up on the Caelian,[123] and the famous equestrian statue of the philosopher-emperor was admired there until 1538, when it was moved to the Capitol. For a long time it was believed to be a statue of Constantine.

Under the Empire the Quirinal and the Viminal also developed considerably. Along the top of the Quirinal, starting from the central point, where the *Thermae Constantinianae* stood in the fourth century A.D., a long straight sunny road, the *Alta Semita*,[124] ran to the *Porta Collina*. In the course of the building operations carried out recently on this high ground, many fragments of lead piping have been discovered, originally used to draw water into private houses. The names of the owners stamped on them show that a large number of the most famous families of Rome lived on the Quirinal in spacious and luxurious houses. In the age of Cicero, T. Pomponius Atticus[125] lived there, in the Imperial age the Flavii,[126] while still private citizens. There were also tall apartment houses,[127] human rabbit-warrens for the poor, in one of which Martial lived; if the central and southern parts of the hill were completely aristocratic in character, the sides surrounded by the walls had humble dwellings where the poor and destitute could hide.

There was an atmosphere of wealth and refinement on the Viminal, and, as might have been expected, a constant coming and going of obsequious clients. Juvenal regards 'going to the Viminal'[128] as the equivalent of going to ingratiate oneself with one's master. The house built there by C. Aquilio[129] in the last days of the Republic dimmed the memory of the houses of Crassus and Catulus on the Palatine (see p. 19). Diocletian added splendour to this light and airy hill when he built his baths there; their imposing ruins still strike the eye on emerging from Rome's Central Station.

The Pincian, *collis hortorum*, was always covered with gardens. Nearby on the Quirinal the *Horti Sallustiani* spread out, one of the most magnificent parks in Rome, on whose beautification the historian Sallust had lavished the fortune dubiously acquired during his governorship of Numidia. Immersed in his studies in the midst of this park, from which the extensive view embraced the whole of Rome, he penned his elegant pages burning with contempt for luxury, corruption and love of riches. Possibly he was not the man best suited to lend conviction to such sentiments, but he is not the only man to have behaved in this way.

At the beginning of the Empire, the *Campus Martius* and the Esquiline were the two districts to change their appearance most.

From the edge of the Forum the green level ground of the *Campus Martius* spread to the bend in the Tiber, across the middle of which today the Corso Vittorio Emanuele runs (see map at end of book). A patch of marshland here had been reclaimed by Agrippa in the year of his aedileship (36 B.C.).

From the restriction of the dark narrow streets and the feverish agitation of the Forum one came almost unexpectedly into the sunlight and open air. One breathed again, and felt pleasure in the countryside and the sense of relaxation which open spaces give to the weary. The Romans felt themselves irresistibly drawn to these wide green spaces. Young men went there to train,[130] and young women were not averse to the locality. Everybody went there to take the air, to cool themselves and to watch. The stroll to the *Campus Martius* was the simple, pleasant attraction which the city offered her people.

But this great empty space invited the buildings of the city to spread and occupy it. Groups of houses were built there. The *Saepta* (see p. 13) stood nearest the Capitol with the *Porticus Octaviæ* and the theatre of Marcellus, further on the *Ara Pacis*, the Baths and Pantheon of Agrippa, the temple of Isis and Serapis, the Mausoleum of Augustus. Nero built his luxurious baths on the *Campus Martius*, Domitian the *Stadium* and the *Odeon*, Hadrian the basilicas of Marciana and Matidia, Antoninus Pius the temple of the deified Hadrian; Marcus Aurelius erected a great sculptured column there to rival Trajan's (Plate 3).

Modern Rome has long since completely invaded the ancient *Campus Martius*, making its centre here, as it shifted from the ancient Forum towards the bend in the Tiber. The present Corso Umberto, which follows the course of the ancient *Via Lata*—the first stretch, within the walls, of the *Via Flaminia*—runs through a compact mass of brick buildings, broken only by the most beautiful squares in the world.

The Ottobuoni-Fiano Palace stands on the ruins of the *Ara Pacis*, and the foundations of the ancient monument are mingled with the walls of its cellars. Agrippa's Pantheon is today choked by a network of streets and houses, which crowd round three sides of it, paying little respect to its mass; modern Romans refer to it irreverently as 'The Rotunda'. Hadrian's temple in the Piazza di Pietra, now reduced merely to the frontal colonnade, displays its beautiful Corinthian columns and seems almost to beg for permission to keep its place in a world no longer its own. The façade of the Mausoleum of Augustus had disappeared behind a growth of modern buildings, and when recently an attempt was made to free it, only a ruined skeleton was revealed. Modern Rome has robbed the *Campus Martius* of all its green beauty.

But large cities are always advancing aggressively, irresistibly recognising no obstacles. Genoa, bold and haughty, has destroyed a mountain, Venice with its great square has trampled on and hidden the lagoon, Amsterdam has largely swallowed up its canals. The street names in the heart of Paris recall fields, windmills, shepherds, those in other cities valleys, gardens, reed beds and wooden bridges. The city stamps its mark on everything, suppressing the countryside, burying streams, digging out the subsoil for drains and underground railways, diverting and imprisoning rivers, driving back the sea. The modern swallows up the ancient, and when it does not destroy it, spoils and strangles it. Cities are inexorable, both their inhabitants and buildings.

It is many centuries since the *Campus Martius* ceased to exist with its green fields on the banks of the Tiber. A slow line of Martial,[131] enumerating the joys of the peaceful life, has come down to us like a voice from the past with its nostalgic echoes:

Campus, porticus, umbra, Virgo, thermae.

The *Campus* comes first in his list, the *Campus* with its sun, its welcome nooks so inviting to those with time on their hands, who wish to enjoy life quietly. But progress has turned Martial's *Campus* into streets and denied us the enjoyment of the simple pleasures of Rome's most faithful lover.

The appearance of the Esquiline also changed surprisingly during the first years of the Empire, almost by accident. Up to the time of Augustus it remained an uninhabited, unhealthy, gloomy district, used as a cemetery for the poor and slaves,[132] and as a place for the execution and burial of criminals.[133] Many heads rolled on these slopes, and many crosses were planted there for the punishment of slaves.[134] Horace calls it the ' black Esquiline';[135] 'gloomy', 'a district whitened by bones', [136] deserted by day, haunted by night. Among the famished curs which scavenged there witches went at dusk to cast their spells (see p. 288). The superstitious gave it a wide berth. It was a gloomy sight: lonely gardens, tombs, traces of fresh blood. From below, the confused hubbub of the *Subura* could be heard.

Within a few years the Esquiline had completely changed into one of the most beautiful and aristocratic districts of Rome.[137] Maecenas built a large park there, the *Horti Maecenatis*; shrines, villas, palaces[138] and fountains sprang up. Nero brought his *Domus Aurea* up to it.

It is a commonplace that the volume of a city's traffic and the different character and animation which a city presents at various points are largely dictated by the actual physical layout of the city. Ancient Rome was no exception, but it had this peculiarity, that after it had grown to a circumference of twelve miles including the suburbs, it presented the unusual appearance of one city within another, a walled city within an open city, since the inner part of the city was surrounded by the Servian Wall; though it was occasionally broken down to allow a way through or incorporated in more recent buildings, this wall remained completely intact for long stretches. When the Aurelian Walls were built later, in the third century A.D., Rome gave the appearance of a larger walled city surrounding a smaller one. With this appearance Rome entered the Middle Ages, to face her new fate. The outer area, once unwalled, became a great ring between two circles of walls, and anyone who wished to leave the centre of Rome had to pass through two gates in succession: for example, the *Porta Capena* in the Servian Wall and then the *Porta Appia* in the Aurelian Wall, the Colline gate and the *Porta Salaria* or *Nomentana*.

The Servian gates,[139] which were restored and decorated at various times, opened in a wall whose construction was attributed to Servius Tullius, but which was actually built in 378 B.C., immediately after the destruction of the city by the Gauls. The walls were particularly substantial in the north-east stretch, a mighty rampart (*agger*) made up of a triple system of fortifications.

After passing the gates in the Servian Wall one still remained in the city; it was no longer the *Urbs*,[140] but it was still Rome; and the stream of pedestrians, controlled and directed by traffic regulations, had its own character at each gate, according to the time and district, not only in numbers but also in the rank of the people passing through.

A steady stream of labourers and businessmen came and went through the *Flumentana*, *Carmentalis* and *Trigemina* gates, which led from the centre to the large markets; it was the same at the three southern gates of the Aventine, which led to the granaries and warehouses. The gates opening on to the Pincio gardens from the Quirinal and Viminal were used by very different people; they were the favourite gates for strollers. A great crowd of soldiers passed through the Colline and Esquiline gates which led to the *Castra Praetoria*. The *Porta Capena*, where the *Via Appia* began, presented a varied spectacle of movement of pedestrians and coaches. Travellers for Campania, nobles with their villas in the country-side south of Rome,[141] smart young men about town, who were only happy racing their fine horses along the *Via Appia*,[142] showing off their teams and themselves, all passed through this gate. Many *cisiarii*, public coachmen, were always on duty there, as they were more likely to pick up a fare at this gate than else-where. During the daytime a small nearby square, the *Area carruces*,[143] was the rank for travelling waggons, which were only allowed to cross Rome during the hours of darkness, and here among their poles and wheels a great number of draymen yawned away their hours of idleness. The *Porta Capena* was the gate for travellers, those bound for the country and all the idlers who were quite happy wherever there was bustle and a large crowd to watch. They squeezed and pressed in their efforts to step aside and avoid being knocked down by the carts blocking the *Via Appia*, ignoring the showers of water which streamed down on the heads of passers-by from the arch of the gate, over which the aqueduct of the *Aqua Marcia*[144] ran. Once through the *Porta Capena*, the first stretch of the road (*via tecta*)[145] was flanked by colonnades, which ensured pedestrians a measure of safety from the dangers of this chaos.

Between the gates long stretches of wall prevented traffic, particularly to the east. This was the *Summoenium*, a dead area amidst the activity of Rome. At the foot of the vast wall, which cut

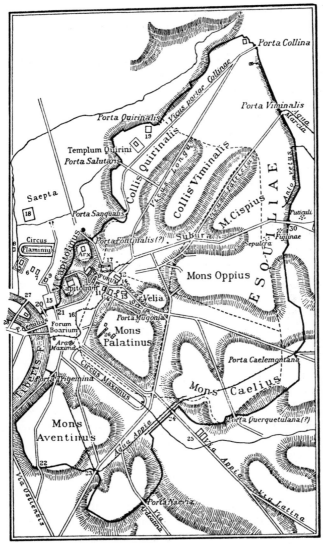

9. THE COURSE OF THE SERVIAN WALL

off light and air, the wretched life of the city stagnated; dirty alleys, filthy houses, treacherous corners, nests of corruption and infamy.[146] To speak of 'a lady of the Summoenium'[147] was hardly complimentary.

29

Ancient Rome was never, like modern Rome, London or Paris, a city divided by a river. The city developed entirely on the left bank; the Tiber did not mark the centre, but the western boundary of Rome. Only in the last stage of its growth did Rome overflow beyond the Tiber, and hovels, houses, buildings, villas and shops sprang up on the right bank, but even then *Trans Tiberim* was only an appendix to the main body of the city. This explains the very small number of bridges in Rome; today there are twenty-two; in ancient Rome there were only eight inside the Aurelian Wall, nine[148] including the Milvian bridge in the northern stretch of the Tiber beyond the wall. The rest were built later.

In the Republican age up to the second century B.C., after crossing the Tiber in a ferry or by one of the infrequent bridges, one was immediately in the country among ploughed fields, meadows, rustic cottages, cows and peasants. This was *Trans Tiberim*. In the long plain, with the Ianiculum and its prolongations in the background once stood the small farm (*Prata Quinctia*),[149] which Cincinnatus was ploughing with his oxen when the deputation from the Senate found him and informed him of his appointment as Dictator. Here also was the piece of land (*Prata Mucia*),[150] which Rome allotted to Mucius Scaevola as a reward for his courage and as compensation for his lost arm.

The centuries passed by, and it was a long time before any houses stood on the right bank of the river. The district opposite the Palatine and the Capitol was the first to be inhabited. The enormous traffic of the docks and the large markets (see p. 17) compelled Rome to cross the river at this point. A working-class district slowly grew up on the right bank, inhabited by workmen, fishermen, and the poor. Later, shops were built, extensions of those on the overcrowded left bank. From this starting point *Trans Tiberim* spread northwards opposite the *Campus Martius* and southwards opposite the *Emporium*, without ever going back far from the river. Many areas remained open, entirely occupied by farms, whose proximity to the city made them extremely profitable.[151] But even in the inhabited area, a man who went from the right bank of the Tiber in the direction of the Ianiculum, once through the narrow trading and working-class district, found himself at once in unspoilt countryside. And a splendid countryside it was; on one side, to the west, the gentle silhouette of the *Montes Vaticani*,[152] on the other the view of Rome across the river. The Romans were admirably skilful in discovering suitable sites for their villas, and they were not slow to appreciate the attractions of a riverside villa, and to build the most beautiful ones there; '*villaque flavus quam Tiberis lavit*', says Horace,[153] to describe a welcome and enjoyable retreat which the owner, on his death, left with the same sorrow as he parted from his beloved wife. The famous barrister, M. Aquilius Regulus[154]—whom Martial loaded with compliments, knowing him to be wealthy and generous, but Pliny the Younger[155] cordially detested for his disgraceful avarice and treachery—had a luxurious villa on the right bank.[156] It had spacious colonnades and an immense park, and a large number of statues stood along the river bank. Regulus may have been unscrupulous as a politician, but he had money and noble tastes.

The slopes of the Ianiculum were also sprinkled with magnificent suburban villas. The view to be enjoyed from there was truly—the cliché for once is justified—unique. Here one was in the country with the city a stone's throw away. One could breathe the pure hill air without feeling utterly cut off from the life of Rome; the city was always there. One could enjoy Rome without being at its mercy, one could see the streets full of people, the river crowded with ships, without hearing the bawling of the busy throng and the clatter of carts. 'The coachman can be seen but the noise of the wheels cannot be heard', says Martial:[157]

> *Gestator patet essedo tacente.*

What pleasanter view could be imagined? The eye could see all the seven hills of Rome:

> *Hinc septem dominos videre montes*
> *Et totam licet aestimare Romam;*

and in the distance the Alban Hills and Tusculum, also covered with splendid villas standing out among the green woods and parks,[158] and the view of the ancient towns of Fidenae and Rubrae. Was the poet really wrong when he said that the gardens of the Hesperides did not have so many marvels to offer as a villa on the Ianiculum?

Caesar planned to build an extensive sports ground, a larger rival of the *Campus Martius*, on the vast plain between the river, the Ianiculum and the *Montes Vaticani*.[159] Both Augustus and Domitian built a *Naumachia* there, Hadrian his mausoleum (now the Castel Sant' Angelo), which he connected to the *Campus Martius* by a bridge (*Pons Aelius*). Here some of the largest parks and gardens in Rome afforded a favourite rendezvous for lovers (see p. 238).

Up to the Italian occupation of Rome, those oases of fields and gardens, called the Prati di Castello, were all that remained of this countryside. Today only the name of Prati (Park) remains, and the area is occupied by blocks of houses.

Rome was a vast city with the strong colour of the South, breathing the pride of her imperial power, but we must guard against attributing to this densely packed mass of humanity a stately solemnity in their way of life, forgetting that men are men and cities cities.

The greatest cities present the greatest contrasts. At Rome where the favourites of fortune spent huge sums on a banquet, decorating their houses with rare and precious objects, even in buying a dwarf,[160] others spent the night under bridges.[161] The wealth and pride of the rich were built on a foundation of humiliation and misery; *mendici, mimae, balatrones*, to quote Horace again. The people who asked for *panem et circenses*,[162] when bread did not come from heaven like manna—and it could not come every day—were obliged to obtain it by a thousand devices. Hovels, where hunger was all too familiar, clustered around the marble palaces.[163] In winter many people trembled with cold.[164] In the apartment houses the rooms were small, cold[165] and dark.[166] Even the upper storeys of shops were inhabited,[167] and a garret was often shared by different families;[168] in these rats' nests there was little air, little light, many bugs[169] and rickety beds.[170] Those without beds slept on mats.[171] Pomp, wealth and imperial splendour were not universal. The real and living ancient Rome was not the glittering Rome of romantic paintings and the cinema. These contrasts make it more human and nearer to us. In fact only thus does it become intelligible, whatever unrealistic pictures may have been painted of it.

The appearance of the different districts and the life which went on in them, matched these contrasts. The plebeian quarters had a peasant character, which the powerful rhythm of city life

i

ii

iii

iv

vi

v

vii

4. Coins illustrating Imperial buildings.

i Claudius—Triumphal Arch.
ii Nero—Triumphal Arch.
iii Vespasian—Temple of
  Augustus.
iv Trajan—Bridge over the
  Danube.
v Trajan's Column.
vi The Trajan Forum.
vii Antoninus Pius—The Templum Urbis et Veneris.

5. Pompeii. Shop sign of M. Vecilius Verecundus.

6. Sarcophagus of a wine merchant. (Third Century A.D.)

7. Marble relief showing a poultry shop. It will be noted that the owner is a woman.

did not succeed in suppressing here any more than elsewhere. In certain districts and at certain hours it was a life of gaiety and colour. Innumerable strolling pedlars sold matches,[172] or bartered them for broken glass,[173] and bought and sold old shoes;[174] humble auctioneers, surrounded by the people in their tunics, sold poor trifles under the hammer.[175] The *libelliones*[176] dealt in secondhand books. The owners of *popinae*, shops where cooked food was sold, and the salt-provision dealers (*salarii*)[177] sent their boys round the streets and baths offering cooked sausages and similar food, crying out in their own peculiar note (as some shopkeepers still do today in Naples) to catch the attention of passers-by and to tempt them to buy their wares.[178] The Romans were gluttons for pease-pudding,[179] and the man who went the rounds selling it had a gold mine.[180] Even then there were roving salesmen of rugs and carpets,[181] known, just as today, for offering their wares at one price and later accepting a lower one, and the purchaser was expected to spend a little time arguing and bargaining before buying.

Some earned their living through one of the trades of the desperate, by which those who have neither skill nor ability always manage to wring money from the simple-minded. It was a common sight in Rome to see a snake-charmer[182] playing with his dangerous pets before an enthralled crowd, a sword-swallower[183] or a monkey trainer,[184] whip in hand, teaching an ape with a shield and helmet to hurl a javelin at a target. Here an extemporary poet[185] was surrounded by a crowd of admirers, or an eloquent mountebank described the miraculous powers of the medicine he was peddling. 'All stand to listen', says Cato,[186] 'but nobody, if he is ill, trusts his own life to it', though they must have found a ready market among the simple if this crew of robbers had taken firm root in Rome from the very earliest time. They found their customers and admirers among the inhabitants of the poorest districts, particularly those who lived under the wall of Rome (*in aggere*).[187]

The number of shops was unlimited, from large luxury shops to the dark holes of craftsmen who worked on commission. In certain streets, as in the older quarters of many cities, all the shops were of the same type. Cicero mentions the street of the scythe-makers.[188] There was the *Vicus Unguentarius* of the scent shops, the *Vicus Vitrarius*[189] of the glass sellers, and, near the temple of Flora, a street called *ad tonsores*. As we shall see (p. 145), this peculiarity served a practical purpose in enabling people to indicate fairly precisely a district in Rome and those who lived there. Shoemakers and booksellers[190] predominated in the *Argiletum*, and men of letters walked through the smell of leather and pitch to cast an eye over the new books displayed on the stalls of the *tabernae librariae*, or advertised in the normal way on the columns of neighbouring buildings.[191] The doorposts of bookshops were completely covered with advertisements.[192] There were other bookshops in a small street which opened on to the *Argiletum* and took its name from the cobblers who made or repaired sandals (*Vicus Sandaliarius*).[193] To us, with our respect for literature, this casual promiscuity of books and shoes may seem disrespectful; but the explanation is that both publishers and shoemakers used dressed leather.

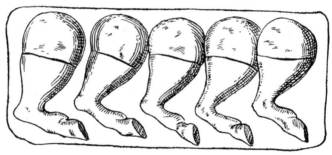

10. BUTCHER'S SIGN
(FROM BLÜMNER, *Die römischen Privataltertümer*)

Shopkeeping was a very profitable business, and the owner of more than one shop was well on the way to amassing a fortune.[194] Each man called attention to his wares with advertisements painted on the walls with symbols of his trade or goods; barbers displayed scissors or mirrors outside their shops,[195] cutlers a row of their products high up in the air (Plate 46), wine-sellers pitchers, bowls and jars also in line (Plate 6), butchers reliefs with joints of meat (fig. 10), poulterers hens and geese hanging from a hook by their necks (Plate 7), alehouses pictures of drinkers holding cups (Plate 5). Others represented with effective sculptured or painted figures the purpose of their trade: the *fullones* (see p. 134) each occupied in his own task, the carders sitting at their bench, the dyers busy about the furnace and the owner displaying the finished goods. The inscription, not always strictly grammatical,[196] encouraged customers;[197] the craftsmen promised careful work, the baths pleasant relaxation.

Above all there was a head-splitting din in Rome, and progress through the streets could only be made by relentless pushing and shoving:

> *Luctandum in turba et facienda iniuria tardis.*[198]

Collisions were common. 'Where's your head—with Maecenas?'[199] shrieked an enraged man at Horace, who, advancing confused through such a crowd, tried to lengthen his step and in his clumsiness had knocked the man carelessly in the back. Walking through Rome was full of danger. 'One man digs an elbow into me, another a hard sedan-pole; one bangs a beam, another a wine cask, against my head.'[200] Among the perpetual building operations, to have to pass near a crane, when a block of stone or a beam was being raised, involved a good chance of a broken head for the careless.[201] The law which forbade the passage of waggons through Rome during the day (see p. 28) specifically exempted carts carrying materials for the building of temples and public works, or the removal of rubble,[202] and the streets and squares, including the Forum itself, were choked with these heavy carts. Besides these there were mule carriages and porters bent under their heavy baskets.[203] All were in a hurry and free with their language. Somebody called out from a distance, reminding you of something in a loud voice. From time to time some sturdy figure running towards you would send you flying head over heels,[204] or mad dogs and escaped pigs rushed between your legs.[205] It was far from peaceful.

Some became intoxicated by all this uproar and confusion; to earn a dinner some hungry clients would perform the most humiliating and laborious services. They were seized by a passion for movement for the sake of movement, for business, for running, and they ran madly, throwing themselves into everything.

> They run to and fro [says Seneca],[206] rambling about houses, theatres, and marketplaces. They mind other men's business

and always seem as though they themselves had something to do. . . . They wander purposelessly about seeking for something to do, and do, not what they have made up their minds to do, but what has casually fallen in their way. . . . You would pity some of them when you see them running as if their house was on fire; they actually jostle all whom they meet, and hurry along themselves and others with them, though all the time they are going to salute someone who will not return their greeting, or to attend the funeral of someone whom they did not know; they are going to hear the verdict on someone who often goes to law, or to the wedding of one who often gets married; they will follow a man's litter, and will sometimes even carry it.

The noisiest trades seemed to be concentrated in the centre of Rome.

Schoolmasters in the morning [Martial complains[207]] do not let you live; before daybreak, bakers; the hammers of the coppersmiths all day. On this side the money changer idly rattles Nero's coins on his dirty table, on that the hammerer of Spanish gold-dust beats his well-worn stone with burnished mallet; Bellona's raving throng does not rest, nor the canting shipwrecked seaman with his swathed body, nor the Jew taught by his mother to beg, nor the blear-eyed huckster of matches. He who can count the losses lazy sleep must bear, will say how many brass pots and pans city hands clash when the eclipsed moon is being assailed by the Colchian magic wheel.[208]

Near the baths there was complete confusion, and wretched were those who found themselves living in their vicinity, where crashes, shouts and cries resounded night and day.

For all its beauty and its size Rome inflicted these tortures on its citizens. Happy the man who could stop his ear and run far from it. In fact most escaped to their villas whenever they could:

O rus, quando ego te aspiciam?[209]

The city dweller appreciates the countryside more than the countryman; the fierce pace of city life makes the peace of the fields more attractive, and the desire to escape from the anxiety and worry of work more imperative. None of the inhabitants of the great cities of antiquity appreciated the poetry of nature and the lure of country life so much as the Romans. The civilisation which built the Colosseum also gave us the poems of Virgil.

By night it was pitch dark in the streets. Whoever wished to avoid the risk of a broken leg or an unwelcome encounter was accompanied by a slave with a light. Slaves with torches accompanied their masters to banquets and squatted for hours on the steps, while their masters drank and amused themselves. Even young roisterers engaged on amorous expeditions were preceded by slaves to light the streets.[210]

From time to time the measured tread of the night watch could be heard, as they went the round with axes and buckets ready to put out fires, as well as to arrest malefactors. Anyone with an uneasy conscience gave them a wide berth.

Nightfall only partly interrupted the activity of the city where life never stood still. Noises died down but never stopped. Life at Rome was lived *inter strepitus nocturnos atque diurnos.*[211] With sunset the movement of waggons through the streets, forbidden during day-time, began again; creaking files of huge transport waggons (*plaustra*) passed by, laden with salt, food and all the goods which Rome accumulated in her warehouses on the Tiber, and which were distributed from Rome to the south. The world supplied Rome, Rome Italy. From the *Porta Trigemina*, in the market district near the river, to the Colline gate, where the *Via Salaria*, the road to the north, began, there was a steady stream of *plaustra* which broke the silence of the night as their heavy weight crunched dully over the street. Travelling carriages, which were also halted during the day near the gates (see p. 28), crossed the streets of Rome in every direction, preceded by a *servus praelucens*[212] who ran in front of the horses with his torch to clear the street. There were light elegant carriages, massive roomy ones, inside which a whole family dozed.[213] They went at great speed through broad and narrow streets alike, followed by the curses of those who had narrowly missed being knocked over, as the noise of their wheels faded into the distance.[214]

The night is made for sleep, but not everybody slept in Rome. As always, the student deep in his studies continued to work by lamplight during the hours of darkness.[215] *At te nocturnis iuvat impallescere chartis*, says Persius.[216] Epicures feasted. Bakers worked[217] so that the earliest riser would find fresh bread in the morning, and schoolboys their breakfast.[218] Those in office remained awake till late, engaged in business; the cares of empire left little time for sleep. Caligula even had executions performed at night and heads rolled by lamplight.[219]

In the streets the occasional passer-by stumbled over the wretches who slept in the open air,[220] and drunkards went their staggering rounds till dawn. Even Cato of Utica,[221] a man of sterling character, who was not, however, averse to wine, spent his night like this. The red glow of torchlight pierced the darkness as boisterous parties went by. From dark alleys came invitations to debauchery.[222] Footpads[223] went their rounds, thugs, aroused by wine, ready to come to blows at any excuse.[224] Unrepentant nocturnal wanderers finished the night in the *popinae* which stayed open till the very latest hours.[225] There they drank with loose women, gambled, and frequently brawled.

Ladies, returning late at night from a banquet, could never feel secure against attacks by ruffians. Darkness encouraged such behaviour; and bold spirits, like the libertine Caelius[226] and the mad Nero[227] took full advantage of it. Scandals were quickly born, and enraged husbands avenged themselves with their fists.

Young men, including those of the best families, took advantage of the darkness to indulge in the most disgraceful orgies. To their mistresses they showed disturbing brutality,[228] when they found the door closed against them. It seemed to them a mere trifle to batter down the door, set fire to the house, and beat up the porter.[229] As well as torches (see p. 82), they carried levers and crowbars in case of need, and apparently even arms,[230] to render their advances irresistible. Their behaviour did not always have the excuse of love, and their worst excesses were prompted only by a desire to pass the time. The Emperor Nero[231] distinguished himself in nocturnal activities of this type. So that he might have more chance of enjoying himself without discovery, he wore a cap to cover his face, or a peasant's cloak. He amused himself by beating up those who were returning home late, and he threw those who resisted into the sewers.[232] He broke down shop doors, laid his hands on all that he found and held an auction of this glorious booty among his friends. Naturally enough he was frequently involved in a brawl and more than once the imperial Mohock ran the risk of broken bones.

Sometimes the solitary passer-by was subjected to another ordeal, invented by soldiers, called *sagatio*.[233] They forced him to lie down on a cloak (*sagum*) spread out on the ground, and grasping the cloak by the corners they tossed the unfortunate man up and down into the air, until they grew tired of the sport and their wretched victim was left feeling shaken and dazed. The police were on the watch, but they could not be ubiquitous.

When the street was narrow and every window was a source of danger, how was it possible to foresee what might fall on to the head of the passer-by? The humbler houses took advantage of the cover of darkness to get rid of their refuse; from all sides scraps, sweepings and rubbish rained down, and the passer-by could consider he had had a lucky escape if he got away with a soaking or a few light bruises. But more serious accidents were frequent.

See [says Juvenal[234]] what a height it is to that towering roof from which a potsherd comes crack upon my head every time that some broken or leaky vessel is pitched out of the window! See with what a smash it strikes the pavement! There's death in every open window as you pass along at night; you may well be deemed a fool, improvident of sudden accident, if you go out to dinner without making your will.

It is fair to say that the state intervened with fierce laws. The Praetor's Edict[235] laid it down that the inhabitants of a building were collectively responsible for damage sustained by pedestrians from any liquid (*effusum*) or solid object (*deiectum*) thrown down from it into the street. The imperial code[236] declared it to be in the public interest for citizens to be able to pass through the city *sine metu et periculo*. But edicts and codes were of small comfort to a man with a broken head, and if he died from the blow, his heirs could only try to extract from those responsible the indemnity of fifty gold pieces[237] laid down by the Praetor as the worth of a man's life in their scale of values.

There was no public lighting system. Every man had to provide his own, and the solitary traveller who had to be content with a humble candle went his way with fear and trembling.[238] Some experiments at public illumination were made in special places on particular occasions. Nocturnal hunting spectacles and gladiatorial contests took place by the light of large lamps.[239] Domitian had the pleasant idea of lighting the Circus with a great circle of torches hung high in the air.[240] Before him Caligula[241] had illuminated the whole of Rome on the occasion of a nocturnal theatrical performance. Nero, too, produced a magnificent illumination for his gardens by burning Christians alive after covering them with pitch.[242] But these were exceptions; normally at night Rome was plunged in the deepest darkness, full of unpleasant and dangerous surprises. A man who had no reason for going out, stayed at home if he was sensible.

Further reading

S. B. Platner and T. Ashby, *A Topographical Dictionary of Ancient Rome* (Oxford, 1929), remains the standard work. It is fully illustrated and brought up to date in the two volumes of E. Nash, *Pictorial Dictionary of Ancient Rome* (London, 1961–2). M. R. Scherer, *Marvels of Ancient Rome* (London, 1955) provides some good illustrations. T. Frank, *Roman Buildings of the Republic* (Rome, 1924), and M. Nilsson, *Imperial Rome* (London, 1926) deal with the buildings at particular times.

Special studies include:

C. Huelsen, *The Forum and the Palatine* (New York, 1928).

T. Ashby and W. Dougill, *The Capitol* (Liverpool, 1927).

I. A. Richmond, *The City Wall of Imperial Rome* (Oxford, 1930).

A. Boethius, *The Golden House of Nero* (Ann Arbor, 1960).

NOTES

Chapter I

1. The greater part of this information is drawn from a description of Rome in the time of Constantine, which has come down to us in two editions, one by the name of *Notitia* (A.D. 354), the other *Curiosum* (A.D. 375).

Other evidence, which helps us to correct the details and draw a complete picture from the information provided by these exceptionally important texts, and generally to reconstruct the topography of Rome, besides purely archaeological data such as the remaining monuments and the result of excavations, etc., can be gained from the following: (1) The marble fragments of a plan of Rome made under the Emperors Severus and Caracalla, and displayed to the public on the north wall of the *Templum Pacis*, which later became the Church of St Cosmas and St Damian. (2) The description of Servian Rome in Varro's *De*

Lingua Latina. (3) The information preserved by Pliny the Elder (N.H., III, 66–67) about the survey of Rome carried out by Vespasian. (4) Inscriptions with topographical references, particularly the *Monumentum Ancyranum* and the Capitoline bases. The *Monumentum Ancyranum* is a copy on stone, discovered in 1555 at *Ancyra* (modern Ankara, the capital of Turkey), of the *Index rerum gestarum*, which Augustus wrote in A.D. 14 and which was placed in accordance with his will, inscribed on two bronze tablets, on the front of the Mausoleum which he had built for himself (28 B.C.) in the *Campus Martius*. The *Monumentum Ancyranum* is in Latin with a Greek translation. Fragments of a Greek copy of the *Index* were discovered in excavations at Apollonia in Pisidia; other more important fragments of the Latin text at Antioch (*Monumentum Antiochenum*) were published in 1927, and made a more accurate reconstruction of the *Ancyranum* possible. The best edition is that of J. Gagé (1934). The other inscription (CIL, VI, 975) of A.D. 136 gives information about the *vici* of Regions I, X, XII, XIII, XIV. (5) Coins and reliefs showing views of temples, and inscriptions on bricks and lead water-pipes (see p. 24).

Occasional evidence can be obtained from the precise information or allusions scattered in the writers of every age. Even medieval sources can provide useful information about ancient Rome, in particular an *Itinerarium* (called *Einsidlense*, because it is preserved in an eighth century manuscript at Einsiedeln) in which seven streets leading from the centre of Rome to the gates are described; it was a guide book for pilgrims to the Holy City. Some collections of legends and the *Mirabilia Romae*, not without useful information, are derived from a complete description of Rome in the twelfth century.

The following are the basic works on Roman topography: H. Jordan, *Topographie der Stadt Rom im Altertum* (Berlin, 1871–5); O. Richter, *Topographie der Stadt Rom* (Monaco, 1901); S. B. Platner and T. Ashby, *A Topographical Dictionary of Ancient Rome* (Oxford, 1929); G. Lugli, *I monumenti antichi di Roma e suburbio*, Vols. I–III (Rome, 1931–8; Supplement, 1940); *Roma antica, il centro monumentale* (Rome, 1946).

The question of the population of Rome at the period of its greatest development is one of the problems connected with topography. Beloch (*Die Bevölkerung der griechisch-römischen Welt*, 1886) was the first to conduct a scientific investigation and estimated 800,000 inhabitants; U. Kahrstedt (in *Friedländer Darstellung aus der Sittengeschichte Roms*, 10th edition, IV, p. 11 et seq.) estimates the population of Rome at the period of its greatest density at above a million, Carcopino at less than 1,700,000. The more recent studies are: G. Lugli, *I monumenti antichi di Roma e suburbio* (Supplement, 1940, II, p. 71 et seq.), and A. von Gerkan, 'Die Einwohnerzahl in der Kaiserzeit' (in

Mitteilungen des deutschen arch. Instituts, 55, 1940); 'Weiteres sur Einwohnerzahl Roms in der Kaiserzeit' (ibid. 58, 1943); G. Calza, 'La popolazione di Roma antica' (in *Boll. della Commiss. archeologica di Roma*, 69, 1941); F. Lot, 'Capitales antiques, capitales modernes' (*Annales d'histoire sociale*, 8, Paris, 1945). Lugli estimates the population at about 2 million, von Gerkan reduces it to a maximum of 600,000, trying to prove that there would not have been room for a larger number (see the map on p. 4). According to Lot the number of inhabitants was just above 200,000.

2. In a general sense, *Capitolium* is a temple dedicated to the Capitoline triad, Iuppiter, Iuno, and Minerva. Even outside Rome, the place where the temple of the triad stood was called the *Capitolium*, for example at the northern end of the Forum at Pompeii. The oldest such temple (apart from that on the Capitol) in Rome was on the Quirinal and was called *Capitolium vetus* or *antiquum*.

3. The Romans also called their seven hills *montes*; but we are not dealing with them here, as the *Septimontium* included only the Palatine and part of the Esquiline. According to an ancient reference (Festus, p. 458, 1) the *Septimontium* comprised the *Palatium*, the *Velia*, the *Cermalus*, the *Oppius*, the *Cispius*, the *Fagutal* and the *Subura*. The ancient unity of the *Septimontium* was preserved by a festival which the inhabitants of this area continued to keep even in later times, when Rome had grown into a large city. The site of the *Fagutal* is uncertain, and the fact that the *Subura* is called a *mons* makes it doubtful whether we are dealing with a different district to that which we know by that name, or whether the name handed down to us is incorrect.

4. The city of the four regions was made by the inclusion of the Caelian, the Viminal and the Quirinal, and included the rock of the Capitol. The new *pomerium* (see p. 47) of the city remained unchanged till the time of Sulla. The four regions were: the *Suburana* (I), the *Esquilina* (II), the *Collina* (III) and the *Palatina* (IV). On March 16th and 17th the festival of the 'Argei' celebrated the new boundaries of the enlarged city with a solemn procession.

5. Vespasian made some modifications to Augustus' boundary, by a new arrangement of the regions and of the city limits (Pliny, N.H., III, 66-67); the limits were extended for the last time by the emperors Marcus Aurelius and Commodus (CIL, VI, 1016).

6. See the map on p. 4. The fourteen regions were: I, *Porta Capena;* II, *Mons Caelius;* III, *Isis et Serapis;* IV, *Templum Pacis;* V, *Esquiliae;* VI, *Alta Semita;* VII, *Via Lata;* VIII, *Forum Romanum;* IX, *Circus Flaminius;* X, *Palatinus;* XI, *Circus Maximus;* XII, *Piscina Publica;* XIII, *Aventinus;* XIV, *Trans Tiberim*. The names do not go back to Augustus, who indicated them simply by a numeral; region IV is called after the *Templum Pacis* built by Vespasian.

7. The *Campus Martius*, which was a topographical whole, was divided between regions VII and IX, each of which included a part of the Pincian; the suburb of *Porta Capena* was also made up of two separate regions, I and XII. Region XII, which from the third century onwards was famous for the *Baths of Caracalla* (*Thermae Antoninianae*), owed its name to the public pool, which had disappeared before the time of Augustus (Festus p. 232, 12), and had in ancient times been situated near the *Porta Capena*, according to the Italian practice of building a pool near a gate. The most central and thickly inhabited part of the Esquiline was outside the region called *Esquiliae* (V) and formed part of III (*Isis et Serapis*); the latter did not receive its name from the large temples of Isis and Serapis in the *Campus Martius* (Region IX), but from a small shrine on the south slopes of the Esquiline.

8. There were in all seven cohorts of *Vigiles*, under the supervision of a *Praefectus Vigilum*.

9. Suetonius, Aug., 30.

10. See p. 207.

11. *Vicus* can mean (1) a village, (2) a subdivision of a *regio*, or quarter, (3) one of the large streets which ran right across Rome.

12. Strictly speaking, the Forum consisted only of the western side of the valley, bordered by the Capitol; later the name was extended eastwards to the present site of the Arch of Titus. After the building of the Forums of the Emperors (see p. 7 and fig. 5) the Forum was called *Forum Romanum* or *Forum Magnum*, but it continued to be known simply by the name of *Forum*.

13. The construction of the *Cloaca Maxima* was traditionally attributed to Tarquinius Priscus (Livy, I, 38, 6). Originally an open ditch, it later became a large subterranean channel. In the haphazard rebuilding of Rome after its destruction by the Gauls, houses were built on ground under which the waters of the *Cloaca* ran (Livy, V, 55, 5). There were other drains in Rome, some of which were open (Suetonius, Nero, 26, cf. p. 38).

14. The *Basilica Porcia* was built by M. Porcius Cato in 184 B.C., the year of his Censorship. Today no trace remains of it, the *Basilica Sempronia* (170 B.C.) or the *Basilica Opimia* (121 B.C.).

15. Curculio, ll. 470 et seq.

16. Varro, De Ling. Lat., V, 147: *Haec omnia, posteaquam contracta in unum locum quae ad victum pertinebant, et aedificatus locus, appellatum Macellum.*

17. The characters of Plautus go to the *Macellum* for all the necessities for a banquet (Aul., 2, 264). We know from Martial that the *Macellum* supplied a very wide range of foods for the tables of the rich (X, 37, 19; 59, 3), including fish (ibid. XIII, 85). A large number of fish bones have been found in the subsoil of the *Macellum* at Pompeii.

18. Livy, XXVI, 27, 2: *Eodem tempore septem tabernae, quae postea quinque, et argentariae, quae nunc novae appellantur, arsere.*

19. Besides the new *Macellum* on the Esquiline, another was built on the Caelian at a considerable distance from the first, towards the end of the first century B.C.

20. The ancient *Rostra* were situated between the *Comitium* and the Forum in front of the *Curia*; it was the place where orators spoke, and was so called because in 338 B.C. it was decorated with the prows (*rostra*) of the ships of the Antiates conquered in a sea battle. Caesar built new *Rostra* in front of the Temple of Concord, using part of the old, which had been pulled down.

21. I, I: *Equus maximus Domitiani imperatoris.*

22. After the murder of Domitian, the Senate decreed that all his statues should be destroyed and his name deleted from inscriptions. (Suetonius, Domit., 23); the *equus Domitiani* was certainly a victim of this iconoclastic fury.

23. For a long time an equestrian statue of Marcus Aurelius was believed to represent Constantine.

24. Phocas probably had his statue placed on the top of an already existing column.

25. The *Vicus Iugarius* left the Forum after passing (see fig. 4) between the *Templum Saturni* and the *Basilica Iulia*; then it followed the line of the foot of the Capitol, ran up to the *Porta Carmentalis*, and probably reached the Tiber (*Porta Flumentana*). In antiquity the name *Vicus Iugarius* was connected with the fact (Festus, p. 92, 29) that an altar to *Iuno Iuga* (*quam putabant matrimonia iungere*) stood on it; the origin of the name was probably similar to that of the *Vicus Unguentarius*, *Vicus Vitrarius* and *Vicus Sandaliarius* (see p. 34); the *Vicus Iugarius* was so called because there were many yoke-makers' shops on it.

26. The short, narrow *Vicus Tuscus* ran between the *Basilica Iulia* and the temple of Castor; it was one of the narrow streets of the ancient centre with many shops and people of every kind (Plautus, Curc., 482: *In Tusco vico ibi sunt homines qui ipsi sese venditant*; c.f. Horace, Sat., II, 3, 228). Latin authors give various derivations of the name, but they are always connected with an Etruscan settlement in Rome.

27. The *Via Sacra* probably took its name from the temples which stood along it, among them the most honoured in Rome: the temples of Vesta in the Forum, of the Lares near the present site of the Arch of Titus, and of the Penates on the Velia.

28. The Velia was a rise in the ground between the *Carinae*, a slope of the Esquiline, and the Palatine; the temple of the Penates of Rome, rebuilt by Augustus, stood there (*Mon. Ancyr.*, IV, 19: *Aedem Larum in summa Sacra Via, aedem deum Penatium in Velia . . . feci*).

44

29. CIL, VI, 960.
30. Martial, IV, 8, 3–4:

> In quintam varios extendit Roma labores,
> Sexta quies lassis, septima finis erit.

On the Roman system of dividing the day into hours see p. 82.
31. Horace, Sat., I. 6, 120–1.

> Obeundus Marsya, qui se
> Vultum ferre negat Noviorum posse minoris.

(cf. Porphyrion, Duo Novii fratres illo tempore fuerunt, quorum minor tumultuosus fenerator fuisse traditur). The so-called statue of Marsyas (in fact a stout Silenus with a wine-skin, taken from a Greek city, probably Apamea, where it originally decorated a fountain) stood near the Praetor's Tribunal, in front of the Tabernae argentariae of the Forum, and was a meeting place of the more unscrupulous money-lenders in Rome. It is shown under a fig tree on the two wells near the Rostra (see p. 6).
32. Martial, XII, 57, 7–8.

> Hinc otiosus sordidam quatit mensam
> Neroniana nummularius massa.

33. Places struck by lightning were regarded as holy, and surrounded with a stone wall (puteal). Besides the puteal Libonis, the best known (Horace, Epist., I, 19, 8), also called Scribonianum (Festus, 448, 28), or simply puteal (Cicero, pro Sest., 8; Horace, Sat., II, 6, 35; Persius, 4, 39), there were also in the Forum the puteal Iuturnae, a true well from the Fons Iuturnae, a short distance from the first (to the east of the temple of Castor), and the puteal of the Comitium near the statue of Attus Navius and the sacred fig (Dion. Hal., III, 71, 5).
34. Persius, 3, 103.
35. Seneca, Apocol., 12, 1: Tibicinum, cornicinum, omnis generis aeneatorum tanta turba, tantus concentus, ut etiam Claudius (the Emperor whose funeral is being described) audire posset.
36. Horace, Sat., I, 6, 42–43; Epist. II, 2, 74.
37. Bruns, X, 4,= Cicero, De leg., II, 25, 64.
38. Ovid, Fasti, VI, 148; Petronius, 3.
39. Martial, VII, 73, 1; XII, 18, 3.
40. Catullus, LVIII, 4–5; Propertius, IV, 7, 19–20.
41. Catullus, X, 26; Propertius, II, 33; Ovid, Amores II, 2, 25.
42. Martial, IV, 64, 21.
43. Juvenal, 4, 116: Caecus adulator, dirusque a ponte satelles.
44. Ibid. 117, Dignus Aricinos qui mendicaret ad axes.
45. See p. 101. Cf. Horace, Epist., I, 7, 65.

45

46. 3, 60 seq. The last two lines are from Johnson's *London*, a free translation of Juvenal's third satire.
47. Catullus, X, 14.
48. Martial, VI, 77, 4; IX, 2, 11, 22, 9.
49. Juvenal, 7, 132; 9, 143; Tertullian, *Ad uxores*, 1, 6.
50. Juvenal, 3, 240.
51. Martial, II, 57, 5; IX, 22, 10.
52. Juvenal, 1, 32–33, 65–66.
53. See p. 106. Cf. for the custom of displaying rings Juvenal, 1, 28.
54. Cicero Ad. Att., VI, 1, 25. Cicero is speaking of one Vedius, whom he had met in the provinces, but certain types of ostentation must have been usual in Rome.
55. Juvenal, 3, 241–2.
56. Seneca, Epist., 4, 2.
57. Cicero, Ad Qu. fr., III, 1, 3, 7; *Romae respirandi non est locus.*
58. Ars Am., I, 79–80.
59. Seneca, De benef., 1, 9.
60. Sat., I, 2, 1–2.
61. Horace, Epist., I, 7, 46; Martial, IV, 8, 4.
62. Horace, Sat., I, 6, 113–14.
63. Ibid. Epist., II, 1, 269–70.
64. Martial, XII, 18, 2; *clamosa . . . in Subura.*
65. Juvenal, 11, 51: *Esquilias a ferventi migrare Subura.*
66. Martial, VII, 31; X, 94.
67. CIL, VI, 9284, *crepidarius de Subura;* 9399, *ferrarius de Subura;* 9491, *lanarius de Subura;* 9526, *in Subura maiore . . . lintearius* etc.
68. Martial, II, 17.
69. Livy, III, 13, 2: *Se . . . in iuventutem grassantem in Subura incidisse; ibi rixam natam esse, fratremque suum . . . pugno ictum . . . cecidisse; semianimem inter manus domum ablatum.*
70. Persius, 5, 30 et seq.
71. Suetonius, Divus Iulius, 46: *Habitavit primo in Subura modicis aedibus; post autem pontificatum maximum in Sacra via domo publica.*
72. Martial, XII, 3, 9–12.
73. Ibid. XI, 61, 3–4.
74. Ibid. VI, 66, 1–2.
75. The *Saepta Iulia*, begun by Caesar and completed by Agrippa, were intended for the meetings of the *Comitia*; expensive wares were displayed for sale in the colonnades of neighbouring buildings. Cf. Martial, X, 80, 4: *Tota miser coemat Saepta feratque domum*, meaning 'to buy everything of the best', an expression similar to that used by Horace, Sat., II, 3, 229–30 (quoted in Note 91).
76. Martial, II, 57; IX, 59.
77. Ibid. IX, 59, 3–6; X, 80, 3–4.

78. Only faint traces remain today of the impressive ruins still visible in the sixteenth century.

79. LXIX, 4.

80. Aelius Spartianus, Hadr., 19, 12.

81. Dion. Hal., III, 43, 1; X, 31, 2.

82. Varro, De Ling. Lat., V, 43; *Olim paludibus mons erat ab reliquis disclusus.*

83. Aulus Gellius, XIII, 14, 7.

84. Varro, De Ling. Lat., V, 158.

85. Ovid. Fasti, V, 293–4:

> *Qui tunc erat ardua rupes,*
> *Utile nunc iter est Publiciumque vocant.*

86. Martial, VI, 64, 13; X, 56, 1–2.

87. Plautus, Capt., 489.

88. CIL, VI, 9671; *negotiator penoris et vinorum de Velabro.*

89. Martial, XI, 52, 10; XIII, 32.

90. Horace, Sat., II, 3, 229–30;

> *Cum Velabro omne macellum*
> *Mane domum veniant.*

91. See p. 134.

92. VIII, 98 et seq.

93. The *pomerium* was the sacred line marking the boundaries of the city. The name (*pone* [= *post*] *moerum* = behind the wall) literally means the strip of ground on either side of the surrounding walls, but the history of the *pomerium* of Rome is not connected with the architectural history of the city. The earliest *pomerium* was outside the walls of *Roma Quadrata* on the Palatine; it was later enlarged to define the boundaries of the city *Quattuor Regionum* (see fig. 2) and remained unchanged until Sulla (Aulus Gellius, XIII, 14, 4); consequently the Aventine, although inside the Servian Walls, was for a long time outside the *pomerium*. After Sulla, the *pomerium* was further enlarged by Caesar, Claudius, the Flavii (Vespasian and Titus) and Hadrian.

94. Valerius Maximus, II, 1, 6.

95. Cicero, De domo sua, 38, 101; cf. Livy, VIII, 19, 4 (331 B.C.): *Aedes fuere in Palatio eius, quae Vacci prata, diruto aedificio publicatoque solo, appellata.*

96. Cicero, ibid. 38, 102; this speech has also preserved the other instances in the text.

97. It was on this occasion that he delivered his two speeches *De domo sua* and *De haruspicum responso* in 57 B.C.

98. Cicero, Ad Att., IV, 3, 2–3.

99. Ibid. 2, 5.

100. Suetonius, Aug., 56.

101. Suetonius, Cal., 22. *Consistens saepe inter fratres deos, medium adorandum se adeuntibus exhibebat.*

102. Ibid. Nero, 31.

103. Ibid.: *Eiusmodi domum . . . hactenus comprobavit, ut se diceret quasi hominem tandem habitare coepisse.*

104. Ibid. Nero, 39:

> *Roma domus fiet; Veios migrate, Quirites,*
> *Si non et Veios occupat ista domus.*

See p. 271.

105. Ibid. Nero, 39: *Nihil eum patientius quam maledicta et convicia hominum tulisse.*

106. See p. 147.

107. *Liber Spect.*, 2, 11–12.

108. See p. 76.

109. Virgil, Aen., VIII, 351–4.

110. Horace, Odes, III, 30, 8–9.

111. Cicero, pro Fonteio, 21, 48: *Virgo Vestalis . . . cuius preces si di aspernarentur, haec salva esse non possent.*

112. Juvenal, 6, 412.

113. Horace, Odes, I, 9, 18.

114. Ars Poet., 245–6.

115. Phaedrus, V, 6, etc.

116. Propertius, IV, 7, 19–20, etc.

117. Tacitus, Annals, IV, 65, 1.

118. Pliny, N.H., XXXVI, 48: the Mamurrae were the first to introduce the custom of lining walls with marble.

119. Martial, XII, 18, 4–6.

120. Ibid. II, 59.

121. Juvenal, 10, 17.

122. Tacitus, Annals, XV, 49, 2, and 60, 1. Plautius Lateranus was consul designate in A.D. 65, when he fell a victim to Nero as a result of the part he played in the Pisonian conspiracy. On the site of the palace of the Laterani, which became the imperial residence under Constantine and later the seat of the Popes, was built the basilica of St John Lateran.

123. Iulius Capitolinus, M. Antoninus, 1, 5.

124. The present Via XX Settembre.

125. Cicero, De Leg., I, 1, 3; Ad Att., XII, 45, 2, etc.

126. Suetonius, Dom., 1.

127. See p. 56.

128. Juvenal, 3, 71: *dictumque petunt a vimine collem.*

129. Pliny, N.H., XVII, 2.

130. Strabo, V, 236: 'The extent of the plain is wonderful, allowing a free space for driving chariots and performing any other exercise on horseback for the very large number of youths who train there at ball, discus throwing and wrestling.' Cf. Horace, Odes, I, 8, 4.

131. V, 20, 9.

132. Horace, Sat., I, 8, 8–11. From Cicero, Phil., IX, 7, 17, it is clear that in some parts of the Esquiline there were tombs of men of higher rank.

133. Suetonius, Claudius, 25.

134. Plautus, Cas., 354; Mil. gl., 359; Pseud., 331. Plautus always uses the term *extra portam* clearly referring to the *Porta Esquilina* (cf. Tacitus, Annals, II, 32, 4: *Extra portam Esquilinam . . . more prisco advertere*).

135. Sat., II, 6, 32–33.

136. Ibid. I, 8, 15–16.

137. Martial (V, 22, 2) and Juvenal (3, 71; 5, 77) mention the Esquiline as a hill inhabited by aristocrats.

138. Some of the best frescoes of the Roman age come from a palace on the Esquiline (Plate 19).

139. The gates in the Servian wall were: *Porta Trigemina* (from the Aventine to the river); *Porta Flumentana* and *Porta Carmentalis* (from the Forum and the great markets to the *Campus Martius*), *Porta Fontinalis* (from the Capitol to the *Campus Martius*); *Porta Sanqualis, Salutaris* and *Quirinalis* (from the Quirinal to the Pincian); *Porta Collina* (from the Quirinal to the *Castra Praetoria*); *Porta Viminalis; Porta Esquilina; Porta Cælimontana; Porta Querquetulana* (from the Caelian to the eastern continuation of the hill); *Porta Capena* (at the beginning of the *Via Appia;* see p. 50); *Porta Naevia; Porta Raudusculana; Porta Lavernalis* (in the south wall of the Aventine). The gates of the Aurelian Wall were placed at regular intervals, and, as they led to the outlying suburbs or the open countryside, the volume of traffic must have been smaller than at the Servian gates. In the stretch of the Aurelian Wall *Trans Tiberim* were the *Porta Portuensis, Porta Aurelia, Porta Septimiana*; northwards, at the *Pons Aelius,* another gate whose name is uncertain. From there, in the north stretch the *Porta Flaminia* (now the *Porta del Popolo*) and to the east, the *Porta Pinciana, Salaria* and *Nomentana.* South of the *Castra Praetoria* was another gate, whose name is unknown. On the east side the *Porta Tiburtina* (now the *Porta San Lorenzo*), *Praenestina* (*Porta Maggiore*), *Asinaria, Metrovia* and *Latina.* To the extreme south the *Porta Appia,* and continuing towards the river, the *Porta Ardeatina* and *Ostiensis* (*Porta San Paolo*).

140. *Urbs* refers only to the walled city, *Roma* to the whole inhabited city, cf. Paulus Ad Edictum, 1, *Urbis appellatio muris, Romae autem*

continentibus aedificiis finitur, quod latius patet, Marcellus, Dig., XII: *Ut Alfenus ait, urbs est Roma quae muris cingeretur, Roma est etiam, qua continentia aedificia essent.*

141. Martial, III, 47.
142. Horace, Epodes, 4, 14.
143. Mentioned in the *Notitia* and the *Curiosum*; see p. 40.
144. Martial, III, 47, 1; Juvenal 3, 11.
145. Ovid, Fasti, VI, 192.
146. Martial, I, 34, 6; XI, 61, 2.
147. Ibid. III, 82, 2; XII, 32, 22.
148. Going up the Tiber from south to north: *Pons Probi,* facing the Aventine (rebuilt in marble by Theodosius); *Pons Sublicius, Pons Aemilius* (in front of the Forum and the markets, which continued the Forum to the Tiber); *Pons Fabricius, Pons Cestius* (in front of the Theatre of Marcellus; they were connected to allow the crossing of the Tiber across the Isola Tiberina); *Pons Aurelius, Pons Agrippae* (opposite the *Campus Martius*); the *Pons Aelius,* which linked the *Campus Martius* and the Mausoleum of Hadrian. Outside the Aurelian Wall was the *Pons Milvius,* the most northerly and the furthest from the centre. It is probable that in the late Empire another bridge south of the *Pons Aelius* joined the arches of Valentinian and Theodosius on the left bank with the arches of Theodosius and Arcadius on the right *Pons Neronianus.*
149. Livy, III, 26, 9; Pliny, N.H., XVIII, 20.
150. Livy, II, 13, 5.
151. Cicero, pro Sex. Roscio Amer., 7, 20.
152. All the ground on the right bank of the Tiber, including the *Ianiculum* and its northern slopes as well as the Mons Marius, was called by the general name of *Mons Vaticanus.* The *Ianiculum* itself is sometimes referred to as *Mons Vaticanus* (Horace, Odes, I, 20, 7-8; Juvenal, 6, 344) and *Montes Vaticani* (Cicero, Ad Att., XIII, 33, 4). Properly speaking, the *Montes Vaticani* are the extensions of the *Ianiculum.* The name *Vaticanus* came later to be applied to the level space at the foot of the *Ianiculum,* which became the centre of Christianity.
153. Horace, Odes, II, 3, 18.
154. I, 12, 82; III, and *passim.*
155. I, 5; II, 20; IV, 2.
156. Pliny, Epist., IV, 2, 5: *Tenet se trans Tiberim in hortis, in quibus latissimum solum porticibus immensis, ripam statuis suis occupavit.*
157. IV, 64, 19.
158. Strabo, V, 12.
159. Cicero, Ad Att., XIII, 33, 4.
160. See p. 98.
161. Martial, XII, 32, 25; Juvenal, 5, 8.

162. This well-known phrase comes from Juvenal, 10, 81.

163. Cicero, Ad Att., XIV, 9, 1; Martial, XI, 32, 56; XII, 32, and *passim*.

164. Persius, 1, 54; Juvenal, 1, 92–93.

165. Martial, VIII, 14, 5–6.

166. Ibid. III, 30, 3; Juvenal, 3, 225.

167. See p. 66.

168. Ulpian, Lib XXIII *ad Edictum; Si . . . plures diviso inter se cenaculo habitent . . .;* cp. para 1: *Si quis cenaculariam exercens modicum sibi hospitium retinuerit, residuum locaverit pluribus.*

169. Martial, XI, 32, 1; 56, 5.

170. Ibid. XII, 32, 11.

171. Ibid. XI, 32, 2; Juvenal, 5, 8.

172. Martial, XII, 57, 14.

173. Ibid. I, 41, 4–5.

174. Quintilian, VI, 3, 74.

175. Horace, Epist., I, 7, 65.

176. Statius, Silvæ, IV, 9, 21–22.

177. Martial, I, 41, 8–16.

178. Seneca, Epist., 56, 2.

179. Horace, Ars Poet., 249.

180. Martial, I, 41, 6.

181. Juvenal, 7, 220–1:

> *Et patere inde aliquid decrescere, non aliter quam*
> *Institor hibernae tegetis niveique cadurci.*

182. Martial, I, 41, 7.

183. Apuleius, Met., I, 4. Apuleius places the scene in the provinces, in the *agora* at Athens; but it is known that jugglers of every type were very popular with the people of Rome, and there must have been sword-swallowers at Rome.

184. Juvenal, 5, 154–5.

185. Martial, I, 41, 11.

186. Aulus Gellius, I, 15, 9; cf. Phaedrus, I, 14.

187. Juvenal, 6, 588.

188. Cicero, Cat., I, 4, 8: *Dico te venisse . . . inter falcarios.*

189. Mentioned in the *Notitia* and the *Curiosum;* see p. 40.

190. Martial, II, 17, 3: *Argique letum multus obsidet sutor;* however in I, 3, 1, he mentions the *tabernae librariae* of the Argiletum (*Argiletanas . . . tabernas*) and in I, 117, 9, the shop of the bookseller Atrectus, also in the *Argiletum.*

191. Horace, Ars Poet., 372–3:

> *Mediocribus esse poetis*
> *Non homines, non di, non concessere columnae.*

192. Martial, I, 117, 10–11.

193. Aulus Gellius, XVIII, 4, 1.

194. Juvenal, 1, 105–6:

> Sed quinque tabernae
> Quadringenta parant.

195. This practice, for which there is evidence in Greece and Italy in the Roman age (Alciphron, 3, 30; Lucian, Ind., 29) and which is probably very old, must have been introduced in Rome when barbers arrived from Greece (see p. 108).

196. E.g. CIL, XIV, 4015: IN HIS PRAEDIS AVRELIAE FAVSTINIANAE BALINEVS LAVAT MORE VRBICO ET OMNIS HVMANITAS PRAESTATVR, where *balineus* will be noticed for *balineum*. Cf. X, 7296 (Dessau 7680) which is in Latin and Greek and contains mistakes in both languages.

197. A stonemason and marblecutter enticed clients thus: TITVLOS SCRIBENDOS VEL SI QVID OPERIS MARMORARI OPVS FVERIT HIC HABES (CIL, VI, 9556 = Dessau 7679).

198. Horace, Sat., II, 6, 28.

199. Ibid. 29–31.

200. Juvenal, 3, 245–6.

201. Horace, Epist., II, 2, 73.

202. CIL, I, 206 (= Dessau 6085) (*Lex Iulia Municipalis*), 11, 56 et seq.

203. Horace, Epist., II, 2, 72 Martial, V, 22, 7–8.

204. Seneca, De tranq. anim., 12, 2: *Impellunt obvios et se aliosque praecipitant.*

205. Horace, Epist., II, 2, 75: *Hac rabiosa fugit canis, hac lutulenta ruit sus.*

206. De tranq. anim., 12, 2–4.

207. XII, 57.

208. To stop eclipses, regarded as ill-omened, recourse was had to such measures, including blowing trumpets. Tacitus, Annals, I, 28, 3.

209. Horace, Sat., II, 6, 60.

210. Horace, Odes, III, 26, 6.

211. Ibid. Epist., II, 2, 79.

212. Suetonius, Aug., 29.

213. Juvenal, 3, 10. Many travellers took baggage, slaves, and a large suite with them. (Cicero, pro Milone, 10, 28: *qui . . . cum uxore veheretur in raeda, paenulatus, magno et impedito et muliebri ac delicato ancillarum puerorumque comitatu . . .* cf. Ad Att., VI, 1, 25; Suetonius, Nero, 30.)

214. Juvenal, 3, 236–7.

215. Horace, Epist., I, 2, 35; Ars Poet., 268–9.

216. V, 62.

217. Martial, XII, 57, 5.

218. Ibid. XIV, 223, 1:

> Surgite; iam vendit pueris ientacula pistor
> Cristataeque sonant undique lucis aves.

219. Seneca, De ira, III, 18, 4.

220. Juvenal, 5, 8.

221. Pliny, Epist., III, 12, 2.

222. Catullus, LVIII, 4–5; Propertius, IV, 7, 19–20.

223. Juvenal, 3, 302; 5, 54–55.

224. Ibid. 3, 278.

225. Ibid. 8, 158.

226. Cicero, pro Caelio, 8, 20; cf. Ovid, Amores, I, 6, 55.

227. Suetonius, Nero, 26.

228. Horace, Odes, I, 17, 25–28.

229. Terence, Eunuch, 771; Tibullus, I, 10, 53–54; Propertius, II, 5, 21–24; Ovid, Amores, I, 9, 20; Ars Am., III, 567, etc. The idea of such violence, realistically represented in Terence (Adelphi, 155) comes from Greek sources but it existed in Rome. Even Seneca (Nat. quaest., IV, praef. 6) regards it as quite normal for a girl, finding her lover's door closed, to knock it down: quemadmodum (ostium) opponi amicae solet; quae si impulit, grata est; gratior si effregit. If girls could behave like this, we may well imagine that boys had even less scruple in doing so.

230. Horace, III, 26, 6–8.

231. Suetonius, Nero, 26.

232. See p. 43, Note 13.

233. Suetonius, Otho, 2: Ferebatur . . . vagari noctibus solitus, atque invalidum quemque obviorum, vel potulentum corripere ac distento sago impositum in sublime iactare; cf. Martial, I, 3, 8.

234. 3, 267.

235. Digest, IX, 3, 1.

236. Ulpian, Lib XXIII ad Edictum: Publice enim utile est sine metu et periculo per itinera commeari.

237. Ibid.: Si eo ictu homo liber perisse dicetur, quinquaginta aureorum iudicium dabo. The aureus was worth one hundred sesterces (about £1). The regular minting of aurei began under Julius Caesar (49 B.C.).

238. Juvenal, 3, 286.

239. Suetonius, Domit, 4.

240. Statius, Silvae, I, 6, 85.

241. Suetonius, Cal., 18: Scaenicos ludos fecit . . . quondam et nocturnos, accensis tota urbe luminibus.

242. Tacitus, Ann., XV, 44, 7–8.

CHAPTER II

The Roman House

The two main types of Roman house. The aristocratic Roman house (Pompeii). The apartment house (Ostia). General characteristics of the aristocratic house. The different parts: vestibulum *and* fauces, *the door,* posticum, atrium, tablinum, alae, andron, peristylium, exhedra, oecus, *bedrooms,* triclinium, *kitchen, slave quarters,* tabernæ. *Other parts. Wall paintings, stuccos, mosaics. Plans of Pompeian houses.*

THE Roman house, as described by Vitruvius and seen in the ruins of Pompeii, was divided into two parts: the first grouped round the *atrium*, the second round the *peristylium* (fig. 11).

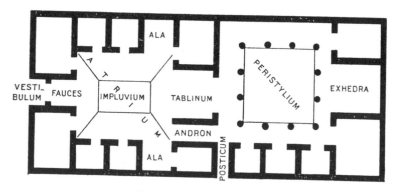

11. PLAN OF A ROMAN HOUSE

The early Italian house consisted only of the *atrium* and the surrounding rooms, with, in most cases, a small garden at the back. An example of this primitive type of house can be seen today in the so-called House of the Surgeon at Pompeii (fig. 12). Out of the small plot at the back of the early house developed the *peristylium*, a garden surrounded by colonnades on to which rooms of various sizes opened on all sides, the largest and most handsome one at the back, at the farthest distance from the *atrium*. The

54

peristylium, both in general appearance and in name, reproduced the men's rooms of a Greek house. While the names of the front rooms of a Roman house are Italian (*atrium, fauces, alae, tablinum*) those of the back are Greek (*peristylium, triclinium, oecus, exhedra*).

This is the typical Roman house, corresponding to the general plan of Pompeian houses and to the literary references to aristo-

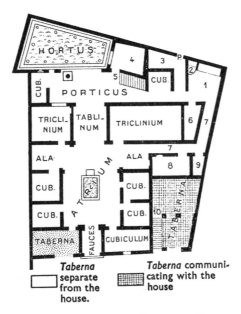

12. THE HOUSE OF THE SURGEON, POMPEII

CUB = *cubiculum*   i = *impluvium-compluvium*   P = *posticum*
1. Kitchen 2 & 3. Lavatories 4. Room of uncertain purpose (possibly summer dining-room) 5. Stairs leading to the upper floor 6. Storeroom 7. Servants' passage 8. Dark room (probably storeroom) 9. Small open courtyard 10. Stair leading to a *pergula*

cratic houses. But recent excavations at Ostia and some evidence in the literature of the Imperial age (Juvenal, Martial and the Digest) allow us to compare this type of Roman house with the huge blocks of apartment houses, the solution to the housing problem in most large cities, particularly Rome; these human rabbit-warrens resembled modern houses more closely than the Pompeian type, both in appearance and in arrangement of rooms. The two types will be dealt with separately.

The typical Roman house was generally occupied only by one family, and differed from the modern house in the following ways: (1) It faced inwards, not, like our houses, outwards. Light and air penetrated from the two central open spaces round which the other rooms were grouped: the *atrium*, which drew the air and light enjoyed by the surrounding rooms from the opening in the middle of the roof, and the garden of the *peristylium* which was even lighter than the *atrium* because it was more open and normally more spacious.

(2) It had no view outwards. Outside windows are rare, small and irregularly placed. Even when they do exist they never have an outside frame. This is a fact familiar to anybody who walks through the streets of Pompeii and, comparing the splendour and magnificence of the inner rooms with the grim, rough outside wall, is reminded of a modern prison or a convent rather than an aristocratic mansion.

(3) It is normally on one floor only, and even when there is more than one floor there is only a limited number of rooms on the upper floor, proof that such rooms were built to meet individual needs, and not according to any definite plan.

(4) The different rooms were intended for one purpose only: for example, the *cubiculum* as a bedroom, the *triclinium* as a dining room, the *tablinum* as a reception room, etc.

The large apartment houses, on the other hand, discovered in the excavations at Ostia (see p. 55), reveal the housing conditions of the lower and lower-middle classes at Rome, and resemble modern houses in the following ways:

(1) They are higher than Pompeian houses, sometimes rising to three or four storeys (about 50 feet).

(2) There are many windows and balconies in the outside walls (see Plate 8). Being economically built, to make the best possible use of the space available, the houses at Ostia were ventilated from outside.

(3) The exterior walls are pleasant to look at.

(4) The rooms are not intended for a fixed purpose (as, for example, the *tablinum*, the *oecus*, etc., in the Pompeian house); they have no special characteristics, either in arrangement or construction and the inhabitants used them as the needs of the family required.

8. Ostia. View of the Via di Diana showing the ruins of houses with balconies. (*p. 56*)

9. Pompeii.   A *taberna* with marble-covered counter.   (*p. 66*)

10. Pompeii.   Mill and oven.   (*p. 66*)

11. Pompeii. Peristyle of the House of Marcus Lucretius. (p. 64)

12. Pompeii. Peristyle of the House of the Vettii.

13. Pompeii. House of the Silver Wedding. View of the peristyle from the atrium. (*p. 62*)

14. Pompeii. Mosaic fountain.

There is no doubt that the lower-class houses of Rome were of this type; we read of interminable stairs to the top floor,[1] of windows so close to each other that neighbours could shake hands.[2] These cramped houses were inconvenient and dangerous, usually without any inside water supply,[3] exposed, furthermore, to the risk of fire and collapse. 'We', says Juvenal,[4] 'inhabit a city supported for the most part by slender props; for that is how the bailiff holds up the tottering house, patches up gaping cracks in the old wall, bidding the inmates sleep at ease under a roof ready to tumble about their ears.'

This was no exaggeration; Cicero writing to Atticus[5] informs him of the lamentable condition of one of his lodging houses. 'Two of my *tabernae* have collapsed; in the others the walls are all cracked; not only the tenants, but even the mice, have left.'

Noise from all sides penetrated into these apartments balanced precariously on top of each other with the windows opening onto the street. Seneca (see p. 225) complains of a bath on the floor below, Martial[6] of a school, Juvenal[7] of every type of noise rising from the street. Only aristocratic houses were satisfactorily protected by their design from outside noise. It was another social injustice that peaceful sleep at night was a privilege of the rich.[8] 'Sleep in Rome is expensive', says Juvenal (*magnis opibus dormitur in urbe*). Inside the house was a series of ill-lit rooms, all narrow and cramped. The poor, envious of the peristyles of the rich, relieved their misery by growing flowers in window boxes.[9] Nature, it has been said, cannot 'be driven out with a pitchfork',[10] and men have always contrived to recall it somehow.

The typical Roman house most adequately met the needs of the family life of Italy when the imported Greek culture had reached its fullest development. In the last stages of its growth it has aristocratic characteristics; it is a convenient, refined and beautiful house, which only the rich citizens of Rome or the inhabitants of a prosperous city like Pompeii could afford, and its sprawling plan caused a land hunger which made it difficult to meet the housing needs of a growing population. Built as it was, this house invited —almost enforced—an open-air life; it is so much a house of a southern people, that when the Romans began to build their palaces in northern Italy or the north European provinces, they adopted a complete system of heating, circulating warm air along

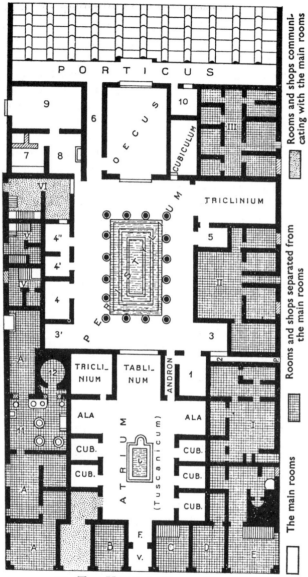

13. THE HOUSE OF PANSA, POMPEII

CUB = *cubiculum*   F = *fauces*   P = *posticum*   V = *vestibulum*
1. Room opening on to the *peristylium* 2. Passage leading to the *posticum*
3. 3′ Rooms opening on to the *peristylium* 4. 4′4″ Rooms along one side of
the *peristylium* 5. Room connecting the *triclinium* and the *peristylium* 6.
Passage 7. Stables 8. Kitchen 9. Shed 10. Storeroom
A, A, A, Baker's shop (11. Room with grid-stones 12. The oven) B. *Taberna*
C. *Taberna* with stairs leading to the *pergula* D. *Taberna* with back shop
E. *Taberna* connected with a small upper room I, II, III, Small rented apartments IV, V, Small rented apartments with upper rooms VI, Small apart-
ments with upper rooms, connected with the main building

hollow walls, in this resembling modern methods (see p. 226). In the Pompeian type of Roman house, the inmates were always in contact with fresh air, which came down from the *impluvium*, spread in from the garden, circulating among corridors and rooms. The rooms surrounding the *atrium* and the *peristylium* were dark and airless when closed; a sensible man used them as seldom as possible. When the weather was fine and the temperature mild, the family ate in the garden.

The Ostian house contained a succession of rooms and corridors, a network of inside and outside staircases varying from house to house, and this lack of uniformity strengthened the resemblance to modern houses. Every room in the Pompeian house, on the other hand, had its own purpose and name, a knowledge of which is necessary, if only to understand the frequent allusions to them in literature.

Vestibulum and *fauces.*—A Roman house was not entered, like a modern house, through a door opening straight on to the street; the door stood half-way down a passage leading from the street into the *atrium*. The passage was thus divided into two distinct parts: (1) the *vestibulum* in front of the door, (2) the *fauces* beyond it. Normally the *fauces* seemed to be simply a continuation of the *vestibulum*, with which they formed a single passage, broken only by the door. The *vestibulum* could, however, be even narrower than the *fauces*; the house of Epidius Rufus at Pompeii offers an example of this.

We know, though archaeological confirmation is lacking, that two neighbouring houses might share a *vestibulum*.[11]

The *vestibulum* of the aristocratic houses in Rome differed in not forming part of the main body of the building, but being built between the street and the door of the house; normally the floor was raised,[12] and steps led up to it.[13] Statues, chariots and arcades of magnificent columns decorated the *vestibulum*. Here the clients were herded together waiting for the *salutatio matutina*[14] (see p. 23).

The door; *posticum.*—The door (*janua*), in the widest sense, consisted of:

(1) *Limen:* the threshold (*limen inferum*), slightly raised above the floor of the *vestibulum*, and the lintel (*limen superum*); the threshold was generally, and the lintel often, of marble.[15]

(2) *Postes:* the door-posts (*postes*), protruding from the two side walls of the *vestibulum*, were faced with a covering of wood

(*antepagmenta*), stucco or marble. On the thresholds of Pompeian houses the holes can be seen in which these coverings were fixed.

(3) *Fores:* the actual door (*fores*), usually consisted of two or more leaves (*valvae*). These *valvae* were not attached to the door-posts by hinges, as in modern houses, but turned on wooden pivots covered with iron or bronze which creaked as they opened.[16]

Besides the main door there was a servants' entrance, the *posticum*. To judge from the almost universal rule at Pompeii, it was not situated in the back of the house, as the name might suggest, but opened in one of the side walls on to an alley. It was used by slaves and humble visitors, such as errand boys from the shops which supplied the kitchen, and sometimes even by the master when he wanted to slip out without being seen by his importunate clients: *Atria servantem postico falle clientem.*[17]

Atrium.—As we have seen, the front part of the Roman house centred round this, and the smaller rooms opened on to it. The *lectus genialis*[18] stood opposite the entrance, recalling the days when for the mother of the family the *atrium* was work room, reception room and bedroom combined. It was a large room with a wide opening in the roof, under which a rectangular tank[19] with beautifully decorated sides (Plate 13) was dug in the floor to catch the rainwater. An opening in one of the upper edges of the basin, surrounded by a cylindrical *puteal*, was connected with a subterranean tank.

Vitruvius[20] describes five types of *atrium:*

(1) *Tuscanicum*, without columns, where the weight of the roof is borne entirely by the rafters.

(2) *tetrastylum*, with one column at each of the four corners of the *impluvium*. (The House of the Silver Wedding[21] at Pompeii provides an excellent example of this: Plate 13.)

(3) *Corinthium*, similar to the *tetrastylum*, but with a greater number of columns and a larger opening for light.

(4) *displuviatum* (there is no certain surviving example of this). Here the roof was built sloping towards the side walls. The rainwater ran off the roof through outlets at the corners.

(5) *testudinatum*, a covered *atrium*, the few examples of which are found only in small and unimportant houses.

Although the heavy wooden beams made both its construction and maintenance very expensive, the **atrium Tuscanicum** seems to

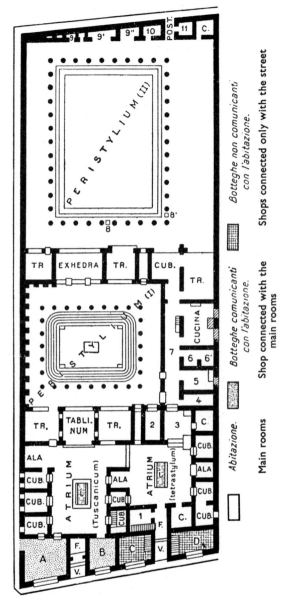

14. THE HOUSE OF THE FAUN, POMPEII

C = *Cella*   CUB = *cubiculum*   F = *fauces*   i = *impluvium-compluvium*
TR = *tricoinium*   V = *vestibulum*
A, B *Tabernae* communicating with the main rooms C, D *Tabernae* separated
from the main rooms, each with a staircase leading to the *pergula* 1. Room
for the doorkeeper (ostiarius) with steps to the upper floor 2. Room opening
on to the *peristylium* 3. Passage to the servants' quarters 4, 5. Stables
6. 6′ Bathrooms 7. Passage with windows looking on to the *peristylium*
8. 8′ Well heads 9. 9′ 9″ Alcoves with tall pedestals for statues 10. Storeroom 11. Room for the doorkeeper responsible for the porticus

have been the normal type of *atrium* in the Roman house. This seems a legitimate inference from the overwhelming prevalence of this type of *atrium* in Pompeian houses. Besides the strong influence of tradition, which preserved in this type the primitive form of the Italian house, other practical and aesthetic considerations contributed to this: the *atrium Tuscanicum*, as it had no columns, allowed the glance of the visitor upon entering to travel across the *atrium* and the *tablinum* to the light and airy peristyle with its garden and decorations.

At one time the domestic hearth burned in the *atrium*, the heart of the primitive house; during the day master and servants gathered there, and the whole life of the family centred round it. But with the gradual development of the back of the house, the centre of family life moved inwards, to the *tablinum* and the peristyle. The *atrium* remained a large richly furnished sitting room, but, except in unusual circumstances or in families where ancient customs were deliberately maintained, it ceased to be the centre of domestic life. So the search for the household hearth in the *atrium* of Pompeian houses, which literary references had led us to regard as an essential element of this part of the Roman house and from which the very name seems to have been derived,[22] proved fruitless. The small marble table (*cartibulum*) (Plate 13), placed inside the *impluvium* against the back wall, is a survival of the household hearth of earlier times. Normal decorations of the *atrium* were a chapel for the *Lares* (*Lararium*), the household safe (*arca*) (Plate 29) and sometimes a herm with a marble bust of the master of the house.

Tablinum.—This was a large room opening for its whole length along the wall of the *atrium* facing the door. At the entrance to the *tablinum* the corners of the walls were shaped into pillars, thus forming an effective interior view. The entrance was not closed by a door, but a curtain, as the magnificent bronze supports found in some Pompeian houses show. On the other hand, a second opening on to the peristyle in the farther wall was closed by a screen or door. In good weather, when the screen was removed, the peristyle could be seen from the *atrium* through the *tablinum*. In the earliest period the *tablinum* was the study of the *paterfamilias*.

Alae.—This was the name given to the two symmetrical rooms opening their full length on each side of the *atrium*, normally at the end, sometimes in the middle. Their use remains uncertain.

Probably, rather than serving a particular purpose their general arrangement of the rooms, they were a survival moe of an ancient form of house. We know that in early Italian houses, where the *atrium* was covered, the *alae* allowed the entrance of light and air and provided a connexion with the outside by means of a window or door.

Rooms round the *atrium*.—It is necessary to distinguish the following rooms built round the *atrium*, according to their situation:

(1) In the entrance wall. These rooms normally gave on to the street and were used as *tabernae* (see p. 66), but if they opened inwards they were used as servants' rooms, bedrooms, or even small dining rooms.

(2) On the two sides of the *atrium*: bedrooms (*cubicula*) with only one door on to the *atrium*.

(3) In the back wall of the *atrium* next to the *tablinum*: rooms which generally opened on to the peristyle, but sometimes communicated directly with the *atrium*.

Andron.—A passage, called the *andron* by a misuse of the Greek word, led from the *atrium* to the peristyle.[23]

Peristylium, exhedra, oecus.—The peristyle, the inmost part of the Roman house, consisted of a garden surrounded on all sides by a colonnade generally on two storeys. This is the typical peristyle, but in practice varieties and adaptations were introduced to meet the demands of space, or the personal fancy of the architect or owner. At Pompeii, for example it is not unusual for the colonnade to run only along one side of the peristyle, or even to be missing altogether, thus giving the impression of a plain garden. In the rooms surrounding the peristyle—bedrooms, dining rooms and reception rooms—there is a greater variety of distribution and appearance than in those round the *atrium*.

Some rooms, larger and more richly furnished than the others, had special names: the *exhedra*, a spacious room, opening for its whole length on to the arcade at the far end of the peristyle, corresponding to the *tablinum*, and the *oecus* (from the Greek οἶκος, house or room), perhaps a larger communal dining room. If decorated inside by columns, it was called *oecus Corinthius*.

The small secluded garden, protected from the winds and the curiosity of neighbours, was as carefully looked after as a drawing room. Herbs and flowers were grown in symmetrical rows, particularly roses, violets and lilies. Small works of art were scattered everywhere, tables, statues, columns, slabs with fine reliefs (Plate 11). Marble ornaments stood on the paths. They sprang up among the bushes at evenly spaced intervals or hung from the roof of the colonnade. This may be beautiful, but to our taste it seems artificial and vulgar. Art demands too much of nature and all these costly toys tend to divert the spectator from his pleasure in the greenery and the open air.

There was often a pool in the middle of the garden. If the garden was large, a canal, the *Euripus* ran through it between brick walls. Numerous fountains added to the attraction of the place, and, where space allowed it, a stone dining table.

The Bedrooms.—We have already observed that in the Pompeian house each room had a definite purpose, which made it impossible, as in the houses of Ostia and today, for the same room to be used for different purposes according to the wishes of the occupants and the needs of the family. At Pompeii the position for the bed in the *cubiculum* was distinguished from the rest of the room in various ways:

(1) The mosaic in the floor on the spot intended for the bed is white and usually surrounded by a particular motif.

(2) The wall paintings are different both in colour and style.

(3) The ceiling above the bed is lower than in the rest of the *cubiculum* and is always vaulted.

The bed therefore stood in a niche. The bedrooms round the *atrium* differed from those round the *peristylium*; the former were smaller but higher and were entered by a single narrow door, while the latter usually opened on to the arcade of the peristyle for all, or almost all, their length, and had a second entrance in one of the side walls.

Sometimes in front of the bedroom there was an antechamber *procoeton* (προκοιτών), where a trusted servant slept (*cubicularius*, or *servus a cubiculo*).

Triclinium.—Only with the development of civilisation did the Romans begin to build rooms (*triclinia*) to be used exclusively as dining rooms. This happened when the Greek practice of dining in a reclining position was introduced into Rome (see p. 92). Previously the Romans had dined in the *atrium*, the *tablinum*, or a room above the *tablinum* (*cenaculum* in its early sense (see p. 92)).[24] The dining rooms of Pompeian houses can only give us a

15. Pompeii. Mosaic of a cat killing a partridge. (*p. 67*)

16. Rome. Mosaic of the ἀσάρωτος οτκος. (*p. 95*)

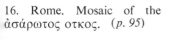

17. Rome. Mosaic of a skeleton. (*p. 97*)

18. Pompeii. Detail of a fresco showing hunting scenes.   (*p. 66*)

19. Rome. Detail of a fresco from a house on the Esquiline.   (*p. 66*)

very approximate idea of the sumptuous *triclinia* of the aristocratic houses of Rome, huge rooms intended for the entertainment of a crowd of guests. Those of Pompeii are comparatively small. There was scarcely room for the three couches even when placed right against the walls, and very little space remained for the slaves who were waiting. The *oecus Corinthius* (see p. 63) was more convenient if it was used, as seems likely, as a dining room. The dining couches stood in the inner space between the columns so that an open passage remained between them and the walls.

The Kitchen.—Seneca[25] wrote: *adspice culinas nostras et concursantes inter tot ignes coquos,* and we imagine a vast room with space for many fires, brick ovens and portable stoves, round which are occupied cooks, undercooks and scullions, a veritable army under the orders of the head cook (*archimagirus*), the supreme ruler of the kitchen. The complexity and splendour of the Roman banquet necessarily leads us to think of a spacious and busy kitchen, extensively equipped with a large variety of utensils. This type of kitchen must certainly have been an exception, a very rare exception, in the largest houses; the normal custom is reflected by the very humble kitchens which we find at Pompeii as well as at Ostia and the *Domus Liviae* on the Palatine; they are poky little holes, largely occupied by a brick oven, where it is difficult to see how more than one cook could have managed at a time without confusion. The room was small and dark. The smoke found its way out as best it could through a window or a hole in the roof, because chimneys were rarely built and there were no chimney stacks on the roof.[26] As a result, there was no draught at all; this was both inconvenient and dangerous. For a kitchen to catch fire, as described in one of Horace's[27] *Satires,* must have been a fairly common occurrence:

> *Nam vaga per veterem dilapso flamma culinam*
> *Volcano summum properabat lambere tectum.*

In addition to the fire there was a small oven for baking bread and a sink (*confluvium, fusorium*) to allow water to drain away.

The kitchen was the most neglected part of the Roman house, with no fixed position reserved for it in the normal plan; we find it in different positions, wherever there is a little free space, to fit in with the general plan of the building. This should not cause any surprise, for reserving a room specially for use as a kitchen is a refinement of civilisation. The ancient Romans had no kitchen; they prepared their dinner in the *atrium*, or sometimes in the open air, like the Homeric heroes who lived in splendid palaces without kitchens.[28]

The lavatory and bathrooms were next to the kitchen.

Slaves' quarters.—These too (*cellae servorum, cellae familiares* or *familiaricae*) had no fixed situation; only the room for the door-keeper (*ostiarius*) was naturally next to the door.

The *tabernae.*—In the general plan of the Roman house, the *tabernae* form part of the rooms surrounding the *atrium*; like them, they were tall and narrow, but opened on to the street. Usually at the entrance there was a brick counter used to display goods for sale (Plate 9). Inside were one or more backrooms separated by a dividing wall. Normally a mezzanine floor divided the *taberna* into two rooms; the upper room (*pergula*) was reached by a staircase inside the shop or straight from the street. This cramped space was usually the house of the very poor. This explains why *taberna* and *pergula* can also mean 'hovels' as in the proverb, *qui in pergula natus est aedes non somniatur*;[29] the *tabernae*, to which Horace[30] alludes in two well-known lines, are hovels:

> *Pallida mors aequo pulsat pede pauperum tabernas*
> *Regumque turres.*

Subsidiary parts.—Other parts of the Roman house are the baths reserved for the exclusive use of the family (see p. 221); in some houses an outside part was used as a mill and leased to a baker (Plate 10).

Wall paintings, stuccos, mosaics.—The inside of a room was decorated to suit its use. Skilled craftsmen decorated the floor, ceilings and walls of the large reception rooms. The walls were painted (Plates 18, 19, 47) with panels of brilliant colour, architectural or floral motifs, hunting scenes, cupids variously occupied, etc. Some copied famous ancient paintings; to this indirect evidence we owe our knowledge of many lost masterpieces.

The ceiling of the most magnificent houses was coffered (*lacunar*) with inlays of gold and ivory[31] or, especially where the ceiling was vaulted, with stucco (Plate 18). These stuccos were executed partly by moulds, partly with tools, sometimes corrected by a light pressure of the finger, and the subjects depicted were chosen with rather excessive preoccupation with variety, but with a pleasant humour: rural scenes, open air sacrifices, mythological scenes, or imaginative and ornamental motifs of every sort; rosettes, lines, bearded heads, winged victories, griffins, many-branched candlesticks. At times these works are carelessly executed, but they reveal in the artist an intelligent feeling for effect and great quickness in appreciating the interplay of light and shade.

The mosaic floors were magnificent; the materials were of the costliest, including precious stones, such as onyx, rare marbles, crystal, and even cubes of pure gold. The workmanship of the surviving mosaics varies considerably; many are the products of a purely industrial art, but some are to be numbered amongst the finest ancient works of art, small mosaics like the doves of the Capitoline Museum,[32] larger ones such as the battle of Issus. There is a great variety of motifs also in the mosaics. The tendency is to suit the subject to the room; fish, tritons and river scenes are depicted in the baths, the watch-dog in the hall, dead animals or scenes of feasting in the dining room (Plate 15).

The careful study of the plans reproduced in this book is recommended. The first (fig. 11) does not correspond to any actual house, but shows the plan of a typical Pompeian house. The aristocratic Roman house, though more splendid and complex and differing in some details, was built on this plan. The second (fig. 12) is the plan of the House of the Surgeon at Pompeii, so called because some surgical instruments (now in the Naples Museum) were found there; this house is an example of the survival of the primitive type of Italian house, consisting essentially of the *atrium* and the surrounding rooms. It has no peristyle, but a small garden at the back, which in the plan of the house appears as a simple addition. The third (fig. 13) is the plan of the so-called House of Pansa at Pompeii. The sides are occupied by small houses and shops, but its interior comes nearest to the ideal plan. The House of the Faun (fig. 14) owes its name to a bronze statuette of a dancing faun which decorated the *compluvium*. It is also known as the House of the Great Mosaic because the floor of the *exhedra* was decorated with the famous mosaic of Darius and Alexander at the battle of Issus (the finest ancient mosaic we possess, now in the Naples Museum). This magnificent mansion shows the complexity and development of which the primitive plan of the house with *atrium* and peristyle was capable. There are two adjoining *atria*, and two communicating peristyles. Of the *atria*, the *Tuscanicum* and its surrounding rooms were used by the owner's family. The tetrastyle, on the other hand, with its surrounding rooms and those to which it leads, was in the humblest part of the house, reserved for slaves. Of the peristyles, the rear one is merely there to ensure as much light and air as possible for its occupants. The one leading out of the *atrium Tuscanicum*, on the other hand, is magnificent; spacious rooms opened on to it, among these, corresponding to the *tablinum*, the *exhedra* with its great mosaic floor. If we isolate the *atrium Tuscanicum* and the first of the two peristyles in our imagination, they reproduce the plan of a typical Roman house. This plan resulted from the expansion of the primitive nucleus of the *atrium* and the peristyle with their surrounding rooms.

Further Reading

For this chapter and the succeeding one see D. S. Robertson, *A Handbook of Greek and Roman Architecture* (Second edition Cambridge, 1943).

For an account of the Ostian house, see R. Meiggs, *Roman Ostia* (Oxford, 1960), Chapter 12.

NOTES

Chapter II

1. Martial, I, 117, 7; VII, 20, 20.
2. Ibid. I, 86, 1–2.
3. Ibid. IX, 18.
4. 3, 193–6.
5. Ad Att., XIV, 9, 1.
6. IX, 68.
7. 3, 234.
8. Juvenal, 2, 235, cf. Martial, XII, 57, the liveliest description of the uproar in Rome.
9. Martial, XI, 18, 2. *Sed rus est mihi maius in fenestra.*
10. Horace, Epist., I, 10, 24.
11. Paulus, I, VI ad Sabinum (D.X, 3, 19, para. 1).
12. Aulus Gellius, XVI, 5, 3–9.

CHAPTER II, NOTES

13. Seneca, Epist., 84, 12: *praeteri istos gradus divitum et magno adgestu suspensa vestibula.*

14. Seneca, Ad Marciam, 10, 1; ad Polyb., 4, 2; Suetonius, Tib., 32; Juvenal, 1, 132.

15. Horace, Epist., I, 18, 73: *Intra marmoreum venerandi limen amici.*

16. Lucretius, II, 450: *Aeraque quae claustris restantia vociferantur.*

17. Horace, Epist., I, 5, 31.

18. Ibid. I, 1, 87; it is also called *lectus adversus.*

19. The names of the opening and the tank below are interchangeable. It seems (Varro, De Ling. Lat., V, 161; Festus, 96, 10) that technically the former was called *compluvium* the latter *impluvium.* But other writers use the words with the opposite meanings.

20. VI, 3, 1.

21. So called because the excavation was carried out in the presence of the King and Queen of Italy in 1893, the year of their silver wedding.

22. Isidore, XV, 3, 1.

23. In Greek ἀνδρών is the men's apartments. As Vitruvius expressly mentions (VI, 7, 5), many other Greek words applied by the Romans to the parts of their houses, have lost their original meaning.

24. As the *cenaculum* formed the upper half of the *tablinum* the word came to mean 'ceiling'.

25. Epist., 114, 25.

26. The exterior of a house is shown in some Pompeian paintings, and there are no chimneys in the roof. This absence of chimneys is confirmed by the way the stove is built in the kitchen of the *Domus Liviae* on the Palatine.

27. Sat., I, 5, 73-74.

28. G. Finsler, *Homer* (Leipzig, 1914), p. 121. But a sizeable room in the West House at Pylos was 'certainly used as a kitchen'. *The Mycenae Tablets,* III. Ed. J. Chadwick, p. 23.

29. Petronius, 74. *Somniatur* is vulgar Latin for *somniat.*

30. Odes, I, 4, 13-14.

31. Cf. Horace, Odes, II, 18, 1-2.

> *Non ebur neque aureum*
> *Mea renidet in domo lacunar.*

32. An imperfect copy of a famous mosaic by Sosos (Pliny, N.H., XXXVI, 184).

The Roman Villa

Villa rustica *and* villa urbana. *General plan of the* villa rustica. *The* villa rustica *at Boscoreale near Pompeii.* Villa urbana. *Pliny's villas. The surroundings of the villa.*

THE Romans usually had two buildings on their country estates, the *villa rustica*, to house the slaves engaged in agricultural labour under the superintendence of the *vilicus* (a trusted slave in charge of the *familia rustica*, rather like a bailiff), and the *villa urbana* or *pseudourbana*, where the owner stayed when visiting the country. In building the first, the only consideration was the practical needs of an agricultural community; the latter, in a picturesque and airy site, offered all the amenities to which city life had made men accustomed. Not every estate had a *villa urbana*; when the owner was not particularly wealthy, he occupied a corner of the *villa rustica*, or at the most built a small easily-run house. Cicero and Pliny had splendid *villae urbanae*, unlike Horace who lived on his Sabine farm together with his bailiff and his slaves.

The *villa rustica* had two courts (*cortes*), an inner and an outer one, each with its own tank (*piscina*). In the inner court the tank was used for watering animals, in the outer one for different agricultural purposes, such as softening leather and soaking lupin seeds. Brick buildings surrounded the first court, forming the *villa rustica* in its most limited sense, the part of the farm occupied by the slaves. A large kitchen stood at the centre; on the farm the kitchen was not, as it was in the city, only used for the preparation of food, but was a meeting place and workshop as well.

Near the kitchen, so as to make full use of the heat it produced, were the slaves' bathrooms, the cellars and the stables for cattle (*bubilia*) and horses (*equilia*). If possible, the henhouse was also near the kitchen, because smoke was thought good for chickens. Far from the kitchen, and if possible facing north, were the buildings which required a dry situation, such as the granary (*granaria*), the barn (*horrea*) and the fruit stores (*oporothecae*). The store-houses most exposed to the danger of fire might also form a building (*villa fructuaria*), completely separate from the *villa rustica*. Close to the *villa rustica* was the threshing-floor, with sheds nearby, such as the barn for agricultural implements or waggons (*plaustra*) and the *nubilarium* where the grain was temporarily stored in case of sudden storms.

It is not certain where the slaves lived. We know, however, that there were their bedrooms (*cellae familiares*), the *ergastulum*, a kind of prison where recalcitrant slaves were punished with hard labour (see p. 125) and the *valetudinarium* for sick slaves. When there was no *villa urbana*, the better rooms were reserved for the owner.

An example of the Roman *villa rustica* is found in the villa of Boscoreale near Pompeii, famous not only for the importance of its ruins but also for the silverware found there (now in the Louvre, Plates 20–23). Its plan deserves attention (fig. 15).

The *villa urbana* stood where a wide view of the countryside or sea could be enjoyed; it was a purely luxurious building, having no practical purpose or function like the farm; this villa in the complexity and richness of its rooms reflected the tastes, and bore witness to the wealth, of its owner. Some villas had no farmland attached, but stood in their own grounds surrounded by woods, parks and gardens. Such villas, sometimes called *praetoria*, increased in number during the Empire. Remains of them are found in Italy, France, Switzerland, southern Germany, England and North Africa.

The practical spirit of the Romans, who fully appreciated the pleasures of life, introduced these large commodious villas, well cooled in summer, well heated in winter, wherever their armies and civilisation penetrated.

Many different types of this villa are to be found. Classical authors describe as a characteristic of the *villa urbana* that its peristyle was entered directly from the *vestibulum* and not, as in city houses, the *atrium*. But there seem to be exceptions even to this. In Pliny's[1] Laurentine villa, for example, there was an *atrium* through the *vestibulum; cuius in prima parte atrium frugi nec tamen sordidum*. The rooms were variously grouped in separate buildings (*conclavia, diaetae*) connected by covered corridors (*crypto-porticus*), often fitted with windows.

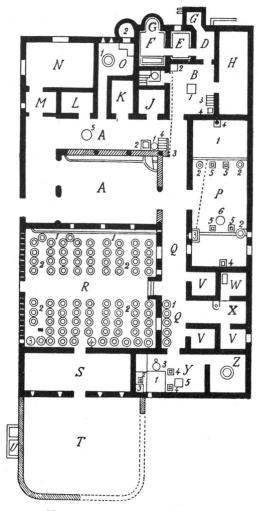

15. The villa rustica at Boscoreale

(from Blümner, *Röm Privataltertümer*, adapted).

A. Courtyard (1 and 5. Wells 2. Brick pool 3. Lead tanks (for storing bath-water) 4. Stairs)
B. Kitchen (1. Fireplace 2. Lead tank 3. Stairs, leading to the upper floor over DEF 4. Drain)
C–G Bathrooms (C. Furnace and cauldron D. *Apodyterium* E. *Tepidarium* F. *Caldarium* G. Lavatory)
H. Stables
J. Storage room for farm implements
K–L. *Cubicula*
M. Corrida
N. Dining-room

The most important parts of the villa were:

(1) The dining rooms (*triclinia, cenationes*).—There were winter and summer dining rooms, for large receptions and small intimate suppers; from the large windows the guests could view the surrounding countryside.

(2) The *cubicula.*—Besides bedrooms, there were *cubicula diurna* for resting or studying during the day. In front of the *cubiculum* there might be an antechamber (*procoeton*).

(3) *Studies*—such as the *bibliotheca* and the *zotheca*; this latter name was applied to a *cubiculum* used as a study; in the niche, where the bed normally stood, were statues which gave the room its name.

(4) *The bath* (fig. 16)—built like the great public *thermae*, had all the essential rooms: *apodyterium, caldarium, tepidarium, frigidarium:* i.e. dressing room, hot bath, warm bath and cold bath, as well as all the additional rooms such as the *piscina* for open-air swimming, and a space for exercise after bathing (*gymnasium, sphaeristerium*) (see p. 223).

(5) *The arcades.*—These stood everywhere, supported by long rows of columns; some were used for walking under cover in bad weather (*ambulationes*), others, wider, and longer, could be used for riding on horseback or in a litter (*gestationes*).[2]

In two letters (V, 6; II, 17) Pliny the Younger has left us a detailed description of his villas in Tuscany and nearby Laurentum. They are vital for illustrating and completing the evidence provided by the remains of the countless Roman villas in Italy and elsewhere. Unfortunately Pliny is a precise writer who loses himself in detail, without concerning himself with readers who would like to know how these details combined and to imagine the

---

O. Bakery (1. Mill   2. Oven)
P. Wine press (1. Site of the press   2. Clay jars for holding the wine   3. Tank for dregs   4, 5, 6. Holes in the ground)
Q. Passage (1. Sunken jars with their lips at ground level)
R. *Cella vinaria* (1. Drain for dregs from P.2 jars   3. Lead cauldrons with fire—probably used to make *defrutum* or *sapa* by heating the juice   4. Tank
S. Barn, or *nubilarium*
T. Threshing floor
U. Tank to collect rainwater from T
V. *Cubicula*
W. Room with a press
X. Room with hand mill
Y. Oil press (1. Site of this press   2, 4. Drains and holes   3. Oil jars   5. Drain)
Z. Room for press

building as a whole. The reconstruction of these villas has been an archaeological problem for centuries;[3] the mere list of those who have attempted this difficult task (to be found in the notes) proves that. The proposed reconstructions are so different that it is sometimes hard to believe that we are dealing with the same villa.

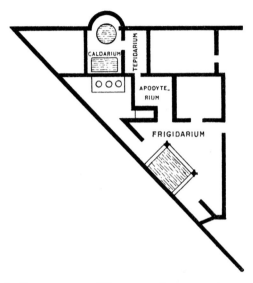

16. Baths in the Villa of Diomede, Pompeii

The fault is Pliny's, who could have been clearer. In the two plans in the text the reconstruction of Winnefeld is reproduced (figs. 17, 18).

Even when it did not stand on a farm, the villa was always surrounded by an estate, parts of which might be used as a garden (*hortus rusticus*); in the remainder (the *xystus*) clumps of rare shrubs (laurels, plane trees, pines), alternated with formal gardens with myrtle clipped into geometrical shapes and flower beds; round and across the flower beds ran small open paths. Here and there statues, fountains and benches added variety to this carefully cultivated, but artificial, landscape.

The land round the villa was crossed or surrounded by wide tracks, called *gestationes*, because they could be used for outings in a litter.

The *hippodromos* was a particular feature of the park. It is rarely mentioned and perhaps, as the *gestationes* could also be used

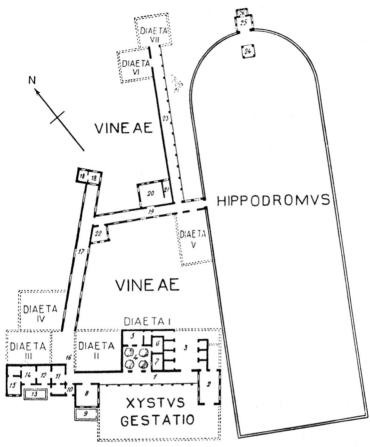

17. PLINY'S VILLA IN TUSCANY (Epist., V, 6)

(WINNEFELD'S RECONSTRUCTION)

Figures in brackets indicate the section of Pliny's letter where these items are described.

Xystus (16)   Gestatio (17)   Vineae (28-30)   Hippodromas (19)   Diaeta I (20)
Diaeta II (27)   Diaeta III (27)   Diaeta IV (27)   Diaeta V (28)   Diaeta VII (31)
Diaeta VIII (31)

1. Porticus (16) 2. Triclinium (19) 3. Atrium (15) 4. Areola (20) 5. Cotidiana cenatio (21) 6. Dormitorium cubiculum (21) 7. Cubiculum with fountain (22-3) 8. Cubiculum (23-4) 9. Piscina (23) 10. Hypocauston (25) 11. Apodyterium (25); superimpositum sphaeristerium (27) 12. Frigidaria cella (25) 13. Piscina (25) 14. Cella media (26) 15. Caldaria cella (26) 16. Scalae (27) 17. Cryptoporticus (27 et seq.) 18. Cubicula (28) 19. Aestiva cryptoporticus (29) 20. Triclinium (29) 21. Scalae (30) 22. Cubiculum (30) 23. Porticus (31) 24. Stibadium (for al fresco meals) (36) 25. Cubiculum (37) 26. Zothecula (38)

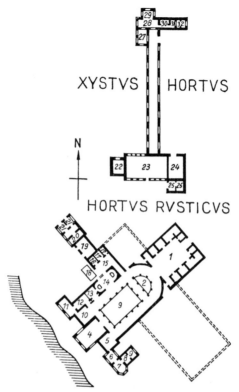

18. PLINY'S LAURENTINE VILLA (Epist. II, 17)
(WINNEFELD'S RECONSTRUCTION)

Figures in brackets indicate the sections of the letter referred to.
Hortum Rusticus (15) Xystus (17-20) Hoetus (13-15)
1. Atrium (4) 2. Area (4) 3. Cavaedium (5) 4. Triclinium (5) 5. Cubiculum amplius (6) 6. Cubiculum minus (6) 7. Cubiculum in apsida curvatum (8) 8. Transitus (9) 9. Dormitorium membrum (9) 10. Cubiculum politissimum (10) 11. Cubiculum grande (10) 12. Cubiculum cum procoetone (10) 13. Cella frigidaria (11) 14. Unctorium (11) 15. Hypocauston (11) (but see note on p. 227) 16. Propnigeon (11) 17. Cellae (11) 18. Piscina (11) 19. Sphaeristerium (12) 20. Turris (12) 21. Diaetae duo (12) 22 Turris (13) 23. Apotheca (13) 24. Triclinium (13) 25 Diaetae duo (15) 26. Cryptoporticus (16) 27. Heliocaminus (20) 28. Cubiculum (20) 29. Zotheca (21) 30. Cubiculum noctis (22) 31. Hypocauston (23) 32. Prococton et cubiculum (23)

for riding, the name was derived from its enlarged form, of which we have evidence in the *hippodromos* of the *domus Flaviana* on the Palatine (built by Domitian (A.D. 81–96) and probably surrounded with arcades by Septimius Severus (A.D. 193–221)). In Pliny's

Tuscan villa[4] the *hippodromos* is described as part of the park with tall trees, myrtle hedges and flower beds, clearly a park. Naturally, this does not rule out the possibility that the long tracts of the *hippodromos* were also used for riding, as we gather from one of Martial's[5] epigrams: *Pulvereumque fugax hippodromon ungula plaudit.*

NOTES

Chapter III

1. II. 17, 4.
2. Martial, I, 12.
3. Many archaeologists have tried to reconstruct the plans from Pliny's details: Scamozzi (1615), Felibien des Avaux (1707), Castall (1728), Marquez (1796), Mazois (1825), Hirt (1827), Winnefeld (in *Archaeol. Jahrb.* VI (1891), p. 201 et seq.: 'Tusci und Laurentinum des jüngeren Plinius'), Tanzer, *The Villas of Pliny the Younger*, New York (1924) (cf. Schuster, 'Zu Plinius' Beschreibung seines Landgutes bei Laurentum', in *Comment. Vindob.* 1, 1935). It should be noted that in Epist. II, 11, 12 and 13, the *turres* are clearly superimposed not juxtaposed, as Winnefeld understands. (*Hic turris erigitur, sub qua diaetae duae, totidem in ipsa, praeterea cenatio, quae latissimum mare, longissimum litus, villas amoenissimas prospicit. Est et alia turris. In hac cubiculum, in quo sol nascitur conditurque, lata post apotheca et horreum, sub hoc triclinium, quod turbati maris non nisi fragorem et sonum patitur eumque jam languidum ac desinentem; hortum et gestationem videt, qua hortus includitur.*) In section II (*unctorium hypocauston*) hypocauston is adjectival (Mau); he is dealing only with one room, not two. (*Adjacet unctorium hypocauston, adjacet propnigeon balinei, mox duae cellae magis elegantes quam sumptuosae.*) In Epist. V, 6, 29–30, the *cubiculum* (22) does not seem to back on to the *cryptoporticus* (17) (*in fine cubiculum, cui non minus iucundum prospectum cryptoporticus ipsa quam vineae praebent*; I take *in fine* to refer to *triclinii* not *cryptoporticus*). *Diaeta V* must have been a larger extension running from the *cryptoporticus* to the *hippodromus*. The *aestiva cryptoporticus*, the dining room, stairs and *cubiculum* are not separate from *Diaeta V*, but form part of it. Tanzer and Schuster, op. cit. disagree with Winnefeld's plan. A villa in the Castel Fusano estate, about five miles from Ostia, has sometimes been identified with Pliny's Laurentine villa, but it is of the wrong date and in the wrong place. See R. Meiggs, *Roman Ostia* (Oxford, 1960) p. 69.
4. V, 6, 32.
5. XII, 50, 5.

CHAPTER IV

Furniture

Difference between Roman and modern furniture. Instrumentum *and* supellex. *Furniture of the Roman house: beds; chairs; tables; cupboards; lamps. Mirrors and clocks.*

THE rooms of a Roman house were not filled with furniture as ours are. Indeed, with the exception of the *atrium* and the *tablinum*, intended for the accommodation of the whole family, and reception rooms like the *triclinium* and the *exhedra*, the rooms were very small. We see this clearly at Pompeii; the *cubiculum*, though decorated with the finest paintings and mosaics, is always a small room, where it would be impossible to turn round if even the humblest furniture of a modern room were placed in it. Special rooms were used for storing objects and clothes, rather than any type of cupboard or chest (*armaria, capsae, cistae, scrinia*)—an archaic habit which modern taste would not tolerate and hygiene would forbid. We regard the recesses and wall cupboards of our old houses as relics of a past age; our ancestors regarded them as one of the amenities of a house, but they are not to modern taste. But this method of storage was extensively used by the Romans, from the niches in the walls of libraries where books were stored, to the numerous *cellae* used as store rooms, wardrobes and safes. The much smaller amount of furniture is a result of this custom. To the Romans our rooms would have seemed grossly overcrowded.

Differences of taste and convenience mean that Roman furniture differed from modern in design and purpose. Two further general differences must be borne in mind:

(1) In modern furniture wood is commoner than other materials (marble, metals, etc.) which are used only for ornament and decoration. The Romans had other tastes. To this circumstance we owe the preservation of Roman furniture, which would have vanished if it had been made of wood.

(2) The ancients did not distinguish, as we do, between industrial and fine art; there were, it is true, examples of good and bad craftsmanship, but there was no distinct difference between works of art and mass-produced articles. This also has been to our advantage, since exquisite masterpieces have been preserved among the furniture found in ancient houses. Even where the furniture itself has been destroyed, beautifully made ornaments and handles have survived.

Everything used for furnishing the house was called by the collective name *supellex;* the Romans distinguished the *instrumentum domus* from the *supellex*, intended *ad tutelam domus*, and not like furniture, *ad voluptatem*, for the personal use of the family.

Instrumentum. The *instrumentum* included the *vela Cilicia*, covers placed over the roof as a protection against bad weather, the store of beams and tiles for urgent repairs, the small arsenal needed for fighting fires (ladders, pails and hoses) with which the house of a prudent *paterfamilias* was always stocked. In this connexion we must not forget that in the ancient economy many of the duties which are today entrusted to large industries or public services were part of the household arrangements. The *instrumentum* of the *villa rustica* was even more important and varied, including not only the implements, but also the animals and slaves.

Supellex. The furniture consisted of: (1) Everything used to decorate the house (pictures, canopies, the drapery round columns, etc.) and to make it comfortable, like the talc (*lapis specularis*) used to perform the function of glass in windows (see p. 156), or the sheets (*velaria*) which were stretched over open spaces (*hypaethri*) as a protection against the sun; (2) The furniture in the narrower sense of the word, such as tables and chairs, weighing machines (Plate 27), candlesticks (Plate 28), braziers (Plate 32), etc.

The following are the most important items of Roman furniture:
The bed (*lectus*, Greek κλίνη). Although the Roman house was not so extensively furnished as ours, there were more beds than nowadays. Besides the sleeping bed (*lectus cubicularis*) and beds used as sofas, the study bed (*lectus lucubratorius*) for example, the custom of eating lying down made dining couches necessary. The sleeping bed was higher than ours and steps or a stool were needed

to climb into it, while the dining couch was lower and more richly decorated.

The frame of the bed consisted of a wooden rectangle (*sponda*), supported on four feet (rarely on six). A back was fitted to this frame on the side against the wall (*pluteus*) and a support (*fulcrum*) at one end for the head. The most luxurious beds were of wood finely inlaid with ivory, tortoise-shell and gold. The bed of the poor (*grabatus, scimpodium*) was extremely simple, and probably had no *pluteus* or *fulcrum*.

A network of webbing (*institae, fasciae, lora*) was stretched over the *sponda*, and a mattress (*torus, culcita*) and cushions (*pulvini*, also *cervicalia*, if used to support the head) were placed on top. Covers (*stramenta, stragula, peristromata*) were spread over the mattress and cushions, and a linen valance (*toral, plagula*) surrounded the bed.

Chairs. There were three common types of chair: the stool (*scamnum subsellium*) a simple seat supported by four legs; the *sella* with arms but no back: the *cathedra* with a high curved back and essentially a ladies' chair; Martial[1] used *stare inter cathedras* to describe a ladies' man, and the *cathedralicii* were young slaves of a delicate and effeminate beauty; men sometimes used the *cathedra* in bedrooms and reception rooms, where in our houses also chairs are softer, less practical and more elaborate. Differing from the feminine *cathedra* or *supina*, was the magistrates *cathedra* with a straight back, shown in wall paintings and bas-reliefs (Plate 33).

As the art of upholstering was not known, chairs always had cushions.

Tables. Their use, shape and quality varied. There is a distinction between the tables (*abaci*) used to display silverware (*argentum escarium*, or *potorium*) during a banquet, and those which stood close to the dining couch for the guests' plates and food, the *repositorium* (see p. 93). In shape, there were tables with one, three and four legs (Plate 34). The first, the *monopodia*, is mentioned as particularly expensive; the *mensa tripes*, was a very humble item of furniture. *Sit mihi mensa tripes*, Horace[2] makes a man say, who wishes to show his modest ambitions, and Martial[3] notices among the battered furniture of a poor man who is moving house that the table is *bipes* and the bed *tripes*; both are missing a leg. But there was also a three-legged table of great value (Plate 34), the *Delphica*, called after the tripod (*cortina*) of Delphi.

20. Boscoreale hoard. Silver libation bowl (*patera*) and ladle (*cyathus*). (*p. 71*)

21. Boscoreale hoard. Silver drinking cups. (*p. 97*)

22. Boscoreale hoard. Drinking vessel (*cantharus*) and salt cellars (*salinum*).

23. Boscoreale hoard. Cup (*scyphus*).

24. Pompeii. Lamp standard for three lamps and lamp holders.

25. Pompeii. Lamp with figure.

26. Pompeii. Lamp holder in the form of a human figure. (*p. 82*)

27. Pompeii. Weighing machines.
(*p. 79*)

28. Pompeii. Lamp standard for four lamps. (*p. 82*)

No other article of furniture in the Roman house offered so great a variety in value, from the ordinary rough wooden table to the most expensive, one of which could be worth a fortune when made with precious materials and elaborately decorated. Such luxurious tables had two distinct parts, the central support (*trapezophorus*) and the top (*orbis*); the *trapezophorus* was of metal or carefully carved ivory, sometimes in the shape of a man or an animal, such as a drunken Silenus, or a sphinx (Plate 34); the *orbis* was of precious wood; the most precious of all was the thuja (*citrus*), a tree of the cypress family, found in the region of the Atlas Mountains (Morocco). As the habit of eating out of doors was very common among the Romans, a marble or stone table, or a support for a table during the course of a banquet, was built inside the space made by the brick dining couches.

Cupboards and safes. The heavy type of cupboard resting on the ground was the same shape as ours; this is shown by a cupboard found at Boscoreale near Pompeii (the wood has perished and its shape has been recovered by pouring plaster of Paris into the impression left by the wood in the earth). Other smaller cupboards were attached to the walls; we are told that the cupboards in the *alae* (see p. 62), where the *imagines* of the ancestors were kept, were of this type. They were all made to lock and seal.

Valuable objects and important documents were kept in a low, heavy metal-bound safe (*arca*) (Plate 29).

Lamps. The Romans had three means of illumination: torches (*taedae, faces*), tapers (*candelae*), and oil lamps (*lucernae*). Torches were only lit on special occasions, such as marriages and funerals; they were probably still used in the country, just as today peasants still use burning straw for light, but for domestic lighting tapers and oil lamps were regularly used. Tapers, unknown to the Greeks, had been known to the Romans from the earliest days before the cultivation of the olive in Italy. They were made by first dipping a wick of a marsh plant (*papyrus*) in a bowl of wax or tallow; the tapers thus obtained, were twisted together, into large torches called *funalia* (or *funales cerei*, or simply *cerei*) from their resemblance to a rope. These torches were either held by a slave (for example, when accompanying his master home late at night), or put in holders; good examples of these of various heights (from four inches to four feet) survive. Oil lamps were commoner than candles and torches (Plate 26), and excavations have brought them to light in thousands. The shape of this lamp is well known; it consisted of a long flat holder with a handle at the back and a nozzle (*rostrum, myxa*) in front, from which the wick protruded. There might be more than one nozzle (*lucerna dimyxos, trimyxos, polymyxos*). In the centre of the lamp was a hole, which made raising the wick and refilling the lamp with oil possible while it was still alight. There were also hanging lamps with chains and hooks. Naturally they were hung high up, either on (Plate 28), or hanging from, candelabra (*lychnuchi*) (Plate 26) of various shapes and heights. Lights could also be attached to hooks in the ceiling. A small low tripod was used as a stand for lamps on a table, when somebody was reading late at night. Oil lamps were used in every room, the dining room, bedroom, study and bathroom. They had to be used in large numbers to defeat the darkness; before we envy the Romans their famous banquets, we should remember that a thick oily pall hung over these nocturnal revels, laden with smoke and the smell of tapers.

Lanterns like ours were also widely used (fig. 19); the light was protected by transparent sides of horn (*lanterna cornea*), bladder (*lanterna de vesica*), and later of glass.

We shall deal later with the most comprehensive, varied and expensive type of Roman furniture—that for the dining room (see p. 94). To conclude this chapter an account must be given of mirrors and clocks, which formed part of the furniture of every well appointed house; their interest lies more in the comparison with their modern equivalents than in their actual importance.

Mirrors. The mirror among the Romans, and still more the Greeks, was a personal and female object, despite the fact that in the Imperial age it came to be used by men and wall mirrors are mentioned in addition to hand mirrors. Being essentially intended for the dressing table and not for display, it was small and easily handled, a round or oval sheet of polished metal with a finely wrought handle. Glass, which was being slowly but steadily introduced for domestic purposes during the Roman era (see p. 156), had not yet begun to replace metal in mirrors.

Clocks. The Roman hour was not the equinoctial hour of sixty minutes which divides the day into twenty-four equal parts. Daylight, the time during which the sun remained above the horizon, was divided into twelve equal hours (*horae*) and the hours of summer were consequently much longer than those of winter. The sixth hour was midday. The observation of the sky, in fine weather, continued to be one of the normal ways of telling the time. Clocks, which were as rare then as they are common today, were of two types: sun clocks and water clocks. Pendulum and spring clocks, using cogs and wheels, with which we are all familiar, appeared only at the end of the Middle Ages; the Romans

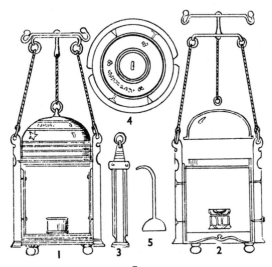

19. LANTERNS
(FROM OVERBECK, *Pompeii*)

1. Closed lantern 2. Open 3. Side support 4. Cover 5. Snuffer

with their primitive and inexact methods of reckoning had to resign themselves to having only an approximate knowledge of the time. Today, when we are accustomed to dividing our time into small and exact fractions and to making a watch the indispensable companion of our feverish lives, it seems almost impossible that the ancient Greeks and Romans lived in blissful uncertainty of the passage of time, which even modern peasants are no longer able to enjoy. But perhaps our clocks have robbed life of some of its poetry, reduced the essential unity of the day, the unity of sun and light, to atoms, and substituted for *carpe diem* an anxiety to grasp every fleeting instant. The tick of the clock has penetrated deep into our hearts, imposing a rhythm on the human spirit as rigid as steel and as uniform as a machine. Let us not therefore pity the Romans for their lack of accurate clocks, if telling the time was such a serious problem as to make a philosopher like Seneca[4] describe the situation by saying, 'It is easier for philosophers to agree than clocks'.

According to a statement of Varro, the great Roman antiquary, preserved for us by Pliny the Elder,[5] the first sundial known to the Romans was brought to Rome by the consul Manius Valerius Messalla from Catania in 263 B.C. during the first Punic War. Naturally after its move it no longer showed the correct time, and in 164 B.C. the Censor Q. Marcius Philippus had a sundial constructed adapted to Roman time. From then on the superintendence of the public sundials, whose use spread steadily, was in the hands of the censors. In shape these sundials were similar to our own modern ones; an iron marker (*gnomon*, from the Greek γνώμων) cast a shadow on to a semicircular marble slab, divided into sections so as to allow the calculation of the time. It will be realised that as the sundial was the commonest form of clock, and not, as it is with us, a relic of the past with no practical use, it was much more perfect; portable ones were also made, which could be used even when travelling, and which indicated the equinoctial hour.

The first *clepsydra*, or water clock, was introduced into Rome in 159 B.C. There were two types of this *clepsydra*:

(1) Those used only to measure a fixed period of time, while the water in the upper container dripped into the lower one.

(2) Those which took twenty-four hours to empty, where a marked scale in the lower container made it possible to tell the exact time. Of this second type, whose invention is attributed to Plato and its perfection to Ctesibius of Alexandria, there were two sorts: in its simpler form it divided the day into twenty-four equal hours. In the more complicated form a varying scale was used, or the size of the hole through which the water dripped was regulated, to mark the hours of daylight and darkness according to the season of the year.

Further Reading

G. M. A. Richter, *Ancient Furniture, Greek, Etruscan and Roman*, (Oxford, 1926) examines the archaeological evidence exhaustively.

NOTES

1. III, 63, 7; X, 13, 1.
2. Sat., I, 3, 13.
3. XII, 32, 11.
4. Apoc., 2, 3. *Facilius inter philosophos quam inter horologia conveniet.*
5. N.H., VII, 214.

CHAPTER V

Food

Difference in taste between the Romans and ourselves. The chief Roman foods. Garum *and* allec.

THE austerity of the early Romans was proverbial, but their descendants, especially in the Imperial age, had a passion for the delights of the table which shrank from no trouble and spared no expense. The pleasures of the banquet were prepared with meticulous care and forethought. On the *villae*, fish, game and birds were scientifically reared; there were *piscinae, aviaria, leporaria*, etc., for the purpose. Methods of fattening not only chickens, hares and dormice, but even ostriches, had been perfected. Trade provided what Italy could not produce; from all parts of the known world fine wines and delicacies poured into Rome. In spite of this, if one of us had to participate in a Roman banquet, both his palate and his digestion would almost certainly be outraged. Cooks, purchased for huge sums, lavished all the secrets of their art and the most expensive ingredients on the preparation of dishes which we would find quite uneatable.

Human taste, contrary to what might have been expected, is capable of great differences from nation to nation and from one generation to another. Describing the Tartars, Marco Polo wrote: 'They also eat the rats of Pharaon, which abound in the summer everywhere throughout their plains. They also eat horse and dog flesh and generally any type of meat.' (Those with weak stomachs should not allow their imagination too much rein over the 'generally'). Even in our day the results of the widespread researches of ethnologists are amazing. In addition to their famous birds' nests, the Chinese eat dogs, cats and rats. 'The first sight to catch the traveller's gaze is of rows of rats hanging up by the tail from the roofs, like maize in Italy and onions in the north of Europe. For the Chinese mole soup is the height of luxury.'[1] The Japanese, on the other hand, consider chrysanthemum salad seasoned with a

86

sauce of fish brine and sugar a delicacy. Of the Asiatic people, the Camschiadali eat raw fish which has been allowed to rot in a trench; if it is not sufficiently rotten, they will not eat it. The Zealanders live on insects, dogs and baked bracken stems washed down with rancid oil. The Kaffirs in Africa are gluttons for the raw entrails of goats and cows, and eat everything, including ants. There are many people for whom reptiles, including snakes, are the highest delicacy; if it were not so well known, one would hesitate to believe it. On the other hand, it is very hard to understand how people living in very different parts of the world, although not accustomed to turn up their noses at food which would revolt us, have an aversion to cheese and butter. Even in the use of sauces the most dissimilar tastes are shown. We find palm oil used, as well as sea water and human fat (among the Niam-Niam) and similar delicacies.

Granted this, the great differences in taste between the Romans and ourselves will cause no surprise. It is difficult to be precise on this subject, since it is not always possible to identify foods and sauces exactly, but it is certain that we should consider it a grave abuse of God's good gifts to make a pigeon stew according to Apicius'[2] recipe with pepper, dates, honey, vinegar, wine, oil and mustard, besides other ingredients which cannot be precisely identified; or to cook birds in a sauce of vinegar, honey, oil, currants (or damsons), wine, mint, pepper and innumerable sharp-flavoured herbs, instead of simply roasting them.[3]

The difference in taste between ourselves and the Romans is even greater than it might seem if we allowed ourselves to be taken in by apparent resemblances. Like us, the Romans enjoyed mushrooms, but they cooked them in honey;[4] they enjoyed good peaches, but cooked them rather like jellied eels;[5] they appreciated many of the fish which we still like to see on our tables, but they prepared them with overpowering mixtures, made from a wide variety of ingredients including plums, crushed apricots and quince puree. It would be a mistake to allow this to set our teeth on edge. We should remember that while the Romans preferred fresh cheese, we enjoy Gorgonzola only when it has begun to smell; the more worm-eaten the cheese, the better it is thought and the more it costs. The Romans refused to eat high game; we regard it as a waste to eat it fresh, and only eat it when it has hung long enough to become high. What we regard as the right taste for game would have nauseated the Romans. It is certainly true that tastes are not a subject for argument.

It should be remembered that modern European taste shows a marked preference for certain types of food and drink which were unknown to the ancients; the Romans had no coffee, tea, sugar, liqueurs, truffles, potatoes or French beans; tomatoes were unknown, dried herbs rare and imported. Sweets were made with honey, cooked must, and sometimes, like *placenta*, with honey and cheese. The only intoxicating drink was wine; even in bars (*thermopolia*) which, to judge from Pompeii, were as common then as they are today, hot wine was drunk. Moreover, the technique of cooking was different. Amongst other things, the binding qualities of egg were not generally appreciated in giving consistency to dishes of many ingredients. As the Romans loved variety in their dishes and sauces, they resorted to stuffing innumerable skilfully cooked ingredients into a pig's bladder. The skill of a cook consisted above all in the preparation of *botella* and *farcimina*.

The fact, frequently referred to by classical writers, that even among the Romans the same food was at different times highly thought of or despised, should be attributed to the whim of fashion rather than to fundamental differences of taste.

Let us now make a rapid review of the commonest foods and drinks among the Romans. The use of bread seems to have become general only at the beginning of the second century B.C. In the earlier centuries grain was used in the preparation of *puls* (a corn gruel, distinguished by the authors from *polenta*, the μᾶζα of the Greeks, made of roast ground barley).

Besides special types of bread, like barley and spelt bread, there were three main grades: (1) Black bread (*panis acerosus, plebeius, rusticus, castrensis, sordidus*, etc.) made of coarsely ground flour. (2) *Panis secundarius*, whiter but still coarse. (3) The best quality bread (*panis candidus, mundus*). Bread made with bran (*panis furfureus*) is also mentioned. Bread was baked in ordinary ovens, or in special containers like the *clibanus* (*panis clibanicus*).

The commonest vegetables were broad beans, lentils and chick peas, and amongst green vegetables, lettuces, cabbages and leeks; laxative herbs, such as mallows and beetroot, were also extensively used. Asparagus and artichokes (*carduus*) were rarer than they are with us, and were only seen on the tables of the rich. The Romans were great devotees of mushrooms, especially *boleti*, as is shown by many references, particularly in Martial. The olive, which we regard simply as an hors d'oeuvre, was much more highly esteemed.

With the exception of citrus fruits, which were introduced from the East and began to be grown in Italy during the fourth century A.D., the commonest fruits were those which we still have; apples (*mala*), pears (*pira*), cherries (*cerasa*), plums (*pruna*), grapes (fresh, dried, or preserved in jars (*uvae ollares*), walnuts, almonds (*nux amygdala*) and chestnuts. The cultivation of the cherry was introduced from Pontus during the Mithridatic wars; previously only a wild species, the *cornum*, was known. Among hard fruits the quince (*malum Cydonium*) was the best known, and even then was used to make jams. The apricot (*malum Armeniacum*, or *praecox*) was introduced from Armenia, and was used in the preparation of certain dishes, for example, chopped ham.[6] Dates (imported from warmer countries) seem to have been very common (*dactyli, palmae, caryotae*).

The animal world contributed its flesh to the Roman table a little more widely than it does to ours. Besides beef and pork, of which they were very fond, the Romans ate venison, the flesh of wild asses (*onager*) and dormice, to the raising of which tremendous care was paid in the *gliraria*. The Romans thought little of the humble chicken and preferred game, which was usually raised in the same way as domestic animals, a method which must inevitably have spoilt its flavour. Animals which have disappeared from our tables, but which were much prized by the Romans, were the flamingo, of which the tongue was particularly highly esteemed, the stork, the crane and even the *psittacus*, a small talking-bird of the parrot family. The peacock, an unusual food for us, was an object of great gastronomic enthusiasm among the Romans.

The Romans, however, preferred high-quality fish to every other food. All types of fish were widely used at Rome; from the small fish preserved in brine (*gerres, maenae*, etc.), part of the staple diet of the poor, to rarer fish, such as turbot, mullet, especially if very fat, scar (*cerebrum Iovis paene supremi*, as Ennius calls it), sturgeon, etc. There is no point in giving a list which difficulty of identification would make uncertain. It is worth pointing out that, although cooking methods may alter, two types of fish, mullet and sole, seem immune from changes of taste and the whims of fashion, and have the unusual privilege of being always highly appreciated.

The difference in taste between ourselves and the Romans appears in their sauces even more than in their foods. We have seen that it was usual for them to mix sour and sweet flavours, since they mixed on the same plate vinegar and mint with honey, cooked must (*defrutum*) and dried fruits. But the chief characteristic of Roman cooking was its extensive use of certain fish sauces, not prepared for each occasion, but produced by a long and elaborate process, and stored in jars in the cellar. There were few dishes which were not improved with a dash of this sauce. These sauces had various names: *garum, oxygarum, liquamen, muria, allec*. They were prepared in a thousand different ways, the difference in taste depending partly on the method of preparation and partly on the quality of fish used. From a detailed recipe[7] preserved for us in a Greek agricultural manual, we learn that *liquamen* was prepared as follows: fish entrails were placed in a receptacle and mixed with finely chopped fish, or small whole fish, and pounded and stirred to produce a homogeneous sauce. This sauce was placed in the sun and frequently stirred and beaten until it fermented. When the quantity of liquid had been much reduced through evaporation a basket was placed in the vessel containing the *liquamen*. The liquid which filtered slowly into the basket was *garum*, the choicest part; what was left, the dregs of the *garum* so to speak, was *allec* (ἅλιξ). *Muria* was a general term applied to salt water or brine, but was later the name of a special type of *garum*.

The flavour of a dish depended largely on the cook's skill in adding *garum*. Sometimes a mere suspicion was enough; two eggs with a dash of good *garum*[8] made a simple and delicious meal.

The production of *garum* required care, work and costly ingredients, which made it extremely expensive. However, it was so widely used that centres for its production were found even far from Rome. For example, the *garum* industry flourished in industrial Pompeii; the finest came from Spain. It is impossible to tell with any accuracy what it tasted like; from the recipe for its production it is easy to gather that it must have been sharp, acid and nauseating. An epigram of Martial[9] confirms this:

Unguentum fuerat quod onyx modo parva gerebat;
Olfecit postquam Papilus, ecce garum est.

('Papilus' breath is so strong that it can change the strongest perfume into *garum*.') Our stomachs would probably revolt at a dish prepared with *garum*.

Further Reading

The recipes of Apicius (a collection dating from the late Empire) have been translated into English with a detailed introduction on Roman cooking: Apicius, *The Roman Cookery Book*, translated by B. Flower and E. Rosenbaum (London, 1958). See also C. G. Harcum, *Roman Cooks* (Baltimore, 1914).

NOTES

1. The information in this paragraph is drawn from A. Cougnet, *Il ventre dei popoli*, 1905.
2. Apicius, VI, 4, 2 (224).
3. Ibid. V, 1 (227).
4. Ibid. VII, 15, 5 (318).
5. Ibid. I, 12, 11 (26).
6. Ibid. IV, 3, 6 (176).
7. Geoponica, XX, 46, 1.
8. Martial, XIII, 40.
9. Ibid. VII, 94.

CHAPTER VI

The Banquet

The meals of the day. The course of a banquet.

THE early morning meal, or the snack which the schoolboy carried to school, was called *ientaculum,* the midday meal *prandium.* Sometimes the *prandium* was served in the *triclinium,* but the normal practice was to swallow a mouthful of cold food, usually left over from the day before, without even bothering to sit down: *sine mensa prandium, post quod non sunt lavandae manus.*[1] The principal meal was *cena* (dinner). The early Romans dined in the *atrium,* and later, in a room (*cenaculum;* see p. 64) above the *tablinum.* But when the Greek custom of eating lying down had become general, a special room, the *triclinium,* was reserved for

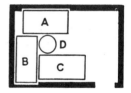

20. DINING ROOM

A. *Lectus summus*   B. *Lectus medius*   C. *Lecturimus*   D. *Mensa*

the *cena.* Summer and winter dining rooms differed in the extent to which they were open to the air. Open-air dining rooms, such as Pliny describes (see the plan on p. 75), and brick dining rooms, such as are seen in some Pompeian gardens (Plate 12), were common.

The arrangement of the couches in the *triclinium* is shown in the accompanying figure (20), illustrating a Pompeian dining room. The three couches were called, reading from right to left, *summus, medius* and *imus,* and the three places on each couch were called, reading in the same direction, *locus summus, medius* and *imus*. There is some uncertainty about the place of honour; it seems to have been the *imus in medio*, called the *locus consularis*, the place where it was possible to receive messages from the back of the couch. The couches in the cramped dining rooms however, were usually so close to the wall that none of them was easily accessible from behind. At the dinner in Eutrapelos' house, described by Cicero,[2] the orator, the most distinguished of the guests, does not occupy the *imus in medio* but the *medius in medio*. At Nasidienus'[3] dinner this place is occupied by an *umbra*, a minor character, if not an actual parasite. The custom clearly varied, and among friends little attention was paid to such niceties. The *locus summus in imo* was the host's place, and the most important guest was normally placed next to him. But even this rule was not invariable; in the Horatian satire Nasidienus was not next to Maecenas.

The custom of having three dining couches set at right angles to each other was replaced in the Imperial age by a curved couch, where six, seven or even eight guests could be accommodated (*exaclinon, heptaclinon, octoclinon*), called *sigma* from its resemblance to the cursive Greek sigma (C), *stibadium* or *accubitum*. The place of honour was at the edge (*cornua*) where the guest was less cramped.

We have already (p. 80) dealt with the tables, the most handsome furniture in the house, of which men were as jealous as women of jewels. The table used by the guests as they reclined on the dining couches was usually round; the dishes and a wine holder (*lagoena*) were placed on it, leaving the guests free to help themselves as they liked. The salt cellar (*salinum*) (Plate 22) and the vinegar bottle (*acetabulum*) were also always available. A special piece of furniture called *repositorium* was used to hold the plates with the food. This method was convenient, but it gave rise to awkwardness unless everybody showed some discretion in helping himself. At large banquets, where many dishes were offered and there were many waiters, the dishes were changed rapidly; some even maintain that they were merely offered without being placed on the *repositorium*.

The towel (*mantela*) appeared in the first century A.D. A napkin (*mappa*) was provided by the host, but some guests used to bring one with them to hold the remains of their dinner, an ill-mannered practice tolerated by Roman society.

The guests ate lying at an angle, with the elbow of their left arm supported by a cushion and their feet turned to the right. Places were separated by cushions placed—as seems certain—not above, but below the cover of the dining couch. The plate (*patina, patella*, or if deep, *catinus*) was held in the left hand; food was eaten in the fingers, as the fork had not yet been introduced. It was polite to eat with the tips of the fingers, taking care not to allow the face or hand to become dirty:

> *Carpe cibos digitis (est quiddam gestus edendi);*
> *Ora nec immunda tota perungue manu,*

orders Ovid.[4] Before being served, the food was cut by a slave (*scissor, carptor, structor*) into small pieces (*pulmenta*). This made a knife almost unnecessary, though we still see it in the hands of some guests in reliefs showing banqueting scenes. The use of spoons (*cochlear* or *ligula*) was more common, and they varied in shape according to the purpose for which they were used (fig. 21).

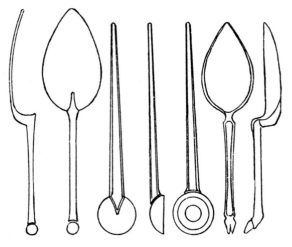

21. Spoons
(Blümner, *op. cit.*)

Dishes and cups were of the finest quality. Though the poor used earthenware (*vasa Saguntina*), the plates and dishes at large banquets were of silver (*argentum escarium* or *potorium*, see Plate 21), the cups (*pocula*) of crystal, electrum,[5] gold and *murra* (*murrina*), a rare and very expensive opaque stone said to improve the bouquet of the wine. These cups were seldom plain (*pura*); more often they were decorated with embossed reliefs or gems (*pocula gemmata*). Their shape also varied; they could be broad and without handles or feet (*paterae*), deep with feet and handles, which in some cases spread above the rims (*calices*), in the shape of a boat (*cymbium, scaphium*), or of a horn (*rhytion*), etc.

As it was the Roman custom to drink wine warm and watered— neat wine was used only for ritual libations—wineholders (*oenophorus*), hot-water vessels (*caldarium*; Plate 30) and mixing bowls (*cratera;*) were other essential items of dining-room equipment. The *cratera* was a large bowl, in which wine and water were mixed in fixed proportions, and from which the liquid was transferred to the cup by a long-handled ladle, the *cyathus*. A filter (*sacculus, colum*) was used, for winemaking had not advanced sufficiently to ensure the production of perfectly clear wine; *liquare*, 'to filter', is used in poetry as a synonym for 'to mix'.

The guests wore a loose gown (*synthesis*) (see p. 103) and sandals (*soleae*) (see p. 104).

The slaves engaged in waiting were divided according to their skill and good looks. The most handsome served the wine (*ministri, pueri a cyatho*), or cut up the food, taking care to perform their duties gracefully. Their clothes were of various bright colours, and their hair was long and curled. The slaves engaged in minor and heavier duties in the dining room wore coarser clothing and had shaved heads. Among these were the *scoparii* (replaced later by the *analectae*) who had to collect and carry away the remains of the banquet thrown under the table by the guests, as was the custom (Plate 16).[6] Ancient manners were not up to the standard of modern behaviour. Every guest brought with him a faithful slave, who was probably young and handsome (*puer ad pedes*) and throughout the banquet attended to his master's needs, even performing humiliating and degrading services for him if, as sometimes happened, he had overeaten. A *tricliniarcha*, experienced in etiquette, was entrusted by the host with superintending the course of the feast.

When the guests were lying down in their places, slaves brought water to wash their hands, and the feast began. The *cena* was divided into three phases:

(1) The *gustus* or *gustatio*, hors d'oeuvres, consisting of light dishes intended as appetisers. *Mulsum*, a mixture of wine and honey, was drunk with it. Egg dishes were usual; Horace's expression *ab ovo usque ad mala*,[7] meaning from the beginning to the end of a feast, is well known.

(2) The *cena* proper, of various courses each of which was called *ferculum* or *cena*, i.e. *prima, secunda, tertia cena*, during which wine was drunk.

(3) *Secundae mensae*, dessert, which at large feasts developed into a drinking party, or *comissatio*. Dry, salt food was eaten to arouse a thirst, and drinking was heavy. Between the *cena* and the *secundae mensae*, the statues of the Lares were carried in and placed on the table, when libations were poured and words of good omen uttered.

The main part of the banquet was therefore the *cena*, during which were served course after course of the rarest and most delicate food. Culinary skill was developed to the utmost to devise unusual dishes, where one sort of food was concealed under the appearance of another. The guests ate

> *aves, conchylia, pisces,*
> *Longe dissimilem noto celantia sucum.*[8]

At the feast of Trimalchio the guests discovered that a goose surrounded by fish and smaller birds was made entirely of pork.[9] 'There couldn't be a better man than my cook', cries the host.[10] 'If you like, he can make a sow's belly into a fish, a side of bacon into a pigeon, a ham into a dove, a sirloin into a chicken.' Macrobius[11] tells us of animals stuffed and cooked with other animals. Trimalchio had peacocks' eggs served, stuffed with beccaficos in pepper sauce, and a boar stuffed with live thrushes.[12] Even granted that all this is exaggerated, it reflects the customs of the time.

During the *comissatio* the guests wore garlands of flowers and scented themselves liberally with perfume. A *rex convivii* (or *magister* or *arbiter bibendi*) decided the proportions in which the water and wine should be mixed and when the drinking should take place (see p. 97). This was a Greek custom (*Graeco more bibere*), but so ancient that Cicero[13] regards it as an institution of the early Romans: *magisteria . . . a majoribus instituta*. During the *comissatio* numerous toasts were drunk to fellow guests, to the

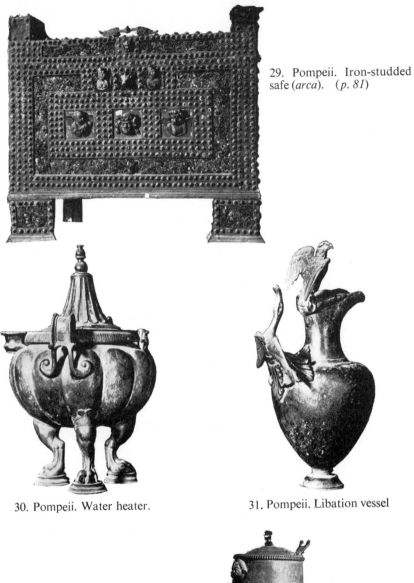

29. Pompeii. Iron-studded safe (*arca*). (*p. 81*)

30. Pompeii. Water heater.

31. Pompeii. Libation vessel

32. Pompeii. Water heater.

33. Pompeii. *Bisellium*.

34. Herculaneum. Tripod.
(*p. 80*)

absent, to ladies, and, in the Imperial age to the emperor and the armies. The commonest method of toasting a fellow guest was to fill a cup with wine, drain it in one breath to his health, and send the cup, refilled, to him, so that he might drink in his turn.

In this drunken atmosphere to remember the inevitability of death was both a warning and an invitation to enjoyment.[14] One man drank cheerfully from a silver cup skilfully decorated with gesticulating skeletons (Plate 21). These macabre images added flavour to the wine. At Trimalchio's dinner,[15] after the *gustatio*, a little silver skeleton, articulated so that it could bow and dance while the host expounded his philosophy, was displayed. The mosaic floor of one Roman dining room was decorated with a huge skull with hollow eyes; another showed a skeleton (Plate 17) twisting on the hook-like flames of a pyre, 'Know yourself' (γνῶθι σαυτόν) is written underneath. All this, doubtless, led to deep thoughts without, however, causing any loss of appetite.

In the Republican age, senatorial decrees and laws (*leges sumptuariae*) attempted to restrict the luxury of banquets by limiting their cost, the types of food served, and even the acceptance of invitations by leading magistrates.[16] But the last of these laws was passed under Augustus, and they were the type of law which falls into immediate disuse. In the Imperial age the luxury of banquets increased; the rich were surrounded by a swarm of clients, induced by the prospect of a good dinner to perform the most humiliating duties and to indulge in the most fawning flattery. The ostentation of enriched freedmen exceeded all limits. For many, giving a banquet was like the distribution of alms, but on a rather more liberal scale than the wretched sum of money, the *sportula*, normally given to clients. The poor guests were made to feel the gulf between themselves and their host. The custom of not offering all the guests the same food and wine was fairly common, but was disapproved of by the more refined. 'I invite my guests to dine and not to be humiliated', wrote Pliny.[17]

With the ancients the banquet lasted for hours on end, roughly from three in the afternoon (*hora nona*) to late at night. It was the normal and generally accepted method of meeting friends. Today we entertain friends at restaurants, theatres and cinemas. The theatre no longer has any connexion with ritual or cult, which made theatrical performances rare and solemn occasions in antiquity (see p. 256). Theatrical spectacles have become a regular type of entertainment, and have taken on a great variety of forms to meet the tastes of the public. In Rome this was not the case. By day anyone wishing to gossip and pass the time with his friends went to the baths or the barbers' shops, but he could only find relaxation in the evening by joining his friends at a banquet.

Naturally, we must not suppose that these long hours were spent entirely in eating and drinking. Besides conversation and argument, which has always been a favourite relaxation for the educated, there were entertainments and diversions of different kinds. Those whom Pliny would call 'the noble' and Martial 'the bores', considered readings by a slave (*lector, anagnostes*) the most enjoyable; recitations by a *comoedus*, who declaimed with extravagant gestures and loud voice, or musical performances were other forms of entertainment; professional lyre-players (*lyristae*) or singers (*choraules*) performed for lavish rewards. Not all, however, favoured such forms of relaxation, and the fashionable preferred gambling or being diverted by the buffoonery and insolence of clowns or by spectacles which today have largely been relegated to the music hall: the soft dances of the girls from Cadiz (*Gaditanae*) (that they were all from Cadiz was not guaranteed), the clattering of castanets (*crotalistriae*) the gyrations of effeminate dancers (*cinaedi*) and the performances of acrobats (*petauristarii*).

Entertainment was also provided by the *moriones*, half-idiot dwarfs, whose coarseness kept the company merry. Martial[18] tells us of one 'with pointed head and long ears, which move like a donkey's'. Such creatures became very fashionable in the Imperial age, and were so popular that even the educated enjoyed laughing at them.[19] The stupider they were, the greater was their price, and there was reason to suspect that at times they were not so stupid as they tried to make out.[20]

At the most lavish banquets *apophoreta*, or presents, were distributed by lot; the great difference in their values added greatly to the excitement of the draw.

That gladiators were regularly summoned to fight and kill each other during banquets is one of those statements we owe to the habit of regarding the exceptional as ordinary. Some emperors certainly provided such spectacles in their search for novelty; it is not, however, true that the Romans enjoyed banquets where blood flowed as freely as the wine.

Further Reading

C. Seltman, *Wine in the Ancient World* (London, 1957) also gives an account of some of the games played at dinner parties.

NOTES

1. Sen. Epist., 83, 5.
2. Ad fam., IX, 26.
3. Horace, Sat., II, 8, 20.
4. Ars Am., III, 755-6. cf. Chaucer's Prioress. Ne wette hir fyngres in hir sauce depe. Canterbury Tales, Prologue, 129.
5. Electrum was an alloy of gold and silver, not to be confused with amber (*sucinum*).
6. This was the general practice in antiquity; the artist Sosos designed a mosaic floor which appeared to be covered in rubbish, the so-called 'unswept room' (ἀσάρωτος οἶκος); cf. Pliny, N.H., XXXVI, 184.
7. Sat. I, 3, 6-7 (to begin *ab ovo*, however, comes from Ars Poet., 147).
8. Horace, Sat., II, 8, 27-28.
9. Petronius, 69.
10. Ibid. 70.
11. III, 13, 13.
12. Petronius, 33 and 40.
13. De Sen., 14, 46.
14. The practice is very old; Herodotus (II, 78) tells us that at Egyptian feasts a small wooden coffin with a skeleton inside was carried round by a servant who said to each guest: 'Look on this, drink, and enjoy yourself; you too will die.'
15. Petronius, 34.
16. Macrobius, III, 17; Aulus Gellius, II, 24.
17. II, 6, 3; *Eadem omnibus pono; ad cenam enim, non ad notam invito cunctisque rebus exaequo quos mensa et toro aequavi*. See Juvenal Sat. 5 for an account of the humiliation of clients.
18. VI, 39, 15-16.
19. Pliny, Epist., IX, 17.
20. Martial, VIII, 13.

CHAPTER VII

Clothes, Shoes and Jewellery

Roman clothes in general. The tunica. *The* toga. *Cloaks. Women's clothes. Shoes and Hats. Jewellery.*

THE official Roman garment was the *toga*; in early days only a simple loincloth, *subligar*, or *subligaculum, campestre, cinctus*, covering the lower part of the body, was worn under the *toga*, which was therefore for the most part in contact with bare flesh. The *subligar* was retained only by conservative families which clung to ancient customs (*cinctuti Cethegi*, says Horace,[1] implying 'old-fashioned'); in a more civilised age it was worn only by labourers when working and by those exercising on the *Campus Martius*; hence its commoner name of *campestre*; as a garment to wear under the *toga* it was replaced by the *tunica*. Over the *toga*, or the *tunica* when it replaced the *toga*, cloaks of various kinds (*laena, lacerna, abolla*, etc.) were worn as a protection against the cold. Women covered the *tunica*, which feminine modesty required to be longer and fuller than the male *tunica*, with a flowing garment called the *stola*. If necessary, women's cloaks (*ricinium, palla*) could be worn over the *stola*. Thus the clothing of the Roman man consisted of the *tunica*, the *toga* and the cloak; and for women, the *tunica*, the *stola* and the overcloak.

The *tunica* proper (not to be confused with the linen shirt, *tunica interior, subucula* or *strictoria*) was a woollen garment, consisting of two pieces of material sewn together so that the front part reached just below the knees and the back to the calves, and fastened round the waist by a belt. Fashion forbade the wearing of the tunic too long or going *discincti*, without a belt. Only during the third century A.D. did *tunicae* with long sleeves reaching to the wrists, previously regarded as the height of effeminacy, come into fashion (*talares et manicatas tunicas habere apud Romanos veteres flagitium erat, nunc autem honesto loco natis, cum tunicati sunt, non eas habere flagitium est*[2]). The richest form of these tunics was known as the *Dalmatica*, of linen, silk or wool, which many wore to replace the *toga*. A special sleeveless form of the *Dalmatica* was called *colobium*. Fully-cut tunics with sleeves were also worn in the worship of Mithras and in early Christian rites in the oriental manner. In the same age long close-fitting trousers were widely worn.

The commonest decoration of the tunic was the *clavus*, a purple stripe which also indicated membership of a particular order; senators wore the *latus clavus* (or *laticlavium*), the *equites* the *angustus clavus*. The *tunica palmata*, embroidered with palm leaves and worn by a *triumphator* during his triumph, was worn only on exceptional occasions, and was not, as has been maintained, a normal garment.

In the provinces and the country, or in the privacy of his own home, a Roman wore the tunic. If he was cold, he put on a cloak or increased the number of tunics (like Augustus, who was terrified of chills and wore four tunics besides wraps of various kinds[3]), but he took care to get out of his *toga*, a garment which was as dignified as it was impracticable, as soon as he had escaped from official life into the heart of his family. When, however, he had to perform a public duty the *toga* was obligatory, and anyone who did not wish to be taken for a slave or a workman had to be seen in Rome in a *toga*. The wealthy, whose vanity was flattered by a long train of clients in their wake, naturally insisted on their wearing the official Roman garment. This explains why the *toga*, the symbol of the magistrates' authority, the dignity of the politician and the national superiority of a people born to empire (Virgil[4] wrote: *Romanos rerum dominos gentemque togatam*), degenerated into the livery of a client. The client's obsequiousness is *opera togata*.[5]

The *toga* was made of a heavy white woollen material, all of one piece and cut in an elliptical shape. It was a difficult garment to put on, and the help of the *vestiplicus*, a slave who arranged the folds the night before, was therefore invaluable. Some men wasted a great deal of time over its arrangement, others, like Horace,[6] never brought themselves to care greatly about turning themselves out fashionably. A long and famous passage of Quintilian,[7] assisted by a study of the countless toga-clad statues which survive, makes it possible to gather how the *toga* was put on; its interpretation, however, is not altogether easy and some details remain obscure. The material was completely folded lengthways into two unequal parts—one edge fell in front from the left shoulder to the feet (about a third of the length). The rest was made to fall down behind and then wound under the right arm, and the remainder thrown once more over the left shoulder. The centre of the garment remarkable for the folds and pleats, to which the fashionable paid meticulous attention, was the *sinus*; as the cloth of the *toga* was folded in two, the upper edge of the *sinus* had to be beneath the arm-pit, the lower fell half-way down the leg. When the *sinus* had been arranged and the last part of the *toga* thrown over the left shoulder, the first edge was drawn up from below to the *sinus*, enlarging it and making it protrude. In this way a *nodus*, or *umbo* was formed which held the completed garment together.

In war only the *sagum militare* was worn; there is, however, abundant evidence that even in the earliest times certain sacrificial rites in the camp were normally performed in a *toga*; in this case the *toga* was passed under the right arm and wrapped round the chest like a belt, leaving the arm free (*cinctus Gabinus*).

In the majority of cases the *toga* was *pura*, without decoration. The *toga praetexta* with a purple stripe, was the dress of boys— the toga was not worn until the age of 17—high magistrates and some priests; the *toga picta* was worn during a triumph; the *trabea* was a striped *toga* worn by augurs and other priests during rites.

The *toga* came to be replaced, particularly during the Imperial age, by more practical garments: the *pallium*, the *lacerna*, the *paenula*, etc., which were sometimes worn over the *toga*, but more often replaced it.

The *pallium* (the Greek ἱμάτιον) was worn over the tunic very like the *toga*, but being shorter and not folded, it did not hinder movement so much.

The *lacerna* was originally a military cloak, on the lines of the Greek chlamys (χλαμύς); under the Empire it began to be extensively worn especially by the middle class. The material and colour varied considerably. The common people wore a dark one, which was cheaper, but anyone who aimed at smartness wore *lacernae* of various brilliant colours.

The *paenula*, a very simple type of cloak, was used especially as a protection against cold and bad weather. It was put on by placing the head through a central hole, and thus remained on the shoulders without the need of any fastening. It was normally fitted with a hood. From the way in which they were used, we gather that some were water-proof (*paenula scortea*, of skin) or very heavy (*paenula gausapina*, of felt). Women wore them for travelling.

The *laena*, also called *duplex*, either on account of the thickness of the material, or, alternatively, because it was worn folded on the shoulders, was a round cloak of heavy material like the military *sagum*. The *laena* worn by the poor was short and dark, while there were richly coloured ones for covering the shoulders at banquets in cold weather. The cloak referred to as the *abolla* does not seem to have differed much from the *laena* in shape or use.

The *cucullus* (literally 'hood'), or *bardocucullus*, the *birrus* and the *caracalla* were heavy hooded cloaks; the last, which reached to the feet (*caracalla talaris*), is famous for having given M. Aurelius Antoninus, who wore it habitually and introduced its use to the army, his surname (hence the name of *caracalla Antoniniana*). This long hooded cloak must apparently be distinguished from the lady's *caracalla*, a light, sleeveless linen wrap.

The *synthesis* (*vestis cenatoria*, or *cenatorium*) was a very smart, well cut, elaborately embroidered garment worn at banquets and in Rome during the festival of the Saturnalia, when everybody, including the magistrates, left their togas at home.

The *endromis* or *endromida*, a heavy cloak mainly worn in sudden showers or thrown over the shoulders when the body was heated from exercise, took its name from a Greek shoe.

In women's dress the following garments must be distinguished: (1) the *tunica*, (2) the *stola*, which was as much the national costume for women as the *toga* was for men, (3) the overgarments.

(1) Roman women wore a shift (*tunica interior, subucula, interula*) next to the skin with a *fascia pectoralis* (*mamillare*, or from the Greek, *strophium* or *taenia*) worn under or above it to support the breasts. They also wore the *subligar* (p. 100), but apparently only when bathing.

(2) In early Rome women wore the *toga*, and men and women dressed in the same fashion: *olim toga fuit commune vestimentum et*

diurnum et nocturnum et muliebre et virile,[8] but very soon female clothing became different from male clothing, and women were made to wear the *toga* only as a sign of immorality. The matron wore the *stola,* a long garment reaching to the ground and belted at the waist. A purple strip (*instita*) was sewn on to the edge of the *stola;* this is a detail on which, through lack of archaeological evidence (it is impossible to recognise the *instita* on the *stolatae* statues) we must resign ourselves to not knowing for certain whether those authors are right who speak of it as a *tenuissima fasciola,* or those who describe it as *longa.* It has been equally impossible to establish what the difference was between the *stola* of the matron who had obtained the *jus trium liberorum* and others, although it is certain that there was a difference. In the third century A.D. the *stola matronalis* was replaced, like the male *toga,* by the *Dalmatica* and the *colobium* (see p. 101).

(3) As an overgarment for going out in public, Roman women in the early days of the Republic wore the *ricinium,* a simple square cloak covering the shoulders and perhaps, as has been maintained, the head. But in the last centuries of the Republic and in the Empire the *ricinium* was replaced by the *palla,* a much longer garment worn like the Greek ἱμάτιον.

There were three main types of footwear:
(1) Sandals (*soleae, sandalia*) held on by leather thongs (*habenae, amenta, obstragula*) round the toes. To wear sandals in public, and not, as good manners demanded, *calcei,* was a grave solecism. When Cicero[9] wants to describe Verres as a man who has forgotten his dignity both as a magistrate and as a citizen, he says: *Stetit soleatus praetor populi Romani cum pallio purpureo tunicaque talari.* ('He stood—a praetor of the Roman people—in sandals with a purple cloak and a long tunic reaching to the ground.') Outrageous behaviour! It was equally ill-mannered, however, to wear *calcei* in another's house when invited for the evening. The floor of a house had its rules no less than the street. When invited to a banquet, a Roman had a slave to carry his *soleae* to his host's house so that he could put them on before entering the dining room; if he was poor and short of slaves, he carried them himself in a bundle, like Horace's *conviva tribulis*[10] who arrived at a party clutching his sandals under his arm.
(2) Slippers (*socci*).

(3) *Calcei*, the proper footwear of the Roman citizen, which together with the *toga* formed the national dress. The *calceus patricius* and the *calceus senatorius* differed from the common *calceus*: the former, originally red, was bound by four leather thongs (*corrigiae*) and closed with a leather tongue (*ligula*) decorated with a semicircular ivory buckle (*lunula*); but in the Imperial age the *lunula* ceased to be the privilege of the aristocracy and was used merely as a decoration for smart shoes; the *calceus senatorius*, similar in shape to the patrician, was of black leather.

Other rougher types of footwear were: the *pero*, of undressed leather wrapped round the feet; the *caliga*, the military sandal; the *sculponea*, a wooden-soled clog, worn by peasants and slaves.

It is remarkable that there was no difference between men's and women's shoes; women also wore *soleae*, *socci* and *calcei*; in particular, women's shoes were of softer leather and brighter colours (red and gilt were the most common) and richer ornaments, sometimes precious (pearls, etc.).

Out of doors the Romans normally went bareheaded; at the most, if it rained, they put on a hood (*cucullus*), or if they had to travel on a summer journey, or stand still for long hours in the sun at the theatre, a broad-brimmed hat (*petasus*, *causia*). At the Saturnalia, when the smart, well-cut *synthesis* replaced the *toga*, everyone, including the Emperor, wore a cap (*pilleus*).[11] On other days a cap was the sign of a freedman. During the dinner of Trimalchio,[12] a slave, freed on the spot, immediately put on a cap, and Trimalchio, that tireless jester in deed no less than in word, had a pig served wearing a cap[13] which on the day before had been served at the end of the meal and been *dimissus* ('sent back untouched to the kitchen', but the word can also mean 'freed') by the guests. Certain types of headgear worn by priests, which were a late survival of early fashions in dress, do not need to be discussed here.

Ladies' hats were unknown; girls went bare-headed indoors and out, and ladies preserved their matronly dignity by covering their heads with a corner of the *palla* when they wore it in public.

Articles conceded only to feminine vanity were the bag (Plate 37), the fan (*flabellum*) and the parasol (*umbella*, or *umbraculum*; Plate 36). The fan and parasol were usually carried by the slave accompanying his mistress.

Jewellery.—The only male jewellery was the ring. Under the Republic only one ring was allowed, which was generally worn on the ring finger of the left hand and was used as a seal. Only freemen could wear it, as an ancient jurist says: *veteres non ornatus sed signandi causa anulum secum circumferebant . . . Nec cuiquam nisi libero, quos solos fides deceret quae signaculo continetur (habere licebat).*[14] A seal was the ancient equivalent of a signature, authenticating a pledge and evidence. Before he died, Petronius[15] smashed his ring so that it might not be misused to compromise others. In the Empire, many other rings, in addition to a signet ring, were worn for display. Some of the wealthiest men had their fingers loaded with them. These rings set with precious stones, were sometimes of enormous value, and were kept in a special box, the *dactyliotheca*. A remarkable difference between the Roman world and today is that male vanity expresses itself in expensive clothes and furniture rather than jewellery.

Female jewellery, however, was of the greatest variety. In addition to rings, which differed from men's in being of finer workmanship as well as having a sign of good luck cut in the jewel, women wore brooches (*fibulae*), hair combs (*acus crinales*, or *comatoriea*), band of gold and precious stones skilfully inserted into the hair (*vittae, mitrae*); earrings (*inaures*), bracelets (*armillae*), necklaces (*monilia*, a word which came to be applied to every type of feminine jewellery), later huge chains of gold round the neck and big rings round the ankle. A law which tried to check female luxury, the *lex Oppia* of 215 B.C., and caused a great outcry, in spite of the recent disaster of Cannae, fell into immediate disuse. Roman ladies carried their dowries on their bodies, in Seneca's[16] phrase, especially in their ears. Earrings reached a fantastic price; besides wearing more than one in each ear (which were called *crotalia* from the tinkling they caused), a fashion very unattractive to modern taste, Roman women wore earrings of enormous pearls (*elenchi, uniones*) and huge precious stones (with the single exception of diamonds, which because of their high price were used only for rings). A Roman matron saw nothing strange in turning herself into a walking jeweller's shop. Pliny the Elder's[17] statement that Lollia Paulina, Caligula's wife, used to wear jewellery worth 40 million sesterces, need hardly be regarded as an exaggeration.

Further Reading

L. M. Wilson, *The Roman Toga* (Baltimore, 1924), and *The Clothing of the Ancient Romans* (Baltimore, 1938).

R. A. Higgins, *Greek and Roman Jewellery* (London, 1962).

NOTES

1. Ars Poet., 50.
2. St. Augustine, De doctr. Christ., III, 20.
3. Suetonius, Aug., 82.
4. Aen., I, 282.
5. Martial, III, 46, 1; *Exigis a nobis operam sine fine togatam.*
6. Horace, Sat., I, 3, 31–32; *rideri possit, eo quod rusticius toga defluit*; Epist., I, 1, 96: *si toga dissidet impar.*
7. XI, 3, 139–41.
8. Varro, in Nonnius, 541, 2–4.
9. Act II in Verrem, V, 33, 86.
10. Epist., I, 13, 15.
11. Martial, XIV, 1, 2: *Dumque decent nostrum pillea sumpta Jovem.*
12. Petronius, 41.
13. Ibid. 40.
14. Atrius Capito, in Macrobius, VII, 13, 12.
15. Tacitus, Ann., XVI, 19.
16. De Benef., VII, 9, 4.
17. IX, 117.

CHAPTER VIII

Beards and Hairstyles

Beards. Hairstyles.

THE strange practice of wearing a round or pointed beard covering the face, and shaving the upper lip clean, which was common among the Greeks of the archaic age and the Etruscans, never seems to have taken root among the ancient Romans; this practice was also the fashion with the Homeric heroes, and compels us to imagine the handsome Achilles with a smooth upper lip and an aureole of facial hair which gives a simian look even to the hand-somest features.

The ancient Romans allowed their hair, beards and moustaches to grow freely; they were ruggedly dignified and unkempt: *illo austero more ac modo,* says Cicero;[1] *illa horrida (barba) quam in statuis antiquis atque imaginibus videmus.* Only with the second century B.C. did the habit of cutting the hair and shaving the beard begin to be at all common. Varro[2] has preserved for us a note derived from the records of Ardea, according to which the first barber came to Italy from Sicily in 300 B.C. The information is probably correct, but we should not exaggerate its significance and believe, like Varro, that the use of scissors and razor was unknown to the Romans before 300 B.C. The razor appears very early among archaeological finds, and is a feature of the earliest Italian civilisation; furthermore the story of Attus Navius,[3] who cut a whetting stone with a razor in the reign of Tarquinius Priscus, is familiar. Such evidence makes it impossible to draw so positive a conclusion from Varro's statement as some have attempted. It is probable that the *tonsores* of whom he speaks came to Italy to set up public barber shops, which would be evidence, not of the first introduction of shaving into Italy, but of its spread. Before this time, the few who shaved used the services of a slave (*tonsor*), which still continued to be the practice in noble families.

It is certain that the third century B.C. (the century of the Punic Wars) saw the victory of the razor. Scipio Africanus,[4] a champion of every novelty, began the fashion of shaving daily, and Claudius Marcellus, the conqueror of Syracuse, was the first great Roman to appear clean-shaven on his coins. We should not forget that, particularly in the last decades of the third century B.C., Greek culture began to influence Rome not only in literature and in matters of deep spiritual importance, but in customs as well, and it came to Rome almost entirely with the form and characteristics it had acquired in the Hellenistic age. The change of fashion which took place in the Alexandrian age, when the previously rare and despised practice of shaving became established among the Greeks, is reflected in Rome by the slow process which culminated at the time of the Second Punic War. This trifling detail of male toilet fits in with the general picture of Hellenistic influence on Rome. The main path for the penetration of such influences was from Magna Graecia, and it was from there that barbers came to Italy and Rome.

From the end of the third century B.C. to the beginning of the second century A.D. shaving was normal, though those who wished to disregard fashion were naturally free to treat their faces as they pleased. Young men did not shave their first down, but allowed it to darken their cheeks until it was almost a beard; then it was cut and consecrated, normally to a god (*depositio barbae*). The event was considered a solemn family affair and, as among the Greeks, it was a great occasion. When the first beard had been cut, a small beard (*barbula*) continued to be worn, to which young dandies paid the greatest care, until the age of forty, when the first grey hairs begin. At the appearance of these melancholy signs of approaching old age men tried to pluck them out with pincers (*volsellae*), but later the speedier method of shaving the whole face was preferred. This explains why the Romans connected the *barbula* with youth; to begin to shave the beard was to grow old.[5] For Cicero,[6] *barbatuli juvenes* is a synonym for young men. Dante's[7] famous lines

> *quando*
> *per udir se' dolente, alza la barba*

('Since you are grieved by hearing, lift up your beard') would have been incomprehensible to a Roman.

This custom lasted for a long time, but with the Emperor Hadrian there came a change. Hadrian's face was disfigured, and he grew his beard to hide the fact. Consequently beards returned to fashion until Constantine, under whom the use of the razor returned. From Constantine onwards, all the emperors, with the exception of the philosopher Julian, were clean shaven. To sum up, five phases can be distinguished in the Romans' treatment of their beards:

(1) Up to the third century B.C. they were usually unshaved.

(2) In the third century the practice of shaving began to spread.

(3) From the Second Punic War (end of the third century B.C.) to the time of Hadrian (first half of the second century A.D.) the use of the razor was common, but only amongst men over forty.

(4) From Hadrian to Constantine (first decades of the fourth century) the beard returned to fashion.

(5) Thereafter men were once more clean-shaven.

A man in mourning did not shave, but allowed his hair and beard to grow long (*barbam demittere, promittere, submittere*). So too did anyone facing a criminal charge, who appeared before the judges untidy and with hairy cheeks, in addition to being dirty and badly dressed (*sordidatus*). Philosophers also, especially the Cynics and Stoics, wore thick, impressive beards. This singularity went back to the Greek custom of the Hellenistic Age when shaving became universal, and only philosophers retained the ancient custom of long beards; traces of this custom survive in the beards of the clergy of the Greek Orthodox Church. The beard became a mark of its wearer's profession and mission, an object of scorn to others. This practice has left its mark on literature, for there is still a proverb that 'the beard does not make the philosopher'.

Only young freedmen and slaves engaged in special duties wore their hair long. Working slaves were shaved; free adults cut their hair either to a certain length (*per pectinem*), or cropped (ἐν χρῷ, *strictim*). Fops curled their hair with irons (*calamistrum*), scented it freely and spent hours at the barbers. From the time of Marcus Aurelius onwards, the fashion of shaving the head began to spread. Early Christians wore their beards and hair short.

Women's hair-styles never favoured short hair. Young women arranged their hair very simply, gathering it into a bun at the nape of the neck or in tresses coiled round the head so as to form a knot on the top. Married women's hair-styles were more complicated, and varied according to the rules of fashion or personal whim. Every woman chose the style which suited her best.[8] An absurd fashion, adopted from the Etruscans, of massing all the hair on the crown and keeping it tight with ribbons (*tutulus*) seems fortunately to have quickly disappeared, remaining the privilege of certain priestesses. The age of the Flavii[9] was the age of high hair-styles with the hair arranged on different levels. The hair was arranged in semicircles (*orbis*) and fell down in countless small ringlets (*anuli*), each held in place by a large pin (*acus*). This fashion required expert hairdressers as well as false hair and a net to keep the whole complicated structure in place (Plate 35); it was essentially a court hair-style, used by women of fashion, probably only for large parties. Female statues which can be certainly dated to this age show that it was not a general fashion, and was not as widespread as has been believed.[10]

False hair, wigs, dyes and lotions to preserve the colour of the hair were very commonly used not only by women, but frequently by men as well.

An exclusively feminine vanity was for a brunette (the normal hair colour in Mediterranean countries) to desire to seem blonde. To obtain this effect a dye (*sapo, spuma Batava* or *Chattica, pilae Mattiacae*) was used to bleach dark hair, and the coiffure was completed with false tresses of hair from some northern race. One of a Roman woman's ambitions was to obtain barbarians' hair, and there was a flourishing trade in this commodity.

Further Reading

For the numismatic evidence for hair-styles see M. Grant, *Roman History from Coins* (Cambridge, 1958).

NOTES

1. pro Cael., 14, 33.
2. *De Re Rust.*, XI, 11, 10: *Omnino tonsores in Italiam primum venisse ex Sicilia dicuntur post Romam conditam anno CCCCLIII, ut scriptum in publico Ardeae in litteris exstat, eosque adduxisse P. Titinium Menam. Olim tonsores non fuisse adsignificant antiquorum statuae quod pleraeque habent capillum et barbam magnam.*

3. Livy, I, 36, 4.
4. Pliny, N.H., VII, 211.
5. Juvenal, VI, 105.
6. Ad Att., I, 14, 5; 16, 11.
7. Purg., XXXI, 68.
8. Ovid, Ars Am., III, 135.
9. Cf. Martial, II, 66.

> *Unus de toto peccaverat orbe comarum*
> *Anulus, incerta non bene fixus acu,*

and Juvenal, 6, 502–3

> *Tot premit ordinibus, tot adhuc compagibus altum*
> *Aedificat caput.*

10. Cf. Mrs. A. Strong, *Roman Sculpture from Augustus to Constantine* (London 1907), p. 365.

CHAPTER IX

Women in the Roman Family

The education of women. Marriage. Wedding rites.

UNLIKE the Greeks, who kept their wives imprisoned at home, and always spent their leisure hours away from their families gossiping in shops and public places,[1] the Romans were very strongly attracted by family life. This is one of the most characteristic sides of their civilisation, which brings the Romans nearer to the customs and feelings of our own day. In every age the Roman's wife was her husband's companion and helper; she was next to him at parties and banquets (behaviour which would have seemed scandalous[2] to a Greek), shared his authority over the children and slaves, and participated in the dignity of his position in public life. *Quem enim Romanorum pudet uxorem ducere in convivium? Aut cuius non materfamilias primum locum aedium tenet atque in celebritate versatur.*[3] This freedom, particularly under the Republic, had a certain austerity and reserve about it; although she joined in a dinner party, a Roman matron sat throughout and did not recline;[4] she did not join in the *comissatio* (p. 96), and she did not drink wine but *mulsum* (see p. 96). This ban on wine drinking seems to have been very strict in the earliest times. With the advance of civilisation it grew less severe. But unless we pay too much importance to the raging of the embittered Juvenal,[5] or to gross caricatures such as Martial's epigrams V, 4, and I, 87, Roman women do not seem to have had the same addiction to wine which Aristophanes so often ridiculed in Athenian women.

The education of women was also sensibly broadminded. From the earliest days boys and girls grew up together, sharing their activities and their games. The elementary schools, where reading, writing, counting and shorthand were taught (see p. 167), were attended by both sexes. In an epigram of Martial[6] a school master (*ludi magister*) is described as an object of hatred to boys and girls (*invisum pueris virginibusque caput*). When primary education was finished, girls of aristocratic families continued their education privately under the guidance of *praeceptores* who grounded them in Greek and Latin literature; at the same time they learnt to play the lyre, to dance and sing.

This liberal education, common among the wealthier families in the last days of the Republic and throughout the Empire, did not prevent Roman women from occupying themselves in the ordinary household tasks. They supervised and directed the slaves, and themselves worked at the lighter tasks. As the Greek woman was an expert weaver, so the Roman woman excelled at embroidery (*acu pingere*). In earlier days the matron spun with the maids, but there is every reason to believe that this was only an ancient custom; a sepulchral epitaph[7] recording spinning as a particular virtue of a Roman woman has become famous; *casta fuit, domum servavit, lanam fecit.*

The Roman custom of giving girls a husband while still very young compelled them to lead a retired life until they became adults, when they gave their dolls to the Lares and began to wait for their fathers to find them a husband. Flirting in respectable Roman society must have been very rare; for one thing, there was no opportunity for it. The marriage of young people depended almost exclusively on their fathers.

With marriage, however, the Roman woman acquired comparative freedom of behaviour and action, luckier in this also than the Greek woman of the classical age, whom marriage changed from being a prisoner in her father's house to a similar role in her husband's; the mistress of slaves, she was a slave herself. Roman matrons enjoyed their husband's confidence and nobody required them to lead a secluded life. They left their houses freely, exchanged visits, went out for business and shopping. In the evening they accompanied their husbands to banquets and returned home late.[8]

The study of Roman marriage and its ceremonies is part of legal history and has only an indirect bearing on customs. It will be enough to refer here to the two forms of marriage which were successively popular.

(1) Marriage by *conventio in manum*.—This was the more ancient form, by which the woman came to form part of her husband's family and was subject to his marital power (*manus*) in the same way as children were subject to his *patria potestas.*

She found herself in the position of a daughter (*loco filiae*) in everything connected with family rights and inheritance. This bond could be created in three ways:

(i) *confarreatio*, a sacred rite originally found only in patrician families, which took its name from the spelt cake (*libum farreum*) shared by the couple during the ceremony; in priestly families its use survived till much later;

(ii) *coemptio*, a sale (*mancipatio*), originally genuine, later symbolic, of the wife by which the father conveyed his legal power over her to the husband;

(iii) *usus*, uninterrupted cohabitation of the couple for a year, a way of acquiring the *manus* which quickly fell into disuse.

(2) Free marriage, or *sine manu*.—The wife continued to belong to her father's family, subject to his *potestas* and retaining the rights of inheritance of her own family. This was not a formal marriage, like the ancient marriage *cum manu* or like ours, but depended on the cohabitation of the couple and their continued desire to be considered man and wife (*affectio maritalis*); consequently it could be annulled by the mere separation of the couple; it was enough for the husband to tell his wife, personally, by letter or through a slave (a freedman in the Empire): 'Take back what is yours' (*tuas res tibi habeto*), and she had no choice.⁹

Throughout the classical period, up to the last days of the Republic, marriage *sine manu* remained in force; it would, however, be a mistake to argue from the ease with which the marriage bond could be broken that the Romans did not adequately appreciate its strength. They were, on the contrary the first to realise that marriage has such social, religious and emotional foundations that law must be limited to controlling only some of them. *Nuptiae sunt conjunctio maris et feminae et consortium omnis vitae, divini et humani juris communicatio.*¹⁰ The *repudium*, in spite of its simple form, was always regarded as an act of exceptional importance. The second marriage of a woman, even a widow, did not meet with public approval. To have had a single husband was considered a feminine virtue, and the epithet *univira* is one of the chief titles of honour in the sepulchral epitaphs of married women. Women who regarded conjugal loyalty lightly incurred severe disapproval. The *connubium* was thus in every way a very powerful bond among the Romans, who founded their empire and their civilisation on the sanctity of family life.

The marriage ceremony was not essential to form a legal bond between a couple, but tradition and the sacred nature it had acquired made it the most important event in family life.

The wedding day was chosen with great care from a jungle of days and months of ill omen which the superstitious Romans avoided more carefully than we avoid Fridays (see p. 283). May was a singularly ill-omened month, and the most propitious time for marriage was the second half of June.

On the eve of her marriage, the bride dedicated her childhood toys to the Lares; in the evening she put on her wedding dress in place of the *praetexta*, the garment of girls, and an orange coloured veil on her head, and then went to bed. For the wedding day the house was decorated as for a holiday. The door and doorposts were hung with wreaths of flowers, branches of evergreen trees such as myrtle and laurel, and coloured ribbons. Carpets were spread at the entrance. In patrician houses, the cupboards containing the wax images of the ancestors (see p. 81) were opened, as was the custom on all solemn days. The bride as she dressed for the ceremony was naturally the centre of attention; her hairstyle and veil formed an important part of the bridal toilet. For the first time the bride put ribbons (*vittae*) in her hair; this was dressed in a special way, called *sex crines*, and divided into six plaits. To part the bride's hair, iron was used, always apparently the point of a spear,[11] *hasta caelibaris*, kept specially for this purpose. The wedding dress was a plain white tunic reaching to the ground, similar in cut to the matron's *stola*, held in at the waist by a belt whose ends were fastened with a special knot (*nodus Herculeus*). The *flammeum* fell from the bride's head over her face; we must assume this veil to have been orange in colour if we are to reconcile the epithets of 'red' and 'yellow' which are both applied to it. This explains why *nubere* (strictly to 'veil the head') came to mean taking a husband. The fact that reliefs depicting marriage scenes show the bride unveiled, contrary to the positive evidence from many literary sources, must be explained by the technical difficulties of the sculptor.

Throughout the ceremony the bride was attended by the *pronuba*, a matron who, to qualify for this honourable office,

35. Rome. Female bust with hairstyle of the Flavian age. (*p. 111*)

37. Relief showing sandals and handbag.

36. Relief showing parasol and comb. (*p. 105*)

38, 39. Roman jewellery. Necklaces, bracelets, ear-rings and (below) br ooches.
(*p. 106*)

39.

must have been married only once (*univira*). The ceremony began with an augural sacrifice, when the auspices were taken. A propitious sacrifice was a sign that heaven favoured the union.

After the sacrifice the signing of the *tabulae nuptiales*, the marriage contract, normally took place in the presence of ten witnesses. Then the *pronuba* took the right hands of the pair, and placed them in each other. This was the *dextrarum junctio*, the most solemn moment of the ceremony, the silent exchange of vows between the young couple and mutual promises of their desire to live together. The scene is shown on many sarcophagi and the symbolic act, which the church has retained in the wedding ceremony, still has meaning and value today.

When the marriage took place by *confarreatio*, the pair were made to sit veiled on two adjacent chairs, over which the skin of the sacrificial animal had been spread. The pair then walked round the altar preceded by a servant (*camillus*) carrying a chest (*cumerus*) holding the sacred vessels. But, as we have said, in the classical age this rite was only celebrated on exceptional occasions.

When all the formalities had been completed, the banquet (*cena nuptialis*) took place. Afterwards, towards the evening, the *deductio*, the ceremony of conducting the bride to her husband's house, began. An attempted rape gave the signal for it. The husband unexpectedly pretended to snatch his young wife, terrified and resisting, from the arms of her mother, or, if she were absent, her substitute—a mere formality in which the memory of the rape of the Sabine women was perpetuated. A procession was then formed to the bridegroom's house. The bride advanced carrying a spindle and distaff, symbols of her new activities as mother of the family, and accompanied by three boys, *patrimi* and *matrimi*, whose parents were both alive; two held her by the hand, the third went in front waving a hawthorn torch (*spina alba*), kindled at the hearth of the bride's home. The charred remains, which were believed to bring good luck, were distributed among the guests, just as we distribute the flowers from the bride's bouquet, a custom which has the advantage of being less messy. A noisy crowd followed shouting the marriage cry, 'talasse' or 'talassio' (the meaning of the words is uncertain) and hurling coarse jests. The satirical and Fescennine (see p. 271) spirit of Rome was unbridled.

When the bride had reached the bridegroom's house, she decorated its thresholds with strips of wool and anointed it with pig's fat and oil; in the light of this custom the etymological fantasy of certain ancient writers had no compunction in deriving *uxores* from *unxores*![12] As she entered the house her husband, who had preceded his wife, stood on the threshold and asked her her name, to which she replied clearly, '*Ubi tu Gaius, ego Gaia*'. Then those who accompanied her lifted her up bodily so that she might not touch the threshold with her feet and carried her into the house.[13] The husband received her with a religious ceremony, called *igni atque aqua accipere*. Then the *pronuba* seated the bride on the *lectus genialis* (see p. 60) facing the door, where she pronounced the ritual prayers to the god of her new home. This ended the ceremony, the wedding party broke up and the guests went home.

On the following day the wife, wearing the clothes of a matron for the first time, made an offering to the Lares and Penates and received presents from her husband. Then an intimate banquet for the relations of the couple took place (*repotia*).

Further Reading

C. Seltman, *Women in Antiquity* (London, 1956).
P. E. Corbett, *The Roman Law of Marriage* (Oxford, 1930).
J. P. V. D. Balsdon, *Roman Women* (London, 1962).

NOTES

1. Lysias, Pro Invalido, 20.
2. Among the Greeks it was improper for a woman to take part in a banquet (Isaeus, De hered. Pyrrhi, 13).
3. Cornelius Nepos, Praef., 6.
4. Valerius Maximus, II, 1, 2: *Feminae cum viris cubantibus sedentes cenitabant.*
5. 6, 425.
6. IX, 68, 2.
7. CIL, I, 1007.
8. Cicero, pro Caelio, 8, 20; Ovid, Amores, I, 3, 55; Suetonius, Nero, 26.
9. Cicero, Phil, II, 69.

10. Digest, XXXIII, 2, 1.
11. Plutarch, Quaest. Rom., 87.
12. Servius on Aen., IV, 458; Isidore, IX, 7, 12.
13. Classical writers give various explanations for this custom; it probably sprang from the fear that the bride might stumble. To have done so on the first day of her married life would have been very ill-omened.

CHAPTER X

Slavery

The slave trade. The number of slaves in a Roman family. Familia rustica *and* familia urbana. *Slave labour as an investment. The legal position of slaves and their treatment in the Roman family.* Peculium; contubernium; *punishment of slaves.* Manumissio.

THE prosperous and comfortable life which the Romans enjoyed from the last centuries of the Republic onwards and their economic stability were largely the result of carefully organised slave labour. With the passage of time and the progress of civilisation, the numbers of slaves increased steadily, while their organisation and employment in a wide variety of industrial and domestic tasks became highly efficient.

There was no scarcity of slaves in the ancient world. To those who were slaves by birth, children of slave women, was added the large number of freemen enslaved for various reasons: prisoners of war, who had become the property of a hostile state and been sold by auction to private citizens; children kidnapped and sold by pirates and brigands, or sold or exposed by their fathers; those guilty of crimes incurring the loss of liberty, or who had become the property of their creditors as the result of a cruel law which rigidly protected the rights of the creditor—all these in various ways helped to swell the ranks of slaves and supply the markets in human beings throughout the world.

One of the results of the growing power of Rome was that from markets everywhere slaves of both sexes, of every nationality and of the most varied abilities streamed into the great city; there were gigantic *lecticarii*, carefully matched for size and build and sold in teams, young handsome boys sold as cupbearers, skilled cooks, learned *Graeculi*, musicians, architects, waiters, dancers, dwarfs, etc. Under the supervision of the aediles the slave dealers (*mangones*, or *venalicii*), sold their wares publicly, either in the open Forum or in shops; not surprisingly their shrewdness and unscrupulousness in extolling their wares became proverbial, and *mangonicare* came to mean 'to make something appear better than it is'. The slaves for sale stood on a revolving stand (*catasta*); those just brought from abroad were exposed with one foot whitened with chalk (*gypsati*). From the neck of each hung a placard (*titulus*) with all the information required by prospective purchasers: nationality, abilities, good and bad points, etc. The best slaves were to be found in the *Saepta* (see p. 10) near the Forum, the meeting-place of the fashionable world, where the best shops were.

Prices varied according to the age and quality of the slave. There are references to fabulous sums and very small prices. One *grammaticus*, for example, fetched 700,000 sesterces,[1] a small fortune. We can imagine from this how much attention must have been paid to protect such expensive slaves against the risk that a common chill might send a man worth more than a factory to the grave. The fact that intelligence and learning were the two qualities which most enhanced the value of slaves argues well for Roman civilisation. Next came good looks, skill at particular duties, as well as various less pleasant qualities, such as being half-witted, dwarfed, or terribly disfigured (see p. 98). But an exceptional price was only fetched by particular circumstances of life and education or the buyer's whim. Generally a good slave was worth about twelve times as much as an untrained slave.

The early Romans were content with a small retinue of slaves, but in the Empire the ranks of slaves began to swell almost into armies. According to Athenaeus,[2] who quotes his sources conscientiously, some Romans possessed ten or twenty thousand slaves. We must treat such evidence cautiously, because there is no suggestion that such a host was wholly employed in the personal service of their master. The cultivation of the *latifundia*, the industries, such as tanning and the manufacture of bricks and pottery which the Romans associated closely with agriculture, and all other industries and investments where the slave, like the machine in modern industry, was an essential element, offered a limitless field for the exploitation of slave labour. Ordinary household needs also required more manual labour than with us, because industry had not yet begun, as it has nowadays, to relieve the household staff of many minor duties. Today the care of clothes, the body, lighting, etc., does not impose on the modern house the labour it demanded among the Romans, when the carpets were made and looked after in the home and all washing and ironing was done in the house (a custom which is becoming increasingly rare outside Italy). The master's bath required the attendance of more than one slave, and lighting was not the simple matter of flicking a switch that it is today; the single chore of preparing innumerable lamps and cleaning from the walls and ceilings the smoke which blackened them, involved many hours' labour. Nevertheless, it is certain that at Rome even those of very moderate means expected to be well served. Horace,[3] who dined simply, had three slaves; speaking of the spendthrift Tigellius he tells us that sometimes he had two hundred slaves, sometimes only ten, that is, either too many or too few. A slave (*paedagogus*) was used to take children to school.[4] Even the poorest took at least three slaves with them to the baths.[5] Not to have one slave was a sign of the most degrading poverty.[6] When there were many slaves—as there were in all well-to-do families—they were divided into groups of ten, each under the orders of a foreman.

The Romans made a fundamental distinction between the *familia rustica* and the *familia urbana*. At the head of the *familia rustica* was the bailiff (*vilicus*) helped by his wife (*vilica*), sometimes with a subordinate accountant (*actor*); when there was no *actor*, the bailiff himself was usually responsible for keeping the books. Subordinate to the *vilicus* were the *magistri officiorum* or *operum*, who directed and supervised the slaves (*operae*) trained in agricultural labour. Other slaves were employed to look after all these men, preparing their food, caring for their clothes, acting as their *tonsores*, and in the large ranches even as their doctors. The country slaves were well treated and fed. Every *villa rustica* had its bath (p. 75), but the slaves led an exhausting life, subjected to a vigorous discipline and tied to the hard work of the land; a transfer from the town to the country establishment was regarded as a punishment. Horace warned a talkative slave:[7] *ocius hinc te ni rapis, accedes opera agro nona Sabino*. The city slaves, the *familia urbana*, were directly under the orders of their master, or of a slave or freeman responsible for the running of the household, the *procurator* (in an earlier age, the *atriensis*). They were occupied in different tasks of varying importance; according to their abilities, some were trained in running the house, like the *dispensator* responsible for book-keeping, the *arcarius*, the treasurer, the *sumptuarius*, the accountant; others cleaned the house and furniture, or looked after the stables and horses. Others attended to the needs of the master or mistress, especially when they dressed or bathed, or had special duties at banquets. When there were children, a number of slaves were allotted to look after them. The kitchen staff, cooks and undercooks, were under the command of the *archimagirus*. The *amanuenses* who copied letters, and the *tabellarii*, strong fast runners entrusted with their delivery, helped with the correspondence.

The variety of duties created distinctions among the slaves themselves. The slave who had fetched a high price was naturally treated with greater care. Slaves were distinguished as *ordinarii*, specialists in some particular duty, and general working slaves (*mediastini*, *vulgares*, *qualesquales*), among whom were included the slaves engaged in the service of other slaves (*vicarii*).

Big capitalists, in addition to the slaves of the *familia rustica* and *urbana*, kept slaves simply as an investment, hiring them out to anybody who needed them. One such speculator was T. Pomponius Atticus, as we learn from references in Cicero's correspondence.[8]

Roman law regarded slaves as chattels (*res*). As chattels they were subject to the unrestrained will of their masters, against which they had no protection. But neither the rigour of the law nor the power of a master can turn a man into a chattel. A slave is a chattel *sui generis*, who feels, thinks and wishes. Above all he has the chance of being freed and turning from a chattel into a person with rights before the law; furthermore a slave's work was obtained with his willing co-operation. Neither threats nor punishment can compel a digger to hoe the ground, a cook to prepare a dish, a lyre player to play, or a *grammaticus* to give a good Greek lesson. A slave is an intelligent being and can only be ordered through his intelligence. Finally, among civilised people an irrepressible sense of humanity gives rise to a feeling of reciprocal obligations and sympathetic feelings between men of different legal standing, and always condemns senseless cruelty, abuse and pointless harshness; even when the law is silent, public opinion makes itself felt and in the most serious cases finds a method of adequate sanction. The master who was senselessly cruel to his slaves, besides becoming an object of scorn, could be prosecuted.

It is therefore unsafe to infer the treatment of slaves in the Roman family solely from their legal position. Relations between slaves and their masters differed very widely. Frequently there was on one side a cold disdain and brutal severity, and on the other a passive indifference sometimes leading to dislike which in the worst cases produced a deep hatred and might even result in murder.[9] Seneca,[10] whose remarks on slavery are particularly humane,[11] and the equally mild Pliny[12] regard the chance of being murdered by slaves as a risk to which everyone is exposed. But there are also examples of devoted attachment between masters and slaves. Not a few cases of a heroic slave's devotion to his master are recorded. Some faced fearful tortures and even death without flinching[13] rather than betray their masters. It would be possible to compile a long list of known cases, contrasting slaves who served faithfully, were kindly treated and became the friends and partners of their master, as Tiro was of Cicero, and slaves who were daily the helpless victims of their master's brutality. Galen,[14] the doctor, noted that many slaves had their teeth broken and their eyes blackened by blows. Kindness to slaves, with the possible exception of sympathy towards the *verna* born in the house, must have been exceptional. To most it seemed weakness, particularly because the degrading conditions of the slave frequently made him deservedly an object of contempt, a talkative, greedy, lazy liar. A man who has lost his sense of human dignity and freedom is compelled to live without any very high standards. The main reasons for the Romans' harshness to their slaves was the conviction that they deserved no better treatment. That this view was not entirely wrong is shown by the fact that the most perverse, vicious and cruel members of Roman society were the freedmen, slaves who had been freed and grown rich. In their new social and legal position they retained the narrow outlook of the slave. None the less, unreasonable and deliberate cruelty was condemned, and it is unhistorical to accuse the Romans of fattening lampreys on the flesh of slaves. The survival of the story of one criminal, Vedius Pollio,[15] who fed his slaves to the lampreys, is due to the horror aroused by this act of criminal madness. Had it been a perfectly normal action, it would have gone unremarked and we should know nothing about it. Vedius Pollio was furthermore a freedman, a former slave pitiless to slaves.

A slave's legal position meant that he could not own property

40. Sarcophagus showing funeral rites.   (*p. 130*)

41. Relief showing marriage rites.   (*p. 117*)

42. School scene. (*p. 168*)

43. Sarcophagus showing scenes in boy's education.

44. Writing materials. To the left are shown two inkwells, one of red clay, the smaller of bronze. The curved pen for writing on parchment or papyrus has a spoon at one end to stir the ink. Two of the *styli* are of metal, one of bone. The wooden tablets were spread with wax.

or contract a legal marriage, and was denied any legal protection against his master's ill treatment, even when this passed all reasonable limits in demands on his labour and infliction of punishment. At various times certain mitigations of the worst consequences of slavery were established; a slave was allowed to put aside from his savings a *peculium*, which he could spend on pleasures, or with which he could buy his freedom when he had saved a certain amount. He was also allowed to choose from among the female slaves a *conserva* as his companion, and to live with her in a form of servile marriage called *contubernium*; although it had no legal status or effect and the children born of such a union were the slaves of the *paterfamilias*, this form had the master's approval, and in the Empire it even found legal protection when masters were forbidden to sell the partners of the *contubernium* separately. Furthermore, in the course of time the master's right to inflict the severest punishments at his mere whim was withdrawn. This necessity of submitting to any punishment inflicted by the master strikes us as the least tolerable aspect of slavery; a slave was defenceless against the whim and caprices of his master, who combined the roles of judge and jury and could impose whatever punishment he chose, without being responsible to any court of appeal. The punishments inflicted on slaves were merciless; transfer to the *villa rustica*, sentence to hard labour in the *ergastulum* (p. 71) or at the mill wheel, which normally involved being placed in chains, were at the bottom of the scale of punishments which rose through other more serious punishments such as whipping, aggravated in various ways, to some of the most unbearable tortures: branding on the flesh with white hot metal rods (*laminae*), racking by the *eculeus* (a wooden instrument which stretched the body and broke the joints), mutilation, *crurifragium* (the violent breaking of the legs), etc. Runaways, liars and thieves were branded (*stigma, nota*) on the forehead with a red hot iron with the letters FUG, KAL, FUR. For the most serious offence the slave was condemned to death, and the method of execution was itself painful and humiliating. Normally a slave was crucified; with his arms stretched and tied to a yoke (*patibulum*) which lay on his neck, he was driven to the place of execution under blows from the whip, where he was hoisted and nailed to a beam fixed perpendicularly in the ground and left to die in slow agony. Other methods of execution consisted of exposing slaves to the wild beasts in the circus (see p. 252) or burning them alive in a cloak impregnated with pitch (*tunica molesta*).

Such were the punishments a master could inflict on a slave without being accountable to anybody. But in the Imperial age an effort was made to restrict this unlimited power of the *dominus*; among the various provisions which guaranteed a slave the integrity of his body, we may remember that Hadrian deprived the master of his power of life and death over slaves, and Constantine regarded the execution of a slave as murder. We may believe that in the earliest times the ancient *mores*, the foundation of Roman society, placed restrictions on the maltreatment of slaves which were confirmed by legal guarantees in the Empire.

Slavery was a wretched state, but not inescapable. The slave could obtain his freedom by means of *manumissio*, which took three forms:

1. *Manumissio per vindictam.*—An *assertor in libertatem* of the slave with the master's approval contested the latter's right of ownership before a magistrate, and when he had been granted possession, touched his head with a rod (*vindicta*) and declared him free.

2. *Manumissio censu.*—The master had the slave entered on the censors' lists as a Roman citizen.

3. *Manumissio testamento.*—Enfranchisement by will. Here the freed slave was released from the bonds which normally bound a freedman to his former master.

These solemn forms are the most ancient. The praetorian law introduced a simpler method which required only the manifestation on the master's part of his willingness to free the slave. Such forms, employed in the Greek provinces, later became part of Roman law: *manumissio inter amicos* (a declaration of the desire to free a slave made in front of friends); *manumissio per epistulam* (a letter by which a master informed a slave of his intention of freeing him); *manumissio per mensam* (when the master invited the slave to lie down at a meal with the obvious intention of freeing him).

The general abolition of slavery took place only later, after the fall of the Western Empire; it was Christianity's greatest victory, and was not attained for many years.

Further Reading

R. H. Barrow, *Slavery in the Roman Empire* (London, 1928), W. L. Westerman, *The Slave Systems of Greek and Roman Antiquity* (Philadelphia, 1958), W. Buckland, *The Roman Law of Slavery: the condition of the Slave in Private Life from Augustus to Justinian* (Cambridge, 1908). See also for a discussion of controversial points and a bibliography, M. I. Finley (ed.), *Slavery in Classical Antiquity* (Cambridge, 1960), a collection of ten essays by leading authorities.

NOTES

1. Pliny, N.H., VII, 128.
2. VI, 272.
3. Sat., I, 6, 116; 3, 11–12.
4. Ibid. I, 6, 78.
5. Martial, XII, 70.
6. Catullus, XXIII, 1.
7. Sat., II, 7, 117–18.
8. e.g. Ad Att., IV, 4, 2.
9. Cf. Pliny, Epist., III, 14, where he tells the story of a freedman, Larcius Macedo, murdered by his slaves while bathing.
10. Epist., 4, 6: *Servorum ira non pauciores ceciderunt quam regum;* ibid. *Nemo non servus habet in te vitae necisque arbitrium.*
11. See especially Epist., 47.
12. Epist., III, 14, 5. *Nec est quod quisquam possit esse securus, quia sit remissus et mitis; non enim judicio domini, sed scelere perimuntur.*
13. Tacitus, Hist., I, 3: *Contumax etiam adversus tormenta servorum fides*; cf. Seneca, Epist., 47, 4, and the well known story of Epicharis in Tacitus, Ann, XV, 57.
14. V, 17.
15. Seneca De Clem., I, 18, 2: *Quis non Vedium Pollionem peius oderat quam servi sui, quod muraenas sanguine humano saginabat et eos qui se aliquid offenderant in vivarium, quid aliud quam serpentium, abici jubebat? O hominem mille mortibus dignum! Sive devorandos servos objiciebat muraenis quas esurus erat, sive in hoc tantum illas alebat ut sic aleret.*

CHAPTER XI

Funeral Rites

The last rites; the displaying of the corpse. The funeral procession. Burial and cremation.

DEATH and burial were occasions for complicated rites among the Romans. Some of these, particularly those whose motive was a delicate feeling of *pietas* towards the dead, have survived to the present day; others have been retained by the Roman Catholic Church in the rites prescribed at the death of a Pope (as when the dead Pontiff is called three timesby his Christian name); most have fallen into disuse.

When a sick man was on the point of death, he was placed on the bare earth; one of his closest relations caught his last breath with a kiss and closed his eyes. Scarcely had he breathed his last, then the *conclamatio* took place, when those present called the dead man loudly by name, a custom dating back to the *Odyssey*.[1] Then began the preparation of the body; the women of the house, or men trained in funeral rites (*pollinctores*), washed it with warm water, and after anointing it with unguents and carrying out a type of temporary embalming, dressed it in its best clothes (the *toga* for a citizen, the *praetexta* for a magistrate), laid it on the *lectus funebris*, and exposed it publicly in the *atrium*. A small coin was placed under the dead man's tongue to pay Charon's fare, a custom which came from Greece.

Lamps and candles burned around the corpse, which was strewn with flowers, wreaths and garlands. As a sign of mourning the fire on the hearth was extinguished, and the women of the household repeated their cries and lamentations at intervals, tearing their hair and clothes, and beating their breasts.

The length of time the corpse was displayed depended on the dead man's position. The poor were buried the day they died, the emperors remained exposed for a week. The corpse was then buried or cremated; of the two rites, burial and cremation, common among the Romans, the latter eventually became the commoner in the Empire, probably through the influence of Christianity. But the solemn ceremony of the funeral (*funus*) preceded both the pyre and the grave.

Men dislike death almost as much as they dislike the idea of not having a decent funeral after death. In every age men have toiled laboriously all their lives merely to save enough to pay their funeral expenses. This human sentiment gave birth to the *collegia funeraticia* in Rome, clubs of men following the same profession formed into a body for religious purposes, especially to ensure their members an honourable funeral. It will not seem strange that these corporations, whose members followed the same profession and had economic and political interests in common, ended by involving themselves in matters unconnected with religion. The *collegia* became, for example, electioneering bodies, and from these pious institutions developed that corporate spirit which the Empire had frequently to fight as dangerous, and which prepared the way for the guilds of the Middle Ages.

The funerals of the poor (*funus plebeium* or *tacitum*) and of children (*funus acerbum*) were hurried nocturnal affairs, while the funerals of adult members of noble families took place in daytime with great pomp, whether the funeral expenses were met by the relatives (*funus privatum*) or the state (*funus publicum*). Even the funerals of the poor were normally entrusted to undertakers (*libitinarii*); theirs was a profitable profession, but so despised that its practice involved a reduction of civil rights (*minima capitis deminutio*). These undertakers employed a considerable number of men who specialised in various tasks: the *pollinctores*, who prepared the corpse for exposing; the *vespillones*, who at poor men's funerals placed the corpse in the coffin and carried it to the pyre or the grave; the *dissignatores*, who arranged and directed the procession at large funerals.

As with us, funeral announcements were made, with the difference that ours are printed, while the Romans' were made by a herald. But the contents of the announcement were the same; the death was announced in an archaic formula preserved for us by Varro[2] and Festus[3]—*ollus* (the name) *Quiris leto datus est*—and the date and time of the funeral. Such announcements were only made for the funerals of important people, which were hence called *funera indictiva*.

The funeral procession (*pompa*), preceded by pipers, advanced to the sound of flutes, horns and *tubae*; behind came torchbearers and the *praeficae*, hired women who raised loud cries of grief (*lugubris eiulatio*); in the intervals one of them sang the *naenia* of the dead, in his honour.

The malicious Fescennine spirit, an indigenous product of Italy, made itself felt even at funerals; dancers and clowns capered and joked throughout the procession, singing ballads that paid scant respect to the dead. As the triumphant general was exposed to the stinging insults of his troops (see p. 269), so a dead man on his last journey was a target for malicious jeers and abuse, the more so if he had been important in life. When Vespasian[4] died, an *archimimus*, wearing a mask and imitating the dead emperor's gait, made ribald jokes about his well-known avarice (see p. 270).

The shrieks of the *praeficae* and the buffoonery of the *mimi* did not rob the funerals of distinguished Romans of the serious and impressive character, which, as Polybius[5] tells us, made such a profound impression on the young: κάλλιον οὐκ εὐμαρές ἰδεῖν θέαμα νέῳ φιλοδόξῳ καὶ φιλαγάθῳ ('an ambitious and virtuous young man could not easily see a nobler sight'). To this the solemn procession of ancestors before the bier mainly contributed. We have seen (p. 81) with what veneration noble Romans kept the masks of their dead ancestors in recesses in the *alae* of their *atria* made for the purpose. Each of these ancestors was represented at the funeral; a man wore the mask and the uniform and insignia of a consul, praetor etc., to show the highest rank achieved by the ancestor he was representing. These ancestors were carried aloft stretched out on a bier; later they stood in a chariot, as was already the custom by the time of Polybius (the Greek historian of the second century B.C., who has left us the most interesting and moving account of a Roman funeral). The impressive procession was ended by bearers of placards recalling by words or symbols the titles or deeds which had distinguished the life of the dead man.

The bier, on which the uncovered corpse lay, came behind the ancestors, preceded by lictors dressed in black bearing the *fasces*, and followed by members of the family in mourning. The women without ornaments and with dishevelled hair, abandoned themselves to transports of despair.

Thus the procession wound on to the site of burial or the cremation. If the deceased had played an important part in public life, the procession halted as it filed through the Forum. The ancestors sat on curule chairs round the *Rostra*, and the son, a close relative or an important official, delivered the *laudatio funebris*.

The last rites had to be paid to the dead outside the *pomerium*. The Law of the Twelve Tables laid down:[6] HOMINEM MORTUUM IN URBE NE SEPELITO NEVE URITO. Burial within the city was a very rare honour granted only for exceptional services to the state.

If the rich sarcophagi of the imperial age show that the rite of burial had spread in the last centuries among leading families, our evidence for the Republic and the early days of the Empire indicates that cremation was the more solemn and elaborate rite. The pitiful rites of burial were confined to the poor and slaves. Social injustice extended even beyond the grave, and the poor were deprived of the honours of the pyre and buried in public cemeteries in humble coffins.

The pyre, the normal rite amongst the rich, was prepared in various ways. Its simplest form was the *bustum*, when a trench was dug and filled with wood and the corpse placed on top. The remains of the pyre, ashes, dust and bones were covered with earth.

Much more widespread was the custom by which cremation and burial involved two separate ceremonies at two different places. In this case the site of the pyre was called *ustrina*, the final resting-place of the ashes *sepulchrum*.

The body together with the bier (*lectus*) was placed on the pyre, which was originally a mere heap, but was later built in the shape of an altar surrounded by cypress trees and decorated with pictures, hangings and statues. Friends and relatives also threw clothes, ornaments, arms and even food on to the pyre, objects which had belonged to the dead or been held dear by him. A very ancient custom which was always observed, required that as he lay on the pyre, the dead man's eyes should be opened and closed and he should receive the last kiss, as a final sign of farewell. Then a relative or friend—in the case of an emperor a high official—set light to the pyre, which blazed while those present threw on spices and flowers. When the pyre had burnt down, the glowing ashes were quenched with wine, and the relative collected the bones, putting them in oil or honey, preparatory to placing them in the urn. After a purificatory ceremony the guests returned home, while the family stayed near the remains of the funeral. The relatives of the dead man were in a state of impurity (*familia funesta*) until the burial took place.

The ashes were placed in an urn, which was then either placed in a *columbarium* with an inscription recording the dead man's name and sometimes with his bust, or a monument was raised above it surrounded by a piece of land, sometimes a pleasant garden, sacred to the dead. These gardens were often the scene of feasts held to celebrate the memory of the dead soon after burial and on the anniversaries of their death.[7]

Further Reading

There is no book dealing exclusively with funeral rites, though most books on Roman religion have a chapter on belief in the after-life.

For burial customs under the Empire see A. D. Nock, Cremation and Burial in the Roman Empire (*Harvard Theological Review*, 1932).

NOTES

1. Odyssey, IX, 65.
2. De Ling. Lat., VII, 42.
3. 304, 2.
4. Suetonius, Vesp., 19.
5. VI, 53.
6. X, 1, Bruns.
7. F. Cumont, *After Life in Roman Paganism*, p. 56.

CHAPTER XII

Pompeii—The Buried City

Pompeii's contribution to our knowledge of Roman life. Pompeii before the eruption. The eruption. After the eruption. Excavations.

OUR knowledge of many aspects of daily life in the Roman world would not be so precise if the excavations of Pompeii had not satisfied our curiosity with such a wealth of information. But we must not forget that Pompeii was not Rome. Pompeii was a small, prosperous provincial city, where public life offered the ambitious no higher goal than membership of the *ordo decurionum* (the colony's town council) or election as *duovir* or aedile. There were bitter struggles for some offices; the walls of Pompeii still preserve traces of hard fought elections in the manifestoes painted on the stucco in neat red letters. Clients awaited the instructions of their patron, and every minor aristocrat had his candidate to recommend. There was in Pompeii, as in all small centres, the usual interplay of rivalry and provincial pride, the usual community of interests and cliques of clients. But life had nothing more to offer than this. Anyone who felt cramped by the limitations of such a life moved to Rome to seek his fortune together with innumerable other adventurers from all corners of the Empire; he risked struggles, humiliation and disillusionment, but he might find wealth and honour.

The difference between Rome and Pompeii is not merely one of size; even in its material and social aspects Rome was an entirely different city, a formidable metropolis, devouring man and money.

Nevertheless, all those who live in the same civilisation, which is dominated by the influence of one great city on its fashions and ideas, inevitably lead a very similar daily life. Today, every French family, even in the most outlying provinces, bears the mark of Parisian manners. The antiquities of Pompeii are not the antiquities of Rome, but anyone studying the latter cannot disregard the former, or ignore the light they throw on the more magnificent life of the capital. Material from Pompeii has been largely used in the chapters on Houses and Furniture, for certain prejudices, tastes and standards of material comfort must have been the same for the wealthy merchant of Pompeii, steadily growing rich on the profits of his *fullonica* or his *garum* factory, as for the high official or influential banker of the capital. Living in the same historical climate inevitably made all men to some extent brothers, especially in the hours when, business over and the long visit to the baths finished, they relaxed in the *tablinum* or the peristyle amongst intimate and congenial company. So a short account of the unique story of Pompeii does not seem out of place here; its disinterment has contributed so extensively to our story, especially in the provision of illustrative material.

In A.D. 79, during the reign of Titus, the ashes of Vesuvius buried three of the most prosperous cities of Campania: Pompeii, Herculaneum and Stabiae. Pompeii, the largest of the three, was rising from the ruins caused by a disastrous earthquake, which on 5 February, A.D. 63, had almost completely razed it to the ground. The city which the excavations have brought to light is a city in the course of reconstruction. Among the buildings of the old city which had survived the earthquake, the new city was rising, richer, more beautiful and more modern. The remains which have come to light prove the energy with which the work was being carried on. Some buildings, like the temple of Isis, were already completed, others in the course of reconstruction. The ruined city was re-affirming its right to life and its faith in the future by its extensive building programme, when, sixteen years after this first disaster, Vesuvius buried it in a sea of ash.

It was a rich and beautiful city; Vesuvius today rises black with lava from the plain of Pompeii and in summer the reflections from its stones when heated by the sun produce an oppressive, almost infernal, sultriness among the ruins. But in those days it formed the picturesque and cheerful background of this prosperous city where every house contained a garden, a beautiful mountain, green and luxuriant, covered with choice vines which produced a famous wine. Nature had been exceptionally kind to this small industrial city whose factories were alive with activity, dye works, bakeries, *garum* factories (see p. 90); the streets, flanked by shops and bars (*thermopolia*), swarmed with people.

The original inhabitants of Pompeii were Oscans, whose primitive language has been preserved for us in a number of inscriptions; some of them informed the citizens of the rallying points when they took up arms during the Social War (91–89 B.C.): *eituns!* (= *eant!*). The town was conquered successively by the Etruscans and the Samnites. With the Samnites it took part in the war against Rome; during the second Punic War it sided with Hannibal along with the other cities of Campania. During the Social War it rose against Rome; when forced to surrender, it was obliged to receive a Roman colony, called after its conqueror Sulla, *Colonia Veneria Cornelia Pompeianorum*.

Living on its industries, Pompeii seems to have enjoyed great economic prosperity in every age. Greek civilisation, which had gradually penetrated into Campania, had given the people of Pompeii a taste for refined luxury and a civilised way of life. For us Pompeii is a model of a Hellenistic city, especially in the design and decoration of its houses.

The catastrophe took place on 24 August A.D. 79 (Pliny[1] has recorded the exact date). An unexpected eruption of Vesuvius rained down a hail of pebbles and ashes upon the surrounding countryside. A violent wind was blowing and it was raining hard. Surprised by the savage fury of the volcano, most people took to flight, leaving their chained slaves to die in hideous agony; others gathered in the inner rooms of their houses to await the end of the storm, until the roof collapsed under the weight of the ashes and crushed them, or the ashes blocked every way of escape and imprisoned them in their houses where they died after a hopeless struggle. Others, who had fled in the first moment of terror, returned later to collect their most precious belongings, but found themselves unable to escape again from the city of death and died near their valuables; at different points throughout Pompeii their bones have been discovered. Others, like the elder Pliny at Stabiae, were suffocated by the choking air, which the ash made impossible to breathe, or by the gases produced by the volcano.

Almost every house collapsed under the weight of the ashes, but the buildings were not completely buried. For many years after the disaster the site where Pompeii had once stood must have had the appearance of a vast field of ash, from which rooftops emerged as from a flood. Through the upper floors which stood above the ashes the lawful owners, or robbers, entered and removed all that they could. This difficult and dangerous salvage work caused further disasters; the walls sometimes collapsed on top of the searchers, burying them in the ruins. The remains of people crushed in this way have been found, enabling us to reconstruct the tragedy.

As time passed, the parts of the buildings above the ash either collapsed or were pulled down for building material. Time and the hand of man levelled this plain of death. The centuries passed, and nobody any longer had reason to imagine that a city lay buried beneath the dry earth, even though the regular elliptical hollow where the amphitheatre was buried must have made men think of a building hidden beneath the earth's crust. Yet the memory of Pompeii lived on, though unconsciously, in the name of 'The City' (*Civita*) which the country people gave to this area. When, between 1594 and 1600, the architect Fontana dug a canal to take the waters of the Sarno to Torre Annunziata and in the course of operations uncovered remains of buildings as well as an inscription with the words *Decurio Pompeis*, it occurred to nobody that they were excavating the site of Pompeii, but they imagined they had found a villa which had belonged to Pompey.

Regular archaeological excavations did not begin until 1748 under Charles III, the Bourbon King of Naples. They were conducted by methods which modern archaeology would condemn, and for unscientific purposes (the ruins were ransacked for works of art in the spirit of an archaeological treasure-hunt). Furthermore, the excavators, although they saw that they were exploring the remains of an ancient city, failed to realize that 'The City' was Pompeii until 1763, when an inscription, bearing the words *respublica Pompeianorum*, identified the city as Pompeii.

In the Napoleonic age, especially through the efforts of Championnet during the Parthenopean Republic (1799), and of Murat during the kingdom of Naples (1806-15), the excavations began to be carried out efficiently with the object of bringing the ancient city to light. But only after the proclamation of the Kingdom of Italy (1861) did a steady and systematic exploration of the site of Pompeii begin. Fiorelli, one of the most brilliant archaeologists Italy has produced, was in charge of the operations; he perfected the method of excavation and showed amazing insight in interpreting the material brought to light, pointing the way to the eminent archaeologists who continued, and are still continuing, his work. In the last few years particularly, the excavations at Pompeii have been singularly active and successful.

Further Reading

Pompeii and Herculaneum; The Glory and the Grief, by Marcel Brion, translated by John Rosenberg (London, 1960) gives an up-to-date account of the excavations, lavishly illustrated. The bibliography lists the works of Fiorelli and Maiuri, which are indispensable for a detailed study of the subject.

NOTES

1. In two letters; VI, 16, and 20.

CHAPTER XIII

Streets, Houses and Addresses

Streets without a name, houses without a number and men without an address. The advantages of numbering in the modern world. Ancient addresses by general references. Proximity to public buildings or places: statues; shrines, temples, sacred groves; public buildings and gates; gardens; city curiosities. Shops. Trees. Vagaries of city nomenclature.

How did a Roman manage when he had to deliver a letter to an unknown address? How did a provincial, in the capital for the first time, discover the person he was looking for? He had to find Aulus Agirius, and he knew that Aulus lived in Rome. But there were so many streets, houses, squares, districts and people in Rome that to find one house whose exact whereabouts he did not already know constituted an enormous problem.

This is no problem today with the name of a street, the number and the floor. But Roman houses had no numbers, and many streets were nameless. The ancients had not discovered the countless practical advantages of numbers. Mathematics is an ancient art, and, long before the time of the Romans, had provided a means of fixing the course of the stars and foretelling eclipses; if, however, the human intellect proved its strength in the science of numbers more than in other fields, it was slow to realise the uses to which they could be put. Alexandrian scholars divided the works of Homer[1] into numbered books; the Romans numbered their legions,[2] Augustus the *regiones* of Rome;[3] but they went cautiously and were afraid of high numbers. The Greek and Roman calendars split up the months into smaller sections;[4] in ordinary usage and in official documents the years were not numbered progressively;[5] there was no era either in popular or administrative practice.[6] Only chroniclers and historians used chronological reckonings and references. In antiquity the advantage of numbering years and houses, with its steady progress to infinity, as a means of precise identification was not appreciated.

Nowadays men rely on numbers to communicate. In all walks of life we use numbers to avoid uncertainty and to identify species, sub-species, places, goods, individuals, grades, offices, chapters and even kings. When the Romans wanted to distinguish between two Tarquinii, they called one *Priscus*, the other *Superbus*; with two Scipios, Catos, Plinys or Senecas, they called one *maior*, one *minor* (translated 'the older' and 'the younger', irrespective of the fact that the older might have died young and the younger old). We speak simply of Louis XIV, who succeeds Louis XIII. That today we travel in trains and the ancient Romans travelled in a *raeda* or on a short-tailed donkey, like Horace,[7] is an obvious and considerable difference between our two civilisations, but there is another which is not so obvious. When we travel, our train has a number, as do the carriages, the compartments, the seats, the ticket-collector, the ticket and the note with which we buy our ticket. When we reach the station we take a taxi which is numbered and driven by a driver similarly numbered; on arrival at our hotel we become a number ourselves. Our profession, age, date of arrival and departure are all reckoned in numbers. When we have booked a room, we become a number, 42 perhaps, and if we are so unfortunate as to forget our number we seem to have forgotten ourselves. If we mistake it, we run the risk of being taken for a thief, or worse. The number is on the disc hanging from the key of our room; it is above the letter rack in the hall; every morning we find it chalked on the soles of our shoes, and we continually see it on the door of our room, and, finally, we find it on the bill. We grow so used to our number that it becomes part of us; if we have a parcel sent to the hotel, we give the number 42; however important we may be, to the porter and the chambermaid we are simply No. 42.

So men who now number everything naturally enough number their houses. The numbers of the houses in our cities follow their own strange course; at Venice they run riot, rushing in and out of alleyways, leaping across bridges, careering round squares, as they grow steadily bigger. At Genoa the numbers of streets are by tradition shown above and the numbers of the blocks below; the numbers of houses are in black, those of shops in red. Florence, with its Tuscan love of order, has the same system as Paris: throughout the city the numbers follow the course of the river, and, in the roads running up from the river, odd numbers are on the right, even numbers on the left.

Today there is no modern city or large country where the streets are not named and the houses numbered, and in large blocks of flats each flat has its own number.

Consequently, every man has his own address, which becomes part of him and follows him wherever he goes; delivery vans need to know it, as well as shops, policemen and many others. Our address, like our surname, Christian name and telephone number, is more useful to others than ourselves, but it is almost part of our personalities, the result of our position as modern civilised men. At moments a man may find himself without money or a job, without hope for the future, but never without an address. Even if he is a tramp, it is not difficult to foretell that he will end up one day in prison, which will then become his address.

On the other hand, the Greeks and Romans lived without addresses and were unable to indicate their houses with that brief combination of a few words and a number, by means of which the whereabouts of a house can nowadays be exactly indicated.

In antiquity a stranger arriving for the first time in a small city or country had no difficulty in finding the house he was looking for. He only had to ask the first person he met to be given the information or conducted there personally, as happens today in smaller towns. But in Rome and other large cities, such as Athens, Syracuse, Alexandria or Rhodes, and even those which were smaller but still densely populated, finding one particular house involved a good deal of luck. It was no small problem to tell a stranger precisely how to find one's own house.

For example, nowadays many travellers attach a leather tag with a card showing their name and address to their suitcases as a precaution against loss or theft (since some honest thieves remove their spoil and return the case to the owner); in the same way the Romans fastened to the necks of slaves who were liable to run away an iron collar with a disc (*bulla*) firmly attached to it bearing the owner's name and address: TENE ME ET REBOCA ME APRONIANO PALATINO AD MAPPA(M) AUREA(M) IN AVENTINO QUIA FUGI[8]— 'Arrest me and take me back to Apronianus Palatinus on the Aventine, near the Golden Flag, as I have run away'; or TENE ME QUIA FUGI, REDUC ME AD FLORA(M) AD TO(N)SORES.[9]—'Arrest me, as I have run away, and take me back to the temple of Flora in the street of the barbers'. Such directions seem precise enough, but anybody who was induced by the promise of a reward, sometimes specified on the *bulla*,[10] to arrest a runaway slave can hardly have hoped to return him to his master's house without further inquiries.

Our modern precision in addresses, achieved by means of street names and numbers, has changed the ancient vagueness of 'living near . . .' into the exactness of our 'living at . . .'. An ancient address could only be approximate, except of course for a public figure, the situation of whose house was known to every citizen. In a case like this the entire neighbourhood took advantage of the fame of their local dignitary and used his house as a point of reference in indicating the situation of their own. In antiquity a man's address usually referred to a nearby and familiar landmark.

How did such references originate and become generally accepted? Partly, they were a spontaneous growth, as much the product of the popular mind as proverbs and idioms. Created and maintained by an intangible and constantly changing public opinion, they reflected the prejudices and whims of the people, and were the product of a tenacious tradition, universally accepted but of unknown origin. As today the centre of London is near the Haymarket, so at Rome there was the *Lacus pastorum*.[11] Some of the names strike a purely rustic note: 'The oxen's heads' (*Capita bubula*);[12] 'The head of Africa' (*Caput Africae*);[13] 'The Gorgon's head' (*Caput Gorgonis*);[14] 'The ten shops' (*Decem tabernae*); 'The white hens' (*Gallinae albae*);[15] 'The twelve gates' (*Duodecim portae*);[16] 'The leaning storks' (*Ciconiae nixae*);[17] 'The pomegranate'.[18] The origin of some is wrapped in mystery, such as 'The sister's beam' (*Tigillum sororium*),[19] connected with the legend of the Horatii and the Curiatii.[20] In the same way in Milan there is 'The street of dark flowers', and at Pistoia 'T street'. A street in Florence is called 'The street of the lost maids', and a street in Genoa 'The street of perfect love'. A Genoese legend tells of a platonic friendship between a lady of patrician family and a king, but the stranger, ignorant of the legend, may well be surprised at the name.

Streets in ancient cities, including Rome, were for the most part nameless and were referred to simply by such expressions as 'The road to . . .'[21']; a few of the more important had names, but most of them were so long that their name by itself was not enough to fix a place with any certainty. At Rome the *Via Lata* ran right across the *Campus Martius*, the *Alta Semita* ran the whole length of the top of the Quirinal, the *Vicus Patricius*[22] started at the centre of Rome, passed the *Mons Cispius* and the Viminal, and reached the *Porta Viminalis* in the Servian Wall (see p. 27). In the interests of precision some further indication had to be added, and so we find expressions such as 'On the *Via Nova*, near the shrine of *Volupia*',[23] 'On the *Via Sacra*, under the *Velia*, where the temple of *Vica Pota* stands'.[24] The house of Tarquinius Superbus stood on the *Vicus Pullius* which ran up the *Mons Oppius* from the *Subura*, near the *Fagutal*;[25] so we know the exact address of this hated king, while it is difficult to say where the poet Ennius' humble house stood, as we only know that he lived on the Aventine.[26] More or less vague terms were used to indicate a part of a district: 'at the mouth', 'at the first road', 'at the centre', of the *Subura*,[27] and, if the street climbed, 'at the highest point',[28] or 'where the ascent stops'.[29] The western part of the Esquiline, where a large market (*Macellum Liviae* (see p. 5)) was built in the reign of Augustus, was known simply as the *Macellum*.[30] In literary references and inscriptions, where some topographical detail has to be made clear, we continually find haphazard circumlocutions: 'Near the place where one goes down from the Palatine to the Forum',[31] 'In the Velabrum at the beginning of the *Via Nova*',[32] 'At the entrance to the *Subura*, where the executioners' whips hang'.[33]

In the following scene from Terence, a slave, Syrus, wishing to fool the elderly Demea, and send him on a wild goose chase round the city solely in order to make him waste time, is directing him to a certain house, near which he will find the brother he is looking for. The comic exaggeration is obvious, but, nevertheless, it gives us an idea of the complicated addresses in those days.[34]

Sy. Well, I can't recall the name of the man he's gone to see, but I know where he lives.

De. Well, tell me the place.

Sy. Down this way. You know the porch beside the butcher's?

De. Yes, of course.

Sy. Pass this way straight up the street, and when you have got so far, there's a slope just in front of you; go down, and after that there lies a little chapel with an alley close by.

De. Where do you mean?

Sy. Where the big wild fig-tree grows.

De. I know.

Sy. Well, go through there.

De. But that's a cul de sac.

Sy. Yes, of course. Heavens! What a fool I am! You must come back again to the porch. Yes, that's also far quicker and less roundabout. Do you know where the wealthy Cratinus lives?

De. I do.

Sy. Well, pass his house, then go left straight down this street, and turn right at Diana's shrine. Before you reach the city gate, just near the pool, there's a bakery with a carpenter's shop opposite. He's there.

To make directions less complicated, recourse was frequently had to statues, columns, temples, public buildings, such as granaries, barracks, colonnades, as well as sacred groves (*luci*) and gardens (*horti*). These points of reference acted as a kind of compass for those who wandered through Rome in search of somebody, or to keep a rendezvous with a friend. Sometimes the indication became so familiar that it ended up by giving its name to a street, or even a whole district. As there was a remarkable number of monuments of the same name at Rome, it was frequently necessary to describe the monument more precisely to avoid all ambiguity: 'The temple of Fors Fortuna, beside the Tiber, outside the city.'[35]

Statues.[36]—The eastern tip of the Quirinal, the present site of the Termini station, where the Baths of Diocletian with their gigantic *exhedra* were built in A.D. 305, was indicated by reference to the *Statua Pisonis*.[37] One of the monuments used to divide into sections the *Vicus Longus*, which ran from the Forum of Trajan to the Baths of Constantine, was a *Statua Planci*;[38] a little street on the slopes of the Quirinal between the *Alta Semita* and the *Vicus Longus* took its name from a *Statua Mamuri*;[39] places on the *Via Sacra*, the most frequented street in Rome, were also the most easily pin-pointed by the large number of monuments along it; among these were such isolated statues as those of Romulus and Titus Tatius,[40] the former facing the Palatine, the latter the *Rostra*, and a female figure on horse-back before the temple of Iuppiter Stator, regarded by the Romans as a statue of Cloelia. From the height of her charger the fiery maid looked scornfully down on the effeminate youths who passed beneath her in one of the most central places in Rome.[41] Money-lenders gathered in the Forum near the statue of Marsyas (see p. 7).

Shrines, Temples, Sacred Groves.—A freedman of Pompey, the orator Lenaeus, opened a school of rhetoric on the *Mons Oppius*,[42] in the district of the *Carinae*; anybody looking for him for the first time had to search for his house near the *Aedes Telluris*.[43] Licinius Sura, an important figure in the age of Domitian, lived on the Aventine near the Temple of Diana,[44] his contemporary, Iulius Proculus, 'on the slopes of the Palatine, near the temple of Bacchus and the dome of Cybele, just on the right as you come from the temple of Vesta'.[45] This last address is one of the most precise, but is hardly simple. The house of the Tetricii, a well known Roman family in the late Empire, was situated on the Caelian 'between the two groves opposite the temple of Isis built by the Metelli'.[46]

Public Buildings and Gates.—Cicero lived on the Palatine (see p. 19) near the colonnade of Catulus. The shop of Atrectus, a bookseller in the Flavian age, stood 'in front of Caesar's Forum'.[47] The house which L. Calpurnius Piso (consul in 58 B.C.) rented after returning from Macedonia was in the neighbourhood of the *Porta Caelimontana*, near the famous house of the *Laterani*.[48]

In the least inhabited areas furthest from the centre of the city, the milestone was the point of reference.

Gardens.—In the districts of Rome where buildings were rare gardens were regularly used to identify a locality, particularly in the thinly populated quarters of *Trans Tiberim* (see p. 30). We find references to the *Horti Aboniani*[49] the gardens of Drusus, Cassius and Lamia, Silius and Scapula,[50] of Galba on the *Via Aurelia*,[51] and of Geta,[52] besides those of Regulus (see p. 27). If the gardens were very extensive, an effort was made to make the identification less vague—for example *Horti Pompei superiores*.[53] Maecenas turned a large part of the Esquiline into a park, and built a tower (*Turris Maecenatiana*) there. From here Augustus' loyal lieutenant used to enjoy the remarkable view in his rare moments of leisure,[54] and from this tower Nero later watched the burning of Rome as he recited poetry in theatrical dress.[55] Both park and tower became regular points of reference. The *horti* and tower in the gardens of Caesar, near the *Porta Collina* were used in the same way.[56] Virgil's house stood near the *Horti Maecenatiani*.[57]

City Curiosities.—Anything which broke the monotony of the long streets became a popular point of reference. Often there were curiosities, antiquities, small, picturesque unusual things, standing out against the uniform face of the city. Even today Rome has the 'Street of the Marble Foot', with a large foot, the remains of a colossal statue, at the entrance to justify its name; at Genoa there is 'Sun-dial Square', at Florence a suburb called 'The Big Madonnas'; in the same way in Rome there was a golden trumpet (*Aureum bucinum*),[58] a golden flag (*Aurea mappa*),[59] an engraved flagstone in a wall, a stone with a hole in it (*lapis pertusus*),[60] and an Orpheus surrounded by wild beasts listening bewitched to his song.[61] Augustus was born in a house on the Palatine near the 'Oxen's heads' (see p. 141), Domitian[62] on the Quirinal in his father's house near the 'Pomegranate'.

A district was frequently named after the type of shop which predominated in it; traces of a similar custom are to be found in the streets of modern cities, like Shoemakers' Street in Florence and Goldsmiths' Street in Genoa; Vegetable Square in Verona still deserves its name. The Athenians in the classical age, when they wanted to find their bearings in their extensive *agora*, used shops as well as buildings: 'near the fresh cheese',[63] 'near the crockery', 'near the grocers',[64] are familiar and natural expressions to the Attic authors. The house of M. Porcius Laeca, a member of the Catilinarian conspiracy, stood 'among the scythe-makers' (*inter falcarios*).[65] We know[66] that the stretch of the Quirinal between the Temple of Flora and the Temple of Quirinus was called after the rouge-makers' shops (*officinae minii*). A booth (*tabernola*) gave its name to a street on the slopes of the Caelian.[67] It is interesting to see how these two methods of identification— by means of buildings and shops—sometimes fused into a single name, easily intelligible for all its absurdity; at Rome there was the *Hercules olivarius*, the *Elephantus herbarius*, the *Apollo sandaliarius*,[68] pleasantly comprehensive ways of saying 'the olive sellers by the statue of Hercules', 'the herb sellers near the elephant', 'the sandal-makers near the statue of Apollo'. Shop signs were particularly useful in indicating the exact point in a street (see p. 34).

145

Finally, trees in Rome, as in all cities ancient and modern, frequently provided a point of reference. Isolated by the city's invasion of the country, they are sometimes honoured for centuries by the invaders, who treat them with respect and almost beg forgiveness for their treatment of them. When they die, the stone slab bearing the street's name becomes their tomb-stone. 'Apple Street', 'Peach Street', 'Elm Street', are common sights. In Paris there is 'Oak Street' (*Rue du chêne vert*) and 'Fig Street' (*Rue du figuier*); in Genoa 'Myrtle Street', 'Walnut Street', 'Olive Street'. Up to a few years ago Florence boasted 'The Pine', a genuine centenarian pine, which bore its many years with dignity and still gives its name to a district of the city. In Homer's Troy a wild fig (ἐρινεός)[69] marked a district near the walls, and a wild fig (*caprificus*) is included among the directions given by Syrus to Demea.[70]

In Rome there were trees even in the Forum: an olive, a vine and a fig near the *lacus Curtius*;[71] we can still see the fig[72] on a corner of each of the two *plutei Traianei** (see p. 302). Near the *Forum Iulium* a large lotus tree blossomed sturdily in the midst of the uproar of the city and its strong roots penetrated into the Forum.[73] We hear of a cypress, whose origins take us back to the earliest days and which fell only in the time of Nero,[74] and of a tree on the Caelian known as 'the holy tree' (*arbor sancta*).[75] Martial lived *ad Pirum*, 'near the pear-tree', on the Quirinal. We do not know whether the pear was still standing in Martial's day or whether the name of the street preserved its memory. Martial clearly considered 'The Pear Tree' as his address. *Longum est si velit ad Pirum venire*,[76] he says, meaning 'it is a long way from the Forum to the Pear Tree, where I live', adding 'without counting the stairs', as he was a poor hungry poet living in a garret.

The most remarkable feature of this popular method of identifying a district by a reference to some topographical feature is the disparity between the importance of the object which lends its name and the attraction of the name; city nomenclature is no respecter of rank, and the dead frequently outlasts the living. The ruined chapel, the vanished tree, the destroyed building, receive

*Reliefs which originally adorned the front of the *rostra* in the *Forum*. (Translator's note.)

an honour never achieved by larger buildings for all their impressive bulk and magnificence. The former, though humble, compel others to live under the protection of their name and to beg for their hospitality. So great sometimes is the power of a vanished building, that a new building, larger but of the same type, may be built after many centuries to justify the name, as has happened in Rome in the 'Piazza dell' Esedra'.[77] The district where the Baths of Caracalla stood still bore the humble name of *Piscina Publica*,[78] even when it was adorned by the most magnificent building in Rome. The *Piscina Publica* was one of the simple tanks which the ancient Italian peoples built near their gates for the use of the inhabitants of the district and as a sign of welcome to strangers.[79] It stood near the *Porta Capena*, witness of other times and other customs. It no longer existed in the first century A.D.,[80] and had probably disappeared in the time of Cicero.[81]

Even the Flavian Amphitheatre owed its name to a neighbouring monument, the *Colossus*, an enormous statue of Nero, commissioned by him from the sculptor Zenodorus,[82] renowned for his skill in work of this sort. It stood in the monumental approach to the *Domus Aurea*, and after Nero's death, as a sign of the disgrace of the fallen Emperor, Vespasian[83] changed it into a statue of the sun, with a head surrounded by rays.[84] For some time it stood on the same spot with a different cult and head; but soon Hadrian,[85] in order to clear the site for the *Templum Urbis et Veneris*, had it moved elsewhere (see p. 14). Commodus[86] changed its head once more, replacing it with his own, but leaving the rays. Then it disappeared, probably ending up in one of the kilns where the later inhabitants of Rome turned marble into lime (see p. 317). But its original site continued to be referred to as *ad Colossum* even after the *Colossus* had been moved and even when it had completely disappeared. Its memory survived and prevented the Flavian Amphitheatre from being commonly called by its own name. As it stood near the *Colossus*, the Flavian Amphitheatre became and remained the *Colosseum*, preserving in its new title throughout the centuries not its own true name, but its ancient address.

Further Reading

There is no book exclusively on this subject. The author's modern parallels from Italian towns have been left unchanged; English readers will have no difficulty in thinking of examples nearer home. How many will be able to give the correct explanation of Friday Street? The practice of giving isolated country cottages high numbers, so that, if houses are eventually built round them, renumbering will be unnecessary, appears to be exclusively English.

NOTES

1. The Alexandrian grammarians divided the *Iliad* and the *Odyssey* each into twenty-four books, distinguished by one of the twenty-four letters of the Greek alphabet. In the Hellenistic age the letters of the alphabet, with special signs and the addition of some letters which were no longer used, also began to be used to indicate numbers.

2. The number of Roman legions varied at different times; from Augustus onwards an epithet was added to the number of the legion, which remained the number given to it during the Republic; different legions had the same number but a distinguishing epithet: thus we have *Legio I Adiutrix*, *Legio I Iulia Alpina*, *Legio I Armeniaca*; other epithets for a *Legio I* were: *Flavia Gallicana Constantia, Flavia Martis, Illyricorum, Iovia, Isauria sagittaria, Italica, Macriana, Martia, Minervia, Noricorum*. Some legions were formed late; others were not re-formed after their destruction; the list of Roman legions does not therefore correspond to the effective strength of the Roman army at a particular time.

3. See p. 4.

4. The Roman Calendar consisted of references to the *Kalendae, Nonae* or *Idus* immediately following the date it was desired to indicate; the day itself was included in the reckoning. The *Kalendae* was on the first day of the month; in March, May, July, and October the *Nonae* and *Idus* fell respectively on the seventh and fifteenth day of the month, in the other months on the fifth and thirteenth. Among the Greeks names of the months varied considerably; the days of the month were indicated in groups of ten; the first group was the ten days of 'the beginning of the month' (ἱσταμένου) indicated by increasing cardinal numbers, the second the middle of the month (μεσοῦντος), the third at the end of the month (φθίνοντος) indicated by decreasing cardinal numbers. The first day of the month was νεομηνία (new moon), the last ἕνη καὶ νέα (old and new moon). *Kalendae* was an exclusively Roman term, hence the proverbial expression 'On the Greek Kalendae' used by Augustus to mean 'never'. (Suetonius, Aug., 87; *In litteris, cum aliquos numquam soluturos significare vult, 'ad Kalendas Graecas soluturos' ait*). Augustus used the expression in connection with payments,

as the Kalends and the Ides were the usual days for the settlement of debts in Rome.

5. The Romans indicated the year by the names of the consuls, the Athenians by the name of the chief archon, who was hence called ἐπώνυμος in the Roman era, but not before, as has been maintained. At Athens the year was also divided officially into ten periods, corresponding to the time that the fifty representatives of each of the ten tribes (φυλαί) held the presidency (πρυτανεία) of the Council (βουλή).

6. The Greek practice of indicating Olympiads (four-year periods reckoned from 776 B.C.) together with the year of the Olympiad was never widely used or incorporated in official documents. From the beginnings of written history many different eras were adopted as a basis for a chronological system, but none became at all widely used. Varro established a Roman era beginning from the foundation of Rome on 21 April 753 B.C. In the late Empire and the Middle Ages a Diocletian era, dating from 29 August A.D. 284, was in use, and was later replaced by the Christian era. In A.D. 297 Diocletian initiated a system of indictions; an indiction was a period of fifteen years during which taxes were collected on all property. Although each of the fifteen years of each individual indiction was numbered, the indictions themselves were not numbered, and so no era could be reckoned from them. This system survived until the Middle Ages, and was originated by Diocletian, not Constantine, as was once thought. The Christian era was introduced by Dionysius Exiguus, a Scythian monk, in 532; but the beginning of this era was fixed after the passage of centuries and based on false calculations, and is three or four years out in the date of the birth of Christ. The Christian era was at first used solely by historians and chroniclers; its use in official documents and its general adoption in every type of writing only came later. The exactness and simplicity of dates is a privilege of the modern world no less than that of exact addresses dealt with in this chapter.

7. See p. 229.

8. CIL, XV, 7182.

9. Ibid. 7172 (= Dessau 8727). The temple of Flora referred to here stood near the Capitol (Varro, De Ling. Lat., V, 158: *Clivus proximus a Flora susus versus Capitolium vetus*).

10. Ibid. 7194 (= Dessau 8731) *Fugi, tene me; cum rovocaveris (= revocaveris) me d(omino) m(e)o Zonino, accipis solidum.*

11. In *Notitia (Regio III, Isis et Serapis); lacus* here = *fons.*

12. Suetonius. Aug., 5: *Natus est . . . regione Palati, ad Capita bubula, ubi nunc sacrarium habet, aliquanto postquam excessit constitutum.*

13. In *Notitia (Regio II, Caelimontium).*

14. Ibid. *(Regio XIV, Trans Tiberim).*

15. Ibid. *(Regio VI, Alta Semita).*

16. Ibid. (*Regio XI, Circus Maximus*).

17. Ibid. (*Regio IX, Circus Flaminius*). The place was even simply called *Ad nixas* (CIL, I², 332).

18. See p. 144.

19. *Fasti Arval.* (CIL, I, 330).

20. *Scholia Bobbiensia*, ad Cic., pro Milone, 3.

21. Dion. Halic., VIII, 79, κατὰ τὴν ἐπὶ καρίνας φέρουσαν ὁδόν, 'on the road to Carinae'. On Carinae see note 28, p. 44.

22. Classical authors mention the *Vicus Patricius* without further details, providing us with no means of discovering where it was or how far it ran; but the memory of it which survived into the Middle Ages (the churches of St Euphemia and St Pudenziana stood *in Vico Patricii*), and the traces of pavement which have been discovered have made it possible to establish the site and length of this street.

23. Varro, De Ling. Lat., V. 169: *In nova via ad Volupiae sacellum* (*nova via* is Scaliger's emendation of the *novalia* of the MSS.).

24. Livy. II, 7, 12: *Deleta confestim materia omnis infra Veliam et, ubi nunc Vicae Potae est, domus in intimo clivo aedificata.*

25. Solinus, I, 26.

26. St Jerome, Ad. Eus.; a. Abr. 1777 (= 240 B.C.): *A Catone quaestore Romam translatus habitavit in monte Aventino parco admodum sumptu contentus et unius ancillae ministerio.*

27. Martial, II, 17, 1: *Suburae faucibus . . . primis;* XII, 3, 9: *prima . . . Subura;* VI, 66, 2: *in media . . . Subura;* cf. IX, 37, 1.

28. Livy, I, 48, 6: *Ad summum Cyprium vicum, ubi Dianium nuper fuit.*

29. See note 31.

30. A trace of this normal method of reference remained in the name given in the Middle Ages to the *Porta Esquilina*, converted into the Arch of Gallienus in the third century A.D.; this arch was described as being *in Macello*.

31. CIL, VI, 450: *In ipso fere Palatini montis descensu.*

32. Varro, De Ling. Lat., VI, 24.

33. Martial, II, 17, 1–2.

34. Adelphoe, 571 et seq. The scene is laid in Athens but is adapted for a Roman audience.

35. Varro, De Ling. Lat., VI, 17: *Fanum Fortis Fortunae secundum Tiberim extra urbem Romam.* Chapels and shrines of Fortune were scattered throughout Rome; they were usually distinguished by an epithet: *Fortuna brevis, Virgo, virilis, equestris, huiusce diei, primigenia, redux, respiciens, publica, mammosa,* etc.

36. Similar systems occurred in other ancient cities. We know that Stephanus of Antidorus, a distinguished politician in the time of Demosthenes, lived in Athens in a house 'near Hermes the whistle-player' (Demosthenes, Con. Neaer., 39: παρὰ τὸν ψιθυριστὴν Ἑρμῆν).

37. Hist. Aug., Vita trig. tyr., 21.

38. CIL, VI, 9673, 10023.

39. The *Notitia* (*Regio VI, Alta Semita*) mentions the *Statua Mamuri*; references to the *Vicus Mamuri* (or *Clivus Mamuri*) occur only in medieval documents, but it seems probable that in the Empire the statue had already given its name to the street.

40. Servius, ad Aen. VIII, 641, *Huius . . . facti in Sacra Via signa stant, Romulus a parte Palati, Tatius venientibus a rostris.*

41. Seneca, ad Marciam, 16, 1: *Equestri insidens statuae in Sacra Via, celeberrimo loco, Cloelia exprobrat iuvenibus nostris pulvinum escendentibus in ea illos urbe sic ingredi, in quo etiam feminas equo donavimus.*

42. See p. 42, note 3.

43. Suetonius, de gramm., 15: *Docuit in Carinis ad Telluris.*

44. Martial, VI, 64, 13.

45. Ibid. I, 70.

46. Hist. Aug., Vita trig. tyr. 25: *Inter duos lucos contra Isium Metellinum.*

47. Martial, I, 117, 9–10.

48. Cicero, in Pis., 23, 61: cf. p. 24.

49. CIL, VI, 671.

50. Cicero, ad Att., XII, 21, 2; 23, 3; 25, 2.

51. Tacitus, Hist., I, 49; Suetonius, Galba, 20.

52. In *Notitia* (*Regio XIV, Trans Tiberim*).

53. Asconius, ad Cic., pro Mil., 37.

54. Horace, Odes, III, 29, 9, 10.

55. Suetonius, Nero, 38: *Hoc incendium e turre Maecenatiana prospectans laetusque 'flammae', ut aiebat, 'pulchritudine' Halosin Ilii in illo suo scaenico habitu decantavit.*

56. Iulius Obsequens, 131.

57. Donatus, Vita Virg., 6: *Habuit domum in Esquiliis iuxta hortos Maecenatis.*

58. In *Notitia* (*Regio IV, Templum Pacis*).

59. See the inscription mentioned on p. 140.

60. In *Notitia* (*Regio VII, Via Lata*).

61. Martial, X, 19, 6–8.

62. Suetonius, Dom., 1: *Domitianus natus est . . . regione urbis sexta ad Malum Punicum, domo quam postea in templum gentis Flaviae convertit.*

63. Lysias, Con. Pancl. 6:

64. Aristophanes, Lysis., 557–8: κἀν ταῖσι χύτραις καὶ τοῖς λαχάνοισιν ὁμοίως περιέρχονται κατὰ τὴν ἀγοράν.

65. Cicero, Cat., I, 4, 8.

66. Vitruvius, VII, 9, G.

67. Varro, De Ling. Lat., V, 97: *Circa Minervium, qua in Caelimonte itur, in Tabernola est; V, 50: Cis Lucum Esquilinum dexterior via in Tabernola est.*

68. In *Notitia* (*Regio XI, Circus Maximus; Regio VIII, Forum Romanum; Regio IV, Templum Pacis*).

69. Iliad, VI, 433-4.

70. Adelphoe, 577.

71. See note 31, p. 45.

72. Pliny, N.H., XV, 77-78.

73. Ibid. XVI, 236: *Radices eijus* (*loti*) *in Forum usque Caesaris per stationes municipiorum penetrant*.

74. Ibid.

75. In *Notitia* (*Regio II, Caelimontium*).

76. I, 117, 6.

77. The *exhedra* was a large building on to which the western side of the Baths of Diocletian opened; on the edge of the ancient *exhedra* the modern Exhedra stands in the square called after it at the beginning of the Via Nazionale.

78. See note 6, p. 62.

79. Festus, 232, 11: *Ad quam et natatum et exercitationis alioqui causa veniebat populus.*

80. Ibid.: *Piscinae publicae hodieque nomen manet, ipsa non exstat.*

81. The mention of it in Cicero (ad Quintum fr., III, 7, 1) seems to refer to a district of Rome rather than to the tank: *Magna vis aquae usque ad Piscinam publicam.*

82. Pliny, N.H., XXXIV, 45.

83. Suetonius, Vesp., 18.

84. Martial, Lib. Spect., 2, 1; I, 70, 6-7.

85. Aelius Spartianus, Had., 19.

86. Aelius Lampridius, Comm., 17.

CHAPTER XIV

Industry

Growth of industry in Italy and Latium. Industry in Rome and Italian cities. Industry in the provinces. The Roman Empire not an industrial empire. Slaves in industry. The free craftsman. Ancient and modern industry. Domestic industry.

AT first Latium was essentially an agricultural region. Its early connexions with Etruria, a country where industry developed extensively, and the growing commercial penetration of the Greek colonists later on the south Italian coast caused an economic awakening in Latium and encouraged the growth of native industry. Vases from Campania and bronze work from Etruria inspired the beginning of pottery and metal work in Rome and the Latin cities. Praeneste was the first centre of the metal industry in Latium and engraved bronze mirrors, pins, cists and various objects of household use, as well as gold jewellery, were manufactured there.

Rome's conquest of Italy did not stifle industry in the subjected cities, but rather had the opposite effect of stimulating it, as Rome provided the largest market for the various products of Italian industry, and, though Italian craftsmen may also have migrated to Rome and started a local industry there, this never produced any serious competition to industries in other cities.

Gradually, as Rome extended her conquests and increased her empire, the growth of the population, the refinement of luxury and the construction of large public and private buildings caused many industries to flourish in Rome to meet the requirements of the capital and the rest of Italy. But Rome, although itself an important industrial centre, was essentially a city of consumers, requiring the greater part of its produce for its own needs as well as many imports. Imports exceeded exports, which were always very limited, with the exception of bronze goods which are found in large numbers in the most distant parts of the Roman world.

Some of the smaller markets for Roman industry, districts where the standard of living was low, lost their dependence on Rome as the result of the Roman conquest which raised the standard of living and encouraged the growth of local industries.

Rome had an absolute lead in the production of luxury goods, especially articles of precious metal, jewellery and engraved cups. The high standard of living in a metropolis makes it the centre of fashion and the unchallenged producer of luxury goods. Foreign craftsmen, mostly Greeks, created small masterpieces in their workshops. Drawing their inspiration from well known ancient models, they decorated flasks and cups with floral patterns, and realistic human figures and animals.[1] The building trade and its allied industries naturally developed incomparably more in Rome than elsewhere.

Industry flourished in other Italian cities besides Rome, especially in the towns which provided the mistress of the seas with ships: Genoa, Ostia and Ravenna. Como, Sulmona, Salerno and Puteoli were centres of the iron industry; the metal was produced in great quantities by the miners of Elba, who extracted the ore by primitive but effective methods. Campania, a rich and productive territory, was remarkable both for its extensive agricultural output, especially of wine, and its industrial products of every sort: bronzes (Capua), terracotta vases (Puteoli, Cumae, Ischia), glass (Cumae, Sorrento, Pompeii), foodstuffs like *garum* (Pompeii).[2] Apulia produced the finest wool (Taranto, Canosa), maintaining an ancient boast of Italy, whose 'noble fleeces of sheep' are no less praised by classical writers than the 'mighty backs of her bulls'.[3] Martial[4] gives a list of wool-producing districts, which may perhaps have been proverbial, 'First for the excellence of its wool comes Apulia, second Parma, third Altinum [near Padua].'

There were many flourishing industrial centres in northern Italy; bronze articles were produced at Bergamo, bricks at Modena, amphorae at Pola; the woollen industry of Istria, Padua and Parma was famous, as were the dye works of Aquileia. Aquileia was a large commercial city, with many flourishing industries (cloth, glass, etc.). The products of northern Europe flowed into it, especially amber, which was found in the Baltic and carved in local workshops, as recent excavations at Aquileia have shown.

Amongst the Romans, objects of amber (*sucinum*)[5] were much more in demand than they are today; amber jewellery indeed was regarded as vulgar and was worn only by women of the lower classes. Matrons wore only gold and precious stones,[6] but it was considered smart for a woman to hold a small ball of amber[7] in the hands and to rub it occasionally to smell its delicate fragrance. This practice should not seem strange. The streets of large ancient cities, usually narrow and airless, with an exceedingly primitive and often non-existent drainage system,[8] congested with heavy traffic, and with elementary cleaning and health services, must have smelt very strongly. Cicero[9] tells us that when Verres went out in public, to protect himself against smells he used to carry a bag full of roses in his hand and wore a garland of roses round his neck. Such a device was not without its practical drawbacks; quite apart from its unattractively ostentatious nature, the perfumed garland swaying about on the chest must have been no small inconvenience. A small amber ball was obviously much more practical for the purpose, besides giving ladies an occupation in public.

Among the many other uses of amber, pieces in their natural state, in which an insect, a reptile, or some other small animal had been imprisoned[10] were used to decorate furniture.

Under the Empire, industries proliferated and grew. Rome encouraged this growth in various ways; technical advances in industry were helped by the unity of the Empire, where ideas could be freely exchanged; the policing of the sea and the improvement of land communications facilitated trade with distant countries. Finally, the needs of the vast civilian population and the military supplies required for the large standing army meant that the city of Rome itself provided an almost limitless market for goods from every land.

The eastern provinces sent to Rome rare and exotic goods produced in local factories or brought to their ports from still more distant regions: silk from China, priceless emeralds from Scythia, perfumes from Arabia, glassware and papyrus from Egypt.

Egypt was the first Mediterranean country where the glass industry flourished; from there, precious crystal cups, turned on the lathe, came to Rome, to be displayed at the banquets of the rich, their owner's pride and the cupbearer's anxiety. The glass industry spread also to Italy, but there it only produced second-rate work. Among the various uses of glass, mention must be made of the cubes for mosaic pavements, where glass alternated with marble, onyx and even gold,[11] and window panes. For from the early days of the Empire the method of closing windows with a translucent material had been discovered, either with very thin sheets of talc (*lapis specularis*) called *specularia*[12] or large plates of glass. Among the rich the use of *specularia* was so widespread, that they were used even in the sides of a closed litter.[13]

The literary references to glass windows are all late, but some fragments of them have been found at Pompeii[14] and the three Gauls;[15] they are about an eighth of an inch thick and are fixed in the walls, or fitted into wooden or bronze frames opening vertically on two pivots at the top and bottom of the centre of the frame. These thick opaque panes allow light and sunshine to enter the room, which is a great advance, but they do not allow the enjoyment of the view of the countryside from inside, once the windows are closed. Furthermore, *specularia* and glass were a luxury which few could afford; the houses of the poor had wooden shutters;[16] when they were shut to keep out the cold, the house was plunged in darkness and lamps had to be lit even in daytime.

In the western and northern provinces also, industries were greatly developed, and together with the eastern provinces they entered into serious, often successful, competition with Italian industries. The Spaniard Martial boasts of the well-tempered steel, the soft wool and the delicious *garum* of his country.[17] Gaul, rich in minerals, was famous for its bronze work, precious metals and the production of clay vases with relief work (*vasa sigillata*). Gallic shoes (*Gallicae*) were exported extensively, along with the products of their woollen industry, materials, cloaks and mattresses. Chariots of the Gallic type became common in Rome.[18] Noricum produced the best arms, the Rhine valley the best earthenware, Batavia certain special hairdyes (*spuma Batava*) made of suet and ashes, incomparable for giving the hair a beautiful bright tint.[19]

The Roman Empire was not an industrial empire; the Romans had other methods of exploiting their provinces. The flow of money to Rome was brought about chiefly through the public offices, in the administration of which officials of every rank, especially in the Republican era, knew how to line their own pockets, and many who left Rome poor returned rich from their duties in the provinces. In particular, the collection of taxes lent itself to various types of financial operations, usually dishonest but always profitable; those who engaged in such practices were promoting the interests of the state as well as of themselves. Furthermore, enterprising Romans found extensive facilities for every form of private activity in the conquered territories. The provinces enriched the Romans, and rich Romans enriched Rome. In spite of this, Rome never systematically insisted on the import of goods produced in the capital into the provinces.

The ruling classes looked down upon trade and industry; only agriculture was considered respectable, and even members of the senatorial order engaged in it, relying almost exclusively on slave labour to run their farms. Furthermore, it was the only occupation which did not seem incompatible with high rank, and was permitted by the law which forbade senators and their sons to possess large cargo ships,[20] essential for large-scale trade. Even in the largest Roman industries over-production never occurred as it does nowadays, requiring a very large field of penetration for its dispersal. Everywhere, including Rome, craftsmanship and small industries flourished, chiefly independent of the activities of high finance, which was in the hands of the *equites* and concentrated chiefly on banking and tax-farming. Larger industries never swallowed up the smaller ones.

The steady increase in the number of slaves imported into Italy from various parts of the world was the largest factor in industrial development at Rome. Slaves used for industrial purposes were divided into gangs (*collegia, classes, decuriae*) under the supervision of foremen (*praepositus*). The individual capacity of each man was the criterion for the distribution of work. The slave gangs, which the Greeks called ἐργαστήριον (strictly speaking, 'factory', but in industrial language 'a gang') were closed groups of specialist workers whose skills were interdependent so that every group constituted a unit which could remain unchanged for years; the rigid structure of such units was favoured by the servile position of the workers, tied to their special job without any hope of escape.

Classical Greece taught Rome the secret of industrial organisation; in Athens the inheritance of a gang of twenty slaves trained in

the manufacture of beds was the subject of litigation;[21] throughout
the vicissitudes of an interminable law-suit in which its possession
was contested, it changed owners many times without anyone ever
thinking of breaking up the component units and shattering the
unity of the ἐργαστήριον with serious economic results. The
owner of trained slaves could exploit them either by using their
labour himself or by hiring them out. There is extensive evidence
for the hiring of slave-labour both in Greece and Italy. The
purchase of slaves in order to exploit their labour in this way was
considered an excellent capital investment. For example, in Athens
in the fifth century B.C., Nicias,[22] the richest man in the city,
invested a large part of his capital in slaves whom he hired out. At
Rome T. Pomponius Atticus,[23] the famous bookseller of Cicero's
day (see p. 184), was particularly skilful in this type of speculation.

Anyone who wanted to carry out a task requiring a great deal of
labour, normally gave the contract for it to a contractor (*redemptor*)[24]
who carried it out with his own workmen. The large public and
private buildings of Rome were built by contractors and it is
interesting to see in Cicero's correspondence[25] how, just as today,
owner and contractor, while in agreement on the general plan of
the building, were in a perpetual state of disagreement when it
came to carrying it out, and were never able to agree about their
mutual obligations.

We need not believe that the work was always as well carried out
as the mighty ruins of Rome might lead us to suppose, nor that
besides skilful and conscientious contractors there were no casual
and careless ones. We know of one architect who was unable to
make columns stand straight,[26] and of contractors whose haphazard methods of construction caused accidents fatal to their
workmen.

Industrial gangs were not normally very large; only in mines,
irrigation works and large industrial organisations were slaves
employed by the hundred, and the high proportion of slaves to
freemen in such tasks might prove dangerous. The possibility of
collective action by slave labourers was guarded against by the
imposition of a discipline so severe that the more humane masters
regarded working under such conditions as a punishment.[27] Even
so it was not always possible to avoid revolts, which often broke
out and were crushed with bloodshed; the revolt led by the

Thracian Spartacus in 73 B.C. was the most serious of the slave risings.

Competition from slave labour hindered the activity and initiative of free labour. It was chiefly for this reason that towards the end of the Republic the Roman proletariat was compelled to live a parasitic life at the state's expense. In spite of this, however, the free craftsman was not eliminated, though life for the lowest classes became increasingly difficult, and the difficulties made the poor idle and all too ready to beg from the rich and the public authorities. But it is a common exaggeration, too often repeated, that the entire Roman people spent every day of the year demanding bread and shows in the circus (*panem et circenses*); to eat, to enjoy oneself, and to do nothing is an ideal life. But the self-respecting poor found themselves work and worked. We must assume that in a city where demand was so great and industrial production relatively limited (see p. 154), it was rare to be unable to find work. What changes least in the history of civilisation is the steady preoccupation of those less favoured by fortune with seeking an honest way of earning their daily bread, and their resignation to God's law of having to work to live, a harsh law, which produces discontents, rebels, idlers and parasites among the weak, its predestined victims; but it also emphasises the humble heroism of the honest, whom the humane Virgil[28] honours in a moving passage when he describes the working class woman, who gets up at cock-crow and spins by lantern light to avoid being beholden to anyone and to preserve her integrity.

At Rome independent artisans worked in their own shops assisted by apprentices and boys; but there was also an organisation of craftsmanship by trades in those fields of industry which demand a more complex distribution of labour. Work was distributed to workers according to their ability; in learning their trade they passed through various grades: epitaphs mention *magistri* and *discentes*.[29] The free workman in the employment of an industrialist worked for a wage fixed without restriction, either on a contract or a daily basis. Diocletian was the first to lay down a fixed scale of wages. The working day lasted as long as the sun was in the sky; generally a compulsory minimum of work was fixed for each day. As among slaves, so with the free craftsmen, independent or not, groups of specialists were formed, a phenomenon which in the late Empire led to strict legislation binding the craftsman to his craft as well as his sons, compelling them to follow their father's trade, and sometimes the daughters, who were only allowed to marry a man practising the same trade as their father, so that a trade became compulsorily hereditary, and the position of the free craftsman was hardly distinguishable from that of a slave.

The craftsmen (Plates 46–48) who had technical methods, basic materials and customers in common, tended to band together. The ironworker, whether he makes ploughs, swords, knives or pins, goes to the same wholesaler and uses partly the same techniques. From this natural grouping of connected trades the craftsmen's corporations developed. These corporations were very old in Rome; tradition traced the foundation of the first eight back to Numa Pompilius:[30] flute players, goldsmiths, woodworkers, dyers, shoemakers, tanners, coppersmiths and potters. The art of the goldsmiths (*aurifices, fabri aurarii*) flourished from the first in Rome, a common phenomenon in primitive societies because of the ease with which gold can be worked; from the goldsmiths' shops came ornaments of various types, as well as fillings for decaying teeth, first mentioned in one of the laws of the Twelve Tables, which laid down that the gold in a man's teeth was the only gold which could accompany him to the grave. Of the baser metals, the first to be worked were bronze and copper, followed by iron and silver; the *fabri ferrarii* and the *fabri argentarii* joined the *fabri aerarii*. The art of pottery was equally ancient, as ancient as pots themselves. As well as craftsmen (*figuli*) the slaves of the *familia rustica* worked as potters, since many of their products were used in agriculture.[31] Italian pottery was of all types, from the humblest earthenware for everyday use, which hardly mattered if it was dropped, to the beautiful *vasa Arretina*, decorated in relief and made in moulds; terracotta statues and clay decorations of houses were works of art continuing a tradition widespread in ancient Etruria. There was a large number of carpenters and woodworkers. The building of houses required the manufacture of beams, doors, wooden staircases, and the framework of roofs by the *fabri tignarii*; there were in addition furniture makers, particularly bedmakers. Skilful craftsmen invented new types of beds which gained popularity either through their beauty or their convenience and low price. Horace mentions

45. Moneychanger's shop.
(*p. 7*)

46. Altar set up by the tool-maker, L. Cornelius Atimetus.
(First Century A.D.)

47. Pompeii. Fresco from the House of the Vettii showing cupids engaged as scentmakers.

48. Relief showing the interior of a metal worker's shop. (Second Century A.D.)

the *lecti Archiaci*,[32] made by Archias, Seneca the beds of Soteri-cus.[33]

Among Roman industries, the ancient art of the dyers (*tinctores, infectores*) also made great advances, especially after the purple industry was introduced into Italy. This had already been flourishing for some considerable time in Phoenicia, the first centre of the trade and the best known both in Roman times and the Middle Ages, in Laconia (in Greece) and on the island of Meninx in North Africa. In Western Europe famous dye works grew up in

22. WORK IN PROGRESS IN A FULLONA
(BLÜMNER, *op. cit.*)

Gaul, Spain and many Italian cities (Ancona, Aquinum, Puteoli, Tarentum, Syracuse). The purple was obtained by extracting the liquid from a mollusc by a complicated process. Although Italian dye-works produced a purple of only second-rate quality, they were very active; consequently purple dyed stuffs were widely used in Italy to make clothes, carpets and bed-covers. Not all purple materials were equally expensive; less rich materials were quite modestly priced; with the more expensive materials the wool had been passed through two successive baths (*dibapha*). The colour of purple varied; brown, violet and red predominated; the belief that in antiquity the colour purple was always red is false; in those days purple was a type of colour produced by dyeing, not a colour itself; the brighter colours were obtained by diluting the fluid with water and urine. This unpleasant process explains the foul smell of clothes dyed in purple. Martial,[34] not surprisingly, considers purple as one of the most malodorous things. Foul-smelling and handsome, with its changing hues, purple was also used at Rome to indicate social position. A purple stripe (*clavus*) at the bottom of the toga indicated, if narrow (*angusticlavium*), membership of the equestrian order, if broad (*laticlavium*), of the senatorial order. There were various departments in a dye-works, and families used to send clothes and linen there for renovation by less perfunctory methods than those employed in the home.

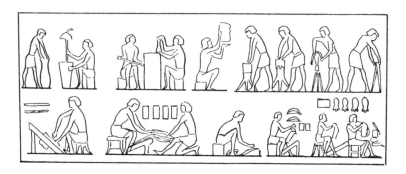

23. TANNING IN ANCIENT EGYPT
(BLÜMNER, *Technologie u. Terminologie*)

The tanning of skins and leather[35] was carried on in the *villa rustica*, or in the shops of the *corarii*; in antiquity the methods of tanning did not differ very greatly from ours, as can be seen from some Egyptian reliefs (fig. 23) in which the various processes of tanning are shown. The leather and skin shops supplied the numerous shoemakers and cobblers (*sutores*) of Rome, as well as the booksellers (see p. 34).

The furnishing of a house, clothing and care of the body provided work for various other craftsmen, whose number grew with the increase in the standard of living in Rome. Skilled workmen were in demand for the decoration of floors (*pavimentarii*), executing mosaics (*tessellarii, musivarii*), inserting glass and talc panes (see p. 156) into walls (*vitrarii, speculariarii*) and decorating the stucco on walls with ornamental motifs (*pictores parietarii*).

Among all these workmen and shops, barbers (*tonsores*) swarmed everywhere, for everyone needed them, as the practice of shaving oneself was unknown in antiquity. Anyone who did not have a slave to whom he could entrust the care of his face, went to a barber's shop, where he found, even in those days, idlers and a rich source of city gossip and scandal.

The organisation of the Roman Empire assisted the most complete industrial development in the ancient world. In spite of this, ancient industry seems very primitive compared to modern industry. If the building industry even from the earliest times has left us masterpieces, like the Pyramids of Egypt, the cyclopean walls of Mycenean Greece, and the baths, arches and aqueducts of Rome,[36] buildings on a grand scale, like Hadrian's Villa at Tivoli

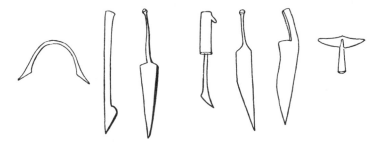

24. TANNING TOOLS

and the Colosseum, ancient industry was in general very far from satisfying all the varied and immense demands of life as it does today. We moderns demand everything from our great industries: from pins to tins of meat, medicine to domestic lighting, textiles of every sort to hotel organisation, sport, entertainment and everything which satisfies our higher cultural needs; we demand the convenience of our houses, the comfort and order of civil life, defence and victory in war. In antiquity this was not the case; industry did not have so complex a function and so tyrannical a rule.

Industrial products also reflect this difference. The products of ancient industry differed from the modern by the slowness of their production and by being less uniform and relatively more expensive. Production was better geared to consumption. We have references to industrial and commercial crises caused by political events (wars, the loss of political, and consequently economic, influence over lands open to imports from a state), but not of serious crises produced by lack of balance between production and consumption.

In antiquity all industry was originally domestic. In ancient Egypt the temple encouraged industry. In Mycenean Greece the palace, the heart of the patriarchal state, was a centre for the development of a primitive but flourishing industry. The same happened in the Roman world; the early Roman house was like a complex factory, producing everything which could be consumed or used. As industry gradually dissociated itself from domestic economy, the house lost its economic independence, but at the same time, industry, isolated from other domestic activities, became more specialised, perfecting its methods and improving its products.

This process passed through various stages, and appears more or less developed in different times and places. In general it may be said, however, that specialised industry never reached the same independence of domestic economy that it has today. In almost every period of antiquity, the house produced for its own needs things which are nowadays almost exclusively produced industrially outside the home, including the majority of those services which today, after being part of private industry, have become public and are managed directly or indirectly by the state or public bodies: sanitary and health services,[37] transport services for people and goods, education,[38] lighting,[39] postal services[40] and fire brigades.[41] These services, which were mostly left to domestic enterprise, complicated the organisation of wealthier homes. The poorer households either did without them altogether, or if they could afford them, had them in a greatly reduced and imperfect form.

Further Reading

M. Rostovtzeff, *Social and Economic History of the Roman Empire* (2nd Edition, Oxford, 1957) is the standard work on this subject.

See also T. Frank, *Economic Survey of Ancient Rome* (1933–40); H. J. Loane, *Industry and Commerce of the City of Rome* (Baltimore, 1938).

M. P. Charlesworth, *Trade-routes and Commerce of the Roman Empire* (Cambridge, 1926).

NOTES

1. Martial, III, 35:

> *Artis Phidiacae toreuma clarum*
> *Pisces aspicis; adde aquam, natabunt.*

III, 41, 2:

> *Lacerta vivit et timetur argentum*

cf. Juvenal, 1, 76.

2. See p. 90.

3. Pliny, N.H., III, 41: *Tam nobilia pecudi vellera, tam opima tauris colla.*

4. Martial, XIV, 155.

5. *Electrum* in the Greek sense of amber is rare in Latin, although the word 'electricity' is derived from this meaning. Amber is normally *sucinum; electrum* is normally applied to an alloy of gold and silver from which the first Lydian coins were made.

6. See p. 106.

7. Martial records the fragrance of these amber balls, when describing the finest scents (III, 65, 5; V, 37, 11; XI, 8, 6); the custom of carrying such balls in the hand seems to have been restricted to women (Ovid, Met., II, 366: *nuribus . . . gestanda Latinis;* cf. Juvenal, 6, 573) and girls (Martial, XI, 8, 6: *sucina virginea . . . regelata namu*); it was not practised by men. From the expression *sucina trita* (Martial, III, 65, 5; cf. Juvenal, 6, 573) we gather that the amber had to be rubbed whenever it was desired to produce its characteristic fragrance.

8. Strabo, V, 8.

9. Cicero, Act. II in Verrem, V, 11, 27: *Ut mos fuit Bithyniae regibus, lectica octaphoro ferebatur, in qua pulvinus erat perlucidus Melitensis rosa fartus; ipse autem coronam habebat unam in capite, alteram in collo reticulumque ad nares sibi admovebat tenuissimo lino, minutis maculis, plenum rosae.*

10. Martial, IV, 32, 59; VI, 15.

11. See p. 67.

12. The manufacture of these *specularia* gave rise to an industry similar to the glass industry, carried on by the *speculariarii* (CIL, VI, 4248, 5202).

13. Juvenal 4, 21: *Quae vehitur clauso latis specularibus antro.*

14. In the Villa of Diomede, the House of the Faun and of P. Caecilius Secundus.

15. Cf. Carcopino p. 318, note 63 ('Peregrine Paperback').

16. Martial, VIII, 14, 3–6; Juvenal, 6, 31.

17. Martial, I, 49, 2, 4 and 12; VIII, 28, 5–6; XIII, 40.

18. See Chapter XX.

19. See p. 111.

20. The *Lex Claudia*, passed by the Comitia in the first year of the Second Punic War (Livy, XXI, 63, 3): *Ne quis senator cuive senator pater fuisset, maritimam navem, quae plus quam trecentarum amphorarum esset, haberet. Id satis habitum ad fructus ex agris vectandos; quaestus omnis patribus indecorus visus.*

21. Demosthenes, Contra Aphobum, 1, 27, 31 and passim.

22. Xenophon. De vectig., 4, 14.

23. Cicero, Ad Att., IV, 4b.

24. Horace, Odes, III, 1, 35.

25. Cicero, Ad Qu. fr., III, 1, 2, 5.

26. Ibid. III, 1, 1, 2.

27. See p. 122.

28. Aen., VIII, 407.

29. Dessau 6419[e], 8676.

30. Plutarch, Numa, 17.

31. See Chapter III.

32. Horace, Epist., I, 5, 1.

33. Quoted by Aulus Gellius, XII, 2, 11; *lecti Soterici.* The context makes it clear that these were of inferior workmanship.

34. Martial, I, 49; 32; IV, 4, 6; IX, 62.

35. See p. 70.

36. See p. 1.

37. See p. 215.

38. See p. 167.

39. See p. 39.

40. See p. 186.

41. See p. 79.

CHAPTER XV

Education

THE literary evidence for the introduction of schools in Rome is conflicting; Plutarch's[1] statement that the first public school was opened towards the middle of the third century B.C. by Spurius Carvilius is incompatible with other references to the school as a much more ancient institution. One thing, however, is certain, ancient Roman custom entrusted a father with the instruction of his son; the greatest men in Rome, like Cato the Elder and Aemilius Paulus, did not consider it a waste of time to withdraw from public affairs and teach their children counting, just as they did not find it undignified to be accompanied by them in the most solemn ceremonies or to take them by the hand in sacred processions, as we see in the fragments of the *Ara pacis*. In this way the father was the constant guide of his son in the first flowering of his intelligence and his first experience of the world, and the spiritual continuity of the race was ensured. But the excellent ancient custom was not universally followed; from the end of the Republic onwards most men either entrusted their sons' education to a tutor, usually a Greek, or sent him to school (*ludus, ludus litterarius*).

In early times the lessons taught were simple; the ancient Roman had learnt enough when he knew how to write, read and count. But in the last years of the Republic and under the Empire, the education became more complicated and involved three stages: instruction by the *litterator* and other elementary masters, and secondly by the *grammaticus*, constituted the normal course of elementary and secondary education; ideally this was followed by a course at the school of the *rhetor*, who trained young men in eloquence before they entered public life; this, however, was not invariable. Elementary lessons took place in the school of the *ludi magister*, a private person who taught reading and writing for a modest salary, meagrely increased by presents on annual holidays.

This was in particular the duty of the *litterator* (the equivalent of the Greek γραμματιστής); when boys had learnt the rudiments of reading and writing, their writing was perfected, and their instruction in mathematics and shorthand begun, under the guidance respectively of the *librarius*, the *calculator* and the *notarius*, who were also elementary masters.

The Romans had no conception of the large school buildings which we consider indispensable; lessons were held in small rented rooms (*tabernae, pergulae*), or even in the open air. The school year begun in March after the *Quinquatrus*, a holiday in honour of Minerva and particularly sacred to schoolboys; there were holidays on festive days and every ninth day (*nundinae*). That a period for the summer holidays was officially laid down cannot be proved,[2] but boys were normally made to rest during the heat of

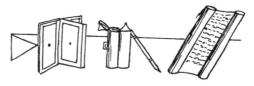

25. SCHOOLBOYS' WRITING MATERIALS
Wax tablets; pencase with pen; papyrus roll

the summer. The school day lasted for six hours; lessons began early in the morning, broke off towards midday, when the boys returned home for *prandium*, and began again in the afternoon.

The furniture of the school was simple. Only in exceptional cases did the boys sit with their master round a table;[3] normally there was no desk either for the master or the boys; the master sat on a chair with arms (*cathedra*) or without arms (*sella*), the boys on benches, holding on their knees the writing tablets which they brought with them together with their pens, paper and ink (fig. 25).

Horace describes his master Orbilius as *plagosus*,[4] 'full of blows'; other masters deserved the epithet no less.[5] Flogging was as frequent at Rome as it was in Greece, from where, perhaps, the example came. Antiquity approved of such educational methods. From the third mime of Herondas we learn that the master was expected to administer corporal punishment even for crimes committed outside the school. A wall-painting from Herculaneum gives a vivid picture of a schoolmaster beating a howling boy.

Once elementary studies were finished, secondary education began under the *grammaticus*. This too, according to the tradition and means of the family, was shared, either in a house or a public school run by a private individual. The first public schools of *grammatici* opened towards the middle of the second century B.C. and multiplied rapidly; there were more than twenty even before the end of the Republic.

It was exceptional for a *grammaticus* to grow rich through his profession, although one or two of the ablest or most fortunate succeeded in doing so; his pay was usually modest. We often meet complaints in the writers of the Empire against the fathers of families who demanded too much and paid too little. Even Juvenal protested:[6]

> Be sure, parents, to impose the strictest rules upon the teacher; he must never be at fault in his grammar; he must know all history and have all the authorities at his finger-tips. If asked a chance question on the way to the baths, or to the establishment of Phoebus, he must at once tell you the name of Anchises' nurse, the name and birthplace of Anchemolus' step-mother, to what age Acestes lived, how many flagons of Sicilian wine he presented to the Trojans.

However, if Juvenal thought it excessive to demand that the teacher should know the rules of grammar, many may feel Juvenal's claim that the teacher almost had a right to be ungrammatical excessive.

The language and literature of Greece and Rome were taught in the school of the *grammaticus*, poetry being particularly studied, and some attention was paid to the fundamentals of history, geography, physics and astronomy, necessary for a complete understanding of the texts. These were normally dictated, and in studying them the scholar learned to pronounce well, read with feeling, bring out the meaning clearly and appreciate the metre. Once the texts had been read, the master required his pupils to learn passages by heart, and to make oral and written explanations of them; these had the same purpose as composition in our schools. It is of enormous importance to the history of Roman literature to discover what authors were most commonly read in schools; the choice of the *grammatici* influenced taste, decided literary tradition, and by its effect on the book trade became one of the most important influences on the fate of authors in succeeding ages. The most noble texts, when they were not read in schools and therefore not in demand, disappeared from circulation and have not survived. Homer was the most widely read of Greek authors; during the Republic ancient writers, like Andronicus and Ennius, were the favourite Latin authors; but a modernistic movement, largely influenced by Horace, drove the literary masterpieces of the archaic age from schools and laid the emphasis on the study of more recent or contemporary literature.

A boy left the school of the *grammaticus* with a sound knowledge of Latin and Greek, the two languages which an educated person was expected to speak. Greek was very widely spoken throughout the Roman world; the contacts which had existed from the earliest times with Magna Graecia, the residence in the oriental Hellenised provinces of many Roman soldiers and merchants, and, above all, the large number of Greek slaves in Roman families from whom children spontaneously learnt a second tongue, made the Romans a bilingual people. Plautus wrote for an audience which understood the Greek words in which his comedies abound; with the passage of time the learning of Greek seemed so essential, particularly in aristocratic families, that elementary and secondary education began with it. Even women knew Greek; girls raved over Menander, and it was thought smart for lovers to speak in Greek.

The *rhetor* was the teacher of eloquence; at his school boys were prepared for public life by enlarging their culture through the further study of classical texts, the emphasis being mainly laid on prose writers, and trained in the difficult art of speaking according to a carefully thought out system. The first schools of rhetoric in Rome were opened in the second century B.C.; in the face of this new invasion of Greek culture there were protests and forebodings, which did not prevent the new teaching from taking firm root, while the ancient Roman custom, by which eloquence was learned through practice or by frequenting the forum from boyhood in company with one's father or some experienced advocate, died out.

The teaching required written and oral exercises from the pupils. The first consisted largely of more varied compositions than those required by the *grammaticus* and were graduated according to their difficulty: stories, eulogies of, or attacks on, celebrated historical characters, brief debates, comparisons, etc. Practical oral exercises in eloquence took the form either of *suasoriae* or *controversiae*.[7] The *suasoriae* were monologues in which famous mythological or historical characters weighed up the arguments for and against their action before taking a serious decision; the *controversiae* took the form of a debate between two scholars, supporting two opposite theses. It was not a lively discussion, based on question and answer, which exposed the scholar to the unexpected, and accustomed him to the quick cut and thrust of the forum, but the continual exposition of two contradictory points of view, in fact true rhetoric in the worst sense of the word. Strange and striking themes were devised to give future orators training in finding effective arguments; this harmed good taste and the very eloquence which such unimaginatively scholastic methods aimed to develop.

The public, especially the pupil's family, was admitted to these exercises in the *rhetor's* school. One can imagine how easy triumphs must have been when parental weakness combined with the vanity of a mercenary *rhetor* to load with praises the stripling, who in the role of Hannibal had produced a splendid argument to persuade himself and the public of the necessity of crossing the Alps.

Nor did the tedium finish there. Once the road was open to easy success in front of a complacent audience, adults also began to delight in tamed applause. The custom of public readings introduced by Asinius Pollio, a contemporary of Augustus, provided the opportunity for this; poems, tragedies, and later even speeches, were read. The object of the readings was to obtain in advance an impression of public opinion from the views of critics chosen from a restricted circle of competent judges. There was some purpose behind the idea, but in fact public readings became an object in themselves. A lecturer with a large scarf round his neck,[8] a curious fashion suggested perhaps by the need to avoid straining the voice, read his verses to an audience of friends who, as they had been applauded themselves the day before, owed a debt of applause, or by applauding for the first time created for themselves a credit for the future. There were also famished clients who stamped their feet and clapped their hands crying 'σοφῶς' ('*euge*') to earn their dinner, and foolish people who went to a reading, as today many people go to lectures, merely to give the appearance of being intellectual.

Pliny attached importance to public readings; Martial, the greatest poet of his age, laughed at them. This diversity of opinion can be explained in various ways: Pliny took everything painfully seriously, Martial turned everything into a joke; Pliny was an aristocrat, living the life of a man of the world and having to accept its fashions and show approval of them, Martial was a cynical and shameless client who only respected those who would give him a dinner. Perhaps it would be malicious to suggest that Pliny's enthusiasm for public readings has another explanation. Martial was so great an artist that he had no use for compulsory applause; vivacity, wit and genius were unquestionably his, and the recognition of his qualities was so wide and assured that he could disregard the successes of the salon; Pliny, on the other hand, had every reason to consider as serious and fair-minded judgments formed in the gossip of the literary coterie, where men went to applaud and to be applauded.

Further Reading

H. I. Marrou, *A History of Education in Antiquity* (New York, 1956) is the best general account.
Special studies include:
D. L. Clark, *Rhetoric in Greco-Roman Education* (New York, 1957).
D. A. Kidd, *Roman Attitudes to Education* (Christchurch, New Zealand, 1958).
A. Gwynn, *Education from Cicero to Quintilian* (Oxford, 1926).
M. L. Clarke, *Rhetoric at Rome: A Historical Survey* (London, 1953).
S. F. Bonner, *Roman Declamation* (Liverpool, 1949).
E. B. Castle, *Ancient Education and To-day* (Penguin Books, London, 1961).

NOTES

1. Quaest., Rom., 59.
2. The question depends entirely on the interpretation of two lines of Martial (X, 62, 10-12):

> *Ferulaeque tristes, sceptra paedagogorum,*
> *Cessent et Idus dormiant in Octobres.*

According to some, there was an official holiday from 1 July to the middle of October, and these lines refer to an over-conscientious master, who kept his school open at a time when it ought to have been closed. In confirmation of this interpretation they adduce a line of Horace (Sat., I, 6, 75) where the poet alludes to the fee paid by the boys of his district to their master. There are two versions of this line: the better manuscripts read *ibant octonos referentes idibus aeris* ('they went to school carrying the fee of eight asses each month'); but those who wish to find a reference in Martial to the supposed official summer holidays, read with the inferior manuscripts: *octonis . . . idibus aera*, ('the fees due for eight months' schooling'). Others who see no connexion between the line in Horace and Martial's epigram, maintain, correctly in my view, that even if it was normal to take children into the country up to the middle of October, it was not a question of real summer holidays, which would make the prayer to the *ludi magister* incomprehensible, but of a custom of going into the country followed by all those who had the chance. Even in summer the school had to remain open, though sparsely attended; Martial is urging the master to close it completely.

3. Martial, X, 62.
4. Epist., II, 1, 70–71.
5. Prudentius, Perist., X, 606; Libanius, Or., XIX, 98.
6. 7, 230–6. So that the reader may not find himself in the same awkward situation as the *rhetor* on his way to the baths, he should know that Anchises' nurse was called Tisiphone, according to the scholiast on Juvenal, that the stepmother of Anchemolus, one of Pallas' victims (Aen., X, 389) was called Casperia, according to Servius. We know from Virgil that Acestes was old (Aen., V, 73) and that he supplied the Trojans with wine (Aen., I, 195), but Virgil does not mention his precise age or the number of flagons, and the father's demand for exact information on these points seems to have been genuinely excessive.
7. Strictly speaking, *suasoriae* gave practice in debate, *controversiae* in legal argument. Seneca the Elder has preserved examples of both; his prodigious memory enabled him to recall the most famous of those heard in his youth from well-known orators (*Oratorum et rhetorum sententiae, divisiones, colores*; one book of *Suasoriae* and ten of *Controversiae*).
8. Martial, VI, 41.

CHAPTER XVI

Books, Correspondence, Papers, Post

Papyrus and parchment; other writing materials. Limited production of writing materials. Papyrus. Parchment. Books. Ink. Pens. Wax tablets. Public notices and papers. Slaves trained as writers. Bookshops; publishers. Public and private libraries. Roman postal services.

THE Greeks and Romans preferred to write on papyrus (*papyrus, charta*)[1] or parchment (*membrana*), but they used other materials as well; the Greeks, like the Egyptians, used potsherds (ὄστρακα) extensively,[2] the Romans tablets of wax and, for certain documents, of ivory; ivory was also used for the manufacture of smart pocket-books.[3] Other materials, to be mentioned later, were also used.

The problem of finding a writing surface was most satisfactorily solved in this age with papyrus and parchment. This problem was born with writing, and the invention of the alphabet, which put writing in the power of a larger number of people, had made it more urgent. But the solution was not as easy as it might seem. For some considerable time after the discovery of writing,[4] men continued to write on anything convenient: walls,[5] tablets of wood,[6] doors, the skins of various animals, especially parchment (see p. 177) and leather, as well as the skins of reptiles and dogs, leaves, fruit skins, panels of silk and linen, and lead tablets. They even had books of lead, in which the public records were kept.[7] Some used bark as a substitute for papyrus.[8] The student of geometry traced his figures on a table covered with sand.[9] Plutarch[10] tells us that when Plato retired to Sicily to the court of the tyrant Dionysius, all his courtiers were seized with such a passion for geometry that there was a perpetual sand storm throughout the kingdom.

When we say that papyrus and parchment played the part of paper today, we should at the same time remember that this paper of the ancient world was not only clumsier and heavier but also much more expensive and infinitely rarer than paper nowadays. This difference between ancient and modern times in the availability of paper is of profound importance and its effects have been so far-reaching that the two ages could be described as the age with too little paper and the age with too much. It is said, with reason, that the discovery of printing began a new era in the history of civilisation, but it is not always realised that this invention would have achieved nothing if some centuries earlier men had not learnt to manufacture the type of paper used today,[11] and the modern world could not have had as much paper as it wanted cheaply and in limitless quantities.

Today more paper is consumed in a single day than the total consumption of papyrus and parchment in many years of the Roman era, even allowing for the fact that the most civilised Romans wrote a great deal in maintaining their correspondence, making receipts, drawing up public and private documents of every kind, making appointments, writing out bills, keeping registers, publishing books and collecting libraries. The modern world is flooded with paper; we are rich and we forget that our paper supply was once poor, and it does not occur to us that without paper the tenor of modern intellectual life would be as impossible as material life without water. There is so much paper and water that we cannot imagine their not existing. But at one time paper did not exist, or existed only in limited quantities. Whether so great a supply of paper is a benefit for which we are indebted to human ingenuity or a universal calamity, is a question which each must answer for himself. The fact remains that for a man who wishes to write, obtaining writing material no longer presents a problem; ideas, common sense, literary and critical ability may be missing, grammar completely non-existent, but paper will never be scarce. The ease with which we can find paper invites us to write on every subject, good, useful or moving, serious or trivial, because sometimes after writing them, we meet approval and even fame.

The production of papyrus began in Egypt, where grew the plant which furnished the basic material for its manufacture.[12] The inner pith of the papyrus plant was cut into long strips (*phylirae*), which were placed together lengthways and other strips were then glued across them, thus making the *charta*.

Egyptian papyrus was rough, because of the unevenness of the fibres. The Romans perfected the process of manufacture, as they succeeded in making the surface of the paper perfectly smooth by pressing it or beating it with a hammer. There were both papyrus shops (*horrea chartaria*) and factories (*officinae*) at Rome; among these the *officinae* of a certain Fannius,[13] from which the best papyrus came, were famous. There was a distinction between the rough Egyptian papyrus called *amphitheatrica* (so called because it was made near the amphitheatre in Alexandria) and the *charta fanniana* which was lighter and smoother. There were various qualities of papyrus; before Augustus the finest was called *hieratica*, but afterwards *Augusta* from the name of the Emperor; the roughest paper, not suitable for writing, *charta emporeutica* (shopping paper), was used for wrapping.

Only one side of a sheet of papyrus was suitable for writing; the back (*aversa charta*) was used only as a last resort; fragments of noble poetry have bills, domestic notes, etc., on their back. On the rare occasions when the papyrus was written on both sides, it was called *opisthographum*. Anybody using an inferior quality of writing paper which was not perfectly smooth, smoothed it before use with a type of ivory comb (from which the paper was called *charta dentata*)[14] or with a seashell.[15]

The shape of the paper varied according to its use. Both letter paper (*charta epistolaris*) and book paper existed. Documents before the age of Caesar[16] were always written across the paper (*transversa charta*), letters always lengthways as with us; in those days also, when there was no further space, additions were written in the margin,[17] a custom which today is for some reason more popular with women than with men.

A book was made from a number of pages (*paginae, plagulae, schedae*), which were dried in the sun, glued together by the longer sides and rolled up. The normal length of each roll (*scapus*) was twenty pages. Papyrus manufacturers sold *scapi* with the pages already glued together. Normally two parallel columns were written on each page, running the whole length of the *scapus* after allowing for a wide margin at the top and bottom. Writing on one of these rolls was not easy; it was necessary to hold it flat both at top and bottom, taking care to prevent it rolling up, or else to stretch it at full length on the ground with the danger that it might be torn or spoilt. Consequently the system of buying

49. Herculaneum. The *apodyterium* of the women's baths.

50. Herculaneum. The *caldarium* of the men's baths.

51. Rome. Sarcophagus showing children's games.

52. Herculaneum. Fresco showing winged cupids playing children's games. (*p. 233*)

the pages cut and having them glued together afterwards, when written on, by a skilful gluer (*glutinator*)[18] came to be preferred.

As has already been said, the use of the skins of animals as writing material is extremely ancient. Sheepskin appears to have been the most widely used.[19] Under Eumenes of Pergamum (197–159 B.C.) a method was discovered of making parchment so fine and supple that, as Egypt had forbidden the export of papyrus, parchment (*membrana*) could replace Egyptian papyrus. But parchment was never used extensively in Rome; it was comparatively expensive, and was only used for books, not, for example, as letter paper. Nevertheless, the parchment industry flourished, and there were shops of *membranarii*. Nor did papyrus and parchment eliminate the use of less suitable writing materials. Men continued to write on potsherds, leather, linen, etc. Public notices were written on boards whitened with chalk (*tabulae dealbatae*), and when it was necessary to preserve them for any length of time, they were engraved on stone, bronze or marble. To this practice we owe the survival of a very large number of Greek and Latin inscriptions with incalculable advantage to our knowledge of history and classical antiquity.

From what has been said the reader will have already formed an idea of the appearance of an ancient book,[20] a long strip of papyrus, which was kept rolled (*volumen*) and was unrolled as it was read. When we think of the ease with which we can read and consult modern books, the inconvenience of the ancient book will be obvious. The reader needed patience merely for the continuous rolling of one part and unrolling of the other which must have been exceedingly tedious; the loss of time involved in unrolling a roll merely to check a reference, compare two passages, trace a particular passage, or make a correction or a note, was obviously considerable.

For a long time parchment books were also in the form of a rolled strip. An innovation which was of decisive importance for the history of the book was introduced when parchment was used differently, being folded and cut into sheets (*quaterniones*); these, when sewn together and bound in a cover (*codices membranei*),[21] had more the appearance of a modern book. The rougher pages (the hair side) were placed together, and so were the smoother ones (the skin side); these, besides being more suitable for writing, had a much clearer colour;[22] but both sides could be used, a notable advantage over papyrus. The use of such parchment *codices* began under the Empire; the first reference to them occurs in the Flavian age.[23] But in spite of their greater convenience, they were not widely used; the high cost of parchment compared with papyrus kept the traditional but inconvenient use of papyrus rolls alive throughout the Roman era. *Codices* in this age never replaced parchment rolls.

The two edges at the top and bottom of the papyrus roll were called *frontes*, and being the only edges unprotected, could very easily be torn; so they were made even by being carefully trimmed to remove every roughness and protuberance and smoothed with pumice; *arido modo pumice expolitum*, says Catullus,[24] to describe a brand new book of smart appearance (*lepidus*). The quality of the book depended on the careful finish of the ends—which were also sometimes brightly dyed.

The papyrus strip was rolled from the bottom round a rod of wood or bone, called *umbilicus*. Usually there was only one *umbilicus*, but in some books one was placed at the beginning and one at the end. The protruding parts of the *umbilicus* were called *cornua*. In expensive books the *umbilicus* was brightly painted or gilded. A parchment[25] label with the title of the book (*titulus, index, σύλλαβος*) was attached to the upper edge of the roll.

A papyrus book ran the risk of decay; if exposed to damp, it rotted, the writing became faint and blurred, the pages lost their shape, and unrolling and rolling up the book became difficult. But the most serious danger was that they would be eaten by insects, the scourge of ancient books, as mice are of modern ones. To preserve the rolls the only remedy was to sprinkle the pages with cedar oil,[26] the best protection against moths and damp. This gave the papyrus a bright yellow colour; when its further preservation was essential, the roll was covered with a brightly dyed parchment wrapper (*membranum*) and kept with others in a box.

Ink was generally black, hence its Latin name, *atramentum*. The ink-well (*atramentarium*) took various simple forms; from the pictures which we have of it, it seems usually to have consisted of two cylindrical containers joined together, each with its own cover. Ink was made by mixing various ingredients: soot, resin, the lees of wine, and the black liquid from the cuttlefish. Gummy substances were always used in its manufacture. A black paste was formed from these which was diluted as required to produce ink. Care had to be taken not to dilute it too much, because this gave the ink a grey and colourless appearance and it ran from the pen.[27] Red ink was also used, but only to distinguish the title. There is evidence that sometimes invisible inks (something like ours) were used for secret correspondence, which could only be read by a

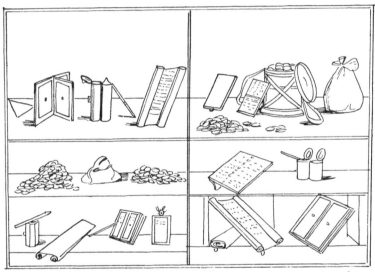

26. WRITING MATERIALS (FROM A POMPEIAN WALL-PAINTING)
(BLÜMNER, *Die römischen Privataltertümer*)

special process.[28] In one system of invisible writing fresh milk was used as ink; the recipient sprinkled the paper with coal dust, and the letters became black.[29]

The durability of ink varied according to its quality; the papyri of Egypt and Herculaneum show that the ancients had strong inks which could last indefinitely as well as weak ones which faded easily. The papyri of Egypt, which remained buried in the sands for many centuries are still perfectly legible. The papyri of Herculaneum are papyrus rolls,[30] which were buried in a layer of damp ash in the eruption of A.D. 79, and came to light in the Bourbon era, when, owing to the peculiar conditions in which they had been for centuries, they had taken on the appearance and consistency of carbon. Opening these rolls is difficult today, because the papyrus has lost all elasticity; when an attempt is made to unroll one, it crumbles into dust. Nevertheless, such is the excellence of the ink, that the pages which are recovered can be read without difficulty. The opaque black of the letters can be perfectly distinguished against the clear black of the background.

But inks were also used which were so far from permanent that in the majority of cases it was sufficient to wipe a wet sponge over the papyrus to remove every trace of it; 'to give the sponge' meant to rub out.

Augustus had begun to write a tragedy on the subject of Ajax, the Greek hero who committed suicide by throwing himself on the point of his sword; when somebody asked him what point his Ajax had reached, he replied *'in spongeam incubuit'*[31] ('he has thrown himself on to his . . . sponge'). Being a shrewd man, he distrusted his ability as a tragic poet and destroyed his tragedy before destroying his hero. Martial advised an indifferent poet to describe the flood of Deucalion, as water was the most suitable material for his poem.[32] This was a polite way of saying 'Rub out everything with a sponge, you tiresome man, and leave the Muses in peace'. Caligula[33] punished the crimes of the pen with the tongue, by compelling indifferent versifiers to lick out their poems.

When today we realise, as we often do, that we have written something foolish, stupid, obscure or rude, as soon as common sense and self criticism have once more gained the upper hand, we rightly tear up these useless pages and toss them into the basket. Such a summary execution of one's writings was impossible in antiquity for two obvious reasons: papyrus and parchment, as has been said, were expensive materials and men thought twice before destroying them, and from a practical point of view the destruction of papyrus and parchment was a far from easy task for a man without strong hands. If one wanted to destroy the papyrus or parchment together with the writing, the whole thing had to be thrown into the fire; otherwise recourse was made to the previously mentioned sponge; either fire or water. Martial proposed the fire of Phaethon as an alternative theme for his indifferent poet. Horace[34] wrote to one of his mistresses, 'Oh daughter more beautiful than your beautiful mother, destroy my verses as you like, either with flame or with the Adriatic sea', again either by fire or water.

Metal pens with a point shaped to serve as a nib were known to the ancient world, and a certain number of such bronze pens have been discovered in excavations, but as writing instruments they were a rare exception; this would seem to prove that they worked extremely badly. Normally for writing on papyrus and parchment a pointed reed (*calamus*) was used or a goose feather (*penna*), similarly pointed and with the end split in two, so that the point had all the appearance of a nib, just like the goose quill of our ancestors. The best reeds came from Egypt or Cnidus. When the reed became blunt it was sharpened with a knife (*scalprum*); an impatient writer changed his pen, and, when writing, bundles of pens (*fasces calamorum*)[35] were always kept ready at hand in a pen-case (*theca libraria*).[36]

Notes, short letters, jottings and receipts, were written on wax tablets (*cerae*) as well as the first draft of a literary work.[37] We know that such tablets were used in certain magical practices and that if an experienced witch wrote the loved one's name on a tablet and then drew his picture and pierced his liver with a sharp needle, the unhappy man later suffered misfortune.[38] The wax was normally dark in colour, which explains the adjective *tristes* which Martial applies to *cerae*;[39] the *sanguinulentus color*,[40] to which Ovid refers, must have been a dark red, deep not bright.

The wax was spread on the inside of the tablet, which had raised edges, so that the wax was kept firmly in place. Normally several tablets were joined together with a cord passed through holes in the edge; the *cerae* were called *duplices, triplices, quin-quiplices*, etc., according to the number of tablets of which they were composed. They were also called by the Greek names of *diptycha, triptycha, polyptycha*. Two or more tablets bound together were called in early times *caudex* or *codex*;[41] each tablet was covered with wax on both sides, but in the *diptycha* only the inner side was waxed, giving it the appearance of a small book (Plate 44); the two outside surfaces acted as a cover. Some people cut their names on the back.

The meaning of the word *caudex* was later extended to include public notices, and later still the parchment books we still call *codices*; in fact we apply the name only to such parchment and paper *codices*. Since, in the later Empire, the Imperial constitutions circulated commercially written on parchment *codices*, a systematic collection of laws came to be called a Codex, either private (*codex Hermogenianus, codex Gregorianus*), or official (*codex Theodosianus, codex Justinianus*), and such collections of laws are still called a code from *codex* (civil code, penal code, etc.). So the meaning of the word has undergone a remarkable change, because *codex* (literally—tree trunk) should strictly be applied only to an object made chiefly of wood, as were the wax tablets, which started the word on its strange history.

The tablets were later called *codicilli* or *pugillares*, especially the smaller ones, as well as *Vitelliani*; the latter, probably much smaller and smarter, seem to have been used for the exchange of lovers' notes.[42]

The shape of the parchment codices was also derived from the wax tablets, since besides wood and wax, they were also made of ivory and parchment; these latter, real pocket-books[43] or smaller versions which were handier to use, especially when travelling (they are first mentioned in Martial),[44] must be regarded as the earliest examples of the parchment codex and therefore of the modern type of book.

Letters were cut on the wax with a long thin, pointed stick, called *stilus* or *graphium*, which was said *arare* or *exarare*, literally to plough a furrow. At the other end of the *stilus* was a small round or flat spatula, which was used to erase any letters already written or to smooth the surface of the wax; *stilum vertere* was to 'correct' or 'alter'.

It will be noted that the origin of some words which are still used in connexion with writing can be traced back to the days when men wrote on wax tablets. Thus *stilus* ended by meaning in Latin the practice of writing, and *exarare* to write even with pen and ink.

The modern 'style', a noble word, meaning the choicest expression of the personality of a writer in his selection and arrangement of words is derived from *stilus*. Buffon said 'Style is the man'; long ago it was a simple stick tipped with iron, bone or ivory, used to cut letters on wax.

Wax tablets were the most convenient method of transmitting private messages, particularly between lovers; in this case, so that nobody except the sender and the receiver might read the contents, they were bound with a cord (*linum*),[45] and sealed. For greater security the cord was passed through a hole in the centre of the tablet.

In spite of the relative scarcity of writing material in the Roman world (see p. 175), from the last two centuries of the Republic onwards a great deal of writing was done. The administration of the state itself demanded a considerable expenditure of paper, as the central authority had to keep in constant touch with the governors of distant provinces and the local magistrates of minor centres.

Fly sheets, copies of the *acta diurna populi*, also circulated, an official publication announcing the more important public events (*senatus consulta*, magisterial edicts, later on, Imperial decrees), in addition apparently to items of daily news, a real city chronicle. The originals were preserved in the public archives and were an invaluable source of information for later historians. The reader, however, must be on his guard against believing that the journal had in Rome the circulation, the variety of contents, and the consequent importance of a modern newspaper. It was only an embryonic and very simple form of newspaper; neither journalists nor journalism existed. The character which the press gives our civilisation was completely absent in Rome, though even then, we gather from a correspondent of Cicero,[46] the rumours which circulated (*fabulae, rumores*) were also reported in the journals. But man has always loved gossip. Copies of the *acta diurna* circulated throughout Rome and were dispatched to the provinces, carrying with them a breath of the life of the capital. But the information they gave was limited; a glance was enough to master the contents. The ancient Roman had no *Times*.

In the higher classes a great deal of paper was consumed. An influential man who played an active part in public life had a thousand reasons for writing; he had to maintain a correspondence with a large number of people, to compose his speeches and, arrange their publication. Many also wrote books; as we have seen, it was very rare for a Roman distinguished in public life not to enrich contemporary literature with some work of a scientific nature, in which experience acquired in some branch of knowledge was preserved, or of a more purely literary character. Caesar, Augustus and many of the emperors were writers and poets. What the Romans called *otium*, the time left free from the conduct of public affairs (*negotia*), was a laborious leisure in which many rolls of paper were annually consumed. The administration of the family estate, which every *paterfamilias* looked after carefully and which required the work of secretaries, accountants and mere writers who spent their entire day writing, involved the use of a great deal of paper. In the wealthiest families a certain number of slaves *librarii* or *amanuenses* (see p. 123) were trained in writing. Slaves employed in writing correspondence from dictation or copying were called *servi ab epistolis* (*a litteris, a codicillis*).

The master also employed the *librarii* to copy books which he had written himself, or those of other authors which he needed for his own library; if possible, he made them correct the copy of a book which he possessed by comparing it with another more exact copy. But during the last days of the Republic, it became increasingly common to go to a bookseller (*bibliopola*) to obtain a book, and either buy a copy which was for sale, or commission one. This must have been the commoner method, as the number of copies on sale was limited by the amount of time taken in copying.

There were many booksellers in Rome; their shops stood in the *Argiletum* (see p. 34) and its neighbourhood. They had a large number of scribes in their employment; when a book was in great demand it was dictated to a large number of slaves simultaneously. The role of the bookseller, in an age without printing and copyright laws, easily merged with that of the publisher; great booksellers and publishers in the age of Cicero were T. Pomponius Atticus,[47] in the Augustan age the Sosii[48] brothers, in the Flavian age Tryphon,[49] the publisher of Martial and Quintilian, besides smaller booksellers like Attrectus,[50] Secundus[51] and others.

In a cultivated society, in which the habit of reading was widespread even among busy politicians, the book trade was as active as it could be so long before the invention of printing. The number of private libraries was large; most aristocratic families possessed several in their city and country houses. There were sometimes considerable libraries, for example that of the poet Persius,[52] which he left in his will to his teacher Annaeus Cornutus. Even in the baths there were libraries for the use of the bathers.

Under the Empire public libraries began to be opened, following a custom of the Hellenistic states. The first was founded by Asinius Pollio, in the *Atrium Libertatis*, the Censors' office; it was a magnificent building decorated with the statues of the greatest authors. The second was opened by Augustus in a building with colonnades next to the temple of Apollo on the Palatine (see p. 21). It held a large number of texts of Greek and Latin authors, and a very extensive collection of legal works. A colossal statue of Augustus as Apollo stood there, and, like the library of Asinius Pollio, it was decorated with busts of famous authors, including the great orators. Augustus added a smaller library to the *Porticus Octavia*.[53] The number of public libraries was rapidly increased by Tiberius (in the *Domus Tiberiana* on the Palatine),[54] Vespasian (adjoining the *Templum Pacis*),[55] and Trajan, who had one of the finest libraries in Rome, the *Bibliotheca Ulpia*, built in his Forum.[56] Still later a library was built on the Capitol.[57] By the fourth century A.D. there were twenty-eight public libraries in Rome (see p. 1).

The subject of books has made this brief account of booksellers and libraries at Rome necessary, and in a chapter dealing with the materials used for letter writing a short description of Roman postal services seems appropriate.

A short while back we observed that the ease with which we can procure paper is one of the fundamental differences between our age and the ancient world. Another is the ease, speed and low cost of our postal services. In antiquity a postal service existed, but it was only used by the state, as the authorities in the capital had to be in constant touch with the civil and military heads of provinces. A state service was first regularly organized in Persia, at the beginning of the fifth century B.C. by Darius the Great, whose postal messengers are referred to by the Greek form of their Persian name, ἄγγαροι. The Hellenistic states, which succeeded the break-up of Alexander's empire, also enjoyed a regular postal service, but the most complete and efficient service was the achievement of the Roman Empire.

The state ensured the regularity of the postal service by establishing at fixed intervals along the most important roads, usually the military highways, couriers or postal waggons, which passed the letters they received as quickly as possible to the next postal station.

In the Roman world, from Augustus onwards, the postal service, called by various names (*cursus publicus, cursus vehicularis, cursus fiscalis, res veredaria*, etc.), developed into an extensive and complex organisation. The Praetorian prefects, trusted servants of the Emperor, were entrusted with the supervision of this service, which reached its perfection under Constantine who assigned its duties to various officials; at the head of it in each province was the governor (*praeses*), who had at his command a magistrate solely responsible for the postal service (*praefectus vetriculorum*).

These magistrates were responsible for the maintenance of everything connected with the service; they had to keep up roads, repair bridges, ensure the regular working of the local offices, etc. For this purpose a province was divided into postal districts, each with a supervisor (*manceps*) in charge, and under him a certain number of subordinate officials and slaves trained in particular tasks: arranging for the change of the post horses (*stationarii*), looking after the animals (*muliones, hippocomi*), or curing them if they were ill (*mulomedici*, or 'vets'), supplying fodder (*stratores*), repairing the carriages (*carpentarii*), etc. The post-horses were strong and swift, and their riders did not spare the whip in their haste; some savage riders, to urge their horses faster, seem even to have employed a stick, and the law had to intervene to protect the horses and forbid such brutal methods. A decree of Constantine,[58] allows the whip, but forbids the stick. The expenses of the postal service were met by the local government.

Only occasionally were private citizens allowed to use the state postal service; normally they had to arrange for the delivery of their correspondence at their own expense; for this purpose they used their own slaves called *tabellarii*, or if letters had to be sent a great distance at speed, *cursores*. If circumstances allowed, the delivery of a letter was entrusted to friends or guests on their travels, business men, or foreign letter carriers from the destination of the letter. When a letter-carrier left for a distant spot, the friends of the sender used him for the dispatch of their own correspondence to his destination or to places on his route. In practice, a kind of mutual assistance society for postal purposes grew up amongst prolific letter-writers. This exchange of services made possible a fairly regular delivery of private letters; but even so, it was not rare for letters to remain lying for some time with their writer waiting for an opportunity to dispatch them.[59] To avoid inconvenience, a man with many political or business friendships maintained a considerable number of private messengers amongst his slaves. But it was always an inadequate service, and, furthermore, an enormously expensive one, if we consider that the cost of the reply must be added to the cost of the slaves; a single letter sometimes involved the expense of a long journey. Today for sixpence we can send a letter from London to Hongkong.

The post is a delicate business, and so in sending letters it was necessary amongst other things to be extremely careful to employ slaves of tested loyalty and intelligence or people whose tact could be relied on. The contents, naturally, remained secret, and as envelopes did not exist, the letters, if written on papyrus, were folded so that the writing remained inside, and were then bound with a thread and sealed. The seal, which performed the task of the signature today, in antiquity guaranteed the authenticity of the letter when it was not in the sender's handwriting, which happened rarely, because letters were normally written by the sender himself.

For official correspondence magistrates, besides having an official staff (*apparitores*) for the delivery of correspondence, regularly used their own private slaves, who travelled by the public postal system.

The choice of a bearer was particularly important in the case of an official letter whose delivery involved a rigid etiquette.

Further Reading

F. G. Kenyon, *Books and Readers in Ancient Greece and Rome* (Oxford, 1950). 2nd Edition.

J. Cerny, *Paper and Books in Ancient Egypt* (Oxford, 1952).

NOTES

1. *Charta*, from which 'chart' is derived, is the Latin for papyrus (from the Greek χάρτης; cp. χαράσσω to scratch, or write).

2. The Athenian 'ostracism', a special sentence of exile for ten years passed on a citizen for political reasons, took its name from the potsherd on which the citizen's name was written by those who wished to exile him (hence in Latin *testularum suffragia*, Cornelius Nepos, Them., 8, 1). Potsherds with the names of Megacles, Xanthippus, and Themistocles have survived. The Romans scratched the year in which the wine had been made, or bottled, on amphorae. (CIL, XV, 4539: *Ti. Claudio P. Quinctilio co(n)s(ulibus)* (=13 B.C.) *a(nte) d(iem) XIII K(alendas) Iun(ias) vinum diffusum (est) quod natum est duobus Lentulis co(n)s(ulibus)* (= 18 B.C.), cf. Horace, Odes, III, 21, i: *O nata mecum*

consule Manlio; Epist. I, 5, 4: *Vina bibes iterum Tauro diffusa,* 'you will drink a wine bottled in the second consulship of Taurus' (26 B.C.). Many inscribed potsherds have been found during excavations in Egypt.

3. Martial, XIV, 5.

4. The spread of the use of papyrus began after the conquests of Alexander the Great and the foundation of Alexandria (Varro, in Pliny, N.H., XIII, 69).

5. Election manifestos and military instructions of great age are written on the walls of Pompeii in red ink (see p. 133).

6. Aristotle, Ath. Pol., 7, 1.

7. Pliny, N. H., XIII, 69.

8. Digest, XXXII, 52 pr: *Volumina in tilia, ut nonnulli conficiunt.*

9. Persius, 1, 131; cf. Aristophanes, Clouds, 177.

10. Dion., 13.

11. The manufacture of paper is a Chinese invention, going back to the second century A.D.; the use of paper was introduced into Europe by the Arabs in the ninth century; the first paper-works were consequently in Spain, a country under Arab influence, from where the paper industry spread throughout Europe (France, twelfth century, Italy, thirteenth, Germany, fourteenth). Paper was made from rags soaked in water. The view that a paper made of cotton once existed has been shown to be unfounded.

12. Pliny, N.H., XIII, 71.

13. Ibid. XIII, 75.

14. Cicero, Ad. Qu. fr., XI, 14, 1.

15. Martial, XIV, 209.

16. Suetonius, Divus Julius, 56.

17. Cicero, Ad Att., V, 1, 3.

18. Ibid. IV, 4a: *Et velim mihi mittas de tuis librariolis duos aliquos quibus Tyrannio utatur glutinatoribus.*

19. Pliny, N.H., XIII, 70.

20. *Liber* is strictly a book of papyrus, because *liber* in its original meaning was the inside of the bark of a tree. The word was later extended to include all books of any shape and material. This varying meaning of the word *liber* gave rise to legal disputes; but the imperial legal system ruled that the word must be understood in its widest meaning. Ulpian (lib XXIV ad Sabinum = Digest XXXII, 52, pr) lays down: *Librorum appellatione continentur omnia volumina, sive in charta, sive in membrana sint, sive in quavis alia materia;* and mentions particularly slates, ivory and wax tablets.

21. Digest, XXXII, 52 pr: *membranas libris legatis.*

22. Persius, 3, 10; Isidorus, Orig., VI, 11, 4.

23. Martial, I, 2, 2–3. The first book of Martial's Epigrams was published in A.D. 85–6, and epigram 1, 2 must have been written just

before that date. The first mention of parchment *codices* can therefore be placed to 84 B.C.

24. Charm., I, 1–2.

25. Cicero, Ad Att., iv, 4a.

26. Vitruvius, II, 9, 13; cf. Horace, Ars Poet., 331–2: *carmina . . . linenda cedro.*

27. Persius, 3, 14.

28. Pliny, N.H., XXVI, 62.

29. Ovid, Ars Am., III, 627–8:

> *Tuta quoque est fallitque oculos e lacte recenti*
> *Littera (carbonis pulvere tange, leges).*

30. Perhaps they formed part of the library of Philodemus, an Epicurean philosopher, who owned a villa at Herculaneum. [But see Cicero, in Pisonem, ed. R. G. M. Nisbet (Oxford, 1961), Appendix IV and references there.]

31. Suetonius, Aug., 85.

32. V, 53.

33. Suetonius, Calig., 20.

34. Odes, I, 16, 1–4.

35. Martial, XIV, 38.

36. Ibid. 19.

37. Juvenal, I, 63; Pliny, Epist., I, 6, 1.

38. Ovid, Amores, III, 7, 29–30.

39. XIV, 5, 1.

40. Amores, I, 12, 12.

41. Seneca, De Brev. Vitae, 13, 4: *Plurium tabularum contextus caudex apud antiquos vocatur.*

42. Ovid, Amores, I, 12, 1–2; Martial, XIV, 8.

43. Martial, XIV, 7.

44. Ibid. 1, 2.

45. Plautus, Bacch., 714, 748; Pseud. 42.

46. Caelius (in Cicero, Ad fam., VIII, 1, 1) describing the *res urbanae*, details *senatus consulta, edicta, fabulae, rumores.*

47. Cornelius Nepos, Att., 13, 1; cf. Fronto, p. 20; Atticus' bookshop continued even after his death, and the books which we find mentioned as Ἀττικιανά came from it.

48. Horace, Epist., I, 20, 2; Ars Poet., 345.

49. Quintilian, Praef.; Martial, IV, 72, 2; XIII, 3, 4.

50. Martial, I, 117, 13.

51. Ibid. I, 2, 7.

52. Vita A. Persi Flacci, 1.

53. Suetonius, De Gramm., XXI; cf. Ovid, Tristia, III, 1, 69.

54. Aulus Gellius, XII, 20, 1.

55. Ibid. V, 21, 9; XVI, 8, 2.
56. Dio Cassius, LXVIII, 16.
57. Paulus Orosius, VII, 16.
58. Cod. Inst., XII, 51, 1.
59. Cicero, Ad Qu. fr., III, 1, 7, 23; *Multos dies epistolam in manibus habui propter commorationem tabellariorum;* and *passim.*

CHAPTER XVII

Law

Dignity of the law at Rome. Essentially political character of the law in the Republic. Differences between Roman and modern legal practice. Law a profession in the Empire. Iuris consultus and orator. Iuris consultus. The orator an adviser, not a representative. Roman criminal procedure. The law a heavy responsibility. The preparation of a case (meditatio). *The case in court. The peroration.* Causidici.

IN every modern society, even amongst educated people who might have been expected to be more reasonable, there is so widespread a prejudice against lawyers of every kind that the word 'lawyer' often has an opprobrious ring.

This prejudice is a longstanding one, perhaps partly literary in origin, as it has been maintained by the rancour of those authors, especially poets, who have been forced by their fathers to adopt the legal profession, while themselves nourishing far different ambitions. The poetical instinct, killed by the subtleties of the law and the depressing spectacle of litigation, produced in them an abhorrence for everything connected with the law, judges or legal procedure. Petrarch[1] went so far as to say that he had not wanted to devote his life to the law, as he found distasteful a profession which allowed no choice between being dishonest and seeming ignorant.

Among the Romans no occupation was considered nobler, more honourable or more useful than the practice of the law. The Forum was the first ring for a politician's training,[2] and even when Republican freedom had declined, Rome, which had spread civilisation and the rule of law, continued to hold oratory in high regard.

Advocates [we read in a late Imperial decree[3]] who illuminate the uncertainties of a case, and both in public and private actions restore the fortunes of those who have fallen and re-establish rights that have been trampled on, are no less useful to the human race than those who risk battles and wounds to fight for the safety of their country and their parents; we feel that it is not only those who are armed with swords, shields and armour who fight for our empire, but advocates as well; theirs too is a service; they defend the life, hopes and posterity of the litigants who trust in the protection of their powerful eloquence.

During the Republic all the greatest men of Rome (with the single exception of Marius, who reached political eminence through his outstanding military ability) were expert speakers. A father took his young sons to the Forum to learn eloquence and study public life, which found its fullest expression in legal discussions. Cato the Censor could never have resisted the bitter attacks of his enemies if he had not been a man of extraordinary eloquence; in spite of being accused forty-four times, he was always acquitted;[4] he succeeded in maintaining a rigid code of conduct in political and civil life because his powers of oratory both in prosecution and defence made him one of the most formidable figures in the Forum. Caius Gracchus was a very young man when he entered public life with the defence of his friend Vettius,[5] and attracted a great deal of attention. Cicero, besides being very young, was a man of humble origins when a parricide case with a political background[6] offered him his chance; his eloquent defence gained him in a few days a leading position in the Forum[7] and laid the foundations of his future political success, although he had previously been completely unknown. For a *homo novus* who was not a member of one of the families where the exercise of power was hereditary, a resounding victory in the conrts opened up the road to the consulship. The defendants of today were the electors of tomorrow, and the nobility who tried to make a closed circle of the magistracies could not afford to disregard anybody who might be a powerful ally or a formidable adversary in the struggles of the Forum. Even Hortensius, an orator of distinction, reached the consulship, though when we examine his character he appears as insignificant as a politician as he was outstanding as an advocate.

But between the advocate of the Republic, when liberty was still flourishing and the great art of rhetoric reached its highest point, and the modern barrister there are some essential differences.

Today the law is a profession; it is quite normal nowadays for a man to make his living from the law alone, and find in his work an honourable, and possibly profitable, occupation. But in Rome the practice of the law was a civil function to which men devoted themselves only for the authority and political prestige it would bring them, and not for any financial reward. Legal assistance, though nominally free, was sometimes financially rewarded by a private understanding between the parties; the *lex Cincia* in 204 B.C. laid down *ne quis ob causam orandam pecuniam donumve acciperet,*[8] but this ban was not rigorously observed later, especially by the recipients. This was one of those laws (*leges imperfectae*) which neither declared that the forbidden actions were *contra legem*, nor laid down punishment for those who committed them; consequently it tended to fall into disuse, even though it was frequently re-enacted, for the last time by Augustus. The situation seems to have been that the client was not obliged to pay a fee nor had the advocate the right to demand one, still less to exact it legally. Demanding a fee in advance was considered particularly dishonourable.[9] However, if at the end of the case one gave and the other received, there could be no objection, though there is no evidence that this always took place. Payment was a private matter and not compulsory and never became an essential part of the Roman legal system.

Throughout the Republican era the practice of the law was inseparable from the many activities of a Roman politician in a world where nobody could triumph without ambition and determination. The financial side of this activity was of minor importance.

With the rise of the Principate, however, the lower tone of public life robbed the law of its essentially political character, and although in the early days of the Empire wealthy men like Pliny the Younger continued the noble tradition of a free defence,[10] the law largely degenerated into a profession, liberal, noble and certainly necessary, but none the less a profession. Claudius[11] ruled that advocates had a right to a fee although he limited it to a maximum of 10,000 sesterces. In the later days of the Empire, advocates, who became merely a professional class, constituted an order (*collegia* or *corpora advocatorum*), with lists of their members (*matriculae*), collective interests to maintain and a set of rules.

To find a more exact correspondence between Roman advocacy and our own, we must wait for the fall of the Republic and the decline of the spirit of liberty which had given birth to it.

If we examine ancient legal procedure other differences become apparent. Today the lawyer who has the confidence of his client, is, according to the circumstances of the case, either consultant or defender. The pure theorist, a professor of law who lives far from the courts, for example, is cut off from the practical field of individual cases and of close personal interest which belongs exclusively to the barrister; whether it is a question of examining the legal basis of an argument or of defending the rights of a plaintiff, the same man is employed; he advises whether or not to start a case, appears in court, and finally prepares the terms of settlement. It is inconceivable to us that a man should first ask a jurist for his opinion and then go to a barrister and instruct him to conduct the case on these lines. Such behaviour would be the surest way of being shown the door.

In the Roman legal system, however, the man who studies the legal aspect of a question and suggests the best method of conducting a case, is not usually the person who presents the case in court; one is the *iuris consultus* who gives opinions, the other is the *orator* who appears in court beside his clients and pleads their case (*orare* in Latin originally meant 'to plead'); one is a man of learning, the other is a battle companion.

This difference between the *iuris consultus* and the *orator* was maintained in Rome in the procedure in civil cases at the time of the so called 'formulary system' in force at the end of the Republic.

Let us try to illustrate the procedure by an imaginary case between Titus, who is, or claims to be, owed a sum of money by Gaius, which he has lent him and which he wishes to recover, and Gaius who refuses to acknowledge the existence of the debt.

In the early days of Roman law an expeditious procedure was allowed; if Titus wished to establish his right to repayment, he issued a summary command to Gaius to appear with him before the magistrates (*in ius vocare*);[12] if he refused, or tried to escape, Titus obtained the evidence of witnesses, arrested him and dragged him *in ius*, before the legal authorities. Later procedure, however, required that the plaintiff, before dragging the defendant before the magistrate, should inform him of the reasons for his action (*editio actionis*), although the right to resort to more energetic methods was still authorised by law if the plaintiff refused to appear.

The legislator, if he authorises private violence, has inevitably resigned himself to allowing disorder, such as Horace[13] depicts when he describes the process of *rapere in ius* of a man who refuses to appear. 'He hurries the man to court; both parties are shouting and there is a general commotion.' In the same way Cicero[14] tells us of the struggle he had, when he wanted to secure the possession of a document, with a man who wished to prevent him from getting it. To decide which of the two was right they dragged each other before the praetor, and disorder resulted:

I tried to seize the tablets on which the decree was written. At once there was fresh trouble and disputation. A man called Theomnastus took the tablets and held on to them— the sort of man whom the boys follow about, and who makes everyone laugh as soon as he opens his mouth. His craziness, however, while it amuses others, was on this occasion a real nuisance to myself. He foamed at the mouth, his eyes blazed, and he shouted at the top of his voice that I was assaulting him, and we were still struggling together as we reached the praetor's court.

In a private case, the two litigants appeared once before the praetor with their various arguments and explained them. This procedure was called *in iure*, and its object was not the final solution of the case, but the examination of the legal foundation of the argument. The case was then settled after a second appearance before a judge[15] (*apud judicem*), chosen by the parties or nominated by the praetor and agreed to by the parties. But most people did not appear before the praetor without first having had their case examined by a *iuris consultus*. Obviously, in fact, the ultimate victory depended largely on the preliminary presentation of the case in court. The praetor did not merely hand down his *formula* from the bench, ordering the parties to appear before a judge, but if both parties seemed prepared to make concessions he helped them to reach a compromise.

To the activities of the *iuris consulti* Rome owes the imperishable glory of having been throughout history the mistress of law to the world. The transfer of the control of law from the priests to the laity, when the interpretation of law ceased to be a monopoly of the *Pontifices* and consequently a privilege of the nobility, favoured the development of law and originated a tradition which lasted for centuries. From then on nobody with education and a legal sense found any limit or obstacle to his ambition of becoming a *iuris consultus.*

The work of a *iuris consultus*, noble in itself and congenial to the practical and well-balanced character of the Romans, served also to further the political ambitions of those who practised it. In Rome, where a ruling class depended for power on the votes of the people, even the nobles had no way of asserting themselves unless they could rely on the support of faithful clients. The assistance freely offered as a *iuris consultus* to his followers and clients and the popularity thus gained opened the way to the *cursus honorum* for a man with political ambitions. The citizen in the *comitium* willingly voted for the man who had advised him when in doubt on the desirability of undertaking a case, the strength of his claims, the procedure of prosecuting or defending or even on the legality of some intended action. He had no other way of showing his gratitude to the man who had helped him than by voting for him.

The aspirant to power in Rome had to be prepared for arduous toil and heavy sacrifices. The mornings of a man in search of prestige and votes by practising as a *iuris consultus* were laborious. The crowd of clients in the *atrium* of his mansion for the *salutatio matutina* were not there simply to greet him, but to ask him for an opinion. He received them, gave them advice and asked for no return. The consultations were not the tête-a-tête interviews of a modern solicitor's office, but took place before a crowd of other clients as well as young aristocrats, aspiring jurists and politicians who listened in order to learn. Some returned for more advanced and less public consultations to ask for further clarification, and other took notes of these pearls of wisdom, destined after a long process of publication and elaboration to survive to our day. Those who attended consultations for practical or personal reasons, were interested in the conduct of a case similar to one in which they were directly concerned, they attended without prejudice to their right to return and consult about their own affairs. In this way an elementary knowledge of law spread even among the people, unlike the period of priestly justice which had turned the law into a mystery.

The necessity of being always at the disposal of the public from cockcrow onwards struck Horace as a great imposition, and he advised (see p. 60) an advocate to escape through the servant's door, imagining the *iuris consultus* sleeping the tranquil sleep of the countryside:

> *Agricolam laudat iuris legumque peritus,*
> *Sub galli cantum consultor ubi ostia pulsat.*[16]

But to escape by the *posticum* to a life of leisure in the country did not seem to the Romans the way best calculated to achieve power. It was impossible to become a master in Rome without beginning as a servant. The greatest *iuris consulti*, Sextus Aelius, the Scaevolas, P. Sulpicius Rufus, were politicians who became consuls. It seems to have been rare for a *iuris consultus* not to pass through the whole *cursus honorum* and reach the consulship; when Quintus Marcius Figulus, one of the most popular *iuris consulti*, suffered such a rebuff and rose no higher than the praetorship, he consoled himself with a jest: *an vos consulere scitis, consulem facere nescitis?*[17]

Unlike the *iuris consultus*, the *orator* assisted his clients in the two stages of the case *in iure* and *apud iudicem*; his abilities as an advocate shone particularly before the judges, because, as still happens today, the discussion of fact formed the most vital part of a case, and provided most scope for surprise; it is at this stage of a case that the greatest reverses occur, demanding the greatest quickness from the defence. *Advocati*, in the original sense of the word, are all those who on the day of a trial lend assistance in any way to a litigant, either by practical suggestions or by their mere presence near him in court.

However much the duties of the *iuris consultus* and the *orator* may have differed to meet the different demands of individual cases and clients, a leading *orator* had also to have a sound knowledge of law. Cornelius Nepos[18] praises Cato, a man of outstanding eloquence, for having been *peritus iuris consultus* and *probabilis orator*; Quintilian[19] gave the same praise to Cicero; Cicero himself, when discussing the training of an orator, does not forget that *neque legum ac iuris civilis scientia neglegenda est*.[20] He regards their limited knowledge of law as a failing in some of the greatest orators, like C. Papirius Carbo[21] 'uncertain in his knowledge of the laws of our ancestors, and unskilled in civil law', and Marcus Antonius,[22] whose *divina vis ingenii* was *scientia iuris nudata*.

Cicero should not therefore be taken literally, when he mocks[23] with good humoured irony at the knowledge of the jurist. The many-sided wit of great advocates is well-known. Certain attitudes may seem suitable and desirable in a particular legal situation and a little 'judicious levity' may be allowed. But it is remarkable that an advocate, *orator*, could publicly declare himself to be so completely different from the *iuris consultus*, that a knowledge of law was no affair of his, a thing which no modern barrister, however ineffective, would dare to do, without implicitly admitting that he was more ineffective than he was.

Another difference is that under the Republic the advocate only helped his client: he stood near him in court, made suggestions, spoke on his behalf; a litigant had largely to fend for himself. Today, however, a litigant in a civil case entrusts its management to a barrister, and does not attend court, or goes there only to see for himself how his case is going or to remind his barrister of some last minute detail which he considers vital to his case.

In criminal procedure also there were differences between modern and Roman law, though there are some similarities: the accused is guaranteed certain safeguards, such as a public trial and the right to cross-examine. Even in the Imperial age, when public liberty was enslaved and eloquence had decayed, there were much publicised criminal trials and distinguished criminal barristers still flourished, including Pliny and Tacitus. Then, as now, poison cases attracted the morbid interest of the public, and enormous crowds attended them and followed their progress; the daily chronicles of Rome were full of them. But the absence of one figure in the Roman legal system strikes us as a grave shortcoming.

In Rome, as in the free cities of Greece, no permanent organisation for public prosecution existed; there was no Director of Public Prosecutions, and it was left to one private citizen to prosecute another; the defence of the law was left to the initiative of the citizen. Consequently, during the Republic the duty of the prosecutor, though sometimes abused, was in itself a noble duty. All the great men of Rome played the part of prosecutors in their time.[24] Except in his prosecution of Verres, Cicero always preferred the role of defender to that of prosecutor. Yet he observed *accusatores multos esse in civitate utile est ut metu contineatur audacia*.[25] His argument was that a man who is unjustly accused always has the chance of being acquitted, while a guilty man can never be condemned if he is not prosecuted; that an innocent man should face a prosecution in which his innocence can be established, was not so great a disaster as it would be for a guilty man never to be accused. A little more than a century later Quintilian[26] stated:

> While to devote one's life to the task of accusation, and to be tempted by the hope of reward to bring the guilty to trial is little better than making one's living by highway robbery, none the less to rid one's country of the pests that gnaw its vitals is conduct worthy of comparison with that of heroes who champion their country's cause on the field of battle.

At Rome the practice of the law was a serious undertaking which demanded a great deal of activity and involved the risk of making enemies (*suscipere inimicitias*). An advocate cannot be any respecter of persons. Even in the Imperial Age the servility of clients towards their patron had not reached the point when they did not demand prompt and energetic support in their lawsuits; otherwise, what was the use of attending on a patron in this humiliating way? Martial complains:[27]

> I have a lawsuit with Balbus: you don't wish to offend Balbus, Ponticus: I have one with Licinus: he, too, is a great man. My next door neighbour, Patrobas, often trespasses on my small field: you are afraid to oppose Caesar's freed-man. Laronia denies that I lent her my slave and keeps him: you ill answer me, 'She is childless, rich, old, a widow.'

Martial means that her husband will be a lucky man, particularly as she is old and may therefore die soon; better therefore not to annoy her with lawsuits; but he concludes: 'It is useless, believe me, to be the slave of a slave, though he is a friend: let him be free who shall wish to be my lord.' It was worse in the Republic. The advocate had always to be on call; not even the consulship protected him from the obligation of defending his clients in court.[28] There is no excuse for one who is asked for assistance until right has triumphed. *Iuris consulti* and advocates sit in their houses from early morning and 'envy the farmer, when towards cock-crow a client comes knocking at the door';[29] if they wish to take an hour of freedom, they are compelled to follow the advice of Horace and escape by the servants' door, abandoning the determined client waiting in the *atrium*.[30]

The great advocate did not appear in court without having first thoroughly mastered the details of the case. The mass of information on Roman eloquence makes it quite certain that no advocates in Rome took their duties lightly. The essential seriousness of the Romans (which had a number of defects—they need no tiresome apologies unbecoming in a historian but not that of frivolity in serious matters) is never so obviously praiseworthy as when we see it engaged in the administration of the law.

Studying a case did not merely involve examining the details with care, testing the value of witnesses in advance, foreseeing the arguments of one's opponent and preparing evidence. Even the most gifted advocate never relied exclusively on improvisation. Every detail of his speech was carefully prepared beforehand, including his gestures and his tone of voice; this was *meditatio, meditari causam*. Every advocate carefully rehearsed in his study the speech which he was to deliver in court. He was not alone but was usually surrounded by slave secretaries to whom he dicatated notes, phrases and entire paragraphs. He later revised the transcript, added, altered or began entirely afresh. He did not cease from this preparation until the most important details of the speech had been completed to his taste.

Some advocates, like Marcus Antonius, endowed with powerful memories, learned the prepared speech by heart and recited it as though it was extemporary;[31] others threw themselves into the *meditatio* with such energy that they believed they were actually in the Forum. Once Servius Sulpicius Galba, when he was about to begin the actual trial in a serious and difficult case, left his study with his face so inflamed and with such a flashing eye 'that one might have said that he had already discussed the case, not that he had merely prepared it'.[32] Behind him filed his unfortunate secretaries, dazed and shattered by the furious oratory of this great man, who shrieked, railed, paced up and down the room and gesticulated extravagantly. It is unnecessary to add that he won the case.

When the moment for the trial arrived, the plaintiff and defendant were surrounded by influential friends; this was much more the case in criminal than in civil proceedings, and even if they had no intention of speaking, their presence beside their protégé helped to give him the support of their authority and prestige.[33] As has been said (see p. 198), in the Republican Age the advocate only assisted his client; consequently, until the *orator* rose to speak, nobody knew for certain who amongst so many *advocati* was the advocate in a particular case.[34]

Speeches probably did not always have the continuity they have in our courts, and which we find in the speeches of Cicero. As they were published with alterations and rearrangements after delivery, it was possible to collect in a single speech the brief discourses delivered at various stages of the case. The·examination of a witness might also lead to what might be described as an incidental speech, as, for example, in the *in Vatinium* of Cicero. In the *actio prior in Verrem*, which is an opening speech, the orator alternated his rhetorical comments with the straightforward presentation of evidence.

In his prosecution of Sextus Roscius, Amerinus Erucius behaved very strangely: 'If an idea came to him, he sat down; then he began to pace to and fro; sometimes he called his slave to him, I suppose, to give orders for dinner.'[35] He spoke as if, instead of being in front of the bench of judges, he was alone in his own house.

The method of speaking naturally varied according to the character and inclination of the speaker; there were impetuous orators and dialectical ones; among some, passion prevailed, as with Galba,[36] C. Gracchus[37] and Marcus Antonius;[38] among others, cold reason, as with Laelius,[39] Crassus[40] and Hortensius.[41] Hortensius was one of those dangerous advocates who can sum up the arguments of their adversary incredibly quickly, divide them into single heads and demolish them one by one, counting them off on their fingers,[42] thus destroying the most persuasive speech, and annihilating his less quick witted opponent.

The greatest advocates knew to perfection the art of varying the tone of their speech to suit the different stages of the trial. Now they reasoned coldly, now they became impassioned and could hardly help arouse sympathy.

At the most dramatic points of their speeches orators were allowed a theatricality which would seem excessive today; their histrionic skill in varying their tone of voice, gestures and attitudes seemed spontaneous, but had been carefully rehearsed during the *meditatio*: stamping the foot, pacing to and fro before the eyes of the public,[43] or turning with a flattering allusion to some member of the upper-class jury, recalling his distinguished career or that of his ancestors,[44] all formed part of their repertoire. Hortensius disconcerted his opponent by his gestures and the attitudes he struck (*gestu ipso et motu corporis*);[45] Servius Sulpicius Galba,[46] when prosecuted and overwhelmed by the evidence, reading his condemnation in the faces of the jury, saved himself by displaying his young son and an orphan nephew whose guardian he was and embracing them publicly, while he continued his impassioned peroration. Marcus Antonius[47] in the difficult defence of M. Aquilius, seeing that he was losing the case, stripped the toga from his client's back, revealing on his naked body the scars of the serious and glorious wounds received in the campaign against the slaves in Sicily, and won by acclamation a case which had previously seemed hopeless.

Behind the *orator* stood a crowd of admiring spectators. When a well known orator was to speak, the news spread quickly and a large audience gathered.[48] In political cases the public took sides.[49] Comments were made on everything, including the personal appearance of the speaker. When the poet Calvus, a distinguished advocate but as small as he was fiery, was finishing his case against Vatinius, one of the public, at such surpassing eloquence coming from so small a body, cried out, 'Good heavens! this little salt-cellar speaks well!'[50]

The legal world has its successes and its failures; some shine brightly, and others earn a meagre livelihood by providing petty services for humble clients. In Rome in the Imperial Age, when the office of advocate was losing its earlier character of an important public duty, great cases and great advocates continued to flourish. At the same time a swarm of indifferent pleaders, the *causidici*,[51] began to infest Rome, greedy and vulgar professionals at the disposal of all—'People', says Quintilian,[52] 'for whom the Forum provides work, who make their voice earn their living, and whom it is fair to describe as competent advocates in private cases'; wordy, gesticulating, inconclusive and vain, they made an affair of state out of some trivial case, and in some wretched argument they found an opportunity for reverberating discourses. The client, deafened by this flood of words, went away unconvinced:

> My action is not one for assault or wounding, or poisoning: it concerns my three she-goats; I complain that they are lost by my neighbour's theft; this is the fact which the judge prescribes to be proved to him. You with a mighty voice and every gesture you know, make the court ring with Cannae and the Mithridatic War, and insensate Punic perjuries, and Sullas, and Mariuses and Muciuses. Now mention, Postumus, my three she-goats.[53]

When some of the more fortunate or more brazen of these *causidici* succeeded in gaining a reputation and making money, their insolence knew no bounds. Some went so far as to place an equestrian statue of themselves in the hall of their houses.[54] The client on entering saw the *causidicus* on horseback, looking fierce and impressive, and paid what he had to with greater goodwill. But, generally, the *causidici* were mediocre lawyers whose legal activities scarcely earned them enough to pay their rent.[55]

Most of them drew their clientele from the poorest classes, unsuccessful and embittered people whose means did not match their acrimonious passion for litigation. Being unable to employ an advocate, they resorted to a cheap imitation; they paid badly, and only when the festival of the Saturnalia came round and everyone by tradition was expected to exchange gifts or remember by some trifle those in whose debt they were, did they fill his house with proof, often edible, of their gratitude. The more the *causidici* received, the prouder they were and they eagerly boasted of their gifts to their friends as a proof of their fame and success. 'The Saturnalia has made Sabellus rich; with reason Sabellus is puffed up; and there is no man, he thinks and declares, among the lawyers, more fortunate.' The malicious Martial[56] goes on to give us a list of these magnificent gifts:

half a peck of spelt and crushed beans, a pound and a half of frankincense and pepper, sausages and a stuffed paunch, a flagon of black must and a jar of fig jelly, onion, snails and cheese; finally a small box with a few olives, a collection of seven cups for his kitchen and a napkin with a coloured border.

Obviously this is a malicious caricature of one of the lowest of his class. But behind it we can see the small pleader at Rome eagerly waiting for the Saturnalia and his clients' gifts. These paltry trifles[57] gave him a chance for ostentatious boasting at a time when that was the fashion.

Further Reading

There are a number of good introductions to Roman Law.

J. Declareuil, *Rome the Law Giver* (London, 1927).

H. F. Jolowicz, *Historical Introduction to the Study of Roman Law* (2nd edn., Cambridge, 1954).

A. H. J. Greenridge, *The Legal Procedure of Cicero's Time* (Oxford, 1901), is a special study.

NOTES

1. Epist. ad posteros: *Piguit perdiscere quo inhoneste uti nollem et honeste vix possem et, si vellem, purites inscitiae tribuenda esset.*

2. Tacitus, Dial. de orat., 34.

3. of A.D. 469, Cod. Just., II, 7, 14.

4. Pliny, N.H., VII, 100.

5. Plutarch, Caius Gracchus, 1, 3.

6. The prosecution of Sextus Roscius Amerinus.

7. Cicero, Brutus, 90, 312: *Prima causa publica pro Sex. Roscio dicta tantum commendationis habuit, ut non ulla esset, quae non digna nostro patrocinio videretur.*

8. Tacitus, Annals, XI, 5, 3.

9. It continued to be regarded as dishonourable even in the Imperial Age, when (see the following pages) charging a fee had become a normal practice. Quintilian, XII, 7, 11: *Paciscendi quidem ille piraticus mos et ponentium periculis pretia procul abominanda negotiatio etiam mediocriter improbis aberit.*

10. Quintilian, XII, 7, 8: *Quis ignorat quin id longe sit honestissimum ac liberalibus disciplinis et illo, quem exigimus, animo dignissimum non vendere operam nec elevare tanti beneficii auctoritatem?*

11. Tacitus, Annals, XI, 7, 8. In the Digest (L, 13, 1, 12) a maximum of one hundred *aurei* was laid down.

12. The Law of the Twelve Tables laid down (I, 1, Bruns): *Si in jus vocat, ito. Ni it antestamino: igitur em capito.*

13. Sat., I, 9, 77–78: *Rapit in jus; clamor utrimque, undique concursus.*

14. Act. II in Verrem, IV, 66, 148.

15. In certain civil cases (e.g. claims for possession) judgment was delivered by a college of *recuperatores*.

16. Sat., I, 1, 9–10.

17. Valerius Maximus, IX, 3, 2.

18. Cato, 3, 1.

19. XII, 3, 10: *Et. M. Tullius non modo inter agendum numquam destitutus est scientia juris sed etiam componere aliqua de eo coeperat.*

20. De orat., I, 5, 18.

21. Ibid. I, 10, 40: *haesitantem in majorum institutis, rudem in jure civili.*

22. Ibid. I, 38, 172.

23. pro Murena, 10, 23.

24. Quintilian, XII, 7, 3–4; Livy, XXXIX, 40, 5.

25. pro Sex. Roscio Amer., 20. 55.

26. Quintilian, XII, 7, 3: *Ut accusatoriam vitam vivere et ad deferendos reos praemio duci proximum latrocinio est, ita pestem intestinam propulsare cum propugnatoribus patriae comparandum.*

27. II, 32.

28. Cicero in the year he was aedile (69) defended Caecina and Fonteius; when he was praetor (66), Cluentius; when consul (63) Rabirius and Murena.

29. See note 16.

30. Epist., I, 5, 30–31: *postico falle clientem.*

31. Cicero, Brutus, 37, 139.

32. Ibid. 22, 87–88.

33. pro Sex. Roscio Amer., I, 1; 21, 59.

34. Ibid. 21, 59–66.

35. Ibid. 21, 59: *Ita neglegens esse coepit, ut cum in mentem veniret ei, resideret, deinde spatiaretur, nonnumquam etiam puerum vocaret, credo, cui cenam imperaret.*

36. Cicero, Brutus, 22, 86; 23, 89; De orat., III, 7, 28.

37. Tacitus, Dial, de orat., 26; Plutarch, C. Gracchus, 2, 5; Fronto, p. 14.

38. Cicero, Brutus, 38, 141.

39. Ibid. 23, 89; 86, 295.

40. Ibid. 38, 143; Quintilian, XII, 10, 10; Macrobius, V, 1, 46; Cicero adds that when the occasion required it, even Crassus could make his oratory impassioned (Brutus, 43, 158: *vehemens et interdum irata et plena iusti doloris oratio*). But it must be remembered that Cicero represents Crassus as a model of an orator endowed with all oratorical gifts and possessing all the skills needed for perfect eloquence; Crassus conforms to Cicero's ideal picture of an orator and Cicero sees him as a reflection of himself.

41. Cicero, Brutus, 88, 303.

42. Cicero, Divin. in Caec., 14, 45.

43. Ibid. Brutus, 38, 141; 43, 158; Quintilian, XI, 3, 126.

44. E.g. Cicero, Act. II in Verrem, IV, 31, 69 and frequently in other speeches.

45. Cicero, Divin. in Caec., 14, 46.

46. Livy, Epit., XLIX.

47. Ibid. Epit. LXX.

48. Cicero, Brutus, 43, 158.

49. Ibid. pro Milone, 1, 3; ad Qu. fr., II, 3, 1, 2, and *passim*.

50. Catullus, LIII.

51. The *causidici* (πραγματικόι) appeared much earlier in Greece. Cicero alludes to them (De orat., I, 45, 198) as *infimi homines mercedula adducti*.

52. XII, 1, 25: *Non enim forensem quandam instituimus operam, nec mercennariam vocem nec, ut asperioribus verbis parcamus, non inutilem sane litium advocatum, quem denique causidicum vulgo vocant.*

53. Martial, VI, 19.

54. Ibid. IX, 68, 6; cf. Juvenal, 7, 125 et seq.

55. Ibid. III, 38, 5–6.

56. Ibid. IV, 46.

57. Juvenal also (7, 119–21) gives a list of the gifts of a *causidicus* which Martial's had no cause to envy:

> *Quid vocis pretium? Siccus petasunculus et vas*
> *Pelamydum aut veteres, Maurorum epimenia, bulbi*
> *Aut vinum Tiberi devectum, quinque lagonae.*

'A dried ham, a jar of pickled sprats, sone old olives and five jars of poor wine'; these are the offerings to Juvenal's pleader.

CHAPTER XVIII

Medicine

Medicine at Rome. Empirical medicine. Professional doctors.

IT was a long time before doctors reached Rome. When Curius Dentatus was roasting turnips in the ashes and Cincinnatus was ploughing his own fields and for long afterwards, the medical profession was unknown. Those who fell ill were either cured with some herbal remedy or died; in neither case did a doctor receive blame or praise for the result.

But while there were no doctors there was still an art of medicine; later Latin writers make it clear that this distinction is necessary. 'There are thousands of people who live without doctors, but who still do not live without medicine', writes Pliny the Elder.[1]

To cure wounds and illnesses certain herbs were normally used; the knowledge of their curative value had been learnt by experience and handed down from father to son. This primitive medicine was essentially a *scientia herbarum* mixed with a little witchcraft, as it is today in the countryside, where old women charm away swine fever with spells. Some of these magical practices seem to have reached Rome from Etruria. Strange formulae were muttered over the patient, and the sickness was believed to obey the witch and disappear.

Antiquity always had an imperfect knowledge of the human body. Where today the advance in medical knowledge makes specific cures possible, then only elementary principles could be applied. It was widely thought that the spleen was the seat of laughter,[2] the bile of hatred (perhaps because of its bitterness), the liver of love (a common idea in poetry),[3] the heart of intelligence and the lungs of pride.

Even when oriental doctors reached Rome, the use of medicine was not restricted, as it is with us, to a limited circle, scrupulously subordinated to the authority of medical science. Rome had no

chemists; their place was taken by shops where medicated ointments, plasters, spices, roots, drugs and herbs were sold at the
mere request of a customer without the necessity of a prescription
and with no supervision by the public authorities—shops of the
unguentarii, the *seplasarii*, the *aromatarii*, the *turarii*, the *pigment-
arii*, etc. The *pharmacopola*, literally 'drug seller', was not a
licensed chemist, but a charlatan who hawked his remedies,
proclaiming their miraculous effects; his success depended more
upon his plausibility than on their effectiveness.

This unrestricted sale of drugs in Rome was assisted by the
fact that in their preparation no actually harmful chemicals were
normally used which might be dangerous and therefore require
strict supervision by the medical profession and the state. The
danger came rather from the fact that many completely in-
experienced people prepared their own medicines, guided only by
quacks and ridiculous superstitions. In Athens in the fifth century
B.C. a young singer died from a draught which was supposed to
improve his voice but killed him instead.[4] Suetonius[5] tells us that
the Emperor Caligula was driven mad by a love philtre given him
by his wife Caesonia. According to an untrustworthy tradition, the
poet Lucretius was also driven mad by a love philtre.[6] Remedies
usually consisted of leaves, roots of plants, animal fat, or harmless
substances such as bread (a very common ingredient in the
medicines of those days),[7] honey, oil, or vinegar. The manufacture
of remedies subjected the patient who relied on them to every
risk and danger. Legally the man who prepared and administered
drugs was responsible for their results.

For centuries in Rome public health, for which medicine is
both a safeguard and a threat, was not at all strictly protected by
the state. Everyone was free to cure himself or be cured as he
chose. Legal punishment only occurred if some great disaster
resulted.

Only in the Imperial age did the state begin to organise medical
aid for the people by expert qualified practitioners. The example
came from the eastern provinces, where from the earliest times
the local magistrates had appointed public doctors to perform
duties similar to those of our public health officials.[8] They were
appointed especially for the care of the poor and they did not
interfere with the professional work of private doctors. As

irreplaceable public servants they enjoyed exemption from certain taxes. In Rome this social benefit was not introduced until very late; only in the fourth century A.D. was a public doctor with the title of *archiatra* appointed in each of the fourteen *regiones* into which Augustus had divided Rome (see p. 2). Their duty was to cure all those who consulted them, the poor free of charge.[9]

As there were no chemists in Rome, and as generally in antiquity no independent pharmaceutical industry existed, the preparation of medicines was one of the essential duties of the doctor, as it is today in homoeopathic medicine, which very closely resembles ancient medicine in many respects. In prescribing cures a doctor was absolutely free, because Roman medicine, transplanted to Rome from Greece, kept all the characteristics of Greek medicine; freedom was a great triumph of Greek medicine, the importance of which we do not appreciate, as we cannot imagine anything else. In fact the principle that medicine is not a rigid application of rules, but the combination of experience with an intelligent and conscientious judgement, developed very late. The oldest form of medicine, Egyptian medicine, famous for the precision of its methods, did not leave a doctor free to adopt his own remedies unless he had first unsuccessfully applied the traditional and cumpulsory cures for four days.[10] If he departed from them during the early days of an illness, he did so at his own risk.

It seems strange to us that a duty so important as a doctor's was never subjected, as it is today, to the double control of a certified scientific training, like our degrees and hospital training, and of supervision to ensure efficiency and care. In antiquity only state doctors were required to provide the proof of training and qualification which is today demanded from all; their appointment by the vote of the citizens had to be confirmed by an examination before a board of experts, qualified doctors of established reputation. But in private everyone could practise medicine, like the cobbler in Phaedrus' fable,[11] who was so incompetent with his needle that nobody ever entrusted their shoes to him, but so persuasive with his tongue, that they willingly entrusted their bodies.

In certain cases public opinion exercised that indefinable control which the State had not yet come to regard as one of its duties; but public opinion is formed by incompetent judges, it is a slave of rumour and prejudice, even if at times it sees further than the authorities themselves. We should not be surprised that charlatans with a superficial smattering of superstitious medical knowledge often found favour at Rome, and that a very large number of people were their own doctors.

As for the scientific training of doctors, only much later were there regular courses in the *auditoria*,[12] the equivalent of university courses today, attendance at which, however, never led to regular examinations or degrees.

In ancient houses the *paterfamilias* prepared medicines for the entire household, women, children and slaves. Cato the Censor,[13] a man of very great learning and a Roman to the core, animated by a furious hatred of professional doctors,[14] boasted that he had reached a vigorous old age and had maintained the good health of his family by the judicious use of his own remedies. Who would have imagined Cato the Censor deigning to pound roots and prepare drugs? Nevertheless he did prepare them, and, according to himself, did it very well.

There was therefore no clear-cut distinction in Rome between scientific and empirical medicine; as the conviction was firmly rooted in many, even men of the greatest learning like Pliny the Elder, that the first was no better than the second, everyone had his own store of medical knowledge, and when someone fell ill, was bitten by a poisonous animal, burnt, wounded, or broke a limb, the whole household was busy pounding herbs and roots, preparing powders, drinks, waxes or plasters. If a doctor was summoned it was only in serious cases, when elementary prudence made complete independence obviously dangerous.

For empirical cures the whole vegetable and, where necessary, the animal world was laid under contribution.

The queen of medicinal plants was called by the Romans *laserpicium* and by the Greeks σίλφιον, 'one of the greatest gifts that Nature has given us'.[15] To be exact, *laserpicium* was the plant, but only the juice from the roots, called *laser*,[16] had the extraordinary curative qualities which made it so precious that the import of *laserpicium* to Rome was an affair of state. In the consulships of C. Valerius and M. Herennius (93 B.C.) it was decreed that thirty pounds of it should be imported into Rome at public expense; Caesar at the beginning of his dictatorship acquired fifteen hundred pounds of it;[17] a wise dictator had to include it in his calculations.

It was also a powerful aid to digestion, and was extensively used in cooking. In the *Cena Trimalchionis*, a slave sings with a loud voice the praises of a *laserpicium* sauce.[18] We might describe *laserpicium* as a distant ancestor of *Fernet*.* In medicine it performed miracles. It had various effects on animals: it made sheep go to sleep, goats sneeze,[19] and serpents vanish.[20] But to men it brought countless benefits.[21] In convalescence, in states of exhaustion, in digestive difficulties, in circulatory and female complaints it was an incomparable tonic. It was used for wounds and bites; it brought boils to a head; it made serpent and scorpion bites harmless. It even cured gout, asthma, dropsy, epilepsy, hysteria and pleurisy. It cured pains of every sort, with the solitary exception of toothache.

This, the most agonising pain of all, resisted every cure so obstinately that not even *laserpicium* could defeat it. On the best cure for toothache the opinions of doctors varied. Some advised filling the hole in the affected tooth with *laserpicium* and sealing it with wax to relieve the pain. Others, like Pliny the Elder,[22] advised against this remedy, quoting the case of a man whose pain became so unbearable as a result of such an ill-considered application, that to end it he jumped headlong from a great height, an effective but desperate cure.

Some alleviation of toothache, however, could be obtained by less violent methods, such as a pulp of sugar, wormwood and salt,[23] or the milky juice from the stem of the mustard plant.[24] It was also believed that to keep the teeth healthy, it was enough to dissolve a little salt in the mouth every morning and evening under the tongue,[25] and to chew anemone roots,[26] or to rinse them three times a year with tortoise blood.[27] Warm vinegar and sugar made loose teeth firmer.[28] But when, in spite of all precautions, the decaying teeth began to ache steadily, one had only to endure it with all the other painful necessities of life.

The ancient belief in the curative power of many herbs has been completely forgotten by modern medicine, or considered of little value. Amongst cures for conjunctivitis an infusion of violets, myrrh and saffron was recommended,[29] or saffron beaten with an

*An Italian aperitif widely used for medicinal purposes. (Translator's note.)

egg.[30] Asphodel, the glory of the fields, the blue aristocratic asphodel sung by all the poets, was reduced in medicine to the humble task of curing running sores and warts, and healing ulcers on the feet.[31] Scalds were cured with asphodel roots, but lily roots cooked in fat and oil were recommended for burns.[32]

Some plants, such as nettles[33] and mustard,[34] were regarded as miraculous. One of the great virtues of mustard was that it made poisonous mushrooms harmless; infused in a cucumber sauce it was a sovereign remedy for epilepsy, but the cucumber sauce was essential.

Remedies against coughs, catarrh, sore throats, epilepsy, scrofula, internal parasites, headaches, eyestrain, pulmonary congestion and the bites of poisonous animals were innumerable. The method of extracting foreign objects which had become imbedded in the body by applying a poultice of honey, bread and narcissus roots was also familiar. For madness nothing was considered so effective as hellebore.[35]

The austere science of medicine has been compelled in every age to lend its assistance to human vanity. So it was among the Romans. Today every chemist's shop has its cosmetic department, and even then herbal medicine had to occupy itself with satisfying the anxiety of both sexes to improve their appearance. Cumin gave the face a pale interesting colour,[36] flax seed improved women's skin[37] and made the nails bright and smooth.[38] Barley sprinkled with salt and honey kept the teeth white and made the breath smell sweet;[39] asphodel roots gave freshness to the skin and whiteness to the teeth;[40] laurel leaves patiently chewed sweetened the breath after excessive drinking;[41] lupin seeds boiled in vinegar restored wounds to their natural colour;[42] maidenhair[43] cooked in wine with celery seeds and mixed with plenty of oil made the hair curly and thick and stopped it falling out; a decoction of leek roots drunk at lunch and again after the meal prevented the foul smell of sweating armpits.[44]

The deep horror which baldness had for the Romans (certainly more than it has for us who, once past a certain age, resign ourselves to it), led them to seek for every sort of preventive. The following[45] elaborate recipe, one of many, was recommended for the partial falling out of the hair: rub the affected part with soda, and then apply a mixture of wine, saffron, pepper, vinegar, *laserpicium* (naturally!) and rat dung. A man who refused to resort to such desperate remedies had to resign himself to remaining half bald. The many other remedies recommended included bear fat.[46] Domitian, who became prematurely bald, wrote a pamphlet *De cura capillorum* to console himself for this misfortune, which made such a handsome man 'wear in youth the appearance of an old man'. Discussing the hair, he wrote with justice, 'there is nothing more beautiful nor so short-lived'.[47]

But man's struggle against nature's attacks on the hair is always a melancholy and losing one. When the hair ceased to cover the head, and medical science could assist no further, men sought every way to conceal the blow to their appearance, which they had tried in vain to keep at bay. Caligula,[48] when he passed through the streets, forbade anyone to look at him from above, because he was uncomfortably aware that he had a bald spot on the top of his head. Caesar,[49] who was very conscious of his baldness, concealed it by always wearing a wreath, and was delighted with the honour decreed to him by the people, which allowed him to hide the nakedness of his noble head with laurel leaves. Some allowed the hair to grow from the temples and trained it up, plastering it down over their bald scalps to create an illusion,[50] a method not unknown today. Others used ointments and paints,[51] false hair or wigs. As the inside of a wig was made of tanned leather, it was said of a bald man who appeared in public with a head of hair as thick as it was false, that his head was well shod.[52]

This empirical medicine of which we have so far talked, was for many years the only form of medicine in Rome, and was always highly esteemed. But at the end of the third century B.C., scientific medicine also made its appearance in Rome, in the form of professional doctors from the Greco-Oriental world. The current of innovation from Greece, which penetrated and transformed the Roman world, included doctors among the many novelties it introduced.

The first doctor to take up permanent residence in Rome was the Peloponnesian Archagathus in 219 B.C.,[53] the year of the capture of Saguntum; after him came a steady flow of doctors. At Rome the followers of Aesculapius found their profession profitable, in spite of the distrust with which their suspect skill and foreign origin surrounded them. 'They have conspired to kill us all,' wrote Cato[54] 'and they charge a fee for it, so that they may be trusted and easily destroy us.' That a doctor should ask for payment for obscure political purposes and present his bill as a mere excuse could occur only to the mind of a Cato. But it illustrates the attitude of mind of Cato and his contemporaries. The evidence that doctors were well paid is clear; 'there is no more profitable profession' (*cum sit ars fructuosior nulla*)[55] we read. Many doctors quickly accumulated huge fortunes. We know of one doctor, Quintus Petronius, whose income was over half a million sesterces a year; and of a surgeon, Alcon (see p. 215), who amassed ten million sesterces.

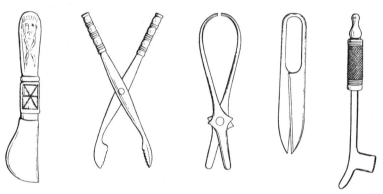

27. Surgical instruments

Wealth brought with it only a limited gain in position and dignity as the prejudice against doctors in Rome never completely disappeared, the more so because it was not always easy to distinguish between the man of science and the charlatan. To pay well is one thing; to show respect and liking is another, and a man is more concerned about his position than his income.

Their skill, which Cicero described as 'sensible and useful',[56] made doctors one of those human instruments of social well-being who are only valued for the aid they give, and do not earn the authority associated with the higher professions. Cicero himself ranked them next to architects and schoolmasters,[57] Varro to dyers and blacksmiths.[58] Neither citizenship nor freedom were necessary for a doctor. Many slaves were doctors as well as teachers.[59] Slaves and freedmen are the most frequently mentioned, because large families had a permanent doctor, concerned exclusively with the needs of the household, in accordance with the tendency of the Roman family (see p. 164), particularly in

Republican Rome, to try to be entirely self-sufficient. In aristocratic houses there were male and female medical slaves, because women when ill were unwilling to consult strange or male doctors. Some doctors were trained in the care of slaves, and where there were many slaves, as was usually the case in the *villa rustica*, there was a hospital for them, the *valetudinarium*.[60]

It was commoner to have a doctor permanently in the house than to employ the professional assistance of a freedman or a public doctor, who, as we have said, reached Rome very late. As might be expected, the first time doctors were employed at public expense to look after a particular class of people was in the army at the end of the Republic. A number of trained and experienced doctors and surgeons were early secured to look after the soldiers, and every legion had its own. In the gladiatorial schools there was a house doctor, who cured wounds and illnesses, prescribed the diet and supervised the training. From their ranks came one of the most famous doctors of the ancient world, Galen of Pergamum. Gymnasiums, theatrical companies and craftsmen's guilds had their own doctors, paid out of the common fund.

In the Imperial age the palace of the Emperors had a court doctor, who from the time of Alexander Severus bore the title of *Medicus Palatinus*.[61] There are also references to the doctors of the Vestal Virgins.

As in our day, doctors either visited the sick, or gave consultations in places[62] called *medicinae*.[63] There were more specialists than general practitioners, since medical skill was divided into watertight compartments to a quite unnecessary extent. Not only were there specialists for diseases of the ears, eyes, teeth and throat,[64] and for feminine ailments, but also for fevers, coughs, etc. and surgeons specialising in amputations, wounds, fractures, and massage (*iatralipta*). Alcon,[65] the famous surgeon of the Flavian age, specialised in operations for hernias and bone diseases.

General practitioners for internal maladies were called *clinici*, and when they visited houses they often gave themselves intolerable airs. The distinguished *clinici* arrived at the sick man's bed followed by a train of medical students; they listened, felt and observed, and in their role of teachers, they made their own students do the same, an unpleasant experience for the patient. Martial,[66] who has something to say on everything, describes the scene vividly: 'I was sickening; but you at once attended me,

Symmachus, with a train of a hundred apprentices. A hundred hands frozen by the north wind have pawed me: I had no fever before, Symmachus; now I have.'

There were many oculists (*medici ocularii*) throughout the Roman Empire. They cured eye diseases with eye-salve, of which there

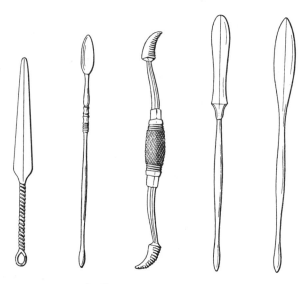

28. Surgical instruments

were two varieties in antiquity—the solid, which was the more used, and the liquid. Solid eye-salve was sold in small sticks, on which was stamped the name of the doctor, the name of the preparation and the purpose for which it was prescribed (for example, see fig. 29;[67] *post impetum lippitudinis*, 'to be used after inflammation from conjunctivitis'; *ad aspritudines tollendas* 'for use in the most acute period'; *ad diathesis tollendas* 'to remove symptoms', as a preventive remedy). For this purpose every oculist had a stone stamp and stamped the information (ἐπαγγελία) on each stick while the preparation, which later solidified, was still viscous. On the stamp were cut instructions for each type of eye-salve the oculist prepared; they always showed the name of the oculist as a guarantee of the standard of the preparation. The commercial purpose of these instructions appears also from the laudatory epithets, intended to recommend the remedy to customers, such as, 'unconquerable' (*anicetum*), 'royal' (*basilicon*) or even 'divine' (*ambrosium, isotheon, theoctiston,* see p. 225). The eye-salve was made of vegetable substances such as myrrh[68] or saffron,[69] or of powdered minerals;[70] sometimes it was prepared on the spot by the oculist; this perhaps explains why the stamp was sometimes in the shape of a small mortar.

Very many such oculists' stamps[71] have been found in the colder and cloudier provinces of the Empire (Germany, France, Britain); they are rare in Italy although eye diseases and the use of eye salves are frequently mentioned.[72] But such diseases must have been more widespread in places where the damp climate and the long hard winters induced them.

29. OCULIST'S STAMP

Spectacles were a later invention, unknown to the Romans. Some attempts at correcting sight by means similar to our lenses must have been made, for Nero, who was exceedingly short-sighted,[73] used a concave emerald to watch gladiatorial combats.[74]

Cosmetic surgery was not unknown; we know of one surgeon[75] who specialised in removing the marks made by the red hot branding-iron on the foreheads of thieving slaves, runaways, or slanderers.[76] The slave became free and, as often happened, rich, and perhaps having become rich because he was a rogue, he went to the surgeon to have the record of his ancient disgrace removed from his skin. Everything can be done with money, and even rascals, when they are rich, manage, despite every precaution, to assume the outward appearance of a respectable gentleman and they could once more hold their foreheads high, restored to their former smoothness by the surgeon's skill.

Further Reading

T. C. Allbutt, *Greek Medicine in Rome* (London, 1921), is the standard authority.
Special studies include: J. S. Milne, *Surgical Instruments in Greek and Roman Times* (1907).

NOTES

1. N.H., XXIX, 11.
2. Schol. in Persium, 1, 12.
3. In the Medea of Euripides (39 et seq.) the nurse expresses the fear that the heroine, betrayed in her love, 'will pierce the liver' of her faithless husband and his new bride.
4. Antiphon, On the Choreutes, 15.
5. Cal., 50.
6. St. Jerome, Chron., 1923.
7. Pliny, N.H., XXII, 138: *Panis hic ipse, quo vivitur, innumeras paene continet medicinas.*
8. Cod. Theod., XIII, 3, 8; Cod. Just., X, 53, c 9.
9. Ibid; *Archiatri . . . . honeste obsequi tenuioribus malint, quam turpiter servire divitibus.*
10. Aristotle, Polit., III, 15, p. 1286b.
11. I, 14.
12. Aelius Lampridius, Alex. Sev., 44, 4.
13. Pliny, N.H., XXIX, 14.
14. Ibid. See p. 213.
15. Pliny, N.H., XXII, 101: *inter eximia naturae dona numeratum.*
16. Ibid. XIX, 38.
17. Ibid. XIX, 40.
18. Petronius, 35.
19. Pliny, N.H., XIX, 39.
20. Ibid. XXII, 106.
21. Ibid. 101, et seq.
22. Ibid. 106.
23. Ibid. XX, 15.
24. Ibid. 239.
25. Ibid. XXXI, 101.
26. Ibid. XXI, 166.

27. Ibid. XXXII, 37.
28. Ibid. XX, 15.
29. Ibid. XXI, 131.
30. Ibid. 137.
31. Ibid. XXII, 68–70.
32. Ibid. XXI, 126.
33. Ibid. XXII, 31.
34. Ibid. XX, 236 et seq.
35. Horace, Satires, II, 3, 82–83; Epist., II, 2, 137; Persius 4, 16, *et passim.* cf. Pliny, N.H., XXV, 54.
36. Horace, Epist., I, 19, 18; Persius, 5, 55; cf. Pliny, N.H., XX, 159.
37. Pliny, N.H., XX, 249.
38. Ibid. XX, 251.
39. Ibid. XXII, 134.
40. Ibid. 75.
41. Martial, V, 4.
42. Pliny, N.H., XXII, 156.
43. Ibid. 62.
44. Ibid. 87.
45. Ibid. 104.
46. Ibid. VIII, 127.
47. Suetonius, Domit., 18.
48. Ibid. Cal. 50.
49. Ibid. Div. Jul., 45.
50. Martial, X, 83.
51. Ibid. VI, 57.
52. Ibid. XII, 45.
53. Pliny, N.H., XXIX, 12.
54. Ibid. 14.
55. Ibid. XXIX, 2.
56. Cicero, De off., I, 42, 151; *Quibus artibus aut prudentia major inest aut non mediocris utilitas.*
57. Ibid.
58. Varro, De Re Rustica, I, 16, 4.
59. See p. 121.
60. See p. 71.
61. Aelius Lampridius, Alex. Sev., 42, 3.
62. Cicero, pro Cluentio, 63, 178.
63. Plautus, Amph., 1013; Epid., 198.
64. Martial (X. 56) mentions among the distinguished doctors of his day the dentist Cascellius, the oculist Hyginus, and the surgeons Fannius and Eros, specialists in throat and skin operations respectively.
65. Ibid. XI, 84, 5.

66. Ibid. V, 9.

67. Illustrated with facsimiles and transcriptions of the inscriptions in G. Ghirlandini, *Notizie degli scavi* (1904), pp. 431 et seq.

68. Called *diasmyrnes* in consequence.

69. Called *crocodes*; in one case the epithet *horaeon* (ὡραῖον) seems to have been added as a guarantee that the saffron was gathered at the most propitious season.

70. Called *diamysus* from *misy*, iron sulphate.

71. The best collection of these stamps is in Esperandieu, *Recueil des cachets d'oculistes romains* (Paris, 1893). [The material for Britain is collected by R. R. James, 'Roman Oculist Stamps in Britain' (*British Journal of Ophthalmology*, 1926).]

72. Cicero, Ad Qu. fr., II, 2, 1, 1: *Parvula lippitudine adductus sum ut dictarem hanc epistolam;* Horace, Sat., I, 5, 30–31: *Hic oculis ego nigra meis collyria lippus inlinere.*

73. Suetonius, Nero, 51.

74. Pliny, N.H., XXXVII, 54.

75. Martial, X, 56, 6.

76. See p. 125.

CHAPTER XIX

The Baths

THE baths played an important part in Roman life, the daily hot bath was a physical relaxation enjoyed both by the very poor and by slaves; the former could use the great baths built especially for the people very cheaply (*quadrante lavatum*, says Horace[1]), the latter had bathing facilities in the house; in the *villa rustica*, *balnea* were built for the slaves (see p. 73) and similar rooms must have existed also in town houses. One part of the *villa urbana* was occupied by the bathrooms, which reproduced in miniature the layout of the *thermae* (fig. 16).

This practice of taking hot baths, which seems to us a typical Roman custom and necessitated the construction of the most grandiose buildings in Rome, was another of the customs introduced into Italy from Greece towards the end of the third century B.C., the century which, as has been said before, was the decisive age for the penetration of Greek civilisation into Italy.

The earliest Romans paid their bodies as much attention as the demands of personal cleanliness and hygiene required. 'Every day they washed their arms and legs which were dirty after working; but they only washed completely every nine days';[2] they also swam in the Tiber, a custom which never completely died out, and they had occasional hot baths in a room (*lavatrina*) next to the kitchen. Only when the custom of a daily hot bath became general, did they begin to build bathrooms (*balnea*) in their houses. The first bath-houses were built in the second century B.C.

There were various types of bathing establishment. The most used were the small private ones with a restricted and regular clientele, frequented by those who wished to avoid the noise and confusion of the larger overcrowded establishments. Examples of such establishments are found at Pompeii where some houses are remarkable for the exceptional development of their bathrooms. Besides these, public bathing establishments were built, the *balnea meritoria*, built and run at private expense for profit, or the public baths (*thermae*) in the fullest sense of the word, a splendid gift to the people from rich citizens and later the Emperors. The *thermae*

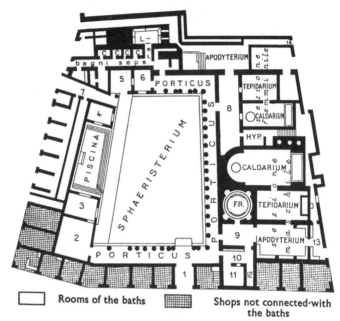

30. PLAN OF THE STABIAN BATHS, POMPEII

C = *cella* (for separate baths)   FR = *frigidarium*   HYP = *hypocausis*
L = *latrina*

1. Entrance to the men's section of the baths. 2. Small *apodyterium* (probably) 3. Small pool (2 ft. deep) 4. Pool originally similar to 3, later filled in and put to other uses 5-6. Rooms for players 7. Side entrance 8. Passage from the women's section to the colonnade of the *sphaeristerium* 9. Passage from the *sphaeristerium* to the men's apodyterium 10-12. Waiting rooms (probably for slaves) 13. Side entrance 14. Entrance to the women's section

The Stabian Baths at Pompeii were part of a vast block of buildings, the northern half of which (not shown here) was occupied by lodging houses, the southern part by the bathing establishment. On the west and south sides (*tabernae*) not connected with the baths open on to the street. It will be noted that, to ensure that only one *hypocausis* was used, the *caldarium* and the *tepidarium* of the women's section are arranged in the opposite order to that in the men's section, and the women's section has no *calderium*.

belonged to the state, but they were let out on contract for a fixed sum to a contractor (*conductor*) who charged a modest entrance fee (*balneaticum*), usually a *quadrans*. Sometimes some rich citizen or magistrate undertook to pay the *conductor* the equivalent of the entrance fees over a certain period, during which entry to the baths was completely free.

The Roman bathing establishments, of which a detailed plan is given in fig. 6, varied considerably in their layout but in all of them the following essential elements are found:

(1) The *apodyterium*, or changing room, with stone benches against the walls; rows of deep square holes in the wall, reaching as high as a man, held clothes. The hole could not be closed, and, as it was not therefore safe to leave clothes exposed amid the activity of the baths, they were left in charge of a slave brought for the purpose.

(2) The *frigidarium* or *cella frigidaria*, a room for the cold bath; usually small, high and dark, with a cupola at the top with an opening in the middle.

(3) The *tepidarium*, a transit room or passage with a marble floor which acclimatised bathers to the difference in temperature between the *caldarium*[3] and the *frigidarium*.

(4) The *caldarium*, the room for the hot bath; the best lit room, provided with basins, tubs, and, in the large baths, with a swimming pool as well.

In some baths, besides the *caldarium*, there was the *assa sudatio* or *Laconicum*, a small heated room, which was used for the sweating bath; it had a dome on top, with a round opening closed by a bronze disc attached to a chain. The bather could regulate the heat by pulling the disc nearer or farther away from the opening.

To these rooms which were used for bathing were annexed the places used for gymnastics (*sphaeristerium*), oiling the body (*unctorium*), and the removal of dust after exercising in the wrestling ring (*destrictorium*). There were also large open-air swimming baths (*piscinae natatoriae*). Anyone who wished to refresh himself after his bath could find food and drink in the numerous *popinae* inside or near the baths.

Many establishments were divided into two sections for men and women, each with all the essential dressing and bathing rooms; where there was no division, a different time for bathing was fixed for the two sexes. Only the *piscinae* were common to both divisions and men and women swam in them together. But ladies who wished to avoid criticism did not frequent the baths.

Later, if required, baths could be taken in separate rooms. There were also medicinal and perfumed baths.

The baths opened at noon, when the furnaces were lit; the entrance and departure of the public varied according to local regulations. The baths in Rome remained open from noon to dusk; the opening and closing signal was given by a gong which took the place of a bell. A restriction was introduced by Hadrian which forbade entrance until two o'clock in the afternoon, exceptions being allowed for the sick.[4] We have references to

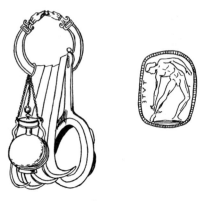

31. STRIGIL
(a) Strigil and oil bottle   (b) Athlete using strigil

baths in provincial cities which remained open for some hours during the night, especially where the bathing arrangements were insufficient to meet the needs of the population.

The method of bathing naturally varied according to taste, age and health, but the object was always to alternate hot and cold baths. A cold bath, whether simply washing or swimming and diving in the *piscinae natatoriae*, was only taken when the body was heated and the pores open from the hot bath, a longer or shorter stay in the *Laconicum* or a vigorous game in the *sphaeristerium*. Less energetic people took a long sun bath (*apricatio*) before entering the cold water.

Bathers took a variety of objects with them to the baths: bottles of oil, strigils (sharp-edged iron scrapers to scrape the oil from the body after exercise), soda (*aphronitrum*) which in the absence of

53. Etruscan fresco from Tarquinia showing slinger and fisherman. (*p. 245*)

54. Mosaic showing huntsman and animals. (*p. 245*)

55. Relief showing chariot racing, perhaps in the Circus Maximus. (*p. 251*)

56. Relief showing incidents from wild beast hunts in the Circus. (*p. 252*)

soap (*sapo*, see p. 111, was a hair dye) took its place, and various towels for drying the body (*lintea, sabana*), the face (*faciale*), the feet (*pedale*), etc. The bathers, except for the poorest, were accompanied by a train of slaves; one helped his master during the bath (*balneator*), another massaged him (*unctor, aliptes*, or, if particularly expert in the care of the body, *iatraliptes*). Another plucked the hair from his arm-pits (*alipilus*). Other slaves brought fresh linen, and stood guard over the clothes, etc. The poorer had to resort to the assistance of the masseurs and barbers who thronged the baths, and when they had undressed, if they did not wish to leave their clothes to the mercy of thieves, they paid the *balneator* or the *capsarius* a small fee for looking after them. The smartest people also took their cup-bearers with them, but this was considered absurdly ostentatious.

The baths in Rome were the chief centre of city life, and when towards the end of the afternoon the people left their work and resorted to them before dinner, there was a chaotic, ear-splitting uproar. From the description which Seneca[5] has left us of a bath (evidently one of the smaller ones, since its upper storeys were let as flats) we can get some idea of conditions in the main baths:

I have lodgings right over a bathing establishment. So picture to yourself the assortment of sounds, which are enough to make me hate my very powers of hearing. When your strenuous gentleman, for example, is exercising himself by flourishing leaden weights; when he is working hard or else pretending to be working hard, I can hear him grunt, and whenever he releases his imprisoned breath, I can hear him panting in wheezy and high-pitched tones. Or perhaps I notice some lazy fellow, content with a cheap rub-down, and hear the crack of the pummelling hand on his shoulders, varying in sound as the hand is laid on flat or hollow. Then perhaps a professional comes along, shouting out the score; that is the finishing touch. Add to this the arresting of an occasional roysterer or pickpocket, the racket of the man who always likes to hear his own voice in the bathroom, or the enthusiast who plunges into the swimming-tank with unconscionable noise and splashing. Besides all those who excel in lung-power, if nothing else, imagine the hair-plucker with his penetrating, shrill voice, for purposes of advertisement, continually giving it vent and never holding his tongue except when he is plucking the armpits and making his victim yell instead. Then the cakeseller with his varied cries, the sausagemen, the confectioner, and all the vendors of food hawking their wares, each with his own distinctive intonation.

An account of the methods of heating the baths remains to be given. A furnace, fed with charcoal and called by the Greek word *hypocausis*,[6] was used for the double purpose of heating the water for the baths and of spreading hot air into the cavities deliberately left under the floor and in the walls. The mouth of this furnace was in a room (*praefurnium*) where a slave watched and stoked the *hypocausis*. The water was heated in the way which *Vitruvius*[7] has described, and which we find in the Villa of Boscoreale (see p. 72) and in the remains of *thermae*.

> Three bronze tanks are to be placed above the *hypocausis*: one for the hot bath (*caldarium*),[8] a second for the tepid bath (*tepidarium*), a third for the cold bath (*frigidarium*). They are to be so arranged that the hot water which flows from the tepid bath into the hot bath, may be replaced by a like amount of water flowing down from the cold into the tepid bath.

The three tanks were therefore communicating and placed one above the other; the cold-water tank must have been at some distance from the *hypocausis*. This ensured a rapid and continuous supply of warm or tepid water as required.

The hot air from the *hypocausis* passed through a large pipe (*vaporarium*) in one wall of the furnace, and was spread by means of the *suspensurae* and the *parietes tubulati* under and along the walls of the *caldarium*, the *Laconicum* and, though less intensely because of the greater distance from the *hypocausis*, the *tepidarium*. The invention of central heating was attributed to C. Sergius Orata[9] in the last century B.C.; the pavements (*suspensurae*) were supported on small brick columns instead of being directly in contact with the soil, thus leaving an empty space in which the hot air could circulate freely under the floor. From this cavity the hot air spread upwards into the cavities of the wall, the *parietes tubulati*, through clay pipes or hollow bricks. This system of the *suspensurae* was completely developed and widely used in the first century A.D.; Seneca[10] speaks of it as a recent invention.

The same system of central heating was used in private buildings, houses and villas. In the colder climate of Britain, central heating was, naturally, used in the villas built by the Romans. Its advantages were so obvious that it was adapted by the Britons themselves and traces of *suspensurae* are to be seen in the remains of many humble British villages.[11]

Excavations at Ostia have shown that rooms were commonly built so that the sun might supplement the supply of artificial heat.[12]

Further Reading

For further plans and reconstructions see G. T. Rivoira, *Roman Architecture*, (London, 1927).

NOTES

1. Sat., I, 3, 137.
2. Seneca, Epist., 86, 11: *Bracchia et crura cotidie abluebant, quae scilicet sordes opere collegerant, ceterum toti nundinis lavabantur.*
3. *Caldarium*, not *calidarium*, a common mistake. In this word the syncope of cal(i)d- is reliably attested.
4. Aelius Spartianus, Hadr., 22, 7.
5. Epist., 56, 1–2.
6. *Hypocauston (-um)* is rarely found in the texts for *Hypocausis*, but is wrongly preferred in archaeological textbooks. *Hypocauston* normally means a room heated by a *hypocausis* (Pliny, Epist., V, 6, 25; II, 17, 123; Digest, XVII, 1, 16) and is a substantive formed from the adjective *hypocaustos*, 'heated by a *hypocausis*'. (Pliny, Epist., II, 17, 11: *unctorium hypocaustom*; cf. Digest, XXXII, 55, 3 *diatarum hypocaustarum*.)
7. V, 10, 1.
8. The same names as are used to indicate the different rooms of the *thermae*, but with a different meaning. Care must be taken to avoid confusion.
9. Valerius Maximus, IX, 1, 1.
10. Epist., 90, 25: *Quaedam nostra demum prodisse memoria scimus . . . ut suspensuras balneorum et impressos parietibus tubos, per quos circumfunderetur calor, cui ima simul ac summa foverat aequaliter.*
11. See R. G. Collingwood, *Roman Britain* (Oxford, 1953), p. 88. Such systems were probably intended for drying grass rather than heating houses, but their existence shows how the advantages of the system were appreciated.
12. R. Meiggs, *Roman Ostia* (Oxford, 1960), p. 414.

CHAPTER XX

Travel

Travelling. Carriages.

THE custom of the wealthier Roman families of sending their sons to Greece to complete their education at the schools of the best known orators and philosophers shows that the Romans had no fear of travelling. The absence of modern means of rapid transport did not stop civilised men of earlier times travelling extensively throughout the world, least of all the Romans with their excellent network of roads; they travelled to reach their places of study, to take up their duties in the provinces, for military or commercial reasons, to visit well known monuments, or simply to drive away boredom. As always, sea travel, which was the most convenient, was the most popular. The absence of decent well-run inns rendered land travel unattractive. The ancients were not familiar with the great hotel industry which is a modern achievement. A traveller who did not have friends with whom he could pass the night, had to be content with a room in one of the many *cauponae* which stood along the main roads or in the great cities. As we can see at Pompeii, these *cauponae* were cramped, undecorated and frequented by carters, drunkards and prostitutes, and the beds must have harboured every sort of insect. We get some idea of the standard of education of those who frequented these inns when we see the obscenities and vulgarities scrawled on the walls of the *cauponae* by the regular clients. This uncivilised custom, even though these masterpieces have been most useful to us for various reasons,[1] does not give us a very favourable impression of the intellectual ability of their authors. The innkeeper was traditionally the typical rogue; *'perfidus hic caupo'*,[2] says Horace; *'cauponibus . . . malignis'*;[3] and the Roman law was extremely severe to innkeepers. All this did not make travelling pleasant, but nevertheless men travelled without anxiety. A people afraid of travelling can never rule an empire.

The travelling garment, except for those going on an official mission which required the wearing of the toga, was a tunic covered by a cloak with a hood (*paenula*) (see p. 103); in the heat of summer a broad-brimmed hat was worn (see p. 105). The tunic was cut so as to make movement as easy as possible; it was very narrow at the waist and reached only to the knees; from the waist hung the wallet (*marsupium*), the ancient suitcase. Most people travelled on a beast of burden which carried the traveller and his baggage at the same time; 'Today, if I will,' says Horace,[4] 'I may go on a bob-tailed mule even to Tarentum, the saddlebag's weight galling his loins, and the rider his withers.' Travelling on foot was even more exceptional than among the Greeks. Nobody had yet conceived the idea of making long journeys on foot for pleasure, as is done today, passing days and months in the rain and sun with a heavy knapsack on the back; among the Romans a hiker would have been regarded as out of his mind. Anyone who wished to travel comfortably, especially if accompanied by ladies, went in a carriage.

The number of words used to distinguish different types of Roman carriages is proof of the variety of their shape, turn-out, solidity, smartness and speed. The Eastern custom of being carried in a litter (*lectica*) or a sedan chair (*sella gestatoria*) is characteristically Roman; in the former men travelled reclining, in the latter seated; both might be provided with cushions (*pulvinaria*) and curtains (*vela*). They were carried by a team of strong slaves, which varied in number from two to eight, of equal height and dressed in livery, a dress similar to that of soldiers but of bright colours. It was a convenient but slow means of travelling, and its use was therefore restricted to the city, when it was the sole means of transport allowed by the law forbidding the passage of carriages during the hours of daylight (see p. 28). Antiquity had a respect for pedestrians, who are neglected today; in those days the possession of a swift vehicle did not confer the right to disregard others. Not only was the circulation of waggons forbidden in the city when the crowd was greatest, but, as appears from Pompeii, the most frequented squares and streets were rendered inaccessible to carts by stone barriers.

There were three types of wheeled carriage:

(1) Carriages for sport and display.—The *currus* with two wheels, which was used for races in the circus and in triumphs.

(2) Transport waggons.—The *plaustrum* with two wheels made of solid drums instead of spokes (a practice still found in the Sardinian countryside), was drawn by oxen, mules or asses; the *serracum*, with lower and more solid wheels, used for the transport of heavy goods; the *carrus*, a military transport waggon, of Celtic origin; the *arcera*, used especially in early days; it was a type of carriage litter for invalids (*quasi arca quaedam magna vestimentis instrata, quo nimis aegri aut senes portari cubantes solebant*).[5]

(3) Travelling carriages.—These were two- or four-wheeled:

(*a*) Two-wheeled.—The *cisium*, a swift light gig for those who wanted to travel fast without baggage. These were hired from the waggoners (the *cisiarii* who had their ranks at the gates); the *essedum*,

32. IMPERIAL BRONZE COINS WITH CARPENTUM

(*a*) Coin of Julia Augusta   (*b*) Coin of Agrippina
(FROM MATTINGLY, *Coins of the Roman Empire*, I, Pl. 23, 18, 30, 6)

a type of travelling chariot whose shape had been adapted from the war chariots of the Gauls and Britons. We do not know its exact form; it must have been a type half-way between the *cisium* and the more solid four-wheeled *raeda*. Smaller ones were driven by the traveller himself, and larger ones by an *essedarius*. The shape of the *carpentum*, however, is known: a smart, convenient chariot of ancient Italian type, with two wheels, drawn by two mules; only ladies of the Imperial family could drive one in the city; so when coins show them driving in a carriage (fig. 32) it is presumably a *carpentum*.

(*b*) Four-wheeled.—The *raeda*, the cart most used for the transport of people or baggage; the *petorritum*, of Gallic origin, like the *raeda*; we know nothing precisely about it; at first probably a richly decorated cart for ceremonial occasions, in the last days of the Empire it became one of the commonest means of travel; the *pilentum*, like the *carpentum*, but larger and with four wheels; originally only priestesses and matrons used them, on feast days, but later they were widely used; the *carruca*, which on account of its comfort—it was actually possible to sleep in it—its elegant fittings and its comparative speed, was a true luxury carriage.

NOTES

1. These *graffiti*, scrawled by illiterate people who wrote as they spoke, are the best evidence for the pronunciation of Latin at the time.
2. Sat., I, 1, 5, 29.
3. Ibid. I, 5, 4.
4. Ibid. I, 6, 104, 5.
5. Aulus, Gellius, XX, 1, 29.

CHAPTER XXI

Sports and Pastimes of Children and Adults

Children's games. Group games; games of Greek origin: the game of King, Jar, etc. Gambling. The tabula lusoria. *Sports on the* Campus Martius. *Other pastimes. Dancing.*

'BUILDING toy houses, harnessing mice to a little cart, playing odds and evens, riding a long stick' were to Horace[1] the first childhood games for Roman children, as nearly all of them are for children today. Only the pleasant pastime of harnessing mice to a little cart and watching them run fearlessly in pairs dragging behind them a lurching wooden toy has disappeared. If the cart was a little larger, big enough to hold a boy, a quiet animal (Plate 43), was harnessed to it, such as a sheep, a goat, a dog, or even another boy who was prepared to pull it. In odds and evens (*par impar*) one boy held some pebbles (nuts, etc.) in his closed fist and challenged his companion to guess whether their number was odd or even. Then he opened his hand and showed whether the guess had been right. Boys also played *capita et navia*,[2] 'head and tails', throwing a coin in the air, and trying to guess before it fell whether the side with the head or with the ship would fall uppermost. They also played *morra** (*digitis micare*), they spun tops (*turbo*) with strings or with whips, and bowled hoops (*orbis, trochus*) with a straight or curved stick (*clavis*). There were large and small hoops; the best were decorated with bells and rings, and the hoop jingled as it ran, giving great pleasure.

When Roman boys were together they played group games of skill. Many games were played with nuts, and Persius says 'When the nuts have been abandoned'[3] to mean 'after growing up'.

---

*An Italian children's game in which one player tries to guess the number of fingers held up by the other. See H. V. Morton, *A Traveller in Rome*, pp. 404–5. (Translator's note.)

Plate 51 shows boys playing with nuts, and the reader can see that the game has not changed much between then and now; one nut was balanced on three others to make a pyramid and the boy who succeeded in knocking them down with a fruit stone won the nuts. A shooting game with nuts was also played which involved trying to throw nuts from a distance into a narrow-necked vase.[4]

Most group games were suggested to boys by their instinctive imitation of adults, as when they played at soldiers, judges or magistrates. The magistrates were accompanied by little lictors[5] with fasces and axes, who, we may suppose, made the ferocious faces of men ready to cut off a head. Plate 51 shows boys playing at horses; the boy who was the horse carried his companion on his shoulders (*humeris vectare*) (Plate 51), or dragged him in a little cart (Plate 51), even resigning himself to being beaten.

Plate 52 shows a game depicted on other monuments; two boys each holding one end of a long rope chase two others, trying to tie them up and reduce them to immobility; the boys pursued, intent on avoiding capture, strike at their pursuers with sticks.

It seems reasonable to suppose that in the period after the invasion of Greek culture all Greek children's games, of which a later writer has left us a minute description,[6] became common in Rome. The innumerable Eastern slaves, who were occupied with the early education of children in Roman families, must surely have imported from their own countries those games which were not already familiar; games which are still exceedingly common amongst us, such as swinging on a rope (αἰώρα) or a see-saw (πέταυρον), kites (αἰετός), catch (ἀποδιδρασκίνδα) and Blind Man's Buff. Blind Man's Buff was called in Greek 'The Bronze Fly' (χαλκῆ μῦια); a blindfolded boy ran round trying to catch one of his companions crying, 'I will chase the bronze fly', and his companions dancing round him with a stick cried out, 'You'll search for him, but you won't catch him', and struck him. A Greek game which must very likely have been introduced into Rome also, was the so-called Jar game (χυτρίνδα). One boy, who remained seated, was the jar; without getting up or leaving his place, he had to try and catch another. His companions came as near as they could without being caught, cuffed him, pinched and tweaked him. The boy who was caught had to take the place of the jar and the game began again. Amongst the games imported from Greece was the game of King (βασιλίνδα).[7] It consisted, like all the others, in a test of skill, which ended with the winner being proclaimed King and the loser 'donkey' (ὄνος), or 'the fool'. During the game the boys chanted '*Rex erit qui recte faciet, qui non faciet non erit*'. When the game was ended, the conqueror was proclaimed king and gave orders to all; the loser, the fool, was sent to Coventry and mocked.

Among all these games, tricks and practical jokes played a part, as when boys glued a coin to the ground and remained at a distance to watch a passer-by, attracted by the small unexpected gain, trying to pick it up.[8] His anger at his failure amused the boys, who watched the faces he made when he found himself tricked, and jeered at him.

The diversions and pastimes of adults were naturally different, except that adults in those days also skipped, as this was considered one of the best forms of exercise, and they played at *morra*, like boys, but with coins, not nuts or similar trifles. *Morra* was the simplest form of gambling for grown-ups; more complicated, and, for those gripped by the passion for gambling, more ruinous, were knucklebones (*tali*) and dice (*tesserae*). Dice in particular provided a chance to win or lose large sums rapidly. Augustus in a letter, preserved by Suetonius,[9] mentions having lost twenty thousand sesterces at the game. Nero[10] was a reckless gambler and only staked the highest sums, four hundred thousand sesterces a throw. But of all the emperors the most fanatical gambler was Claudius;[11] he gambled even when travelling; to prevent the jolting of the coach throwing the gaming pieces into the air, he had the gambling table fixed to the side of the coach. Being a man of letters, he also wrote and published a hand-book on games of chance; for a man of letters, whether an emperor or not, turns everything into literature, even his passion for gambling. Juvenal[12] called the action of young men who lost a hundred sesterces at a game and allowed their slaves to shiver with cold because they had no tunic, madness. Gambling was a pastime apparently confined to aristocratic circles;[13] some lost their entire fortune by gambling.[14] In spite of all this, however, the Romans do not seem to have had that frantic love for games of chance which Tacitus[15] considered a particular characteristic of the Germans.

Knucklebones and dice were thrown on to the gaming table (*alveus, tabula aleatoria*) by hand or from a cup (*pyrgus*, from the

Greek πύργος, a tower, *turricula, fritillus, phimus, φιμός*). The cup was a guarantee of fair play; throwing the dice with the hand encouraged cheating.[16]

The name *alea* was not applied, as some expressions might lead us to believe, to dice or knucklebones, but only to the act of throwing or gambling generally.

Knucklebones and dice had naturally different shapes. It is a fairly common and widespread mistake to think that the *tali* were the equivalent of our dice, to which the Roman *tesserae* in fact corresponded exactly. *Talus*, literally a shin bone, is the little bone (in Greek ἀστράγαλος, whence the Latin *astragali*) found in the leg of most animals, between the shin and ankle; this small bone from calves, sheep, goats and antelopes, or an object of a similar shape made from metal, bone, ivory or stone, was used in the game of knucklebones. Knucklebones had only four faces which could be used; being very long and narrow, they could not rest upright on their two ends. The four faces were rectangular, long and narrow; two were flat, one concave, one convex; each of them had a different value: one (χῖον, in Latin *canis* or *vulturius*), three (πρανές), four (ὕπτιον), six (κῷον, Latin *senio*). The game was played with four knucklebones at a time, and thirty-five combinations were possible; the highest scoring throw was called *Venus* or *iactus Venereus*, when each knucklebone showed a side with a different number (one, three, four, six).

On this point, as on so many others, our source of information is Martial:[17]

> *Cum steterit nullus vultu tibi talus eodem,*
> *Munera me dices magna dedisse tibi,*

two verses accompanying a gift of ivory knucklebones.

Tesserae (Greek κύβοι, our dice, (see p. 234)) offered a larger number of combinations; in dice one was also called *canis*, the other faces were referred to by the numbers which they bore. Dice were made of bone or ivory and were thrown two or three at a time. To ensure a good throw, it was usual when throwing to invoke a divinity or the name of one's beloved. A parasite in Plautus[18] says that in banquets all call him 'the girl'; the girl in fact is *invocata* (invoked by the players) while he is *invocatus* (not invited). A banquet was the occasion for young men to gamble,[19] when their thoughts turned to their beloved.

Roman Law was particularly severe against gambling; it forbade it except during the Saturnalia, the Roman carnival when liberty was granted to all. Gambling debts were not recognised; not only did the creditor have no right to bring an action against the debtor or enforce payment by legal methods (as is also the case in our law), but the debtor had the right to recover what he had paid by a lawsuit. (In English law, gambling debts freely paid cannot be recovered.)

There were also games of skill, depending on ability at moving pieces (*calculi*) according to certain rules on a type of chessboard, called a *tabula lusoria* or *abacus*. Classical authors frequently refer to such games, but they do not give us enough information to enable us to reconstruct the rules at all precisely.

The most popular was the *ludus latrunculorum* or 'game of soldiers'; *latro* in early Latin did not mean as it did later (for example, in the age of Cicero) a murderer, but simply a mercenary soldier; the single pieces were therefore also called *milites*, or *bellatores*.

As usual in games of this type, a mock battle took place between two sets of pieces manoeuvred on the squares of the *tabula lusoria* (also called in this game *tabula latruncularia*); we do not know the details of the game; the *ludus latrunculorum* seems to have partly resembled our draughts, because the object was to hem in one's opponent so that he had no more space to move in (this was called *ad incitas redigere*), and partly chess, because while some pieces (*calculi ordinarii*) moved like our pawns, others (*calculi vagi*) could advance and jump in different directions.

A game like backgammon was called *duodecim scripta*; on a board on which twelve vertical lines were drawn, divided by one horizontal line, each of the two players advanced (*calculum dare, promovere*), or was compelled to withdraw (*calculum reducere*), one of his fifteen pieces according to the throw of dice. The game was a combination of skill and chance.

Certain stone tables which have been found in large numbers in excavations as well as in the Catacombs must presumably have been used for a similar game. They are also shown in some large mosaics. These tables were certainly used for a game with dice and draughtsmen. On the upper edge of these tables some words are inscribed in three lines each of twelve letters, divided in half by a

separation mark (a bird, a flower, etc.) usually six words of six
letters each, for example:

TURDUS	STUPET
MERULA	CANTAT
AUCEPS	CAPTAT

The words are not always so neatly divided, especially when, as
is very common, the thirty-six letters give a phrase alluding
specifically to the game, for example:

SITIBI	TESSEL
LAFAVE	TEGOTE
STUDIO	VINCAM

(*Si tibi tessela favet ego te studio vincam*, 'Even if the dice favour
you, I will beat you by my skill') The game consisted partly of luck
and partly of skill in calculation and foresight, as in our poker and
in card games generally, which are Eastern in origin and only
reached Europe in the Middle Ages.

The rules of the game in which these tables were used have not
been satisfactorily explained in spite of a most penetrating study
on the subject.[20] So the matter must be left to the curiosity of the
reader who wishes to investigate it further.

In the afternoon most people spent many hours in the baths;[21]
but hardy young men preferred to exercise on the *Campus
Martius* and swim in the Tiber, *quo omnis iuventus causa natandi
venit*, says Cicero.[22] Swimming was a sport more widely practised
then than now. A man who did not know how to swim was as
contemptible a rarity in the ancient world as a man who cannot
bicycle is today. The Greeks said of a ne'er-do-well that he knew
neither how to write nor to swim. (μήτε γράμματα μήτε νεῖν
ἐπίστασθαι)[23] It was considered remarkable that the emperor
Caligula, who, although mad, was a man of considerable ability,
did not know how to swim.[24] Sea swimming was also common
from the earliest times; the reader will admire the vivid Etruscan
maritime scene in Plate 53. In summer the beaches were
crowded, especially the beach at Baiae, the smartest summer
resort of Rome, and, like all smart summer resorts, a place of
endless amorous intrigue[25] and gossip.[26] Marine sports in Italy go
back to the earliest times. Winter sports, on the other hand, were
unknown.

Exercise and sports of every kind took place on the *Campus Martius*, and they were an excellent training for the hard life of military service. The passer by saw there the sturdiest of the youth of Rome riding, drilling, driving chariots at great speed and practising all the tricks of the wrestling ring.[27] The neighbouring Tiber challenged the strongest to cross it, sometimes many times, and beat its strong current.[28] The number of sportsmen who gathered on the *Campus Martius* was so great that Caesar[29] (see p. 31) thought of building an even larger *campus* on the right bank of the Tiber.

But there were also young men who preferred strolling in female company in the many gardens which adorned Rome to the hard toil of such exercises. As all Rome, especially the aristocracy, was passionately devoted to gossip (see p. 268),[30] and scandal was quick to be born and spread, there was always a great deal of gossip about these carefully arranged meetings which so many handsome youths made *in hortis*,[31] especially by the censorious who recalled with useless regret the stern times of Appius Claudius. But when Rome became big, Appius Claudius had been dead for many years, and the beautiful gardens were full of discreet nooks.

Dancing was also popular at Rome. The ancient Italian dances consisted of a heavy stamping, which had a solemn and martial effect as the feet struck the earth in a triple rhythm. It was leaping rather than dancing; in fact this form of dancing was called *saltatio*, and was practised in the rites of certain priestly orders[32] and amongst country folk on holidays.[33] At the end of the second century B.C. Greek culture introduced more refined forms of dancing into Rome, and it became the fashion in smart society to dance in the Greek manner. But only women and young men danced. A man of serious disposition was not allowed to do so; the name 'dancer' (*cinaedus*)[34] was the most offensive epithet which could be applied to a man of distinction, and Cornelius Nepos mentions as an example of the difference in Greek and Roman customs that Epaminondas, the grim Theban general, knew how to dance.[35] Ladies were allowed to dance, but with a certain restraint. A woman who danced too well was struck off the Censor's roll,[36] and Horace,[37] when he assumed the office of moralist to support Augustus' efforts to bring about the moral renaissance of Rome, looked with disgust on grown women stricken with a mad desire to learn Greek dancing.

Modern manners are more tolerant towards dancing. Dancing, whoever the dancer, may sometimes seem clumsy or stupid, but not immoral and never in itself unbecoming. Guicciardini[38] maintains that anybody who is politically ambitious should not refuse to dance. One might say that this aphorism is held by all modern people; today it is not unusual for a man holding responsible positions in public life to know how to dance and to do so, and the knowledge may be useful.

The method of modern dancing also gives a greater impression of moral freedom. We have great admiration for dancers, which the Romans would never have shared or approved; our form of dancing, which allows a man and a woman to embrace in public, would have seemed to the ancients disgraceful and even scandalous. We, on the other hand, find nothing to laugh at or criticise in it. It seems to us perfectly natural that those who wish to dance should do so in this way, because we are accustomed to it. Every age has its own customs and its own methods of dancing.

In the Roman world, as in the Greek, it was often the custom for a dancer to be a singer as well, accompanying himself on an instrument; this is very characteristic, and it must not be forgotten that in antiquity to dance was to put oneself on show, to prove one's ability and grace in front of an audience of admirers. As today in the East, dancing was considered an art, and nobody thought of dancing if he had an ungraceful figure or did not know how to. Dancing was a pleasure, but also an exhibition. Today everybody dances if they want to, the old, the fat, the clumsy and the ugly. Dancing, which is in origin a spectacle of beauty, is today simply an occasion for a social gathering, and for individual enjoyment for those who wish to dance, even when they do not know how to. Many people enjoy dancing for its own sake, although they are not natural dancers and have never been to a dancing school; they know that modern society is prepared to look on them kindly and overlook their shortcomings. These poor people (we have all seen them), suffer agonies but they are forgiven. They barge with their elbows, trample on feet, sweat and pant to keep their balance, they are inelegant and ridiculous, and yet they still dance. The Romans showed greater wisdom; not only was the number of those who were allowed to dance more restricted, but a sense of modesty forbade dancing in public without having first mastered the art.

In those days also there were many who longed to dance, especially the young with itching feet. A real passion for dancing gripped Rome in the years after the Punic Wars; it seems to be a law of history that a period of fearful war brings as its aftermath amongst the young a heightened desire to dance. Never, however, have dancing masters opened so many schools and done so much business, as in that age. The phenomenon gripped men's minds, and even in the circle of the Scipios, who were generally so tolerant towards Greek influences and all modern tendencies in Rome, men began to ask where this perpetual dancing of the young would end. Scipio Aemilianus in particular, who publicly denounced this danger and the indecorum of excessive dancing, said[39]

> Our young people are taught indecent tricks. They go to acting schools with dancers where they learn to sing to the harp and lute, which our ancestors considered disgraceful for freeborn men. I repeat, freeborn boys and girls go to dancing lessons with ballet dancers. When I was told this, I could not bring myself to believe that men of noble family would allow their children to be taught such things. But when I was taken to one of these schools, I swear I saw there more than fifty boys and girls, among them—a sight which made me despair of the state—a boy still wearing the *bulla*, not less than twelve years old and the son of a candidate for the consulship, dancing with castanets. Even the basest slave would shrink from performing such a dance.

Wise words, but the passion for dancing was stronger than the criticism of the wise and it continued. In the Imperial age the attraction of dancing, it seems, seized even grown men, but not seriously minded people; the effeminate, the ostentatious and the vain danced. The bore, who in Horace's[40] famous satire torments the poet with his interminable chatter, boasts that he can dance most gracefully. *Quis membra movere mollius (possit)?* A similar character, Atticus, who is presented to us by Martial[41] as the prototype of a vain and foolish man, danced most gracefully. The emperor Caligula[42] also danced, and carried the fury of his madness into this pastime. He danced day and night, and when he was watching others dance in the theatre, he accompanied the

57. A chariot race. This well-preserved mosaic from the Horkstow Villa of the fourth century A. D. shows a chariot race. The *spina* (central wall) is terminated at each end by a pair of *metae*. On the left (*above*) an *auriga* has fallen from his chariot, which has lost a wheel, and is being assisted by a dismounted horseman. To the right, a mounted horseman waves a lassoo. (*p. 251*)

8. Mosaic showing cupids fighting, from Bignor, Sussex. To the left a *secutor*, with a helmet, breast-plate and curved shield and armed with a short sword, fights a *retiarius* armed with a net (*rete*), trident and sword. He is lightly clad in a tunic and girdle. To the right a *lanista*, or trainer, supervises the fight. The block and ring were evidently used for shackling gladiators. (*p. 253*)

9. Death of a fallen gladiator. As the heralds raise their trumpets the victorious gladiator lifts his sword to despatch his fallen rival. (*p. 253*)

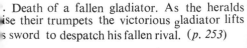

60. Relief showing scene from a comedy. The masked actors recite while a flute player plays.

61. Pompeii. Mosaic showing comic actors.

gestures of the actors with his own and sang their songs with them. Once, at dead of night, he suddenly summoned three men of consular rank; they came at once, torn rudely from their sleep and filled with dread, convinced that their last hour had come. They were invited to seat themselves on a bench; suddenly with a great leap Caligula appeared, magnificently dressed in a mantle and a tunic reaching to his feet. He danced, sang and disappeared; when the spectacle was finished, the three consuls were allowed to return home.

But these were exceptional cases; for grown and responsible men dancing *Romanum non est.*

NOTES

1. Sat., II, 3, 247–8:

> *Aedificare casas, plostello adjungere mures*
> *Ludere par impar, equitare in harundine longa.*

cf. Seneca, De const. sap., 12, 2: *In litoribus harenae congestu simulacra domuum excitant.*

2. Macrobius, I, 7, 22.
3. Persius, 1, 10: *nucibus facimus quaecumque relictis.*
4. Ibid. 3, 50. The game is described in a short anonymous poem, called Nux, errroneously attributed to Ovid in some manuscripts.
5. Seneca, De Const. Sap., 12, 2.
6. Pollux, IX, 122.
7. Horace, Epist., I, 1, 59–60.
8. Persius, 5, 111.
9. Suetonius, Aug., 71.
10. Ibid. Nero, 30.
11. Ibid. Claud., 33.
12. 1, 92–93.
13. Ibid. 11, 176–7.
14. Persius, 5, 57.
15. Germania, 24.
16. Martial, XIV, 16.
17. XIV, 14.
18. Capt., 70.
19. See p. 98.
20. Lamer in Pauly-Wissowa, XIII, col. 900, s.v. Lusoria tabula.
21. See p. 224.
22. Cicero, pro Caelio, 15, 36.

23. The expression is quoted as proverbial by Plato, Laws III, 689 d.
24. Suetonius, Cal., 54: *Atque hic tam docilis ad cetera natare nesciit.*
25. Martial, I, 62, 5–6.
26. Cicero, pro Caelio, 11, 27: 15, 35.
27. See note 130 on p. 49.
28. Horace, Sat., II, 1, 7–8.
29. Cicero, Ad Att., XIII, 33, 4.
30. Cicero, Pro Caelio, 16, 38: *At fuit fama. Quotusquisque est qui istam effugere possit in tam maledica civitate?*
31. Ibid. 15, 38, and *passim.*
32. Horace, Odes, I, 37, 1–2.
33. Ibid. III, 18, 15–16:

> *Gaudet invisam pepulisse fossor*
> *ter pede terram;*

Epist., I, 14, 25–26.
34. From the Greek κίναιδος. In Greece in the Hellenistic age there were stage performances by dancers, a mixture of recitation, music and dancing.
35. Praef., 1; Epam., 2, 1.
36. Sallust, Bell. Cat., 25, 2: *Psallere et cantare (docta) elegantius quam necesse est probae.*
37. Horace, Odes, III, 6, 21–22.
38. *Ricordi politici e civili*, p. 179.
39. Macrobius, III, 14, 7.
40. Sat., I, 9, 24–25.
41. II, 7, 5.
42. Suetonius, Cal., 54.

CHAPTER XXII

Hunting and Fishing

Uncertainty of the origin of hunting as a sport in Rome. Venatio. Aucupium. *Fishing.*

HUNTING and fishing were two of the most popular Roman pastimes. Horace[1] compares the Roman love of hunting with the less manly Greek sports; but if hunting became one of the most popular sports for young Romans and was even enjoyed by women,[2] it seems that hunting as a sport, which was widespread in Greece in the Hellenistic age, reached Rome from Greece only late in the second century B.C. According to Polybius,[3] one of the earliest hunters in Rome was Publius Scipio Aemilianus and his tutors were young Greek aristocrats. Later, hunting became a common recreation for all. An inscription puts hunting amongst the greatest pleasures of life: 'to hunt, to bathe, to gamble, to laugh, that is life' (*Venari, lavari, ludere, ridere, occest vivere*).[4] Cicero mentions its two forms (see p. 244), *venatio* and *aucupium*, as agreeable occupations for the elderly.[5] Even Pliny the Younger,[6] the most literary of literary men of the Imperial age, amused himself in the country by hunting, though he did not forget to take his wax tablets along with him as well as his nets, so that he might devote to composition the time when he was waiting for game to appear. 'Whilst I sat at my nets, you would have found me not with spear (*venabulum*) and dart (*lancea*), but pen and tablet by my side. I mused and wrote, being resolved if I returned with my hands empty, at least to come home with my pocketbook full.' With such a peaceful hunter the animals must have felt reasonably safe.

In a country once so thickly wooded as Italy, to fix an exact date for the introduction of hunting as a sport seems arbitrary. Almost certainly young free men did not wait to be taught by Greece, but spontaneously decided to do as a sport what trained slaves did as a duty in order to destroy animals which were harrying the flocks, or to maintain and vary the table of their masters. Fixing a precise date for the beginning of hunting as a sport in Italy is therefore impossible. The practice is certainly very old, for it is obviously a useful occupation, and even when it became a sport there continued to be professional huntsmen and specially trained slaves. The haughty statement of Sallust[7] that hunting is a *servile officium*, seems contrary to contemporary opinion, although it has some truth in it.

After the invasion of Rome by Greek customs, both recreational and professional hunting acquired the greatest importance in Roman life. The hunting of birds, *aucupium*, differed completely from *venatio*, the hunting of wild animals, such as wolves, bears, boars, hares, etc. The Romans regarded the two occupations as separate and had two different words for them.

The modern use of firearms has resulted in identical methods of hunting wild animals of every type, winged or not, and the same name is applied to both sports. Birds are a difficult prey for a man without firearms, and cunning is usually a more successful method of catching them than shooting at them with slings (Plate 53)[8] or arrows. Of these two types of hunting *venatio* uses force and animals are its prey, while *aucupium* uses guile and is directed at birds; the first is an energetic and strenuous sport, the latter a pleasant sedentary occupation only requiring a certain skill. The genuine huntsman, the Roman Nimrod, is the *venator*, unwearied by any effort, who endures the ice cold nights on the mountains ('forgetful of his tender wife', as Horace says[9]); the fowler, on the other hand, needs no courage to watch the sky and to decoy and capture his prey.

Large scale *venatio*, the driving of game, consisted of tracking down the animals and then pursuing them with dogs and driving them towards nets.

The huntsmen in short tunics (*aliculae*), their legs protected by high boots (*crepidae*) or puttees (*fasciae crurales*), and usually wearing a close-fitting cap to protect their heads against the sun, carried weapons of various types in the hunt: the sling (*funda*), javelins for wounding from a distance (*iacula, lanceae*), a small knife (*culter venatorius*), and, for hunting boars and any other beasts likely to turn and defend themselves vigorously when attacked, the *venabulum*. This was used to keep the infuriated beast at a distance and to finish it off; its long, strong wooden handle, had a broad iron point, long and sharp, with two other iron points (*morae*) at the bottom, the purpose of which was to keep the wounded animal at a distance from the hunter, for it was never wise to take liberties even with a mortally wounded beast. The *venabulum* was not a weapon for a faint-hearted man. Pliny the Younger (p. 243) preferred his pen and his wax tablets.

Before the hunt began, the weapons as well as the nets, dogs, horses, everything in fact which made up the *instrumentum venatorium*, was in the charge of slaves. When hunting, free men willingly faced danger and exhaustion, but they would not stoop to acting as porters.

The companion of man in the chase was, as it always has been, his faithful hound, *fida canum vis*, as Lucretius says;[10] a trusted and intelligent slave (*magister canum*) looked after the breeding, rearing and training of the hounds, and when they were still puppies, he began to arouse their hunting instincts by urging them to worry the skins of wild beasts;[11] as soon as they were capable of enduring the fatigues of the chase they were unleashed with adult dogs against the fleeing game.

When the place for the drive was reached, each hunter took his weapons and went to his position. The slaves (*vestigatores*), with the hunting dogs on the leash, followed the animals' tracks and tried to run them down. As soon as the beast left its hiding place, the pursuit began. Those which, when wounded, stood at bay against their attackers, were finished off in a hand-to-hand fight between man and beast; most fled, with the dogs at their heels, pelted with stones and terrified by cries, and were skilfully guided in the required direction until they were caught and trapped in closely-woven nets. To cut off their retreat towards safer ground, besides the *retia*, to be described later, the so-called *formidines*[12] were used, long ropes to which feathers of different colours, particularly red, were attached. The rustling of these large brightly-coloured feathers was especially used as a scare when hunting deer; the terrified animals turned back to meet their death.

Nets (*retia*) were of different types. The *retia* properly so called, with large meshes, were used to surround the area where the drive was held. They were made in considerable lengths to prevent the animals escaping from the area. *Casses*, small-meshed nets made into loops (*sinus*), were used for enveloping the animals when caught; the skill of the huntsman consisted in driving the animals towards them. The *plagae* were small-meshed nets which were probably used for the double purpose of blocking the passage of fleeing animals at points where they were likely to escape, as well as enveloping them in the meshes.

The large-scale drive was the most spectacular form of hunting, exhausting and dangerous, but exhilarating. However, man's taste for treachery is too great for him to restrain, even with animals, from resorting to deceitful means, such as traps (*laquei, pedicae*) or pits (*foveae*) covered with leaves. Game was often trapped like this and lost life and liberty, the inglorious victim of man's guile.

Sometimes hunting developed into a trial of speed between man and animal; skilful horsemen chased hares on horseback, and when they were exhausted and allowed themselves to be overtaken, the riders tried to hit them with a stick. This sport is mentioned as one of the most exhausting forms of hunting.

In *aucupium* methods still employed by bird catchers today, when guns are not available, were used. Snares concealed among bushes or on branches of trees are the simplest form of deceiving birds; boys and country folk use them today as they were used then. But the art of the *auceps* depended chiefly on attracting birds by song and bait, and then capturing them with carefully laid traps. On the trapping grounds (*areae*) blind birds tied by a string were used as decoys; the ground was spread liberally with food clearly visible, and when a number of birds had arrived, nets hidden on the ground were rapidly closed by means of ropes. This, the most advanced form of *aucupium*, might bring large bags. Men also hunted with birdlime, or decoyed birds with the little owl, or other tame birds, or a *fistula* which imitated their call. *Aucupium* with birdlime required great skill, because it involved making the smeared reeds (*calami aucupatorii*) rise slowly through the branches where the bird was perching, without arousing suspicion. The *auceps* carried with him long thick sticks to reach the bird even if it was sitting on the highest branches of a tree; these treacherous sticks were bound together and rose slowly until the bird perched and was caught.

Martial,[13] always precise, has pictured the scene in two wonderfully descriptive lines:

> *Non tantum calamis, sed cantu fallitur ales,*
> *Callida dum tacita crescit harundo manu.*

Large birds of prey were captured by tying a live dove by the leg and making it flutter, after the surrounding ground had been scattered with large sticks smeared with birdlime.

Hawking was known, but not widely practised.[14]

Fishing, a dangerous and unpleasant trade for those whose living it was, had its devotees, like hunting, and many fished for pleasure.

33. FISHERMEN
(FROM BLÜMNER, *op. cit.*)

There were numerous ways of fishing; the method preferred by professional fishermen consisted of large throwing-nets, held under water by a weight, with large corks at the edges (*sagena, verriculum, tragum,* etc.); fishing in this manner had to be done in parties and involved many hours at sea. A single fisherman who wanted to fish with nets from the land or a rock, used a smaller net (*iaculum*); these nets (fig. 33) were made so that when the fisherman drew them in, the same cord which brought them up closed their mouths, and prevented the fish escaping while the net was still under water.

Single fishermen preferred to use lines (*linea*) and hooks (*hamus*) like ours.

Another method of fishing was to leave osier baskets with narrow mouths (*nassae*), like lobster pots, immersed for a long time in the sea; fish could easily enter these traps but found difficulty, in escaping.

With larger fish, such as tunny, and large molluscs like the octopus, brutal means were used, and they were killed with blows from a trident, as we see in the Etruscan mural painting reproduced in Plate 53. This method of fishing was rarer with small fish, but small tridents were sometimes used to spear them. For this type of fishing we use forks, but, as we know,[15] the fork was not a common object among the Romans, who ate with their fingers.

Further Reading

W. Radcliffe, *Fishing from the Earliest Times* (London, 1921).
A. J. Butler. *Sport in Classic Times* (London, 1931).

NOTES

1. Sat., II, 2, 9–13.
2. Juvenal, 1, 22.
3. XXXI, 29, 3.
4. CIL, VIII, 17938, found on a *tabula lusoria* (see p. 236).
5. De sen., 16, 56.
6. Epist., I, 6, 1.
7. Cat., 4, 1.
8. Persius, 3, 60–61.
9. Odes, I, 1, 25–28.
10. VI, 1222.
11. Horace, Epist., I, 2, 64–67.
12. Seneca, De ira, II, 12, 2; Lucan, IV, 437–8.
13. XIV, 218.
14. XIV, 216.
15. See p. 94.

CHAPTER XXIII

The Ludi Circenses

Ludi circenses *and* ludi scaenici. *Organisation of the* ludi. Ludi gladiatorii. *Chariot racing.* Venationes. *Public executions. Bloodlust of the people.*

THE public shows given to the people of Rome by the generosity of magistrates or private citizens were called generically *ludi*. The *ludi* were of three types: those which took place in the circus (*ludi circenses*), theatrical performances (*ludi scaenici*), and gladiatorial combats (*munera*). These were Etruscan in origin, and in the Republican era were of a private character, performed on the occasion of funerals (*ludi funebres*). The *ludi scaenici* were the most ancient and took place in the Circus Maximus or the Circus Flaminius, later also in the Flavian Amphitheatre, reserved for shows on a larger scale. The *naumachiae* were used for naval battles, and were built so that the centre could be flooded for the occasion. Temporary wooden amphitheatres were also built.[1] For certain shows open spaces were used. When Nero[2] burnt alive the Christians held guilty of the fire of Rome, he used his huge gardens for their punishment, which for that night were extensively illuminated by the smoking brightness of so many human torches.

The celebration of the *ludi* formed part of Roman religion and was an event in the official calendar. This did not exclude the possibility of proclaiming exceptional public *ludi* as well, or *ludi* offered by private citizens; but the most important were the annual *ludi* on certain fixed dates (*ludi stati*). Apart from the *ludi Apollinares* (6–12 July, founded in 212 B.C.) presided over by the Urban Praetor, the task of organising the games in the republican era fell on the Aediles. The plebeian Aediles were in charge of the *ludi plebeii* (4–17 November, founded in 229 B.C., in the Circus Flaminius) and the *Cerealia* (12–19 April, founded in 202 B.C.); the curule Aediles were in charge of the *ludi Romani*, the *Megalenses* and the *Floralia*, in honour respectively of the Capitoline

Triad (Jupiter, Juno and Minerva), the *Dea Mater* and the *Dea Flora*. The most ancient and solemn were the *ludi Romani*, of which the *ludus Troiae*, celebrated by Virgil in the *Aeneid*, formed part;[3] it consisted of manoeuvres by youths on horseback.

Theatrical performances accompanied the *circenses* only at the most important *ludi*. In the *Floralia* mimes were put on and were occasions of licentious displays,[4] in harmony with the cult of the *Dea Flora*, a divinity without thought of morals, the lighthearted goddess of abandoned celebration.

In the Imperial age, when the emperor gave extraordinary games, he appointed *curatores ludorum* to organise them. The *ludi saeculares* had a particular importance; they were supposed to take place every century, but in reality they were celebrated at very irregular intervals. The *ludi saeculares*[5] of 17 B.C., when Horace was the official poet, are well known.

Although the *ludi* were financed by the Treasury, the magistrates responsible for providing them spent their own money lavishly on the games, often huge sums, to win the favour of the mob; many were ruined by such prodigality.

The *ludi circenses* consisted of spectacles of very different types; the most usual were the *ludi gladiatorii*, in which well-trained gladiators fought in various ways (see Plate 59), each trying to wound or kill his opponent; the fate of the wounded man depended on the mood of the public; if all waved their handkerchiefs the fallen man's life was spared. If they held out their fists with down-turned thumb (*pollice verso*) the conquered man was killed, either by the victor or an assistant;[6] the crowd was always curious to see how elegantly he could die. The Emperor Claudius,[7] who delighted in bloody sights, was always ready to condemn a fallen gladiator, particularly if he was a *retiarius*, as the *retiarii* fought with uncovered faces, and Claudius took great pleasure in observing the spasms and sudden pallor on the faces of the dying. Even senators and ladies were compelled to appear in gladiatorial contests,[8] and some emperors[9] descended to fight in the arena of the Circus, overcome by the lure of blood, danger, popularity and exhibitionism.

Gladiators were usually prisoners of war and were trained in barracks (*ludi gladiatorii*), run on military lines with instructors (*lanistae*), trainers and doctors (see p. 215). In the circus they were matched in couples (*paria*); different *paria* of gladiators often fought simultaneously.

Funerals, or any other event which made an act of private generosity to the public appropriate, were also occasions for *ludi gladiatorii;* some speculators bought up pairs of gladiators and hired them to those who required them.[10]

Chariot racing was another of the sports of the circus (see Plate 57); the charioteers drove standing upright in their chariots, and the best acquired a tremendous popularity; their names were on the lips and in the hearts of all; the horses were known as well as the charioteers. Martial[11] says 'I, who am known to the nations and to Rome's people (why do you envy me?) am not known better than the horse Andraemon'. A poet could never compete for glory with a horse. The professional charioteers were of humble origin, but the passion for chariot racing in the circus also gripped high society, and Nero in his mania for self-display often descended into the circus to play the part of charioteer.[12]

The charioteers wore the colours of the sporting parties (*factiones*) which were competing for the prize. There were four *factiones*, the red (*russata*), the green (*prasina*), the white (*albata*) and the blue (*veneta*). The charioteers wore a metal helmet and a short, smart belted tunic. The starting signal was given by the magistrate in charge of the games dropping a small starched napkin.[13] Each race consisted of a certain number of laps. The greatest difficulty in the race lay in keeping as close to the *meta* as possible when making a turn. It was necessary to graze the *meta* to save time but without striking it and overturning the chariot. The *meta* (a broad-based stone pillar with a pointed top) was on the left; the better horse (*funalis*) was usually put on the outside of the team. The race depended largely on the co-operation between the *funalis* and the *auriga*. Every *factio* had its fanatical supporters.[14] Caligula[15] was a devoted supporter of the green faction; he spent hours in the stables amongst the horses and charioteers and even ate there. The rivalry between charioteers was very great, and often broke out in personal hatred (see p. 254).

The *venationes* were wild-beast hunts in the circus; starving tigers, panthers and lions were let out from subterranean cages and killed after a long and dangerous chase by armed gladiators (Plate 56); bulls and infuriated rhinoceroses charged round the circus, enraged by the dummies of red material, called *pilae*,[16] which were thrown at them. Nero[17] descended into the arena unarmed, or armed with only a club, to face and kill a lion. This would have been an act of extraordinary boldness, if he had not been dealing with a *praeparatus leo*, a poor beast, previously made harmless and only fit to be killed. But the public went into ecstasies.

There were also less dramatic hunts, intended to put the audience into a good humour. In the *Cerealia*, foxes with lighted torches tied to their tails were hunted, in the *Floralia* harmless animals like rabbits and hares were pursued.[18]

The public execution of criminals formed part of the *circenses*, when they were thrown *ad bestias* or put to death in some equally cruel way; as the condemned man had to be tortured to death, there seemed no reason for cheating the public, who could never have enough bloodshed, of such a spectacle.

Among the most popular forms of such executions in the circus were spectacles which ended with the mutilation and death of the leading actor. While in normal performances the death of the actor was a fiction and he was replaced by a dummy at the last moment, in the circus the actor playing a character destined to die died in reality. As in the myth, real beasts chased an Orpheus of flesh and blood, who played his lyre until a real bear tore him to pieces.[19] The story of Daedalus and Icarus was also performed.[20] Icarus with his dishevelled wings was hurled from the sky to break his bones in the middle of the circus; a flight, a fall and then a mass of shapeless palpitating flesh in a pool of blood. If Icarus finished in this way, Daedalus did not profit from his foresight, because a ferocious beast sprang out and tore him to pieces. The effect was magnificent and the people abandoned themselves to transports of delight.

Another popular item was the scene of Mucius Scaevola in the presence of Porsenna, reproduced to the life; a heroic Mucius[21] allowed his arm to be burnt, unmoved under the admiring eyes of the spectators, full of sympathy for a man so brave in the face of physical pain. However, it was observed, he could not do otherwise; his choice was clear, either to remain motionless with his hand in the flame or to be burnt alive in a tunic of pitch.[22]

The theme of one ancient mime was the story of the pirate Lareolus, who was crucified after a lifetime of violence and sacrilege. When the Flavian amphitheatre was opened, a perfect production of this mime was staged. The leading actor was nailed to the cross; and an infuriated bear was let loose upon him, which tore the unfortunate man with his paws and reduced him to a blood-stained pulp.[23] The official poet of the scene describes the sight with great complacency. The limbs dripping with blood were reduced to one vast wound; the body which no longer resembled a human body ('in no way at all', *nusquam*, the poet specifies), was still alive and palpitating, a wonderfully entertaining spectacle. It was 'the love and delight of the human race', the emperor Titus, who took this paternal care to provide his subjects with such pleasant pastimes.

The Romans watched gladiatoral shows with the same attitude of mind, almost drunk with the sight of so much bloodshed. 'Kill him', they shouted,[24] 'beat him, burn him! Why does he meet the sword so timidly? Why didn't he fight more bravely? Why does he die so unwillingly?' In the intervals impatient voices could be heard: 'Now let's have some throats cut to keep the action going.'[25] They found it tedious to remain seated without some form of entertainment.

It was a solemn and moving moment when the fallen gladiator was about to be dispatched by his opponent (Plate 59). Hard-faced men and women, eagerly anticipating the sight of blood, stretched out their arms with their thumbs turned down, the sign of condemnation, *pollice verso*. Bleeding and resigned, the loser, already in agony but not forgetting the art of dying well, learnt from the *lanista* in the training school, bared his throat and gathered his last effort in order not to disappoint the spectators by a poor performance. The circus heralds blew loudly on their trumpets, and the conqueror, whirling round his sword in triumph, plunged it into the neck of the wretched writhing man while the people applauded.

All this horrifies us. Over Roman civilisation and its greatness the people's abominable passion for the *ludi* of the circus throws a dark shadow, a stain which cannot be rubbed out. Even in the most barbarous times the human conscience has refused to continue the wicked custom. To say that we condemn this revolting custom is too little, we cannot even begin to understand. The indifference of the upper classes surprises us more than the frenzied excitement of the bloodthirsty crowd; we are amazed that men who seem to us so human and near our own way of thinking in so many ways, should have been so indifferent towards this bestial and wicked practice. Only in the writings of Seneca is a voice of disapproval raised, but it is a weak voice, expressing disgust rather than protest. The first Christians whose bodies torn by wild beasts reddened the sand of the circus, proved the need for new laws, which in their triumph abolished ancient cruelty and made it impossible and incomprehensible.

Amongst the Romans these sights of violence and bloodshed excited the worst instincts. The crowd loved them, and the spirit of partisanship which always seizes men watching a public competition, helped to increase their excitement. They took sides for a particular gladiator, betted and shouted encouragement to their favourites. Women were in ecstasies of excitement, and their hearts too were won by the victorious gladiator. In the provincial amphitheatres local prejudices burst out. The heated atmosphere of the circus and the presence of a closely-packed crowd stimulated insults and riots.

Tacitus tells of a tragic episode which took place at the games at Pompeii in the reign of Nero. An exchange of insults began, as usual, between the people of Pompeii and of Nuceria, who had come in great numbers to watch the show in the amphitheatre. Tempers grew heated, and men came to blows, first with stones and then with knives. A furious riot broke out and the people of Nuceria, whose numbers were smaller, got the worst of it, and left dead and wounded on the ground. Nero punished the people of Pompeii by banning their games for ten years. This did not, however, stop the Pompeians from glorying in the event and recording their victory over their ill-treated and murdered guests in their scribblings on the walls.[26]

Further Reading

L. Friedlander, *Roman Life and Manners under the Early Empire* (London, 1908) Vol. ii, Ch. i.

G. Jennison, *Animals for Show and Pleasure in Ancient Rome* (Manchester, 1937).

W. Warde Fowler, *The Roman Festivals* (Oxford, 1899).

NOTES

1. Suetonius, Nero, 12.
2. Tacitus, Ann., XV, 44, 7.
3. Aeneid, V, 545.
4. Valerius Maximus, II, 10, 8; Martial, I, praef.; cf. Lactantius, Inst., I, 20, 6.
5. An inscription discovered in 1890 has preserved the programme (CIL, VI, 32323 = Dessau 5050).
6. Martial, XII, 29, 7; Juvenal, 3, 36.
7. Suetonius, Claud., 34.
8. Tacitus, Ann., XV, 32, 2: *Spectacula gladiatorum idem annus habuit; . . . feminarum illustrium senatorumque plures per arenam foedati sunt;* Suetonius, Dom., 4: *Nec virorum modo pugnas (edidit) sed et feminarum.*
9. Suetonius, Cal., 54; Aelius Lampridius, Comm. Antonin., 12, 10–12.
10. Cicero, Ad Att., IV, 4b, 2.
11. X, 9.
12. Suetonius, Nero, 22: *Ipse aurigare atque etiam spectari saepius voluit.*
13. Martial, XII, 29, 9; Suetonius, Nero, 22.
14. Petronius, 70.
15. Suetonius, Cal., 55.
16. Martial, Lib. spect., 19.
17. Suetonius, Nero, 53.
18. Martial, I, 44, 1.
19. Martial, Lib. spect., 21, 7–8.
20. Cf. Suetonius, Nero, 12, and Martial, Lib. spect., 8.
21. Martial, I, 21.
22. Ibid. X, 25.
23. Martial, Lib. Spect., 7; see verses 5–6:

> *Vivebant laceri membris stillantibus artus*
> *Inque omni nusquam corpore corpus erat.*

24. Seneca, Epist., 7, 4: '*Occide, verbera, ure! Quare tam timide incurrit in ferrum? Quare parum audacter occidit? Quare parum libenter moritur?*'
25. Ibid: *Intermissum est spectaculum:* '*Interim jugulentur homines, ne nihil agatur*'.
26. CIL, IV, 1298; 1329 (= Dessau 6443[b]).

CHAPTER XXIV

The Theatre

The tradition of the Greek theatre. The Roman theatre continued the tradition of the Hellenistic theatre. The building of theatres at Rome. The parts of a Roman theatre. The organisation of theatrical performances. The audience.

THE modern theatre derives the design of its buildings and the pattern of its performances from the Roman theatre. As the regular Roman theatre was modelled on the Greek, the theatrical tradition of ancient Greece, after various stages of development like the links in a long chain, has come down to our day.

The presentation of plays in the classical world is one of the principal achievements of Athens and goes back to the period of her greatest splendour; in Athens theatrical performances were rare and solemn religious ceremonies connected with the cult of Dionysus. Later, the theatre gradually acquired an independence which made its development as secular entertainment possible, as well as accentuating the literary character of both tragedy and comedy. Many factors contributed to this evolution of the ancient theatre, particularly the drying up of the dramatic genius of Athens; the great tragedians of Athens flourished within little more than two generations in the fifth century B.C., and left no worthy successors. Spreading beyond the boundaries of Attica, the theatre, in addition to new productions, began to present dramas whose reputation was already established; if prizes were awarded on such occasions, they went not to the poet and the trainers of the chorus, as in the dramatic festivals at Athens, but to the actors for their skill in interpreting the play.

An attempt to restore theatrical performances to the old style of dramatic competition, as a stimulus to new productions, was made by Ptolemy Philadelphus (285-247 B.C.), under whom there was an unexpected but shortlived revival of dramatic poetry (the Pleiad of seven dramatists).

In the fourth century B.C., as a result of the extensive spread of the cult of Dionysus in Greece, centres for plays multiplied, and efforts were made in most cities to build permanent theatres. Even in Macedonia and Thessaly, countries which were then barely civilised, there were regular dramatic performances. But at the same time as the spread of the cult of Dionysus and the theatre, a contrary development which was of decisive importance for the independence of the theatre was taking place. Theatrical performances were no longer necessarily bound up with the Dionysiac cult; on the one hand they were introduced into the rites of other divinities besides Dionysus (in the Pythian Games at Delphi, the games in honour of the Muses at Thespiae, the games in honour of Zeus Soter at Acraephia, etc.), while on the other hand, particularly in the Hellenistic age, theatrical performances were put on not only at religious festivals, but also to celebrate a political occasion, such as a royal marriage, a victory or some other important event. Though on such occasions a performance always had a religious side to it, as an act of prayer or thanksgiving to the gods was involved, the ritual element was reduced to a minimum compared with the worldly, secular and literary aspect of the production.

The Hellenistic practice of celebrating important events by the production of famous plays was adopted in Rome, and regular performances also began to be customary in the Roman world. The primitive forms of native drama either fell into disuse or were staged as minor performances. The year 240 B.C. is a vital date in Roman literature, when Livius Andronicus presented translations of a Greek tragedy and comedy.[1] There are references to *ludi scaenici* which took place in Rome in 364 B.C.,[2] but they refer to a pantomime performed by Etruscan actors.

In its external arrangements the theatre was bound up with the celebration of the *ludi*. But even if the occasions for dramatic performances were religious festivals, the Roman theatre no longer presented that ritual atmosphere which we have observed in the Attic theatre. To watch plays was not, as it was for the Athenians and the Greeks generally in the fifth and fourth centuries, to participate in a rite. The Hellenistic age, as we have seen, had accentuated the secular character of the theatre, and the theatre at Rome was essentially secular.

This explains the low esteem in which actors and authors were held. Writing for the theatre, or at any rate wearing officially the garb of a dramatic author, was not thought becoming for a man of high rank. The profession of an actor was one of those which involved a reduction of legal rights, as did all humble and degrading trades;[3] even the Etruscan name *histrio*, which the Romans used for 'actor', was a word of contempt from the earliest days. Actors and authors were usually slaves or freemen.

The *ludi scaenici* were the noblest part of the *ludi*. The common people preferred the amphitheatre to the theatre, but the Roman theatre also had its devotees; Roman dramatic literature produced masterpieces, even though they have largely disappeared, with the exception of the comedies of Plautus and Terence. If the public had tastes which varied according to social classes and the time, and were sometimes questionable, it is still true that the Roman people took an intense pleasure in the theatre; it is an exaggeration to generalise on the Roman public's lack of interest from the misfortune suffered by Terence, when at the first production of his *Hecyra*[4] the spectators deserted the theatre to watch an exhibition of tight-rope walking.[5]

Dramatic writing flourished most brilliantly in Rome between the second Punic war and the age of Sulla. But in this period the structure of the theatre, if it deserves the name, was primitive. The theatre consisted merely of the *scaena*, the stage (*pulpitum*) on which the actors performed, and the *scaena* in its literal sense of backcloth. Both *pulpitum* and *scaena* were large wooden[6] erections put up temporarily[7] and dismantled when the *ludi scaenici* ended. Brick stages were only rarely built, as we know from references going back to the first decades of the second century B.C.,[8] but such buildings, although they might show a magnificent feeling for theatrical decor and be adorned with paintings[9] and silver, gold and ivory ornaments,[10] were equally temporary.

The public in early days stood to watch the performances,[11] senators among the people; later, wooden benches (*subsellia*) were arranged in front of the stage, and a law[12] was passed that members of the senatorial order should sit in the front rows.

We have no archaeological evidence for the theatres of this age, as is inevitable with temporary structures, and we are forced to reconstruct the stage not so much from the few direct references we have, as from the details provided by the comedies of Plautus and Terence. We are thus confined almost exclusively to the stage in comedy. This consisted of a vertical wooden backdrop; it was considered a novelty when painted scenery was introduced at the beginning of the first century B.C.[13] In the backdrop three doors[14] opened on to the stage, corresponding to the three neighbouring houses of the characters in the comedy. If the action required an entrance to a temple, the main door was not shown, but a side door similar to that of the neighbouring houses in the wall (περίβολος) round the temple;[15] at a distance from the temple an altar could, if necessary, be erected on the stage.[16] From the backdrop a porch protruded on to the stage in front of each of the three doors,[17] consisting of a flat roof[18] supported by two columns.[19]

The tragic stage must have been very similar. As Roman tragedy was modelled on Greek, we must suppose that the Roman tragic stage had the same characteristics as the Greek; in the centre at the back of the stage a large door opened, representing the entrance to the palace, with the usual porch;[20] at each side of the palace two other doors opened, through which the actors could enter a private house or a temple.[21]

When in the Imperial age permanent stone theatres were built meticulous attention was paid to every detail of scenery, three types of which were available—for tragedy, comedy and the *saturae*; in these last, trees, caves and mountains were shown.[22]

The first stone theatre was built in 55 B.C. by Pompey,[23] who had been impressed by the theatre at Mytilene and had a model of it made, in order to build a similar one himself in Rome on a larger scale. It stood in the *Campus Martius*. Under Augustus two other theatres were built: the theatre of Marcellus,[24] the building of which was started by Caesar and completed by Augustus, and the theatre of Balbus (smaller, but more splendidly decorated and with four onyx columns)[25] near the Tiber. Both were dedicated in 13 B.C. But the theatre of Pompey remained the largest of all Roman theatres.[26] We have references to other stone theatres.[27] We know, besides, that later wooden theatres still continued to be built,[28] as well as theatres consisting of the stage alone.[29]

It may seem surprising that the Romans, among whom Greek culture penetrated at a fairly early stage (see p. 109), should have resisted for so long the Hellenistic custom of building permanent stone theatres. From the beginning of the cultural growth of Rome, a very strong interest in regular performances had been revealed, for the Italian character finds the theatre particularly congenial. But to the austerity of the ancient Romans it seemed contrary to good habits (*inutile et nociturum moribus*)[30] to encourage the people to sit for long hours watching performances.[31] Consequently if one college of censors, the magistrates responsible for authorising theatrical expenses during their period of office, generously allowed more permanent buildings, even though they were only stages, the succeeding censors might feel it their duty to have them pulled down.[32] Right up to the last years of the Republic there was a regular slaughter of theatres, which were built simply to be destroyed.[33]

When, in the last years of the Republic, and later during the Empire, Rome also had its permanent theatres, the essential parts of the theatre were the same as in the Hellenistic theatres, which had served as a model, except for varieties in shape: the *scaena*, the *orchestra* and the seats (*cavea*) which rose in a semicircle. In the Greek theatre the *orchestra* was an open space reserved for the chorus,[34] but in the Roman theatre it was occupied by seats for magistrates and members of the *ordo senatorius*. The *lex Roscia Theatralis*[35] of 67 B.C. laid down that only *equites* could sit in the fourteen rows behind the *orchestra* and in the first two rows only members of the order who had been tribunes.[36] The law aroused public protests, and during the consulate of Cicero it provoked riots.[37]

The choruses, which only very exceptionally took part in the dramatic action, acted on the stage and not in the *orchestra*.[38]

Another detail, unknown to the Greek theatre, was the curtain (*siparium, aulaea*). The curtain did not come down from above, as it does in our theatres, but was pulled up from below; consequently, 'to raise' and 'lower' the curtain have exactly opposite meanings in Latin. The curtain was only raised at the end of a performance, not between acts.[39]

The custom of protecting the audience from the sun with *velaria* was exclusively Roman.

The use of theatrical machinery to produce more realistic illusions on the stage was late in Rome. In the Greek theatre such machinery had been used from the fifth century B.C. (the age of the great tragedians and Aristophanes) when Greek theatres were still of wood;[40] in the Hellenistic age, when the design and layout of theatres and scenery reached the highest stage of perfection, the use of machinery became more involved and developed. The oldest of these *machinae* were those which announced the unexpected appearance of a divinity[41] with crashes of thunder and flashes of lightning: the βροντεῖον for thunder and the κεραυνοσκοπεῖον for lightning. A winch, μηχανή in its original meaning,[42] used for the appearance of a god from above (θεὸς ἐκ μηχανῆς, *deus ex machina*), was equally ancient. As in some plays, particularly those of Euripides, the intervention of a god helped to resolve a situation to which there seemed no human solution, the term *deus ex machina* is still used today to mean a superhuman and unexpected solution.

It is disputed by archaeologists when the περίακτοι were introduced into the Greek theatre, but they were probably an innovation of the Hellenistic age. The περίακτοι, which were also adopted by the Romans in the Imperial age and of which Vitruvius[43] gives an exact description, had the same theatrical function as our flies, that is to produce scenery suitable to the action of the play. They were revolving prisms, probably triangular,[44] of painted wood, one face of which represented, for example, the country, another a harbour, the city etc. They were situated on the two sides of the central door.

In one of the faces of the περίακτοι was a hollow which also made appearances by divinities possible. Our information on the two methods of staging divine apparitions by the μηχανή and the περίακτοι is insufficient; probably after the introduction of the περίακτοι only the celestial gods appeared *ex machina*, while the gods of earth and sea arrived on the stage by means of the περίακτοι. Apparitions from the underworld, however, arrived through a hole in the floor of the stage, called the 'Stairs of Charon' (χαρώνειοι κλίμακες).[45]

Another machine used in the Greek theatre was the ἐκκύκλημα, on the use of which there is disagreement. According to most,[46] it was a wooden hut on wheels, which at the suitable moment was rolled through the door with a tableau representing actions which had occurred inside the house. According to others it was a movable floor, on which a corpse on a bier or a living man in bed appeared at the door.[47]

Tradition attributed the introduction of theatrical machinery into Rome to M. Claudius Pulcher,[48] as he is mentioned as the first to introduce the βροντεῖον. Even before this, men had tried to produce the illusion of thunder by primitive methods, such as throwing rocks and nails into a brass basin. In the Imperial age, Greek machinery (*pegmata*)[49] was introduced into Rome, and was used not only in the theatre, but also for certain shows in the circus.

In the age of Plautus only one tragedy or comedy was performed in a day; the later custom of producing more than one play made dramatic competitions possible.

Tragedies and comedies were divided into acts according to rules which varied with the time. During the intervals of a comedy a flute player (*tibicen*) gave a performance on the stage.[50]

While in the ancient Greek theatre actors, including the chorus, were chosen and trained for each performance, there were permanent companies (*greges*) in Rome; acting had become a profession (see p. 258). Every company had a manager (*dominus gregis*, or *actor*); the magistrate or private citizen organising the games gave the manager an agreed sum for the payment of the author and the actors. If the performance was not satisfactory, the payment had to be refunded.

Until the middle of the second century B.C. there is no mention of regular dramatic competitions. The magistrate who had the task of organising the *ludi scaenici* decided on his own between competing authors and companies, without consulting others. The later references to theatrical competitions are far from precise, and we cannot be sure on what system admission to the competition was controlled. The winner received a palm as a prize. Dramatic competitions in Rome never had the importance they had in Athens.

The public was admitted free to the ordinary seats for performances in the circus and the theatre. The shows lasted for many hours and people brought their food and drink with them. The official in charge of the show also provided for the distribution of food, drink and sweets (*bellaria*).[51] Spectators began to collect in the public seats even on the night before the show. Everybody was anxious to be in time to secure a good seat, and for that he was prepared to sacrifice his sleep. During the long night wait the public made much noise. It is easy to imagine the cries, jokes, jeers and inevitable brawls, which made sleep difficult for all those in the neighbourhood. Once Caligula, who suffered from insomnia,[52] driven to distraction by the uproar of the mob, ordered his guards to chase them all away and beat them.[53] That night at least the crowd waiting for the *ludi* was silent.

During the show the Roman public was very rowdy, not only in the circus, but also in the theatre; as in Greece, the crowd showed its disapproval noisily with hisses, shouts and other rude noises. In theatrical performances they participated in the rivalry between competing authors and companies, each of which had its own supporters (*fautores*). The *operae*, cliques paid to applaud, contributed to confuse the judgement of the public in dramatic competitions and to disturb the good order of the theatre.

Theatrical performances took place by daylight, and so usually did the games in the circus, although sometimes nocturnal performances were held by torchlight as a novelty. The theatres were open to the skies; only the Odeons for musical performances were roofed. In the summer the sun beat pitilessly upon the crowded public benches of the theatres; umbrellas were used as a protection against the sun.[54] If the wind was not blowing, great covers[55] were drawn over the *cavea*, supported by large poles fixed in iron rings, such as we can see today in the large theatre of Pompeii. An effort was made to cool the theatre by sprinkling the stage with water mixed with saffron,[56] lightly perfumed. As it is agonising to stay seated on stone for a long time women brought cushions with them.[57]

Performances in the theatre and the circus were also a social occasion. In the back seats the people were crushed, but in the seats reserved for officials and aristocrats the smartest of Roman society met as if at a party. The ladies of the nobility could find no better occasion for displaying their smart clothes, elegant hairstyles and jewellery, and encouraging admirers. The front rows offered a magnificent sight with so much female beauty on show, so many fair elderly matrons, tinkling with jewellery and full of gay exuberance. 'They come to see', says Ovid,[58] 'and to be seen themselves' (*spectatum veniunt; veniunt spectentur ut ipsae*); later, Goethe[59] was to say in *Faust*, that women at theatres give a performance without demanding a penny from the manager (*die Damen spielen ohne Gage*). If any lesson is to be learnt from a detailed study of ancient manners, it is perhaps that, while the world changes little, the eternal female does not change at all.

Further Reading

M. Bieber, *The History of the Greek and Roman Theater* (Princeton, 1961) gives a detailed account of the archaeological evidence.
Special studies are:
W. Beare, *The Roman Stage* (2nd edn. London, 1955).
G. E. Duckworth, *The Nature of Roman Comedy* (Princeton, 1952).

NOTES

1. Livy, VII, 2, 3–4.
2. Ibid.
3. A man who practised the *ars ludicra* was deprived of the right of voting and of being elected a magistrate (*ius suffragi et honorum*), and his rights were also limited in private law; he could not marry into a senatorial family (Digest, XXIII, 2, 44, pr.).
4. In 165 B.C. the *Hecyra* was performed on two more occasions; in 163 at the games given by L. Aemilius Paulus, it was equally unsuccessful, but a performance later in the same year was a success.
5. Terence, Hec. Prol., 1–4.
6. Valerius Maximus, II, 4, 6: *scaenam vacuis ante pictura, tabulatis extentam.*
7. Tacitus, Annals, XIV, 20, 3: *subitariis gradibus et scaena in tempus structa.*
8. Livy, XL, 51, 3 (179 B.C.); XLI, 27, 5 (174 B.C.)
9. Valerius Maximus, II, 4, 6.
10. Pliny, N.H., XXXV, 23.
11. Livy, Epit., XLVIII, *populus aliquamdiu ludos stans spectavit;* Tacitus, XIV, 20, 3: *stantem populum spectavisse.*
12. Livy, XXXIV, 44, 5 (195 B.C.)
13. The introduction of painted scenery, which in Greece was attributed to Sophocles (Aristotle, Poet., 1449a) was attributed in Rome to M. Claudius Pulcher (99 B.C.), who is mentioned as the great innovator of theatrical technique.
14. The representation of three doors was traditional, even if one of them was not used. In the *Heautontimorumenos* of Terence the action only requires two doors, but a third is referred to (170).
15. Such as the setting in the *Rudens* of Plautus.
16. The sacred precinct (σηκός) of Semele was shown in Euripides' *Bacchae* (6–12), the altar of Venus in Plautus' *Rudens* (688); there is an altar in front of a private house in Menander's *Perinthia* (Korte 3, p. 130).

17. Plautus, *Mostell.*, 817: *viden vestibulum ante aedis et ambulacrum cuiusmodi.* Ambulacrum is the floor of the porch, probably a translation of ἀντίθυρον (Sophocles, *Electra*, 1433; cf. Lucian, Alex., 16) or πρόθυρον (Euripides, Alc., 101).

18. Certain situations in Greek tragedy and comedy can only be explained by assuming that the roof of the porch was a flat terrace on which movement was easily possible (in Euripides, Or., 1574, Orestes standing δόμων ἐπ᾽ ἄκρων threatens to kill Hermione, without Menelaus, who is on the stage, being able to prevent him; the φύλαξ in Aeschylus Ag. 3 appeared on a similar terrace; cf. Aristophanes, Ach., 283, Vesp., 68).

19. Plautus, Asin., 425: *iussin columnis deici operas aranearum.*

20. Euripides, Alc, 546.

21. Ibid. Andr., 43.

22. Vitruvius, V, 6, 9.

23. Plutarch, Pomp., 42.

24. Augustus, Mon. Ancyr., IV, 21: *Theatrum ad aedem Apollinis . . . feci, quod sub nomine M. Marcelli generi mei esset.*

25. Pliny, N.H., XXXVI, 60.

26. According to Pliny (N.H., XXXVI, 115) it held 40,000 spectators, according to the *Notitia* (see 40) over 17,000. Pliny's figure is probably an exaggeration. In the Theatre of Marcellus there was room for 14,000 spectators (20,000 according to other sources), in the Theatre of Balbus for over 7,000. The latter was destroyed by fire in A.D. 80, and rebuilt later (Ausonius, lud., VII; 39).

27. We have only scattered references to a *Theatrum Traiani* and a *Theatrum Antoni.*

28. A wooden theatre is mentioned in an inscription of A.D. 17 (Eph. epigr., VIII, 233: *Ludos . . . Latinos in theatro ligneo, quod est ad Tiberim*).

29. Ibid. 231, 100: *ludi noctu sacrificio confecto sunt commissa in scaena, quoi theatrum adjectum non fuit.*

30. Livy, Epit., XLVIII.

31. Tacitus, Ann., XIV, 20, 3.

32. Livy, Epit., XLVIII.

33. Tertullian, De spect., 10: *saepe censores renascentia theatra destruebant.*

34. Roman tragic poets, to meet this different use of the parts of the theatre, when adapting Greek plays for their audiences, changed the choral songs into monodies or duets sung on the stage.

35. Livy, Epit., XCIX; Juvenal, 3, 159.

36. Porphyry, on Hor., Epod., 4, 15.

37. Plutarch, Cicero, 13.

38. A chorus of drunken youths was inserted in the *Perikeiromene* of Menander (after line 76) as a mere interlude; choral songs, to mark a

pause in the action, are also indicated in the *Epitrepontes* (after lines 35, 242 and 648) and the *Samia* (at line 270); there is a chorus of fishermen in Plautus' *Rudens* (after line 290; the metre, iambic octonarius is unique), who converse with an actor in the following verses.

39. Horace, Ars. Poet., 154–5.

40. The theatre of Dionysus, the first permanent stone theatre, was built in Athens about 330 B.C. during the administration of the orator Lycurgus. Eudemus of Plataea contributed to the expenses (I.G., 2, 176 = Syll.[3] 288). Previous theatres had been of wood (Plato, Laws, VII, 817e; Xenophon, Cyrop., VI, 1, 54; Demosthenes c. Meid., 17 p. 520).

41. Vitruvius, VI, 4, 8.

42. Other names occasionally used are: αἰῶραι, ἐάρημα, κλάδη.

43. Vitruvius, VI, 4, 8; cf. Pollux, IV, 126.

44. Pollux, ibid.: καὶ θεοὺς . . . ἐπάγει θαλαττίους.

45. Pollux, IV, 132.

46. The evidence on which this explanation rests is extensive and clear, but late.

47. All passages alluding to the ἐκκύκλημα refer to persons who are lying down, either dead or alive.

48. See note 13.

49. Seneca, Ep., 88; Pliny, N.H., XXXIII, 53; Martial Lib., spect., 21; Juvenal, 4, 122.

50. Horace, Ars Poet., 214–15:

> *Sic priscae motumque et luxuriem addidit arti*
> *Tibicen traxitque vagus per pulpita vestem.*

51. Statius, Silvae, 1, 6, 27.

52. Suetonius, Cal., 50.

53. Ibid. 26.

54. Martial, XIV, 28.

55. Ibid. XII, 29, 15–16.

56. Ibid. VIII, 33, 3–4; Sen., Epist., 90, 15; Lucan, IX, 808–9.

57. Juvenal, 6, 352–3:

> *Ut spectet ludos conducit Ogulnia vestem,*
> *Conducit comites, sellam, cervical, amicas.*

58. Ars. Am., I, 99.

59. In *Vorspiel auf dem Theater.*

CHAPTER XXV

Italum Acetum

Roman wit. The satirical epigram. Ribaldry at triumphs, funerals and weddings. Pasquinades and witticisms. Attacks on loquacity, vanity and meanness. Mockery of the ugly. Human shortcomings pilloried.

THE sturdy Romans had a quick tongue, and when there was something to be said, they were seldom inclined to remain silent. This unchecked and determined outspokenness on every subject, an essential element in the Roman character, had its roots in an age-old spirit of liberty; on a people tested in a thousand battles the hardest sacrifices could be imposed and the most stringent military discipline; but to hold their tongues in check when the need for silence had disappeared seemed a pointless restriction and an intolerable outrage to the pride of the masters of the world. *Italum acetum*[1] is a native product, with its own unmistakable characteristics, and the power of wit in Rome was great.

It is no accident that the earliest forms of Italian literature were the *Saturae* and the Fescennine verses, a rustic competition in gross ribaldry and coarse abuse; that the comedies of Plautus show an inexhaustible vein of repartee, rudeness and abuse absent from the comedies of Terence, who kept closer to his Greek originals; that satire in the form originally adopted by Lucilius, and developed later by Horace and Juvenal, was regarded by the Romans as a national achievement;[2] that the satirical epigram was also essentially a national product, although indebted for its form and some general characteristics to a Greek tradition; and above all, that no other literature before or since has been able to produce a Martial.

A terse and pithy wit is an essential part of the sturdy Italian character; it is in accordance with the spirit of a hardy people from whom the refinements of civilisation have never removed the aggressive outspokenness of the peasant; it is a harsh spirit, quick, fierce and revealing itself in an acrimonious exchange of insults and abuse, in a struggle in which deadly blows are dealt and which only ends with victory or defeat. 'Why are you barking?' 'I see a robber'[3]—the repartee is quick and deadly. The natural instinct for satire amongst Italians and in Rome tended to express itself in epigrams. Rudeness has no point unless it is barbed. 'Italian vinegar' was the natural expression of a people, who having conquered by arms, did not forget that words are also arms.

'Our city is a very malicious one', says Cicero,[4] 'nobody is safe from it.' Certainly nobody was safe from him, for he had a very quick tongue and could pick up gossip even in the provinces; on the death of Vindullus he spread abroad a scandal which filled the intimate gazettes of Rome with sniggers. Among the papers of the dead man were found five miniatures of well known ladies of the nobility, which Publius Vedius, a notorious man about town, had entrusted to Vindullus. Cicero hastened to communicate the delightful news to his friend Atticus,[5] poking great fun at one of the heroines of this thrilling change of fortune, using words with a double meaning, and ridiculing the unfortunate husband.

Insinuation and innuendo were not unknown, that deadly perverted malice whose underhand methods always remain the same: saying without actually saying, excusing to condemn, denying credit to gossip while spreading it. Horace[6] provides an example of this: 'Capitolinus has been my comrade and friend since boyhood; he has done much to serve me when asked, and I rejoice that he is alive and out of danger here in Rome—but still I *do* wonder how he got out of that trial.' But this was not the genuine malicious style of Rome. Roman malice is purely brutal, it calls a spade a spade, and tells each man his shortcomings without hesitation and with no respect for persons. It looks its adversary unflinchingly in the face and is not afraid of provoking enmity.

Every nation reveals itself in its sense of humour; a non-Frenchman can appreciate the *esprit* of France but cannot acquire it; outside classical Athens an Aristophanes is incomprehensible; the spirit of Rome is Roman. Roman wit has an unrivalled power of expressing itself with precision and an almost lapidary finality; the nature of the language helped to express an idea pithily and wittily. Roman wit appeals to a part of man—not necessarily the best part—which exists in all ages, and this gives it an timeless quality.

Nobody was a greater master of laughter than Aristophanes, but his jokes cannot be divorced from the theatre where they originated, they are the leaven of his plays whose tone and character depend entirely on them; taken by themselves they lose all attraction and effect. The Roman epigram, on the other hand, lives its own life.

Perhaps that is why the satirical epigram achieved in Rome the heights of the best poetry, which in every other age it has failed to reach. In Rome it found a congenial atmosphere; wit in its most literary form flourished in the country of wit. It preserved the immediacy and efficacy of an oral improvisation, even when written on a wall,[7] collected with others in a political pamphlet,[8] inserted in a comedy[9] or a speech. Nor did it lose this character when the Greek epigram lent its untrained violence the precision of a regular metrical form and native wit took its place in literature, assuming without difficulty all the lightness of Alexandrian literature.[10]

Behind literary wit there always lurks the spirit of a people with a passion for ribaldry. In fact, in literature, as in the conversation of educated men, humour came in from the street, and the people became the masters of the world of fashion and of famous poets. Boorishness became smart without losing any of its energy or its expressiveness. Martial,[11] writing to Domitian to justify the free language of his epigrams says, 'Your triumphs too have been accustomed to endure jests, and it is no shame to a commander to be matter for wit.' The poet appealed to tradition, an effective plea at Rome; Fescennine freedom of speech broke out on every occasion, triumphs, marriages and funerals.

As the triumphal procession of Julius Caesar[12] passed through the streets after his conquest of Gaul, the soldiers behind his chariot reproached him with jeering shouts for the hunger they had suffered at Dyrrachium, and accused him of greed, because the promised rewards had not been distributed with the liberality they had hoped. Caesar knew the custom and allowed them to have their say. But these soldiers were also aware of the intemperance of his private life; he was rumoured to have no hesitation in paying his attentions to the wives of others, and there seemed no reason for silence on this point. They also knew another of his weaknesses: he was bald and did not enjoy references to the fact (see p. 213); and so they sang to the tune of Clementine, 'Romans lock up your wives, we are bringing back the bald adulterer':

Urbani, servate uxores; moechum calvum adducimus.

They might be thought to have gone far enough, but the soldiers began to say things so outrageous[13] that Caesar eventually became angry[14] and protested that they were not true; he had never done such things. But he was reduced to silence by the coarse jeers of his legionaries. Customs are customs, and not even a Caesar can alter them.

A few years afterwards another triumphal procession filed through the streets of Rome;[15] Lepidus, the triumvir, and Plancus, his fellow consul, were celebrating their triumph over the Gauls. The memory of the triumvirate and its proscriptions was still fresh in men's minds, when the streets of Rome had run with blood; there was still an atmosphere of terror, and the picture of Cicero hacked and mutilated on the beach at Gaeta always haunted the more civilised, reminding them of their lost liberty and the ever present threat of death. The soldiers, however, were determined to make their jokes, and, remembering that the brothers of the two triumphant generals had been among the victims, they made a pun on the word *Germanus*, which can mean both German and brother. Behind the triumphal chariot of the two assassins, they sang, beating out the rhythm of the song with their heavy marching tread, 'These two consuls do not triumph over the Gauls, but over the Germans'—'*De Germanis non de Gallis duo triumphant consules*'.

Undeterred from attacking the living, the Fescennine spirit had no scruples in abusing the dead, all the more so if the dead man had been important and revered. When Vespasian[16] died, the piety of his son Titus and the deep sorrow of the Roman people paid the dead Emperor the honours of a solemn funeral. Vespasian had been an excellent general and administrator and a wise and intelligent ruler, but among all these gifts he had one small failing, avarice. The finances of Rome, after the extravagance of the later successors of Augustus, needed the most stringent economy. All were agreed on this point. But Vespasian's interpretation of economy was so rigid and parsimonious that the *plebecula* of Rome, unfortunately accustomed to the crazy generosity of Nero, found it excessive, even actually disgraceful. They reproved him when alive and did not pardon him when dead. During the solemn funeral procession a strange sight was to be seen; the chief clown to the court, Favor, followed the bier, clownishly imitating, '*ut mos est*', says Suetonius, the gestures and speech of Vespasian. From time to time he approached the Emperor's accountants and in a preoccupied manner demanded in a loud voice, 'Tell me, how much will this great funeral cost altogether?' They answered, 'Ten million sesterces', and the pseudo-Vespasian cried out desperately, 'Ten million sesterces? Give it to me at once, and then throw me straightaway into the Tiber.'

The determined insolence of the descendants of Romulus did not wait for great occasions to give vent to its natural bent for ribaldry. All moments were good for it, all places suitable, a smart drawing-room, a dark alleyway, or the confusion of the Forum. All gatherings invited it: marriage ceremonies, banquets, magistrates' receptions, parties of revellers, the licence of the Saturnalia. A bridegroom knew that he had to reckon with the Fescennine freedom of speech. His friends among the guests knew a good deal about his previous life. What better occasion to remind him brutally of all this, than in the presence of his young bride, modestly veiled in her orange *flammeum*, amongst the comments of the guests and the shouting of the crowd?[17]

Jests, scurrilous attacks, outspokenness and witticisms were always to be met. Pasquinades flourished, written by unknown hands in whitewash on the walls of Rome; satirical songs spread rapidly from mouth to mouth, and there was soon no corner of the city where they were not sung. Often the humour of the satier was political. The rapid rise to power of Ventidius Bassus,[18] who had originally been a muleteer before climbing to the top of the *cursus honorum*, caused surprise; suddenly there appeared on one wall, and now on another, and then through the whole of Rome some *versiculi*, proclaiming the miracle of a man who had wiped down mules having become consul. Nero built the *Domus Aurea*, and as he built, enlarged, dug and decorated, he seemed anxious to occupy half Rome. One day a pasquinade[19] appeared on this great house which would soon occupy the whole of Rome and force the *Quirites* to emigrate to Veil (see p. 21).

Wit also seasoned private conversation; the *bon mots* of smart society had a wide circulation and were enjoyed by all ranks of

Roman society. The diligence of those who made collections of
them has preserved them for us. Roman society was gripped with a
passion for indulging in wit; anybody who had something smart
to say had to say it even if this meant incurring the hostility of the
world: *potius amicum quam dictum perdidi*[20] 'I prefer losing a
friend to a joke'—that summed up their attitude.

The improvement in manners in high Roman society from the
end of the third century B.C. onwards made a superficial observation of the rules of politeness and courtesy essential in the fashionable world; there was a genuine devotion to form. It was difficult
to make any request even to an intimate friend without using the
prescribed formulae such as *sis, quaeso, ne graveris*, the equivalent
to our 'if you please'; to leave an unappetising dish untouched
seemed a silent criticism of one's host, and bad food had to be
eaten cheerfully;[21] to invite your friends to dinner, and not to
entrust your wife with issuing the formal invitations was to disregard the normal relationships between married couples.[22]
Anyone who gave a present sought a formula which would avoid
inflicting humiliation.[23] Roman society had rigid rules of courtesy
and etiquette, but it allowed, none the less, a freedom of speech
which would not be tolerated today.

It was a society in which one could be certain that one's shortcomings would not pass unobserved. Politeness did not prevent
criticism, and criticisms were expressed loudly. The ambitious,
the vain, the talkative, and the mean had no hope of having their
failings overlooked, but always found someone to compel them to
look at themselves carefully in the mirror of truth. Ridicule is
educative and teaches everyone what he is and what he can claim
to be; certainly, it is the most effective cure for men with too great
a regard for themselves. A Roman who tried to cover up his weakness was told the truth at once, and advised not to deceive himself
and others.

Roman malice is pitiless and outspoken; the coarse must not
forget their coarseness, nor the greedy pretend to generosity.
Roman wit made its point with infallible accuracy about each
man's standing in public opinion. 'Know yourself' is a wise
maxim, but men must have the lesson knocked into them; at Rome
there were plenty of men ready to give such lessons. Marcus
Caelius was a chatterbox; Cato the Censor[24] attacked him in public

'That man is never silent who is afflicted with the disease of talking, as one in a lethargy is afflicted with that of drinking and sleeping. For if you fail to assemble when he calls a meeting, so eager is he to talk that he would hire someone to listen.' Caelius could also easily be bribed to support or attack a proposal, and Cato said of him, 'For a crust of bread he can be hired to keep silence or to speak.' A bad advocate demanded praise for a speech which he claimed had drawn tears from his audience. 'Certainly,' said Catulus,[25] 'your speech reduced everybody to tears.' On another occasion somebody was displaying an honourable scar on his forehead with the inevitable tediousness of a wounded hero: Augustus[26] turned on him angrily: 'Yes, when you run away, you will always take care not to turn round.'

One of the most popular targets was avarice. In all the extravagance of Roman society meanness was despised. It was easier to excuse a governor returning from a plundered province than a miser whose life was devoted to cheese-paring and bargain-hunting. Domitia, the wife of Possienus, had a reputation for stinginess; it was said, and Junius Bassus took care to spread the rumour, that she sold her discarded shoes. Domitia turned on her slanderer. 'But no,' said Bassus, excusing himself, 'I never said that you sold discarded shoes, I said that you . . . bought them.'[27] A mean host had some fish, left over from the day before, served at his table; they were already half eaten, and the parsimonious host had arranged them so that the part that had been eaten was face downwards on the plate. A witty gourmand, with all the malice of his class, immediately discovered the deception. 'Let us eat quickly,' he said 'other guests are eating with us under the plate.'[28]

Roman wit also assumed the cruel duty of disabusing the ugly of any pretensions to good looks. It was malicious, but malicious wit is enjoyable. No other people have taken so much pleasure in laughing at nature's victims as the Romans. The *cognomina* of many families are enough to prove this; those indicating a physical defect or deformity are frequent: famous names like *Blaesus*, or *Balbus*, 'stammerer', *Plautus*, 'flat-footed', *Varus* ,'knock-kneed', *Valgus*, 'bandy-legged', *Scaurus*, 'with deformed ankles', *Luscus*, 'one-eyed', *Paetus, Strabo*, 'squinter', *Homullus*, 'dwarf'; names derived from some growth an ancestor had had on his head and which earned him a name inherited by his descendants, such as

Verrucosus, Tubero, and *Cicero,* according to whether the growth was only a wen, a wart, or a still larger growth. Finally there was *Lamia,* 'witch', and other names enough in themselves, such as *Naso, Calvus, Macer, Niger, Fuscus, Rufus,* and the names of animals, *Asinius, Catulus, Aper, Bestia, .Brutus.* It would be possible to make the list even longer.

No victim of nature's caprices could feel safe even in the best Roman society. Cicero[29] one day saw Lentulus, his son-in-law, passing in uniform. Lentulus was a small, stunted man and he wore a very long sword at his side, with that ferocious air, we may suppose, which small men tend to assume in uniform. Cicero surveyed his diminutive son-in-law and his large sword, and asked, 'Who has tied my son-in-law to his sword?'

Quintus Cicero, the orator's brother, was equally diminutive. Following a contemporary custom of the nobility, Quintus had had his half-length portrait painted on a shield-shaped surface; the artist had done his job well, and had painted an imposing portrait of the little man from the waist up. Cicero,[30] standing in front of the shield, admired the metamorphosis of the dwarf into a giant, and commented, 'Curious! Half my younger brother is bigger than all of him.'

Galba, an effective advocate and a man of genius, but greedy (it was said 'this genius lives in a humble dwelling'), was one day concluding a case before Augustus.[31] At one stage, with all the guile of a skilled debater, he tried to force the Emperor to give implicit approval by his silence and said, *'Corrige in me si quid reprehendis',* meaning 'if there is anything you disapprove of in my words, please correct me'. But Augustus's quick wit did not fail to realise that in Latin these words might also mean, 'if there is anything in me which you dislike, put it right'. With a benevolent air Augustus replied *'Ego te monere possum, corrigere non possum'*— 'I can give you advice, but I cannot correct you'. His apparently polite reply meant in fact, 'I can give you advice but to put you right is impossible, my dear glutton'.

Obviously not everybody lay down under such insults; once Ovid's son-in-law, Fidus Cornelius, who had an ungainly body and scanty hair, began to cry like a baby because Corbulo had called him a hairless ostrich *(struthiocamelus depilatus)* in the Senate.[32] The insult was undeserved, but this did not detract from the senators' mirth.

Humour directed at physical failings is the unfairest form of humour; sometimes, however, it has a certain point if the victim has provoked it and it is not unjustified, particularly if foolish vanity is regarded as a physical failing. Human beings of both sexes resign themselves with difficulty to the pointless and ironical cruelty of nature, who is harsh towards her own creations, particularly the old. An ageing man wishes to seem young and active; a bald or greyhaired man gives himself a young man's head; a toothless man wears false teeth; an ugly man is anxious to persuade himself and others that he is irresistible with women:[33] this was the case in Rome, as it always has been everywhere. A man who smelt (this unpleasant theme for mockery was too popular to allow it to be passed over), searched for every remedy—sweet-smelling pastilles,[34] laurel leaves chewed in the mouth,[35] ointments for the skin,[36] perfumes and cosmetics to drive away what he wanted to hide; it offended the nose of his neighbour, as well as of *amour propre* of the unhappy man, who in fact, if he smelt even after washing, scraping and cleaning himself, was not really to blame. Such is the duel between nature, which sows ugliness and destruction, and man, who runs to repair it, as obstinate and methodical as she is capricious and malicious.

At certain failings Rome laughed wholeheartedly. When Cicero heard a woman of fifty coolly maintaining that she was thirty, he said, 'It must be so, for I have been hearing you say so for twenty years.'[37] On another occasion, finding himself in conversation with a contemporary who was trying to make himself out to be as young as possible, he said,[38] 'In that case, when we went to school together, you were not yet born.'

On one occasion an old man with grizzled hair presented himself before the emperor Hadrian to ask for a favour, which the emperor refused. Undismayed by the refusal, he persevered, and meanwhile his hair grew steadily whiter and he began to dye it. Finally he returned dark-haired to the emperor, and repeated the request which he had already made when grey headed. Hadrian replied, 'But I have already refused your father.'[39]

In Martial's epigrams, which caricature Rome in Rome's own spirit, all the deformities which most afflict the human race are reviewed in a gallery of ugliness: men with one eye,[40] bandy legs,[41] disfigured faces,[42] pointed heads,[43] toothless mouths,[44] women who are absurdly tall and thin,[45] brazen old age,[46] bald heads,[47] foul mouths,[48] people who stink for all their perfumes.[49] The subjects of these epigrams may have been fictitious, but everybody could recognise old acquaintances in them, and laughed at them amongst his friends with many a sly wink.

Much more could be said, as there are inexhaustible sources for a history of Roman wit. But this sketch of one of the most typical aspects of Italian and Roman society will serve to discredit the fairly widespread legend of a Rome which was invariably austere and perpetually frowning, a romantic and academic substitute for the real Rome. Rome from the very beginning of the Republic was a city genially open-minded and malicious. Its leading men had to fit in with its tastes; Cato was not so much a Cato that he did not take pleasure in submerging his malicious adversaries, the vain and the foolish, in ridicule, and Cicero, a man of great humour, could play other roles besides that of the enraged consul puffing out his cheeks and growling '*Quousque tandem?*'

Further Reading

There is no book on the subject of Roman humour. Aulus Gellius and Macrobius have preserved many other examples of Roman wit. J. W. Duff, *Roman Satire* (Cambridge, 1936), deals with the literary form.

NOTES

1. *Italum acetum* is a Horatian expression (Sat. I, 7, 32).
2. Quintilian, X, 1, 93: *Satura quidem tota nostra est.*
3. Ibid., VI, 3, 8: *Catulus dicenti Philippo, 'Quid latras?' 'Furem video,' inquit.* Philippus, who thought Catulus raised his voice too much, compared him to a dog in two words. Catulus in two more words compared Philippus to a thief, as dogs bark at the sight of a thief.
4. pro Caelio, 16, 38.
5. Ad Att., VI, 1, 25.
6. Sat., I, 4, 96–98.
7. Aulus Gallius, XV, 4, 3.
8. Macrobius, II, 4, 21.
9. Aulus Gellius, II, 7, 4; III, 3, 15.
10. The Greek satirical epigram (σκωπτικόν) belongs to the Roman age; the greatest Greek writer of this genre, Lucillius, lived in the age

of Nero, and we gather from the names we find in his works that the majority of his epigrams were directed against members of Roman society (Anth. Pal., XI). Martial (I, Praef.) mentions only Roman epigrammatists amongst his predecessors, including Catullus (*Lascivam verborum veritatem, id est epigrammaton linguam, excusarem, si meum esset exemplum; sic scribit Catullus, sic Marsus, sic Pedo, sic Gaetulicus*), and he connects his epigrams specifically with the Roman triumphal songs (see p. 270); he maintains the Roman character of the type of epigram which he wrote, when he compares (IV, 23, 27, 6–7) Greek grace (*Cecropius lepos*) with Roman satirical sharpness (*Romanae sal Minervae*).

11. Martial, I, 4, 3–4.
12. Suetonius, Divus Julius, 51.
13. Ibid. 49.
14. Dio Cassius, XLIII, 20.
15. Velleius Paterculus, II, 67, 3–4.
16. Suetonius, Vespas., 19.
17. Catullus, LXI, 122, et seq.
18. Aulus Gellius, xv, 4, 3.
19. Suetonius, Nero, 39.
20. Quintilian, VI, 3, 28.
21. Suetonius, Divus Julius, 53.
22. Cicero, Ad Att., V, 1, 3.
23. Pliny, Epist., VI, 32.
24. Aulus Gellius, I, 15, 8.
25. Cicero, De orat., II, 69, 278.
26. Macrobius, II, 4, 7.
27. Quintilian, VI, 3, 24.
28. Ibid. VI, 3, 90.
29. Macrobius, II, 3, 3.
30. Ibid. II, 3, 4.
31. Ibid. II, 4, 8.
32. Seneca, De Const. Sap., 17, 1.
33. Martial, II, 87.
34. Horace, Sat., I, 2, 27; Martial, I, 87.
35. Martial, V, 4.
36. Ibid. III, 55.
37. Quintilian, VI, 3, 73.
38. Ibid.
39. Aelius Spartianus, Hadr., 20, 8.
40. Martial, III, 8; IV, 65.
41. Ibid. II, 35.
42. Ibid. II, 87.
43. Ibid. VI, 39, 15–16.

44. Ibid. I, 19; II, 41; VIII, 57.
45. Ibid. VIII, 60.
46. Ibid. II, 41.
47. Ibid. XII, 7.
48. Ibid. VII, 94; II, 42 and *passim*.
49. Ibid. I, 87; II, 12; III, 55 and *passim*.

CHAPTER XXVI

Superstitions, Magic and Spells

Children's bogeys. Ghosts and spectres. Werewolves, men from the sea, etc. Magical spells and superstitions. Defixiones. *Love spells.*

PLATO[1] maintained that 'the child is the most intractable of all animals', and this belief was so widely held in antiquity that nurses invented bogeys to control children, and threatened them with being eaten alive by a large, famished wolf with gaping jaws if they were naughty. The Greek Mormo ($Mo\rho\mu\dot{\omega}$),[2] was a terrifying woman with donkey's legs,[3] the Roman Lamia[4] prowled around devouring children; she always had one in her stomach.

The dread of such bogeys survived into adult life and succeeded in ruining the tranquillity of the weaker minded. How could a man be certain that malignant spirits and the souls of the dead were not at large in the unseen world? That a ghost, terrifying in its insubstantial transparency, might not materialise in the darkness? Etruscan religion, which influenced Roman religion so strongly, had populated certain dark corners of supernatural life with the ghosts of the dead (*lemures*), but educated Romans did not take such tales of the next world seriously, and they were only believed by weak-minded old women and nervous children. In spite of this, Lucretius[5] felt it necessary to reassure his readers by providing a rational explanation for the apparition of ghosts; and if Horace[6] considers a disbelief in *lemures* as one of the surest signs of a strong mind, we may suppose that such strength was by no means universal. For the ancients too, the lost souls of the dead wandered in the world of the living, which they had left, to show their love for the body they had lost,[7] or to bring home to those who had survived them the anguish of lying unburied.[8] There were houses which 'had something about them', and, however much the owner might lower his price, he could never find purchasers or tenants. Such houses were felt to be haunted because they had been the scene of a crime;[9] the murderer had killed his guest and hidden his body in the earth, depriving him not only of life but of the rites due to the dead. The dead man came back to life to protest at his treatment. Groans and strange noises were heard and shapes appeared in the darkness. The appearance of a ghost was sometimes accompanied by the clanking of chains.[10] Nobody dared to live within such haunted walls, or even to go near the place, unless he was like the philosopher Athenodorus, whom Pliny the Younger describes in one of his letters. Athenodorus was certainly a courageous philosopher, and what terrified others was to him merely an opportunity for a new experience. He moved into one of these haunted houses and waited at night, writing notes on his tablets. Suddenly, behind his back there appeared a troubled ghost, clanking his chains and beckoning with his finger; he was a filthy emaciated old man with a long beard, and his hair stood upright on his head. He seemed to be asking Athenodorus for something and to be urging him to follow. The unperturbed philosopher gestured to the ghost to be patient; he finished what he was writing, and then took up a light and went off unhurriedly with the ghost in the direction it indicated. Man and spirit passed through the house in silence by the flickering light of the lantern; as soon as they reached an abandoned and overgrown courtyard the ghost suddenly vanished. In the morning the magistrates, summoned by Athenodorus, found bones and iron chains on the spot where the apparition had disappeared.

Some believed in werewolves (*versipelles*[11]), men who could turn into wolves and went round at night attacking flocks in company with real wolves, and later resumed their human shape. If they were wounded during these bestial expeditions, the wound inflicted on the wolf remained on the man. It was whispered that certain old women knew the art of changing into birds;[12] they put on wings and flew off into the dusk on their evil errands. There was talk, too, of strange monsters of the northern seas, half man half beast, which some claimed to have seen.[13] Sea faring folk feared 'the man of the sea'[14] who climbed on to ships at night and pulled them over; if he remained there long, the ship went to the bottom. Witches[15] and vampires[16] made their way furtively into houses where there was a dead man, to rob and dishonour the corpse; they ate its nose, for example. Such talk was so common that even those who did not believe in it could not feel entirely happy.

Most of these superstitions reached Rome at the beginning of the Greco-Oriental invasion, but particularly during the course of the wars against the pirates,[17] when mysticism, magic and the strangest superstitions corrupted the natural sanity of the Roman mind. Magical practices were very ancient in the Roman world, it is true, but they were limited to traditional rites intended to make certain dark powers propitious and to avert danger; it was enough, for example, to write ARSEVERSE[18] on the door of a house to avoid the risk of fire. There were formulae for incantations against hail, diseases of every sort, and scalding; Pliny the Elder assures us that some of them were effective in practice.[19] Superstitions were also very ancient, but for the most part they took the purely superficial form of observing lucky or unlucky omens; careful precautions could then prevent the occurrence of an unhappy event. For example, to stumble on the threshold when leaving home[20] was a bad omen, and it was better to spend the day safely in the house. It was foolish to mention fire at a banquet,[21] but this could be remedied by immediately pouring water on to the table. It was a bad sign for a cock to crow during a party; either the correct spells had to be made[22] or nothing was eaten that day.[23] A bad dream could fill a man with anxiety. If he was a barrister and had an important case on that day, he asked for an adjournment.[24] There were, in fact, primitive superstitions or scruples which could suggest one form of behaviour rather than another on particular occasions, but which never really dominated the spirit of the Romans. Most fears, foolish fantasies and dramatic manifestations of the supernatural reached Rome late, and they influenced only the lower ranks of society, servant girls, the uneducated, weak-spirited or foolish, or they were used as themes by authors seeking sensation.

If the Greeks and Roman seem to us much more superstitious than modern men, a substantial difference in religious outlook between the two ages must be borne in mind. Modern religions condemn superstition; for the ancients, superstition played a perfectly natural and normal part in the relationship between gods and men. The formalism of most ancient religions meant that they imposed no particular creed on an adherent and made no effort to penetrate deeply into his soul; furthermore, the gods were believed to be omniscient and ready in their goodness to share some of this omniscience with mankind.[25] The ways in which it was believed that the gods might reveal the future and warn man of his impending fate were infinite; a stumble, the cawing of a crow or the hooting of an owl, an unfortunate meeting, a word accidentally heard, an unlucky dream, an oil flask falling to the ground, and many other similar accidents might help to foretell the future. Only the irreligious ruled out the possibility of any providential intervention by the gods in human life and denied the truth of omens and mocked at superstitions. The oracle was the most advanced form by which the gods might be persuaded to impart a little of their omniscience for man's benefit. But the methods of questioning the gods were innumerable; they did not merely give answers to specific questions but also spontaneous advice.

This makes it easier for us to understand why men of outstanding intelligence, such as Socrates and Demosthenes, were superstitious, and will explain the enormous number of superstitions among the Greeks and Romans. It was an omen of disaster for a black cat to enter a house, a snake to fall from the roof into the yard,[26] for a beam in the house to split, to spill wine, oil or water, to meet a mule laden with *hipposelinum*, a herb used to decorate tombs,[27] or for a rat to make a hole in a sack of flour.[28] It was worse if the statue of a god sweated blood,[29] crows pecked at a divine image,[30] if pickled fish, when being roasted, began to wriggle as if they were alive,[31] if, through some quirk of nature, a horse was born with five legs, a lamb with a pig's head, a pig with a man's head,[32] or if an escaped bull climbed the stairs of a building up to the third floor.[33]

The anxiety among the ancients was great and not unjustified, when, as happened, or was said to have happened, several times, a thick beard suddenly sprouted on the tender cheeks of a priestess.[34] A bearded women was certainly a serious omen. It seemed no less ominous when horses wept 'hot tears',[35] a statue 'began to laugh immoderately',[36] or an ox began to speak.[37] These were illusions caused by the tendency of superstitious men when excited to attach too much significance to things in themselves unimportant.

The Romans' superstitious instincts also made them believe in the evil eye which they tried to avert with various types of amulets;[38]

they avoided ~~marrying on certain days~~ and in certain months
~~(see p. 116)~~[39] and took care not to cross the threshold with their
left foot.[40] When there was lightning, they whistled at every flash.
Pliny[41] says that this was a common custom among many people;
when the skies were lit up, the whole earth was filled with
whistling. During a banquet both guests and servants had to be on
their guard to prevent any action which might be of ill omen; for
example, if a servant swept the floor when a guest was standing
up, or lifted the table and the *repositorium*[42] while he was
drinking, or if the guest himself let the food fall from his hand to
the ground; in this case the food was immediately restored to the
banqueter, who had to be careful to clean it, even if only by
blowing upon it. The accident would teach him to be more
cautious in future. It was particularly serious if food fell from the
hand of a Pontifex during a ritual meal; here the bad omen could
only be expiated by placing the food on the table and burning it
as an offering to the Lares. It was unpropitious to sneeze while a
waiter was handing a tray; the only remedy was to start eating at
once. For everybody to fall silent at one time, when there was an odd
number of guests at a banquet, presaged a misfortune for each of
the guests.

Cutting the nails only on market days in Rome, while remaining
silent and starting with the forefinger, is mentioned as a superstition peculiar to women. Neither hair nor nails were to be cut
while at sea.[43]

Some of these beliefs even received public recognition. In many
Italian villages[44] women were forbidden by law to walk through
the streets turning their spindle or holding it in sight. Woe to
anybody who saw such a thing! All his hopes of a good harvest
were shattered.

We have already seen (p. 207) that Roman empirical medicine
was influenced by magical practices and superstitions; there was a
widespread belief that medicines, if placed on a table before being
taken, lost all their strength. Pliny the Elder has preserved the
following interesting piece of information:

M. Servilius Nonianus, one of the leading men of the city,
being afraid of losing his sight, hung a charm round his neck
on a thread with two Greek letters, *alpha* and *rho*. Mucianus,
who was consul three times, tied a live fly in a white cloth to

avoid the same fate; these remedies are said to have been successful.

Even highly intelligent men attributed a certain efficacy to such practices, and we can only envy the ancients when we learn that they relied on a simple but certain method of relieving themselves from unpleasant thoughts; a finger moistened with saliva passed behind the ear was enough. We no longer believe in such fantasies; if we did how often should we be inclined to lick one finger and moisten the skin behind the ear!

Hatred and love were the occasions for two more complicated rites among the ancients, *defixiones* and spells. The practice of *defixio* was very ancient, and the evidence for it in Greece goes back to the fourth century B.C.[45] *Defixio* was the consecration of an enemy to the gods of the underworld. It was usually provoked by legal[46] or domestic disasters, business or professional rivalry. A man gave vent to his rancour after an unsuccessful lawsuit by consecrating his opponent, the witnesses on his opponent's side and all those who had spoken for him, sometimes even the books in which the judgement of the court had been recorded (τὰ δικαιώματα);[47] women consecrated those who had stolen their husband's heart,[48] and men the business rivals who had ruined them.[49] But *defixio* might be invoked whenever a man had quarrelled bitterly with another and, seeing no more effective means of revenge, resorted in his impotent rage to imploring the co-operation of the gods. So we read in one inscription of a man who consecrated the whole of a gang which had come to his house, called him outside, tied him up and beaten him,[50] and of a woman who consecrated a slanderer who had accused her of poisoning her husband.[51] Some cursed a faithless trustee who denied the trust, and sold the object entrusted to him instead of returning it;[52] among those consecrated appear the thieves of cloaks, clothes, gold objects, etc.[53] Such naive methods were used chiefly by the lower classes, as the ungrammatical language of the inscriptions shows; the *defixiones* in Greece, when we examine the rank of those involved, take us back to a humble world of traders, craftsmen and poor servant girls. We find the names of schoolmasters[54] (bitter hatreds seem to have been common with them; teachers have always been a cantankerous class), cooks,[55] comic

actors,[56] soldiers,[57] prizefighters;[58] athletic competitions sometimes gave rise to a mass of *defixiones*, when the defeated athlete
avenged his failure by confiding his disappointment to the lead
sheets.

This practice passed from Greece to Rome, especially in the
army, where the festering hatred aroused by the harshness of
commanders sometimes took this form,[59] nor did aristocratic
courtiers refrain from using it against the emperor.[60] The hatreds
arising from the passions of the races in the circus[61] and from
litigation[62] favoured the spread of *defixio*. In the provinces the
sheets discovered in Rhaetia, Britain, Germany and Africa show
how widespread the practice was.

The procedure for *defixio* was as follows: the hated name was
written on a sheet of lead[63] with a formula of cursing, 'dedicating'

34. MAGICAL SIGNS USED IN DEFIXIO

the victim to the deities of the underworld, and the sheet was
placed in a tomb, more rarely in a temple, a well or a spring of
hot water, usually held in position by a long nail passed through
the sheet. Most of these sheets have been pierced, sometimes in
many places. In some sheets we find a long list of people dedicated;[64] the names of those on whom the curse is invoked file by
in procession, precisely catalogued by the hatred of the dedicator.
The name of the dedicated person is always carefully written, from
the fear that an inexact indication might render the curse ineffective; the name of his mother frequently follows the name of
the victim, more rarely the name of his father. Magical alpha-
betical signs (fig. 34) sometimes precede the text, or are inserted
in it; on some sheets a rough figure is traced; in fig. 35 a bearded
demon, with an urn and torch, symbols of death, stands on a boat,
perhaps representing the *cymba* of Charon, as he sails at night
across the waters; on the *cymba* we read '*noctivagus; Tiberis;
Oceanus*'. Magic words are mixed with the formulae of imprecation,
intended to make the curse more efficacious; for example in
Greek ἀρουράς, φρίξ, φρόξ, ἀβρασάξ, etc;[65] in late inscriptions
from North Africa the mysterious words BESCU, BEREBESCU,

ARURARA, BAZAGRA frequently recur, sinister mutterings of hatred transformed into syllables. The formulae of cursing are sometimes simple; 'I write down' (καταγράφω) 'I consecrate' (καταδέω, literally 'I bind'); sometimes solemn and awe-inspiring: 'I consecrate, bury, eliminate from human sight';[66] sometimes passionate: 'May his tongue be pierced . . . may his soul and tongue be

35. DEFIXIO TABLET WITH FIGURE OF A DEMON

(left: CUIGEU, CENSEU, CINBEU, PERFLEU, DIARUNCO, DIASTA, BESCU, BEREBESCU, ARUBARA, BAGAGRA. On the demon's breast: ARITMO, ARAITTO. On the boat: NOCTIVAGUS, TIBERIS, OCEANUS)

pierced'.[67] In some, disasters are invoked upon the victim with a perverse complacency along with the most frightful diseases.[68] 'May burning fever seize all her limbs, kill her soul and her heart; O gods of the underworld, break and smash her bones, choke her, *arourarelyoth*, let her body be twisted and shattered, *phrix*, *phrox* . . .' and so on in this tone. Particular parts of the body of the cursed were consecrated to the infernal deities for greater precision, usually the tongue, or the hands, feet, toes, ears, nose, brain, nails, ankles, eyebrows, lungs, and almost always the mind and soul.

Disaster for all the possessions of the consecrated was also invoked: 'And if he has, or shall have, any money, inheritance or trade, may they all become useless, may he lose them, and all be stricken with disaster and destruction.'[69]

In this rumbling of low passions, among so much wickedness, a more humane voice can occasionally be heard when in the rare love *defixiones* we find the prayers of a tormented lover, who asks for the aid of the underworld to obtain the love of the woman he desires; as when Successus[70] dedicates his wife that she may turn her arms towards him, burning with the love with which he loves her so passionately: 'May Successa burn, let her feel herself aflame with love or desire for Successus.' This prayer from the heart shines through the primitive and superstitious formulae.

The illusion of being able to force the supernatural powers to intervene in love affairs, to help a broken heart or an unrequited passion, was the origin of the practice of sorcery by women. To attract their beloved to them, women became sorceresses, the more determined in their spells the more they felt themselves old, ugly and despised. The woman who was the victim of an unhappy love, tried everything, from potions made to win over the man whose heart she wished to conquer (see p. 208), to more doubtful methods (see p. 288). Sorceresses inspired fear, because of their reputation for acquiring a superhuman power. They used disgusting and fearful ingredients for their charms: the intestines of frogs and toads, the feathers of owls, the bones of snakes, herbs from tombs[71] and powerful poisons (which also gave them the name of *veneficae*); they knew the most powerful spells (*carmina*) capable, as Virgil says, of drawing the moon down from the sky:

Carmina vel caelo possunt deducere lunam.[72]

So convinced were men of their power that some attributed the eclipse of the moon to the spells of women in love.[73] The power of these sorceresses was so great that nobody could feel secure from them, and men tried to protect themselves against them by nailing the beard of a wolf to their door,[74] for a wolf's beard had great strength in spells, both in rendering them effective[75] and in making them harmless. For those who feared spells there was no better method than to meet the beard of a wolf with the beard of a wolf.

One system of attracting a man consisted of a type of magic wheel, which the Greeks called ῥόμβος and the Romans *turbo*;[76] the wheel had four spokes, to which a bird was tied (a cuckoo, it seems, or a wryneck; ἴυγξ in Greek) and it was spun quickly with a cord or whip; then, as if an invisible thread bound the wheel to the man, he felt himself drawn irresistibly[77] and shortly afterwards his lover saw him coming home wreathed in smiles and good humour.

Some spells were more complicated. Unholy preparations were made in cemeteries, and tombs were violated to extract the bones of the dead; recourse was had to all the means suggested by the most practised sorceresses: magic formulae, sinister rites, poisonous and repugnant concoctions. Horace,[78] certainly exaggerating, describes the scene of a spell on the Esquiline. Two ugly old women, Canidia and Sagana, with bare feet and dishevelled hair, their faces deathly pale, and wrapped in black, chant their spells with mournful howlings. They invoke the shades of the dead, they tear up the earth with their nails and pour into a trench the blood of a black lamb which they have torn to pieces. The moon has sunk and hidden its bright face behind the tombs, bathing it in a dark, ill-omened light; dogs and serpents from the underworld gather round the unholy pair to complete the squalor of the scene. No detail is missing. In this spell the final operation consisted of melting a wax doll, representing the beloved, in the fire. Canidia has brought two such dolls with her; one is of wool, and raises its arm in an imperious and threatening manner; the other smaller one of wax stands in a position of supplication, as of one who is about to die dishonourably. The execution takes place. After burying the indispensable's wolf's beard and serpent's teeth in the ground, the two old women throw the wax image on to the fire, where it melts and burns with a bright flame. In the epilogue we learn that all would have turned out satisfactorily if at the last minute an unforeseen incident had not taken place to render all these careful preparations useless. A rough statue of Priapus, the god of gardens, made of fig wood, has watched dumbly, motionless in his office of bird-scarer, with evil intentions and a little fear. Now with typical malice he makes the wood split in two with a dry and sinister crack; the two women disappear terror-stricken; in their hurried flight Sagana loses her wig and Canidia her false teeth.

62. The Colosseum. Engraving by Piranesi.

63. The Forum. Engraving by Piranesi.

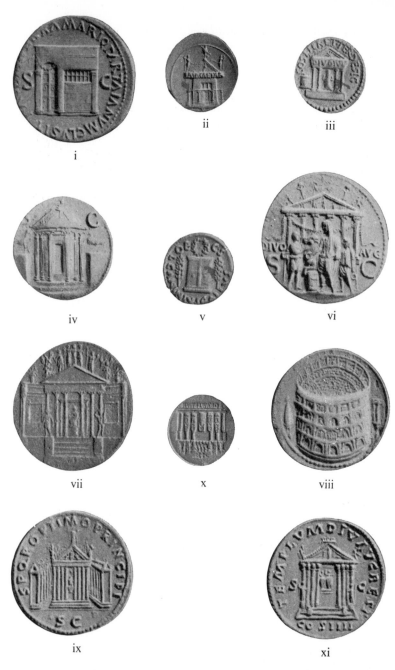

64. Coins illustrating Imperial Buildings.

i Temple of Ianus.
ii The Curia Iulia.
iii Temple of Divus Iulius.
iv Temple of Vesta restored by
   Augustus.
v Door of Augustus' house.
vi Temple of Divus Augustus.
vii Temple of Concord.
viii Flavian Amphitheatre.
ix Temple of Trajan.
x Entrance to Trajan's Forum.
xi Temple of Divus Augustus.

Further Reading

There is no comprehensive work on superstition, though it is dealt with in most books on Roman religion.

W. R. Halliday, *Greek and Roman Folklore* (London and Liverpool, 1927), describes a number of superstitions.

On magic, see L. Thorndike, *A History of Magic and Experimental Science* (London, 1929), J. E. Lowe, *Magic in Greek and Latin Literature* (Oxford, 1929) and, E. Massoneau, *La Magie dans l'Antiquité romaine* (Paris, 1934).

The best collections of texts of the *defixiones* remain those mentioned in note 45.

NOTES

1. Laws, VII, 808d.
2. Ibid. Crito, 46c.; Theocritus, XV, 40.
3. Lucian, Vera Hist., 139.
4. Horace, Ars Poet., 340.
5. I, 132; IV, 722.
6. Epist., II, 2, 209.
7. Plato, Phaedo, 81c.
8. Horace, Odes, I, 28.
9. Plautus, Most., 476; Pliny, Epist., VII, 27, 6.
10. Pliny, ibid.
11. Virgil, Ecl., VIII, 97; Petronius, 62; Apuleius, Met. II, 22.
12. Ovid, Amores, I, 8, 12–13; Apuleius, Met., I, 21.
13. Tacitus, Annals, II, 24, 6.
14. Pliny, N.H., IX, 10.
15. Petronius, 63.
16. Apuleius, Met., II, 21; Petronius, 134.
17. For a more detailed account see F. Cumont, *Les Religions orientales dans le paganisme romain* (Paris, 1929).
18. Afranius (quoted by Festus, 17, 16); *inscribat aliquis* ARSEVERSE *in ostio*. It has been maintained that *arse verse* were Etruscan words meaning 'keeping fire away'.
19. N.H., XXVIII, 25–29.
20. Cicero, De div., I, 40, 84; Tibullus, I, 3, 19; Ovid, Met., X, 452
21. Pliny, N.H., XXVIII, 25, 29.
22. Petronius, 74.
23. Cicero, in Pis., 27, 67.
24. Pliny, Epist., I, 18, 1.
25. Plato, Symposium, 188 c-d.

26. Terence, Phorm., 705.

27. Plutarch, Timoleon, 26.

28. Theophrastus, Characters, 16.

29. Cicero, De div.,: I, 34, 74. There are many similar references in other authors.

30. Plutarch, Nicias, 13; Pausanias, X, 15, 5.

31. Herodotus, IX, 120.

32. Livy, XXXI, 17, 12.

33. Ibid. XXI, 62, 3.

34. Herodotus, I, 175.

35. Suetonius, Divus Julius, 81: *Equorum greges . . . comperit pertinacissime pabulo abstinere ubertimque flere.*

36. Ibid., Cal., 57: *Simulacrum Jovis . . . tantum cachinnum repente edidit ut . . . opifices diffugerint.,*

37. Livy, III, 10, 6; XLIII, 13; Pliny, N.H., VIII, 183.

38. Virgil, Ecl., III, 103; Persius, 2, 34.

39. See p. 116.

40. Silius Italicus, VII, 172; Petronius, 30.

41. Pliny N.H., XXVIII, 25-29, from which the references to other superstitions in this paragraph are drawn.

42. See p. 93.

43. Petronius, 104.

44. Pliny, N.H., XXVIII, 25-29. See Sir J. G. Frazer, The Golden Bough 1, 113.

45. The facts in this paragraph are drawn from the collection of R. Wuensch, *Defixionum tabellae Atticae* (IG, III, 3; Berlin, 1897); Audollent, *Defixionum tabellae* (Paris, 1904); and the texts published by E. Ziebarth, *Neue Verfluchungstafeln aus Attika, Boioten und Euboia*, in Sitzb. preuss. Akad. (Berlin, 1934).

46. The sheets referring to lawsuits are the most numerous.

47. Wuensch, no. 94.

48. Audollent, 5, 10.

49. Ziebarth, 5, p. 1032; cf. Audollent, 92.

50. Audollent, 13.

51. Wuensch, praef., p. XI.

52. Audollent, 42, 212.

53. Ibid. 104 (theft of a cloak), 6 (clothes), 122 (garments and washing), 106 (a ring).

54. Ibid. 33 and 34.

55. Ibid., 49.

56. Ibid., 45.

57. Ibid., 55.

58. Wuensch, no. 68a.

59. Tacitus, Annals, II, 69, 4; III, 13, 3.

60. Ibid., Annals, IV, 52, 2; Suetonius, Cal., 3.

61. The consecration of charioteers at Rome (Audollent, 159–187) and of charioteers and *venatores* in North Africa (ibid., 232, 254, 972, 295) are numerous but late.

62. See Audollent, p. 471.

63. Consecrations written on other metals (gold, silver, tin or bronze) are rare; some are written on marble or pottery.

64. Ziebarth, 14, p. 1037.

65. At first these words, mostly of Egyptian or Semitic origin, were comparatively few and were called Ephesian letters (Hesychius s.v. Ἐφέσια γράμματα); the most ancient seem to have been ἄσκιον, κατάσκιον, λίξ, τέτραξ, δαμναμένευς their number later increased, and a large number of compounded syllables were collected, whose strange sounds earned them the name of barbarian words (Lucian, Menipp. 9).

66. Ziebarth, No. 1a. p. 1023.

67. Wuensch, n. 97, p. 24.

68. Ziebarth, 24, 1–4, pp. 1042 et seq.

69. Wuensch, n. 97, lines 26 et seq.

70. CIL, VIII, 12507. *Uratur Su(c)e(s)sa, aduratur amo(re) vet* (= *vel) desideri(o) Su(c)ce(s)si.*

71. Horace, Epodes, 5, 17; Propertius, III, 6, 27, etc.

72. Ecl., VIII, 69.

73. Martial, XII, 57, 16–17; cf. Tacitus, Ann. I, 28.

74. Pliny, N.H., XXVIII, 157.

75. Horace, Sat., I, 8, 42.

76. Theocritus II, 40 (see Gow's note *ad loc.*); the Greek word *rhombus* is found in Ovid, Amores, I, 8, 7; Propertius, III, 6, 26, etc.

77. Horace, Epodes, 17, 7.

78. Sat., I, 8.

CHAPTER XXVII

The Changing Face of Ancient Rome

Steady change in the appearance of Rome. The heart of Rome at the end of the Second Punic War. In the age of Sulla. Under Augustus. In the last years of the Julio-Claudian era. At the end of the Flavian age. In the age of the Antonines. From Septimius Severus to Constantine. Conclusion.

MOST people fail to appreciate how constantly and completely the appearance of ancient Rome changed, and that within a very short period it might alter out of all recognition. Cicero, Seneca and Martial have each left us an immense mass of detail on the subject, but if we collate these details, the picture of Rome which emerges is different for each author. It is a very common mistake to imagine that a picture of the city càn be drawn which is true for more than one generation, and to think that Cicero walked through a city very similar to that through which his son walked as a grown man, and that Rome looked very much the same to Horace as it did to Martial.

The theme of this chapter, the continually changing face of Rome, will be illustrated in a very simple way. From the age of Cato the Censor to the age of the late Empire, at regular intervals a representative of each generation will be placed at a point from which the widest possible view of the heart of Rome can be obtained, on the Via Sacra, at the western extremity of the Forum, with his back to the Capitol, at the foot of the temple of Saturn, facing the Esquiline. What did our observer see from there?

The sight which the visitor of today sees, when he stops at this same spot during his tour of the Forum, is shown in Plate 1. This is the Forum today, the fantastically confused remains of the history of more than a thousand years, the stupendous result of centuries of building activity and of successive destructions and attacks. Every generation has left its monuments there, and every monument its traces. Between the *Lapis niger*, which ancient legend regarded as the tomb of Romulus (and recent excavations have proved that it was an ancient tomb) and the column of Phocas, raised in the first years of the seventh century A.D. (see p. 6), lie more than a thousand years of history, of which today the venerable ruins of the Roman Forum are our witness. No ancient Roman ever saw the Forum in this state, and if we wish to gain an idea of how it appeared to each generation, and what could be seen from the Forum, we may resort to the fiction already described.

36. THE LAPIS NIGER

Let us imagine our first observer at this point towards the end of the second Punic War, Cato the Censor for example while still a young man, when the Forum was still mostly occupied by houses and shops, and there were no other public buildings besides the ancient temples and the *Curia Hostilia*, where the Senate met; it had not yet been decided that it was essential for the magistrates to have an office for conducting their business. The observer in these years would have seen on his left the *Comitium*, where the people met for discussion, the heart of the political life of Rome during the centuries of political liberty. Excavations in this small corner of the Forum have provided tangible evidence of the political activity of the Romans; a total of fourteen stratifications shows how their feet wore away the pavement when they attended meetings. Private houses and shops surrounded the *Comitium;* to the south the area was bounded by the *Lapis niger* and the *Graecostasis*,[1] a paved area where foreign ambassadors waited to be introduced to the Senate, and to the north by the· *Curia Hostilia*. Facing the *Curia*, not far from the *Graecostasis*, on the extreme western edge of the *Comitium*, stood the *Rostra*[2] (see p. 6); on the *Graecostasis*, Cn. Flavius in 304 had built a small bronze shrine to Concordia.[3]

Up to the beginning of the first Punic War the *Rostra* and the *Graecostasis* were used to tell the time. The reader already knows (see p. 84) that the Greek sun-dial brought to Roma from Sicily in

37. THE SHRINE OF VENUS CLOACINA

263 B.C. had not worked well in a new latitude; sun-dials had not yet been adapted to Rome, and to know the exact moment of midday it was necessary to wait for the servant (*accensus*) of the consuls to make a solemn announcement when he saw from the steps of the *Curia Hostilia* that the sun was between the *Rostra* and the *Graecostasis*.[4]

In the time of Cato, the *Curia Hostilia* was a cramped, antiquated building, which was enlarged only later (see p. 296), and subsequently rebuilt.[5] Towards the east, still to the left, the observer would have seen the ancient *Macellum*; together with the two small markets, the *Forum Piscarium* (or *Piscatorium*) and the *Forum Cuppedinis*, which were dependent on it, it spread southwards to the farthest edge of the Forum. Further south stood the *Tabernae Novae*, built to replace the ancient shops burnt

in 210 B.C.[6] In this northern corner of the Forum stood two very
ancient temples, which later builders always respected: the temple
of Janus, whose doors were closed only in times of peace, and the
temple of Venus Cloacina, where the *Cloaca Maxima* entered the
Forum. This temple was a memorial of the sacrifice of Verginia,
killed by her father to prevent her falling a slave to the power of
Appius Claudius.[7]

If the observer then turned his eyes in the opposite direction, a
mass of shops came into view, the 'old shops' (*Tabernae Veteres*)[8]
and private houses including the house of the Scipios.[9] Still on the
same side, but further east, stood two of the most ancient and
revered temples in Rome: the temples of Vesta and of Castor.
These two temples were still primitive in appearance; the imposing
remains which today bear witness to their ancient magnificence
as they dominate this corner of the Forum belong to buildings of
a later date (see p. 297).

In the age of Cato the Temple of Castor was a simple building
of tufa, said to have been built by the dictator Postumius to
commemorate the divine aid which the two Dioscuri had brought
to the Romans at the battle of Lake Regillus.[10] Nearby stood the
spring (*Lacus Iuturnae*)[11] where, according to legend, the Dioscuri
had watered their horses after the battle. The small round temple
of Vesta, the only temple of the goddess which existed in the
Republican age, where the sacred fire was guarded, was rebuilt
entirely in brick for the first time in 241 B.C., when it was destroyed
by fire, a fate which it frequently suffered (see p. 324).

Near the temple of Vesta stood the 'Palace' (*Regia*) which,
according to tradition, had been the house of Numa,[12] and was the
residence of the Pontifex Maximus[13] in the Republican age. The
Regia too was frequently destroyed by fire; in the age of Cato it
did not have the magnificence which made it one of the most
remarkable buildings in the Forum when Cn. Domitius Calvinus
rebuilt it after a new fire in 36 B.C.[14] and placed two statues in
front of the entrance.[15] The house of the Vestal Virgins near the
temple was also a humble building. The *Atrium Vestae*, whose
ruins can be seen today, is a later building erected after the fire in
the reign of Nero (A.D. 64).[16]

Higher up, still to the right, there stretched before the eyes of
the observer the three peaks which together formed the Palatine
Hill, the *Palatium*, the *Germalus*, and the *Velia*; neither the peaks

nor the valley between them had yet been covered by the large buildings which in the first century of the Empire gave the Palatine an architectural unity. In this area, on the *Via Sacra*, stood the most ancient temple of Iuppiter Stator, which was first restored by Augustus. On the *Palatium*, the largest of the peaks of the Palatine, the aristocratic houses which crowded its slopes in the age of Cicero, when this hill became the favourite residence of politicians, were not yet standing (see p. 19). Looking straight ahead of him beyond the Forum towards the *Velia*, where today the Arch of Titus and the Colosseum mark the end of the Forum, the observer would have seen a closely packed mass of working-class houses with narrow streets where there was intense activity and little fresh air (see p. 13). The fire of Nero was to destroy this human rabbit-warren and to clear the area, which afterwards had the most varied and splendid history in Roman architecture (see p. 21). Still further east stood the gloomy peak of the Esquiline (see p. 27), uncared for and almost uninhabited.

If our observer turned round he saw behind him the temple of Saturn, an ancient building going back to the fifth century B.C.; it was not yet that splendid building which dominated the Forum when Plancus, the loyal follower of Caesar, rebuilt it in 42 B.C. Higher still was the ancient *Porticus Deorum Consentium* with its bronze statues of the twelve principal divinities of Rome,[17] the ancient temple of Concordia, which was later frequently rebuilt, and above the *Graecostasis* the *Senaculum*, where the Senators met, when not in full session, for discussions with the magistrates.[18]

If at our observation point we place a Roman of the time of the dictatorship of Sulla—Cicero, for example, at the beginning of his political career—the view will be very different. On his left stood the *Comitium;* its appearance had changed considerably after Cato had built the *Basilica Porcia*[19] in 184 B.C., the first basilica in Rome, and Sulla had enlarged and modernised the *Curia Hostilia* in 88 B.C. This venerable building was later burnt and destroyed in 52 B.C., when Cicero, now an ex-consul, was fifty-four years old. It was then rebuilt under the name of *Curia Cornelia* by Faustus Sulla, the dictator's nephew, but, as we shall see (p. 298), it lasted in this state only a few years. Further away, still to the left, stood a new basilica, the *Basilica Aemilia*, which M. Aemilius Lepidus[20] had built in his censorship in 179 B.C., together with his colleague M. Fulvius Nobilior, five years after the *Basilica Porcia*. If Cicero wanted to know the time, it was no longer necessary, as it had once been, to wait for the solemn announcement by the *accensus* (see p. 294); he could go to the *Basilica Aemilia*, where a water clock marked the hours.[21] Scipio Nasica had put it there in 159 B.C.[22], and from then on the Romans could always be certain of the time. The *Basilica Aemilia* was still primitive and humble; it was not yet the magnificent building which the people so much admired after L. Aemilius Paulus Lepidus,[23] the brother of the triumvir, had rebuilt it, using some of the ancient material, in 54 B.C. Cicero was then fifty-two, and in one of his letters to Atticus he wrote that there was nothing more beautiful or more splendid.[24] The old basilica was not yet decorated with the gilded bronze shields which M. Aemilius placed there in the year of his consulship,[25] engraved with the portraits of his ancestors;[26] this was done in 78 B.C., when Cicero was twenty-eight, and his defence of Roscius Amerinus had already established his reputation as an advocate (see p. 192).

The district to the right of the observer was still occupied by the *Tabernae Veteres*. This block of shops surrounded two sides of the *Basilica Sempronia*, built in 170 B.C. and destined, like the *Tabernae Veteres*, to be destroyed when the building of the *Basilica Iulia* began. Further on stood the temple of Castor, rebuilt by L. Caecilius Metellus[27] in 117 B.C., not many years before the birth of Cicero.

Further east, the Palatine, not yet, as in the reign of Augustus, covered with buildings, was already showing signs of new life, now that the most distinguished men in Roman politics had begun to build themselves splendid private houses there (see p. 19).

Behind the observer stood the new Temple of Concord, rebuilt by Opimius in the age of the Gracchi, and between this and the *Porticus Deorum Consentium*, the Basilica built by the same Opimius, a remarkable building mentioned by Cicero in one of his speeches,[28] which disappeared when Tiberius rebuilt the Temple of Concord on a larger scale in A.D. 10 (see p. 300).

Very different was the view from our vantage point if, instead of Cicero, we place the ageing Horace to observe the appearance of Rome some years before the beginning of the Christian era. Little more than seven decades had passed, but the great scene had completely changed. The tremendous building activity of Caesar and Augustus had left its mark everywhere. Very close by, to the left of the observer, were the *Rostra*, which Caesar[29] had moved from the western edge of the *Comitium* to the site where we can still see their remains, near the southern side of the arch of Septimius Severus. The area of the *Comitium* had been enlarged and made more regular. The *Graecostasis* had disappeared and been replaced by the *Graecostadium*, near the southern side of the *Basilica Iulia*. By Augustus' orders, a block near the *Rostra*, covered with gilded plates of bronze[30], marked the central point of Rome, from which the roads spread out to the furthest corners of the Empire. Below the *Argiletum*, facing the western side of the *Basilica Aemilia*, now one of the most splendid buildings of the Forum, near the site of the *Curia Hostilia* and the *Curia Cornelia*, whose destruction Horace had witnessed, now stood the *Curia Iulia*;[31] the building had been begun by Caesar[32] and finished by Augustus, who dedicated it in 29 B.C.[33] Facing the south-east corner of the *Basilica Aemilia*, separated from the *Via Sacra*, near the *Regia*, on the spot where the corpse of Caesar had been burnt, stood the *Templum Divi Iuli*, shown on some imperial coins (see Plate 64). The northern edge of the *Argiletum*, beyond the *Curia* and the *Basilica Aemilia*, had been impressively transformed by the construction of the *Forum Iulium*, at the edge of which stood the *Templum Veneris Genetricis*, and of the *Forum Augusti*, with the Temple of *Mars Ultor* nearby (see p. 7). Recent excavations have cleared the remains of these two temples and made a partial reconstruction possible. The façade of the temple of *Mars Ultor*, if the identification is correct, is shown on a relief at the Villa Medici.

Behind the observer stood the splendid temple of Saturn, rebuilt by Plancus, and, higher up the slopes of the Capitol, the magnificent building that housed the public records, the *Tabularium*, built by the consul Q. Lutatius Catulus in 78 B.C. The temple of Concord, rebuilt by Opimius, the *Basilica Opimii* and the *Senaculum* were still standing, but their days were numbered. At his right, along the southern side of the *Via Sacra*, on the site of the *Tabernae Veteres* and the *Basilica Sempronia* in the age of Cicero, stood the massive marble-covered *Basilica Iulia*. Horace was a boy when the Basilica was built for the first time by Caesar, and a grown man when Augustus rebuilt it after the original building had been destroyed by fire.[34] The ancient temple of Vesta, which Augustus had restored and enriched with marble, was living the last years of its life.[35] The temple of Castor was still the same as in the age of Cicero, but in A.D. 6, only a few years after the death of Horace, still during the principate of Augustus, it was rebuilt by Tiberius and his brother Drusus,[36] and was, as the remaining columns still show, one of the most conspicuous buildings of the Forum.

The slopes of the Palatine facing the Forum had undergone no remarkable change, but the top of the hill was altered in appearance. The Palatine, which in the last days of the Republic had become the residence of politicians, became, and remained until the reign of Nero, the residence of the emperors of the Julio-Claudian family. Augustus built the temple of Apollo Palatinus there, to which the two great libraries of Rome were attached (see p. 185). The splendour of this temple, extolled by all the greatest poets of Rome, bore witness to the political shrewdness of a man who, having secured the mastery of the world for himself, kept a humble house for his own use (see Plate 64), and built splendid temples for the gods. Historians have not yet decided whether his motive was genuine austerity or hypocrisy. Facing the observer stood an Esquiline much transformed, and Horace no longer recognised in the magnificent appearance of the hill the solitary desert where, in his Satires, he had pictured a sinister scene of witchcraft (see p. 288). The area between the Forum and Esquiline was still without buildings, as in the age of Cicero. On the *Velia* the temple of Iuppiter Stator (see p. 296) had been restored and beautified by Augustus.

Now let us place the poet Martial at the same observation point. He has a right to this, for nobody observed Rome more closely than he, or described it in greater detail. After his arrival in Rome from Spain he lived there almost uninterruptedly for thirty-four years, from A.D. 64 to 98, and so we shall see through his eyes how it looked when he arrived as a young man, how he saw it change, and how he left it when, after his long exile, he returned grey-headed to his own country. In these years one surprising change had been completed; others no less surprising were in progress.

Martial came to Rome during the last years of the principate of Nero. It is easy for us to reconstruct the buildings near our observation post in the Rome of Nero and of the Flavians, as it is possible to follow their changes almost year by year. When Martial came to Rome, the Roman Forum was for the most part as Horace had seen it in the last years of his life; but the temple of Castor, rebuilt some years after the death of Horace, at the foot of the Palatine, was now one of the most striking buildings in the Forum, and between the *Rostra* and the temple of Saturn stood the arch which Tiberius[37] had built as a memorial of his victories over the Germans, when the armies of Germanicus had avenged the defeat of Varus. The enlargement of the Imperial Forums had not yet begun. The slopes of the Palatine facing the Forum, however, had altered, as on this hill Tiberius had built the imperial palace (see p. 21). Though Augustus had continued to live as an ordinary private citizen, Tiberius built himself a palace on this same hill. Caligula eagerly continued the work of his predecessor on the Palatine; he built the *Templum Divi Augusti*[38] there (whose façade, extremely stylised, appears on a coin of Caligula; see Plate 64), and enlarged the palace, which now extended to the Forum (see p. 21).

Behind the observer's back the slopes of the Capitol presented a new appearance, after Titus and Domitian had built the *Templum Divi Vespasiani* in their father's honour next to the temple of Concord (see p. 297), rebuilt by Tiberius, and below the *Tabularium*. To make way for this new building the *Basilica Opimii* and the *Senaculum* had disappeared. The ancient *Porticus Deorum Consentium* had been restored.

To the east of the Palatine, the future site of the Colosseum looked, in the year when Martial came to Rome, like the scene of a recent catastrophe. Where previously old houses had crowded together in a labyrinth of narrow streets, enormous mounds of charred bricks were to be seen. But soon the removal of the material began, and the site of the catastrophe was swarming with contractors, engineers, Greek artists, hundreds of slave labourers, occupied in an exhausting task; everywhere blocks of stone were to be seen, slabs of marble, statues waiting to be erected; for within a short time this same area offered a spectacle no less magnificent than strange, when Nero had built there his *Domus Aurea*, which was to occupy a stretch of the slopes of the

Esquiline, and whose vicissitudes we have already described (see p. 17).

When the effects of a more rational government began to be seen (see p. 22), Martial himself wrote that the Flavians had restored Rome to Rome.[39] On the still inhabited site of the *Domus Aurea* arose, beside the houses, buildings which have defied the centuries. It seemed that this dominating and aggressive city had chosen this place to proclaim its material power and its pride in its empire. Martial was a daily eye-witness of this feverish activity and miraculous transformation, and to the humble provincial, reared in his small Spanish village perched on the top of a mountain, the way the city changed its appearance and assumed new aspects daily seemed majestically regal; he felt he had come to a city of the gods.

If we now place him on the eve of his departure at the same point, what a different city he was about to leave, how changed from that which he had admired on his arrival! To the east of the *Forum Iulium* on the previous site of the *Macellum*, stood the Forum of Vespasian, considered together with the *Basilica Aemilia* and the Forum of Augustus to form one of the most beautiful groups of buildings in the world.[40] Dominating the Forum stood the *Templum Pacis*, built as a memorial of the conquest of the Jews; here the precious booty removed from the temple of Jerusalem, which is shown in the reliefs on the arch of Titus, was displayed. The extension of the Forum of Vespasian, built by Domitian, was used as a passage from the Forum of Augustus to the Forum of Vespasian; it was therefore called the *Forum Transitorium*, and later, from the name of the emperor who completed it, the *Forum Nervae*. The main building in this Forum was the *Templum Minervae*; recent excavations have brought to light some traces of its surrounding wall and the Corinthian columns with protruding entablature (Plate 67).

We do not know whether the colossal equestrian statue of Domitian, between the *Rostra* and the *Templum Divi Iuli*, which dominated the *Forum Romanum*, and which a court poet, Statius, had celebrated in the first of his *Silvae*,[41] had already been destroyed. On the Palatine the *Templum Divi Augusti*, destroyed by fire, had been rebuilt by Vespasian. Beyond the Forum, only that part of the *Domus Aurea* which reached the Esquiline still remained, and had become the residence of Titus. The Colossus still remained, as has been said (see p. 147), although its head had been changed. The rest had for the most part been destroyed to make way for buildings of greater public, or private, use. Some of the artistic masterpieces which Nero had collected in the *Domus Aurea* had been moved to the *Templum Pacis*; others remained in the *Domus Titi*, where the Laocoön, now in the Vatican Museum, was found.

On the site of the *Stagnum* of the *Domus Aurea* was built the Flavian amphitheatre, whose appearance is shown on a coin before the great building was defaced. Today it has been stripped of its marble, but has lost none of its impressiveness, and is, next to the Pyramids and the Parthenon, the most famous building of the ancient world. Mutilation has only increased its beauty. Next to the amphitheatre was built the Arch of Titus, whose subsequent fate in later centuries we shall mention later (see p. 316); a short distance away stood the Baths of Titus, which were remembered not so much for their splendour, as for the speed with which they were built.[42]

This great city, which Martial had seen change at such prodigious speed, continued its development in the succeeding age, and if we place at the same point some Roman immediately after the death of Antoninus Pius—the aged Suetonius, for example— yet another city met the observer's eyes. In this period of almost fifty years further changes had taken place. In the *Forum Romanum* beside the *Rostra* shone the marbles of the *plutei Traianei* (see p. 146); near the *Basilica Aemilia*, towards the east, the Temple of Antoninus and Faustina had been built, and a new and splendid view was offered from this point to anyone who gazed towards the Forum which spread out before him. A flood of air and light swept over the Imperial Forums from the *Campus Martius*, whose green plain was to be seen not far off as a background for the *Forum Traiani* and the *Basilica Ulpia*. In the age of Trajan an almost miraculous transformation took place. We have seen that from Augustus to Domitian other Forums had been built in continuation of the single Forum of the Republican age, the Roman Forum. In a little more than a century the number of Forums had jumped from one to five; however, even this number was insufficient. They did not offer enough room for the movement of a population which was always growing and which resorted there till noon. The enlarging of the Forums, besides giving an excuse for architectural activity, was a practical necessity. But up to the reign of Trajan an enlargement of the main area of the Forums was hindered by the bottleneck between the Quirinal and the Capitol.

The Forums could only develop northwards, but in this direction the way was barred at one point by the slopes of the two hills, which only allowed a narrow passage between them. Trajan faced the formidable task of removing this natural barrier, and had the most westerly spur of the Quirinal removed. This great work opened up communication between the site of the Forums, packed to bursting point with buildings, and the open plain which stretched down to the Tiber. It was like throwing open a great door between the perpetually overcrowded centre of Rome and the lungs of the city, the *Campus Martius*. We have the impression that only thus did Rome begin to breathe. There then stood to the north of the Forum of Augustus a new building complex, whose area exceeded that of all the other Forums together, and included, beside the *Forum Traiani*, the *Basilica Ulpia*, and further north, the *Templum Traiani*. On the eastern flank of the Forum the Market of Trajan was built. In the centre stood the wonderful column, with its historical reliefs, whose height indicated the height of the slope which had been cut away, and whose reliefs, spiralling upwards, represented in a continuous story the actions and events of the victorious campaign against the Dacians. The entrance to the new Forum was magnificent (Plate 64).

On the Palatine the temple of Augustus, recently destroyed by fire and rebuilt by Antoninus Pius, had become more impressive. From the representations of it which we have on two coins of Caligula and of Antoninus Pius (Plate 64), we can see that the new temple had used some of the architectural elements of the old, but that the number of columns had increased from six to eight.

In the area of the Colosseum, near buildings of the Flavian age, on the slopes of the Esquiline, stood the Baths of Trajan, of which only insignificant traces remain today. But it is possible to obtain an idea of the splendour of their picturesque ruins from a fifteenth-century engraving by Du Pérac. Next to the Colosseum, the most magnificent temple which had ever been seen in Rome or in the world shone with its golden roof, the double temple *Urbis et Veneris*, conceived and designed by Hadrian (p. 14). The Colossus had disappeared from this area (see p. 147).

It might seem that with Trajan and Hadrian the centre of Rome, which we have been studying, had reached saturation point. But for a great city embellishment has no limits. In the age of the Severi, the splendid Arch of Septimius Severus was built in the Forum and has survived untouched to our day. In the first decade of the fourth century A.D. on the southern side of the Forum, to the east of the *Basilica Aemilia*, was built the most magnificent basilica that ever stood in Rome, begun by Maxentius and completed by Constantine.[43] In honour of the same Emperor an equestrian statue was erected in the centre of the Augustan

38. THE RUINS OF THE BATHS OF TRAJAN
(*from a print by Du Pérac*)

Forum,[44] and an arch beyond the Colosseum; the statue has disappeared, but the arch remains intact today and has suffered no outrages from time. Even when the miracle of the city which was continually changing was about to end, every generation continued to see a different Rome from that of their fathers.

But from the end of the second century onwards, most of the principal new buildings of Rome were erected at some distance from the Forum; under Marcus Aurelius the *Columna Antonini* in the *Campus Martius*, under the Severi the *Thermae Antoninianae*, called the Baths of Caracalla, near the beginning of the Via Appia, and the *Amphitheatrum Castrense* beyond the furthest slopes of the Caelian; later the Baths of Diocletian and of Constantine on the Quirinal, and in the district of the Caelian the palace of Constantine on the present site of the Basilica of St John Lateran;

5. Rome. The Arch of Titus.

66. Relief from the Arch of Titus showing the seven-branched candlestick being removed from Jerusalem.

67. Remains of the Temple of Minerva in the Forum Transitorium.

68. Rome. The Pantheon of Agrippa.

facing it was a statue of Marcus Aurelius, which was moved to the Capitol in 1538 (see p. 6).

The reader knows that the object of this chapter has been merely to give an idea of the constantly changing face of Rome, and, to achieve this, what seemed the most suitable observation point has been chosen. From this point, however, though much was visible, not everything could be seen. Other evidence of the continual architectural transformation of the city would be obtained, if after having placed our observer on the *Via Sacra* with his back to the temple of Saturn, we were to place him on the Capitol, the Palatine, the eastern slopes of the Quirinal or at the far end of the *Campus Martius*; but, there seems no need to take our observers to other vantage points in Rome, since our object has already been achieved.

What has been said suggests that the changing appearance of Rome was the proof of its tremendous vitality. Consequently, when, under Constantine, the pulse of the city ceased to beat with its accustomed rhythm after the transference of the capital, this was for Rome the beginning of an agony that was to last for centuries. The changes and mutilations which the ancient buildings underwent were the slow death-throes of the city; for cities, too, die, though they may rise again with a new appearance. This melancholy story of decay is the subject of our final chapter.

Further Reading

See the bibliographical note at the end of Chapter I for books dealing with buildings of the Imperial age.

NOTES

1. Varro, De Ling. Lat., V, 155: *sub dextra huius a comitio locus substructus, ubi nationum subsisterent legati qui ad senatum essent missi; is Graecostasis appellatus.*

2. Ibid.: *ante hanc (Curiam Hostiliam) Rostra.*

3. Pliny, N.H., XXXIII, 19: *Flavius . . . aediculam aeream fecit in Graecostasi, quae tunc supra Comitium erat* (Pliny says *tunc*, because in his day the *Graecostasis* no longer existed and had been replaced by the *Graecostadium* near the south side of the Basilica Iulia).

4. Ibid. VII, 212: *XII tabulis ortus tantum et occasus nominantur, post aliquot annos adiectus est et meridies, accenso consulum id pronuntiante, cum a Curia inter Rostra et Graecostasin prospexisset solem.*

5. Cicero, de fin. v, 1, 2: *Curiam nostram (Hostiliam dico, non hanc novam, quae minor esse mihi videtur, postea quam est maior)*, etc.

6. Livy, XXVI, 27, 2: *Eodem tempore septem tabernae, quae postea quinque, et argentariae, quae nunc Novae appellantur, arsere.*

7. Ibid. III, 48, 5: *Data venia seducit filiam ac nutricem prope Cloacinae ad tabernas, quibus nunc Novis est nomen, atque ibi ab lanio cultro arrepto:* 'Hoc te uno quo possum', ait, 'modo, filia, in libertatem vindico'. *Pectus deinde puellae transfigit.*

8. When the *Tabernae*, which stood on the southern side of the Forum, came to be called *Tabernae Novae* after being rebuilt after their destruction by fire in 210 B.C., the shops to the north of the Forum, where the *Basilica Sempronia* and the *Basilica Iulia* later stood, began to be known as *Tabernae Veteres*.

9. Livy, XLIV, 16, 10: *Tiberius Sempronius ex ea pecunia, quae ipsi attributa erat, aedes P. Africani pone veteres ad Vortumni signum, lanienasque et tabernas conjunctas in publicum emit, basilicamque faciendam curavit, quae postea Semproniana appellata est.*

10. Ibid. II, 20, 12: *Ibi nihil nec divinae nec humanae opis dictator praetermittens aedem Castori vovisse fertur ac pronuntiasse militi praemia;* 42, 5: *Castoris aedis eodem anno idibus Quintilibus dedicata est; vota erat Latino bello a Postumio dictatore; filius eius duumvir ad id ipsum creatus dedicavit.* cf. Cicero, De Nat. Deor., III, 5, 13.

11. Ovid. Fasti, I, 705-8:

> *At quae venturas praecedit sexta Kalendas,*
> *Hae sunt Ledaeis templa dicata deis.*
> *Fratribus illa deis fratres de gente deorum*
> *Circa Iuturnae composuere lacus.*

12. Ovid. Tristia, III, 1, 29-30:

> *Hic locus est Vestae, qua Pallada servet et ignem*
> *Haec fuit antiqui regia parva Numae.*

13. Servius on Aen., VIII, 363: *Domus enim, in qua pontifex habitat, regia dicitur, quod in ea rex sacrificulus habitare consuesset.* The *Regia* lost it importance after the end of the Republic, when the Princeps assumed the office of Pontifex Maximus; from then on the residence of the Pontifex was the Emperor's house on the Palatine.

14. Dio Cassius, XLVIII, 42, 4–5: (Καλουῖνος) ἀπ' αὐτοῦ (= τοῦ χρυσίου τῶν Ἰβρηικῶν) τὸ μέν τι ἐς τὴν ἑορτὴν ἀνάλωσε, τὸ δὲ δὴ πλεῖον ἐς τὸ βασίλειον. Κατακαυθὲν γὰρ αὐτὸ ἀνῳκοδόμησε καὶ εἰκόσιν καὶ καθιέρωσεν, ἄλλοις τέ τισι λαμπρῶς κοσμήσας καὶ εἰκόσιν.

15. Pliny, N. H., XXXIV, 48: . . . . *statuae, ex quibus duae ante Martis Ultoris aedem dicatae sunt, totidem ante Regiam.*

16. Tacitus, Ann., XV, 41, 1: *Numae regia et delubrum Vestae cum Penatibus populi Romani exusta.* That the temple of Vesta was rebuilt shortly afterwards can be gathered from Tacitus himself, who tells us (Hist., I, 43) that Piso, when wounded, took refuge in the temple of Vesta, from which he was forcibly dragged by two emissaries of Otho, and butchered at the door of the temple. This was in A.D. 69, five years after the fire of Nero.

17. Varro, De Re Rustica, I, 1, 4: . . . *duodecim deos Consentes . . . quorum imagines ad Forum auratae stant, sex mares et feminae totidem.*

18. Id. De Ling Lat., V, 155: *Senaculum supra Graecostasim, ubi aedis Concordiae et basilica Opimia, Senaculum vocatum, ubi senatus aut ubi seniores consisterent.* cp. Festus, 470, 8: *(Senaculum) ubi nunc est aedis Concordiae inter Capitolium et Forum, in quo solebant magistratus dumtaxat cum senioribus deliberare.*

19. Livy, XXXIX, 44, 7: *Cato atria duo Maenium et Titium in lautumiis et quattuor tabernas in publicum emit, basilicamque ibi fecit, quae Porcia appellata est.* The *Basilica Porcia* was built near the ancient prison, *Carcer* or *Lautumiae*, on the northern slope of the Capitol. According to tradition, the upper floor was built by Ancus Marcius, the lower, the *Tullianum*, by Servius Tullius (a false etymology, as the name was most probably derived from *tullius* 'a spring').

20. The *Basilica Aemilia* was built in 197 B.C. by the efforts of M. Aemilius Lepidus and M. Fulvius Nobilior; it was first known as the *Basilica Aemilia et Fulvia* (Varro, De Ling. Lat., VI, 4), and then generally *Aemilia*. cf. Livy, XL, 51, 5: *(M. Fulvius) basilicam (locavit) post argentarias novas et torum piscatorium circumdatis tabernis, quas vendidit in privatum.*

21. Varro, De Ling. Lat., VI, 4: *Solarium dictum id, in quo horae in sole inspiciebantur, quod Cornelius in basilica Aemilia et Fulvia inumbravit.*

22. Pliny, N.H., VII, 215: *Tunc Scipio Nasica . . . primus aqua divisit horas aeque noctium ac dierum, idque horologium sub tecto dicavit anno urbis DXCV* (= 159 B.C.) *Tam diu populo Romano indiscreta lux fuit.*

23. Plutarch, Caes., 29: (Καίσαρος) Παύλῳ . . . ὑπατεύοντι χίλια καὶ πεντακόσια τάλαντα δόντος, ἀφ' ὧν καὶ τὴν βασιλικὴν ἐκεῖνος. ὀνομαστὸν ἀνάθημα, τῇ ἀγορᾷ προσεκόσμησεν.

24. Cicero, ad Att., IV, 17, 7: *Paulus in medio foro basilicam iam paene texerat isdem antiquis columnis, illam autem, quam locavit facit magnificentissimam. Quid quaeris? nihil gratius illo monumento, nihil gloriosius.*

25. Pliny, N.H., XXXV, 13: *Post eum M. Aemilius collega in consulatu Quinti Lutatii non in basilica modo Aemilia, verum et domi suae* (*clupeos*) *posuit . . .; scutis . . . continebantur imagines.*

26. See above, p. 296.
27. Cicero, in Verrem, actio II, 7, 59, 154; pro Scauro, 23, 46.
28. Id., pro Sest., 67, 140: *L. Opimius . . . cuius monumentum celeberrimum in toro . . . relictum est.*
29. Dio Cassius, XLIII, 49, 1: τῷ δὲ ἐχομένῳ ἔτει (= 44 B.C.) . . . τὸ βῆμα ἐν μέσῳ που πρότερον τῆς ἀγορᾶς ὄν ἐς τὸν νῦν τόπον ἀνεχωρίσθη.
30. Id., LIV, 8, 4: τὸ χρυσοῦν μίλιον κεκλημένον ἔστησε.
31. Augustus, Mon Ancyr., IV, 19: *Curiam et continens ei Chalcidicum . . . feci.*
32. Caesar built the Temple of Felicitas on the site of the destroyed *Curia Cornelia.*
33. Dio Cassius, LI, 22, 1: τὸ βουλευτήριον τὸ ᾿Ιουλίειον, τὸ ἐπι τῇ τοῦ πατρὸς αὐτοι τιμῇ γενόμενον, καθιέρωσεν.
34. Augustus, Mon. Ancyr., IV, 20: *Forum Iulium et basilicam, quae fuit inter aedem Castoris et aedem Saturni, coepta profligataque opera a patre meo perfeci et eandem basilicam consumptam incendio ampliato eius solo sub titulo nominis filiorum meorum inchoavi et, si vivus non perfecissem, perfici ab heredibus meis iussi.*
35. See note 16.
36. Suetonius, Tib., 20: *Dedicavit et Concordiae aedem, item Pollucis et Castoris suo fratrisque nomine, de manubiis.*
37. Tacitus, Ann., II, 41, 1: *Fine anni arcus propter aedem Saturni ob recepta signa com Varo amissa ductu Germanici, auspiciis Tiberii (dicatur).*
38. Suetonius, Cal., 21: *Opera sub Tiberio semiperfecta, templum Augusti theatrumque Pompei, absolvit.*
39. See p. 48, note 107.
40. Pliny, N.H., XXXVI, 102: *. . . non inter magnifica basilicam Pauli columnis e Phrygibus mirabilem forumque Divi Augusti et templum Pacis Vespasiani Imp. Aug., pulcherrima operum, quae unquam vidit orbis?*
41. Statius, Silvae, I, 1. This poem gives us some precise topographical details. We gather that the statue stood in front of the *Templum Divi Iuli* (22–24):

> *Hinc obvia limina pandit,*
> *Qui fessus bellis adsertae munere prolis*
> *Primus iter nostris ostendit in aethera divis;*

that the *Basilica Iulia* stood on the right of the horse, the *Basilica Aemilia* to the left, and that the Temple of Vespasian and the Temple of Concord stood behind it (29–31):

> *At laterum passus hinc Iulia tecta tuentur,*
> *Illinc belligeri sublimis regia Pauli,*
> *Terga pater blandoque videt Concordia vultu.*

42. Suetonius, Tit., 7: *Amphitheatro dedicato thermisque iuxta celeriter exstructis;* cf. Martial, Lib. Spect., 2, 7: *Hic ubi miramur velocia munera thermas.*

43. The basilica was begun by Maxentius in A.D. 308, hence it was generally called the Basilica of Maxentius. It was completed by Constantine after his defeat of Maxentius in 313.

44. The inscription on its base has been preserved: *Pius, Felix, Triumphator: ob amplificatam toto orbe rem publicam.*

CHAPTER XXVIII

The Architectural Decay of Rome

From Constantine to the invasions of the Goths and Vandals. The siege of Vitiges and its consequences. The hunger for stone. Buildings converted into fortresses. The fate of smaller buildings. Marble turned into lime. Trade in architectural fragments. The work of destruction in the sixteenth and seventeenth centuries. The engulfing soil. Recovery of ancient Rome. 'The Niobe of nations.'

ROME's architectural decay began with the transfer of the capital to Constantinople. The decay was steady, but it was not so rapid or so disastrous in effect as to transform the great city to a chaotic mass of ruins in a short time. We even know of a period of revival under Theodoric, when walls, drains, aqueducts and theatres were restored.[1] The first symptom of the fatal onset of decay was the sudden halt in building activity at Rome after Constantine's departure. The work of continuous renovation, through which the city, like all great cities, changed appearance daily, came suddenly to a stop. Rome's changing face set; for cities, as for men, this is the first sign of approaching death.

The day came when the goats feeding on the Capitol and the cows grazing in the Forum gave them the names of *Mons Caprinus* and *Campus Vaccinus*,[2] but the memory of the generations who had seen the glories of Imperial Rome lasted for centuries.

Rome was not built in a day, and it could not be destroyed in a day. Great cities, monsters of stone and brick, have a vitality which resists the silent onslaught of time and the destructive fury of men. The transfer of the capital to Constantinople reduced Rome's population without emptying it. The official world emigrated to the shores of the Bosporus in the train of Constantine who took with him the government, the insignia of power, the court, the nobility, artists and many leading citizens as well as a large number of statues. The new capital was beautified at the expense of the old,[3] and the example of Constantine's quiet and methodical depredations was followed by a long line of plundering successors.[4] Administratively Rome was no longer the *caput mundi*, but the great historical event did not prevent the Romans of Rome remaining in their humbled city to breathe the air of the seven hills, as they had always done, near the tombs of their ancestors and among the signs of their ancient glory. Gradually the population of Rome decreased, but the depopulation of a great city is a slow process; the daily needs of the inhabitants protect the decaying city from complete destruction. As long as the city walls surrounded men who were born and died and had to solve the innumerable problems of daily life, the very task of keeping alive was a source of energy which kept walls and houses standing. The roof had still to be repaired when it leaked, even if Constantine had removed the eagles to Constantinople.

The legend that the barbarian invasions left Rome a heap of ruins has long been discredited. The sack of Alaric's Goths in August 410 and Genseric's Vandals in June 455 were occasions for extensive plundering, in which Rome was ravaged but not destroyed. Later authors continue to speak of it as a city of unrivalled architectural magnificence.[5] After Alaric's invasion a poet from Gaul, Rutilius Namatianus,[6] could still celebrate the splendours of Rome, the centre of the world; from the *Itinerarium Einsidlense*[7] we learn that the principal monuments of ancient Rome were still standing and recognisable up to the end of the seventh century.

Alaric's sack lasted for two days (24–25 August) and its fury was concentrated against the *Horti Sallustiani* with their innumerable statues, and the aristocratic palaces on the Aventine. The Vandals' sack lasted longer; for fourteen days, while their ships on the river were eagerly loaded with the rich booty, these barbarians, whose ranks included desert robbers, Arabs and Bedouins, raged through the streets, striking terror into the hearts of the inhabitants and venting their wrath particularly against the hills which had formed the heart of ancient Rome; they ruthlessly attacked Rome's most sacred monuments, the imperial residence on the Palatine and the temple of *Iuppiter Optimus Maximus* on the Capitol. When this wave of madness was past, the city still shone with its marble splendour, though there were wounds on its body and there was no hope of revenge; but the barbaric onslaught had not destroyed the buildings, and Rome still stood.

The barbarians came from the north, intent on plunder; they made havoc of statues and works of art, hacking out bronze doors and gilded tiles from the temples. Metal ornaments in particular were the objects of their greedy, childish plunder, for they were fascinated by the blazing splendour of the city glittering under the hot sun, unknown to the gloom of their native land. But they made no effort to destroy the buildings themselves, having neither the time nor the means, nor perhaps the inclination.

The long siege of Vitiges from February 537 to March 538 hastened the decay of the ancient city. In order to overcome the resistance of the citizens, protected by the Aurelian Wall, the besiegers destroyed considerable stretches of the aqueducts in the Campagna. Rome found itself without water; the vast baths, with their water supplies cut, became useless; water no longer splashed in the innumerable beautiful fountains (in the age of Constantine it was calculated that there were one thousand three hundred and fifty two wells and fountains in Rome[8]), the pride of Rome. Some years afterwards (546) a fiercer whirlwind of destruction beat upon the city with the conquest of Totila.

Meanwhile Rome had lost its wonderful countryside. In the age of its imperial splendour the life of Rome had extended to its suburbs, where citizens resorted to their villas to seek fresh air and quiet; the transition from city to country was gradual; even when he had gone through the walls a man still remained in the neighbourhood of Rome as he crossed the suburbs; the houses grew thinner and the green spaces steadily larger, as the country gradually replaced the town. The long straight roads spreading out from the gates rang cheerfully with the *raedae*[9] of the rich, who owned suburban villas among the farms on the right bank of the Tiber, on the Janiculum, the slopes of the Tuscan hills or at Tivoli. But from the early stages of its decline, a desert began to spread round Rome. The airy fields, parks and villas were replaced by a malarial plain and a dense, uncultivated jungle riddled with swamps, imprisoned in the midst of which lay decaying Rome, a heap of stones. The gates no longer saw the cheerful stream of citizens passing through.

Inside the city the population abandoned the hills, and confined itself to the *Campus Martius* and *Trans Tiberim* where the Vatican district was beginning to spring up.[10] This became the heart of the new city; at first, lying unprotected outside the Aurelian Wall, it was particularly vulnerable; later, after the Saracens had sacked the churches of St Peter and St Paul in 846, being unable to capture the walled city, Leo IV surrounded it with walls (the Leonine city). The hills and the Forums, previously throbbing with life, were abandoned to silence and decay, which the ancient buildings still dominated.

The population decreased steadily; in every age internal political struggles, epidemics, famines and sieges combined to reduce the number of inhabitants. Ten years after the Saracens' attack the Tiber flooded, causing incalculable damage. Rome was in ruin and misery. The city which had once been the most densely inhabited in the world[11] had been reduced to a mere seventeen thousand inhabitants, according to an estimate at the time of the Papal secession to Avignon.

The absurdity of this vast city being inhabited by so small a number of citizens was more fatal to ancient Rome than all the violence of its external enemies. The city of brick and marble was dying from its own misfortune; there was an atmosphere of helpless inertia, a complete lack of faith in its own destiny; the self-esteem of the city had been extinguished, and Rome was no longer proud of itself. The diminished population began to regard this city of the past as having no connexion with themselves; as built by another race whose temples bore witness to a cold and severe religion which did not reach the heart as did the good news recently brought from the East. What is large arouses feelings of fear and jealousy in those who are conscious of their own insignificance; men withdraw from what they hold dearest when a feeling of disproportion produces dislike. The Romans felt lost and lonely in this Rome which had grown too big for them. Unmoved by the charm of the ancient monuments, they contributed by their inertia to their steady decay. What falls rises again so long as there is the energy to repair the ruins; but when a ruin no longer causes sorrow and is made permanent by the indifference of those it should concern, the material body has no longer grounds for hope, for the soul is feeble. Buildings can last for ever, so long as they are protected by the love of those who feel a pride of ownership and see in their survival some consolation for their own mortality; the devouring fire, the destructive flood, the shattering earthquake merely mark an interruption in their eternal life. Countless times in Rome did the temple of Vesta[12] fall, the temple of Juppiter on the Capitol[13] and the Pantheon[14] on the *Campus Martius*. But, each time, the age which had seen their ruin saw them rise again, more splendid, from their ashes.

But now the old Rome was dying because it had died in the hearts of its inhabitants, who watched its destruction unmoved. They even accelerated it, as they continued the work of demolition for their own ends, an even more fatal process, because it was steady and uninterrupted. They stripped the buildings of marble slabs, bronze sheets, door posts and lintels to adorn their churches, and carried off the columns to support the naves. In times of siege they broke up statues and used the pieces as projectiles. Such was the fate of many of the statues which had adorned the Mausoleum of Hadrian and the *Pons Aelius* (Plate 64) (see p. 32). Nor did the emperors in Constantinople forget Rome, so long as there was a bronze door or gilded statue to be removed.[15] The defenceless body of Imperial and pagan Rome offered an easy and inexhaustible source of building materials to the new city timidly rising within the same walls, a new, obscure Rome, which, though indifferent and even hostile to the remains of its ancient glory, nevertheless, even while destroying the old city, renewed the promise that it would never cease to exist. Even in the gloomy twilight which lasted for over ten centuries between the city's two great periods of splendour, the Rome of the Empire and of the Pontiffs, the first stirrings of a new life could be discerned. Christian Rome began to rise out of the dying city of the Caesars. The darkness of the Catacombs gave up the ashes of the martyrs for public veneration; their remains were piously interred in great vessels taken from the now abandoned baths. The marble seats in the churches had been removed from the circus, where previously the purple-robed magistrates had watched the bloody games unmoved. Many sarcophagi sculptured with scenes from pagan mythology, were placed in the new cemeteries and held the bodies of the baptised.

Piety, however, was not always the motive for this systematic devastation; new needs arose and the ancient buildings became stone quarries; with the exception of a few which were required for other purposes, the marbles were thrown into kilns to make lime for cement. The city of their ancestors provided the descendants with means of satisfying their insatiable greed for ornaments, stone and lime.[16]

Rome became the prey of private greed. Baths, temples and noble palaces were covered with marble and the vaults of the rooms with stucco; plates of gold and ivory had been let into the coffered ceilings, and the mosaic floors shone with pure gold as well as onyx and rare marbles. All this was stripped, smashed and carried away until everything had disappeared. To the degenerate Romans this was the most obvious advantage of their great inheritance. The daily work of destruction went on, insidiously and persistently like the work of parasites which attack the skin and destroy more than they devour. Rome decayed steadily, and with this decadence its colour changed, as it lost the brightness of marble and took on the grey hue of stone; old and discoloured, it became a dark and gloomy city; the blazing sun pitilessly exposed the red gashes in its white stones. From the pillage emerged the ruins, severe, uniform, solemn, dominating the solitude around them. The inhabited area shrank steadily, as Rome was plunged into a profound silence. The irregular outlines of the ruins stood out against the skyline with a new harmony; the buildings stood free and acquired a strange beauty.

At first the solidity of their construction defeated the efforts of their plunderers; the ancient cement, its strength increased by the passage of time, resisted their attacks; the size of the blocks of stone made the attempt to shift them difficult and dangerous. The hour of their final collapse or demolition came later in a magnificent age of revival. Some buildings survived because they served a new purpose, when scruples at adapting pagan temples to Christianity were overcome and they were converted into churches; Boniface IV (Pope 608–15) consecrated the Pantheon (Plate 68) to the Virgin with the title of *Sancta Maria ad Martyres* in 610 after obtaining the permission of the Byzantine Emperor Phocas (602–610). The *Templum Sacrae Urbis* (Note 1, p. 40), near the Forum, became the church of SS. Cosmas and Damian, the *Curia Iulia* housed the church of St Adrian, the library of the *Templum Divi Augusti* (see p. 185) the church of Santa Maria Antiqua, the temple of Antoninus and Faustina (see p. 6) the church of St Lorenzo in Miranda, originally simply an oratory, later transformed into the present seventeenth-century church, which rises above the older colonnade. Some monuments had the exceptional good luck of being protected by a public or religious authority, like Trajan's Column, which the Roman Senate took into its care, or the Column of the Antonines, which was acknowledged to be the property of the order of the monks of St Sylvester, who threatened to excommunicate anybody who dared lay hands upon it.

Buildings which were used for any practical purpose were also saved from destruction; in this way the central part of the *Porticus Octavia* survived. This colonnade, rebuilt on a magnificent scale by Augustus,[17] remained partly standing, and from the twelfth century onwards it became the city fish-market. It survived in this capacity until the end of the eighteenth century (Plate 63); it disappeared shortly afterwards with the destruction of the ghetto, leaving behind it only the ancient ruins on which it had been built. A memorial of medieval market life still survives today, to the right of the great stone arch, in the form of a slab with a Latin inscription, from which we learn that fish whose breadth, including the fins (*usque ad pinnas inclusive*), exceeded the breadth of the slab, were to be reserved for the Conservatori Capitolini, a tribute to the tables of the municipal authorities.

During the struggles between the people and the nobility in the ninth and tenth centuries, many of the most remarkable Roman buildings were converted into fortresses. This new role, while it slowed down the steady destruction by the inroads of plunderers, involved disfiguring alterations; in addition, the buildings were exposed to the risk, natural to fortresses, of being attacked and destroyed. They took on a new appearance, picturesquely medieval, crowned with towers, sometimes joined together by walls and casemates with iron bars and loopholes. The ancient arches were given battlements, and the gaps between the columns of temples were walled up. Medieval Rome was so rich in towers that the neighbourhood of the ancient Forum of Nerva was called 'Campo Torrechiano' (Field of Towers). The most complete system of fortification rose in the heart of ancient Rome with the Castle of the Franks, whose perimeter included the *Septizonium* (see p. 22) on the Palatine, the Colosseum, the Arch of Titus, the temple of Venus and Rome, the Circus Maximus and the Arch of Constantine. The Colosseum became the formidable centre of the citadel of which the Arches of Titus (Plate 65) and Constantine were merely gates.

In the same way the Orsini converted Hadrian's Mausoleum and Pompey's Theatre into fortresses, the Colonna the Mausoleum of Augustus and the Baths of Constantine, the Savelli the Theatre of Marcellus. The civil wars, which convulsed Rome for centuries, played havoc with them; the nobles could not be defeated unless the bulwarks with which they protected their private power were dismantled. Often these converted fortresses were a stake in the game and emerged damaged from the struggle.

Most of the smaller buildings, sacred as well as profane, disappeared, the victims of the hunger for stone which Rome both aroused and satisfied. From time to time the onslaught of a foreign enemy spread ruin and destruction over the city and facilitated the gathering of building material; the conquests of Rome in 1084 by Henry IV and by Robert Guiscard in the same year, when he drove out the Imperial armies, were particularly violent. Fires and the earthquakes so frequent in the Middle Ages contributed to the work of destruction; the earthquake of 1349 was particularly terrible. Rome's misfortunes were shown in the great heaps of stone, on which the industry of men began to exercise itself with all the patient tenacity of ants attacking a heap of grain.

The palaces of the new Rome rose with the dark hues of ancient stone; among the ruins small houses grew up, incorporating fragments of famous buildings in their walls. Peasants brought their heavy waggons into Rome from the country to remove stones for their farm buildings and walls; many came from great distances to gorge upon this inexhaustible quarry.

Most of the marble was turned into lime, and kilns sprang up all over Rome, where almost all the statues which had survived the successive sacks ended up; emperors' heads, fragments of columns, friezes, capitals, lintels, pedestals and beautifully executed statues of gods were thrown into the fire.

Iconoclasts without rancour, these insignificant pillagers had an easygoing, unimaginative attitude to the havoc which they caused among stone and marble; lazy and concerned solely with their own convenience, they took advantage of the opportunities they found.

The venerable ruins instilled no respect into their hearts, for they served no purpose; the Romans no longer granted the right to exist to the baths where life had ceased, the temples where worship was ended, the altars where grass grew, and all those ancient private buildings, now desolate and uninhabited, on the abandoned hills. The earliest pillagers justified the actions of their successors; the statues vanished from their pedestals, the capitals from the columns, the plaster from the walls, the idols, offerings and even the ceilings from the temples. Every generation continued the work of its predecessors. As with all unimaginative people, their object was to complete the task of destruction, and if they did not succeed, the credit was not man's but of something greater than man.

The feeling for art, which was introduced into the despoliation of ancient Rome, played as great a part in the work of destruction. This more aristocratic motive for the devastation of ancient monuments gave rise to a profitable business in architectural remains in the Middle Ages. The nobility, relying on the rights of private ownership and with the formal permission of the Senate, sold them to marble dealers, or to aristocrats from other cities who were anxious to decorate their own palaces with them. Marble from Rome is to be found in the Baptistry of Florence, the cathedrals of Pisa, Lucca, Montecassino and Orvieto, and even outside Italy. The marble round the tombs of the kings of England in Westminster Abbey comes from Rome. Petrarch regarded such a trade as impious, since Rome belongs to the world, and her monuments are not for sale. To sell the common inheritance is a crime, and the enraged poet has scathing words for 'the petty thieves who ravage as in a captured city' (*latrunculi non aliter quam in capta urbe grassantes*).[18] To the Romans of Rienzi's day he wrote:

After the palaces fell through old age and the arches collapsed . . ., they felt no shame in seeking an ignoble profit and in engaging in a disgraceful traffic in the remains of Rome which had survived their impiety. And now, to your eternal shame, slothful Naples is decorated with your marble columns, the thresholds of your temples, to which men of old came from all corners of the world, and the portraits sculptured on the tombs, in which the venerable ashes of your forefathers lay.

And so, step by step, even the ruins are being reduced, which are the mighty evidence of your ancient greatness.

But if otherwise everything was going to end up in the lime kilns, was this any worse? Theft removed these marbles from the flames of the kiln, and the thief who saved them from complete destruction was performing a praiseworthy task.

At the Renaissance the monuments of ancient Rome were employed on a large scale for the decoration of new buildings. It was no longer merely a question of removing a sarcophagus or a capital, but of destroying entire ancient buildings to make new ones from them. From the second half of the fifteenth century and the beginning of the sixteenth century onwards many of the ancient monuments which were still standing were either totally destroyed or partially demolished: *quod non fecerunt barbari, fecerunt Barberini.*[19] The temples of Iuppiter Capitolinus, Concord, Isis and Serapis, Janus and *Hercules invictus*, the Arches of Gratianus Valentinianus and Theodosius and the *Saepta Iulia* disappeared; other buildings were mutilated, like the Colosseum, the Baths of Caracalla and the Circus Maximus. The last remaining column of the Basilica of Constantine was removed by Paul V in 1613, and placed in front of the Basilica in the Piazza Santa Maria Maggiore, where it still stands, surmounted by a bronze statue of the Virgin and Child. The same Pope took down the columns of the temple of Minerva which stood in the *Forum Nervae* (Plate 67) and used them for building the fountain of the *Acqua Paola* on the Ianiculum. The columns are still visible in one of Cook's prints of a slightly earlier date.

So the destiny of ancient Rome had been reduced to this; the degenerate Romans destroyed Rome, pillaging and tearing it down; in their determined, unconscious impiety they did not scruple to reduce Rome to powder, to burn it in furnaces or to sell it piece by piece. For as long as men could remember, nobody had ever swept out the abandoned houses, and the streets of ancient Rome had forgotten the rude caress of the broom. The results of this neglect were enormous.

It is not hard to imagine what would happen to some large modern city if its population were suddenly reduced, and the municipal authorities were no longer able to maintain the regular cleaning services which are vital in preserving the appearance of all cities.

This is exactly what happened in Rome, especially in those districts which were densely inhabited in antiquity, but were the first to be abandoned—the Roman Forum (Plate 63), the Imperial Forums and the Baths (Plate 62). Dust began to gather in the deserted streets; at first it was only a film, but in the course of time it grew steadily and was changed into mud by the rain. Soon the mud blocked the drains, and when their underground outlets were choked, they brought foul, thick water to the surface and doubled the deposits of mud. A layer of damp earth was thus formed, and when the moisture had dried out a hard, cracked crust was left. Tufts of grass grew out of the mud and gave it a certain solidity as it covered the pavement, preventing the rain from washing it away or the wind from scattering it when the sun turned the mud once more into dust. Low-lying ground where no form of drainage was any longer possible became impassable marshes. The layer of mud grew thicker; men no longer swept the streets, but they still swept their houses, and carried their refuse to these deserted districts. The drains added to the deposit from below, men from above.

During the course of centuries filth and rubbish accumulated on this swamp, whose appearance changed with the seasons, and in time everything ended in the mire which swallowed up a large variety of objects: old rags, broken jars, carcases of dead cats, bones, shells, cabbage stalks, straw, toothless combs, lost coins and a thousand other trivial objects. One day, when the devouring mud is compelled to give back all that it has not destroyed, the patient archaeologist will excavate, catalogue and describe all these objects, and his careful examination of them will help to answer his questions about countless secrets of ancient life.

This deposit absorbed and devoured, rotted and assimilated, as its level steadily rose. The disfiguring covering grew thicker, while the city sank, overwhelmed by the encroaching earth. The streets of an earlier age disappeared from view, while a new Rome, humble, built on mud and giving a rustic appearance to the places which had once been the centre of the world, rose above ancient

Rome. A deep layer of soil concealed the Roman Forum; beneath lay the *Argiletum,* the *Via Sacra* and the *Basilica Iulia*; above was a green meadow where idle shepherds watched their goats and cattle graze. The days of Evander had returned after an interlude which had embraced all Rome's glory. The relentless passage of time humbles the pride of men and makes them realise that their history is no more than a series of interludes in the steady progress of eternity. Where cattle had grazed before Rome stood, they had returned to graze now that Rome had ceased to stand. What had once been grass had returned to grass and rustic silence. In the mud which had become soil the vital force of nature burst out, joyfully producing grass and flowers. In spring daisies covered the fields and butterflies fluttered round the Arch of Titus. The Forum became the *Campo Vaccino* ('Field of Cows'), and a track made by the trampling of the herds went the whole length of this grassy expanse like the pastures in mountainous districts. A desire for beautifying the city was reborn, and the track was turned into a wooded path running from the Arch of Septimius Severus to the Arch of Titus; it became a favourite spot for the people, who went by it to the open countryside; on religious festivals processions filed along it. The ruins which still stood out in this idyllic peace were in harmony with the atmosphere, and helped to give it a feeling of romance and poetry. The friars to whose order this land had been assigned, cultivated their plots among hedges and shrubs, alternately work and prayer. The smell of freshly dug earth and the green grass provided a change from the peace of the monastery which covered the remains of the pride of Imperial Rome. The brothers followed the course of the streets which had once witnessed triumphs, but were now buried many feet deep in the productive soil.

When regular excavations began, many complained of the sacrilege, asking if science had the right to destroy this romantic atmosphere, and if the results of excavating the Forum would justify sacrificing for ever the beauty and peace of the *Campo Vaccino.*

The systematic recovery of ancient Rome began in the early years of the nineteenth century. Excavations in the Roman Forum and the *Forum Traiani* began in 1812. The principal monuments of Rome were freed from buildings which clustered round them;

their lower parts, which had for long been buried in the earth, were cleared, and the monuments were restored to their ancient appearance. At first they emerged only half-way out of the earth which had submerged them, like squatting giants, without vitality and almost without dignity. The vaults of the ancient arches recovered their proportions, and light once more shone through them, the harmonious outlines of temples and baths were again revealed. Bases of columns, shattered pillars, fallen capitals and pavements were brought to light. Ancient Rome returned, but it was dead and gaunt, withered and venerable like the relics of a saint; its rough stones bore witness to a mighty past as well as to the passage of many centuries; it was only the solid ghost of a great and vanished age.

Anyone who stands on a clear summer evening on the Pincio, and sees modern Rome spread out before him, bathed in glittering and reflecting light, watching the whole city ablaze in a magic furnace which burns without consuming, searches in vain for the scanty and obscure remains of ancient Rome. Only the dark mass of the Colosseum stands out among a sea of roofs, office buildings and green patches, with its wonderfully irregular outline cutting the sky. But the awe-struck watcher is offered a sight which cuts short all regrets and prevents all longing for the past. In front of his eyes stands the evidence of a city that does not die. In this light and at this hour he realises that Rome is immortal.

The story of the architectural decay of Rome, briefly sketched in these pages, is only the beginning of a very different story, as glorious as the first is sad. Rome's steady growth in size and splendour was not finished when the conquered provinces first drew light from the dawn of Roman civilisation. In the barbarian west and the civilised east a new age began. Rome gave its language and civilisation to uncivilised peoples, and inspired their faith in order and continuity; in Greek-speaking countries it introduced a practical common sense which overcame local rivalries, looked down upon controversial subtleties and taught the tenacity of purpose from which came enduring achievements. Everywhere Rome built roads, bridges, aqueducts and new cities, introduced beneficial customs and furthered civilisation; everywhere it brought the wisdom of its law and the weight of its immense powers of assimilation, which took and gave, and adapted the better characteristics of its subjects to produce a more complete civilisation. Its trade stimulated industry in the provinces, its navies ensured peace on the seas, its armies guarded the frontiers and guaranteed security for all. True to itself, it actively admired the virtues of other peoples, and absorbed from all sources and spread throughout the world the principles of a varied but harmonious civilisation. It impressed on the united world which it ruled the stamp of its own balanced and tolerant outlook and the basic Roman virtues of a people who, amidst all the glory of the mightiest empire the world had ever seen, retained the solid peasant virtues of devotion to the soil, dogged determination and common sense. Rome was the mother of the provinces, but remained always to some extent their daughter; it spread civilisation, but absorbed what was best in the provinces; without any foolish exclusiveness it remained true to its own principles, and was universal without ever resigning its right of leadership and claim to the distinction which was its destiny. In the fullness of time Rome accepted Christianity and spread it throughout the world, making the Church one of its imperial institutions. And when, 'the Niobe of nations', it saw its long period of power ended and lost the provinces one by one, the active and determined spirit it had nourished in those provinces continued to flourish for centuries. Rome's marbles were shattered the population reduced, barbarian horsemen rode through the deserted streets which had once been alive with peaceful trade, but Roman civilisation continued to flourish in new forms in the territories it had lost, which inherited and continued the tradition when the empire of Rome had fallen but its name was still venerable and holy.

Further Reading

The main authority is F. Gregorovius, *History of the City of Rome in the Middle Ages* (English translation, London, 1897–1906).

Other studies are:

R. Lanciani, *The Destruction of Ancient Rome* (London, 1951).

R. Rodd, *Rome of the Renaissance and Today* (London, 1932).

J. S. Bury, *The Invasion of Europe by the Barbarians* (London, 1928).

J. Hodgkin, *Italy and her Invaders* (Oxford, 1899).

NOTES

1. Cassiodorus, Var., II, 34; III, 30; 53; IV, 51.
2. See p. 321.
3. Most of the classical works of art which decorated Constantinople were destroyed after the capture of the city by the Turks in 1453.
4. In particular Constantine II (337–40), who even stripped the bronze bosses off the Pantheon. The bronze doors of the Pantheon remained intact until they were removed in the papacy of Urban VIII (Maffeo Barberini, Pope 1623-44). Hence the pasquinade *Quod non fecerunt barbari fecerunt Barberini*, which became proverbial (see p. 319).
5. Procopius, De Bello Gothico, III, 22: ' Ῥώμη . . . πόλεων ἁπασῶν οὖσαι ὑφ' ἡλίῳ τυγχάνουσιν οὖσαι, μεγίστη τε καὶ ἀξιολογωτάτη ὡμολόγηται εἶναι.
('Of all the cities beneath the sun, Rome is universally agreed to be the largest and most splendid.')
6. De red., I, 47 et seq.
7. See note 1, p. 40.
8. In the *Breviarium* of the *Notitia* (see p. 40): *lacus* (the *Curiosum* adds: *quod est putea*) MCCCLII.
9. See note 213, p. 52 and p. 230
10. See note 152, p. 50.
11. See note 1, p. 40.
12. The temple of Vesta, whose first building went back to Numa, was destroyed by fire in 241 B.C. (Livy, Epit., 19; cf. Ovid, Fasti, VI, 437 et seq.; Juvenal, 3, 138–9); the memory of this fire lasted for a long time, and was connected with the name of L. Caecilius Metellus, the Pontifex Maximus of the year, who is said to have dashed into the blazing temple to save the statue of Minerva, and to have been blinded. (Modern criticism has shown this to be an unfounded legend, which originated in the schools of rhetoric.) The temple was again burnt in 210 B.C., and then during the fire in the reign of Nero, from 19 to 27 July, A.D. 64 (Tacitus, Ann., XV, 41) and finally in 191 under Commodus.
13. The building of the temple of Iuppiter Capitolinus was agreed to and begun under the Tarquinii (Cicero, de rep., II, 36; Livy, I, 38, 7), and completed in the first year of the Republic (Tacitus, Hist., III, 72); it was dedicated by the consul Horatius on the Ides of September 509 B.C. In 83 B.C. it was destroyed by fire, as we learn from Cicero, who records this disaster as having occurred twenty years before his consulate (Cat., III, 4, 9: *Hunc annum . . . quiesset . . . post Capitoli . . . incensionem vicesimus*); it was burnt a second time during the riots provoked by the supporters of Vitellius, which shook Rome after the death of Nero (Tacitus, Hist., III, 71, 8–9) and some years after (A.D.

80) in the Flavian age (Dio Cassius, LXV, 17), when it was immediately rebuilt by Domitian in 82 (Suetonius, Dom., 8) and remained standing in spite of partial damage by fires until the process of demolition began with Stilicho in the barbarian age.

14. The Pantheon is the best preserved of the buildings of ancient Rome, and throughout its history Romans of every age have felt a particular affection for it. In the Middle Ages the Roman Senate swore to defend St Peter's, the Castel Sant' Angelo and the Pantheon. The first building in 27 B.C. was the work of Agrippa, as is recorded by the Latin inscription on the architrave, which has remained unaltered in spite of subsequent rebuilding: *M(arcus) Agrippa L(uci) f(ilius) consul tertium fecit*. It was destroyed by fire during the reign of Titus and rebuilt by Trajan; a second fire, caused by lightning, destroyed it under Trajan (Orosius, VII, 12: *Pantheum Romae fulmine concrematum*), but it was rebuilt shortly afterwards by Hadrian. An inscription (CIL, VI, 2041) shows that it was extensively restored in A.D. 202 under Septimius Severus and Caracalla: *Pantheum vetustate corruptum restituerunt*. Archaeologists have not yet agreed how much of the original building has survived the successive reconstructions, nor has the connexion between the temple and the Baths of Agrippa, which stood in the same district, been established.

15. Constans, II (337–50) removed the gilded horse which decorated the triumphal arch in the Circus Maximus; Stilicho, the great general of Honorius (395–423), carried off the magnificent bronze doors of the Capitol.

16. Most of these kilns were erected between the Circus Flaminius and the Baths of Agrippa, which gave the district the name of Calcarario ('The lime kiln'). It should be added that the practice of stealing stone in Rome was of very long standing. Suetonius (Dom. 8) tells us that a freedman of Domitian used stone intended for the rebuilding of the temple of Iuppiter Capitolinus (p. 22) to build a sepulchral monument, to his son. The emperor, indignant at the theft and the sacrilege ordered his soldiers to destroy the monument and throw the un-offending body into the sea.

17. Mon. Ancyr., IV, 19: *Porticum ad Circum Flaminium, quam sum appellari passus, ex nomine eius qui priorem eodem in solo fecerat, Octaviam . . . feci*. The portico was built by Cn. Octavius in 168 B.C. in memory of the naval victory over Perseus, king of Macedon; it was later destroyed by fire and rebuilt by Augustus in 33 B.C.

18. Variarum, 48.

19. See note 4.

Index

Figures in bold type indicate references to plates